BEYOND DISSOCIATION

C0-BXA-477

ADVANCES IN CONSCIOUSNESS RESEARCH

ADVANCES IN CONSCIOUSNESS RESEARCH provides a forum for scholars from different scientific disciplines and fields of knowledge who study consciousness in its multifaceted aspects. Thus the Series will include (but not be limited to) the various areas of cognitive science, including cognitive psychology, linguistics, brain science and philosophy. The orientation of the Series is toward developing new interdisciplinary and integrative approaches for the investigation, description and theory of consciousness, as well as the practical consequences of this research for the individual and society.

Series B: Research in Progress. Experimental, descriptive and clinical research in consciousness.

EDITOR

Maxim I. Stamenov
(*Bulgarian Academy of Sciences*)

EDITORIAL BOARD

David Chalmers (*University of Arizona*)
Gordon G. Globus (*University of California at Irvine*)
Ray Jackendoff (*Brandeis University*)
Christof Koch (*California Institute of Technology*)
Stephen Kosslyn (*Harvard University*)
Earl Mac Cormac (*Duke University*)
George Mandler (*University of California at San Diego*)
John R. Searle (*University of California at Berkeley*)
Petra Stoerig (*Universität Düsseldorf*)
Francisco Varela (*C.R.E.A., Ecole Polytechnique, Paris*)

Volume 22

Yves Rossetti and Antti Revonsuo (eds.)

Beyond Dissociation
Interaction between dissociated implicit and explicit processing

DISCARDED.

BEYOND DISSOCIATION

INTERACTION BETWEEN DISSOCIATED IMPLICIT AND EXPLICIT PROCESSING

Edited by

YVES ROSSETTI
INSERM, Espace et Action, Bron, France

ANTTI REVONSUO
University of Turku

JOHN BENJAMINS PUBLISHING COMPANY
AMSTERDAM/PHILADELPHIA

∞ TM   The paper used in this publication meets the minimum requirements of American National Standard for Information Sciences — Permanence of Paper for Printed Library Materials, ANSI z39.48–1984.

Library of Congress Cataloging-in-Publication Data

Beyond dissociation : interaction between dissociated implicit and explicit processing / edited by Yves Rossetti, Antti Revonsuo.
    p.   cm. -- (Advances in consciousness research, ISSN 1381-589X ; v. 22)
   Includes bibliographical references and index.
   1. Consciousness. 2. Dissociation (Psychology). I.Rossetti, Yves. II. Revonsuo, Antti. III. Series
QP411B49   2000
153--dc21   00-037961
ISBN 90 272 5142 8 (Eur.) / 1 55619 665 2 (US) (Pbk.)

© 2000 – John Benjamins B.V.
No part of this book may be reproduced in any form, by print, photoprint, microfilm, or any other means, without written permission from the publisher.

John Benjamins Publishing Co. • P.O.Box 75577 • 1070 AN Amsterdam • The Netherlands
John Benjamins North America • P.O.Box 27519 • Philadelphia PA 19118-0519 • USA

Contents

List of Contributors

Abernethy, Bruce
Dept. of Human Movement Studies
The University of Queensland
AUSTRALIA
bruce@hms01.hms.uq.edu.au

Bar, Moshe
Massachusetts General Hospital
NMR Center, Bldg. 149, Rm. 2301
13th St., Charlestown 02129, USA
bar@nmr.mgh.harvard.edu

Berti, Anna
Department of General Psychology
University of Padua
35131 Padua, ITALY

Bhalla, Mukul
Department of Psychology
Loyola University New Orleans
6363 St. Charles Avenue
New Orleans, LA 70118, USA
bhalla@nadal.loyno.edu

Bridgeman, Bruce
Department of Psychology
University of California, Santa Cruz
Santa Cruz, Ca. 95064, USA
bruceb@cats.ucsc.edu

Chaplin, John
Neurological Rehabilitation Clinic
Stora Sköndal Hospital, SWEDEN

Ciarrochi, Joseph
School of Psychology
University of new South Wales
Sydney 2052, NEW ZEALAND
joseph_ciarrochi@uow.edu.au

Clements, Wendy A.
Laboratory of Experimental Psychology
University of Sussex
Brighton, East Sussex BN1 9QG
ENGLAND

Ellis, Hadyn D.
School of Psychology
University of Cardiff
P.O.Box 901
Cardiff CF1 3YG Wales, ENGLAND

Farnè, Alessandro
Ospedale I.N.R.C.A. "I Fraticini"
50100 Florence, ITALY
Department of Psychology
University of Bologna
Viale Berti Pichat, 5 – 40127 Bologna
ITALY
farne@psibo.unibo.it

Forgas, Joseph P
School of Psychology
University of New South Wales
Sydney 2052, NEW ZEALAND
JP.Forgas@unsw.edu.au
Home page: http://www.psy.unsw.edu.au/
    ~joef/jforgas.htm

Hommel, Bernhard
Faculty of Social Sciences
Section of Experimental & Theoretical
    Psychology
Wassenaarseweg 52, room 2B05
P.O.Box 9555 2300 RB Leiden
The Netherlands
hommel@fsw.leidenuniv.nl

Imanaka, Kuniyasu Ph.D.
Department of Kinesiology
Faculty of Science
Tokyo Metropolitan University
1-1 Minami-Ohsawa
Hachioji 192-0397, Tokyo, JAPAN
imanaka-kuniyasu@c.metro-u.ac.jp
Home page: http://www.sci.metro-u.ac.jp/
    sport/personal/imanaka/imanaka.E.html

Jackson, Stephen R.
Centre for Perception, Attention, and
    Motor Sciences
School of Psychology
University of Wales
Bangor, Gwynedd LL57 2DG
UNITED KINGDOM
srj@psychology.nottingham.ac.uk

Johanson, Mirja
Neurological Rehabilitation Clinic
Stora Sköndal Hospital, SWEDEN

Làdavas, Elisabetta
Department of Psychology
University of Bologna
Viale Berti Pichat
5 - 40127 Bologna, ITALY
ladavas@psibo.unibo.it

Perner, Josef
Department of Psychology
University of Salzburg
Hellbrunnerstraße 34
A-5020 AUSTRIA
josef.perner@sbg.ac.at

Pisella, Laure
Institut National de la Santé et de la
    Recherche Médicale
Unité 94: Espace et Action
16 avenue Lépine, Case 13, 69676 Bron
FRANCE
pisella@lyon151.inserm.fr

Proffitt, Dennis R.
Department of Psychology
Gilmer Hall
University of Virginia
Charlottesville, VA 22903, USA
drp@virginia.eduGeographical

Revonsuo, Antti
Department of Philosophy
Center of Cognitive Neuroscience
University of Turku
FIN-20014 Turku, FINLAND
antti.revonsuo@utu.fi

Rossetti, Yves
Espace et Action
Institut National de la Santé et de la
    Recherche Médicale: Unité 534
16 avenue Lépine, Case 13, 69676 Bron
FRANCE
rossetti@lyon151.inserm.fr
Home page: http://www.lyon151.inserm.fr/
    unites/534-rossetti.htlm
www.lyon151.inserm.fr

Wedlund, Jan-Eric
Neurological Rehabilitation Clinic
Stora Sköndal Hospital, SWEDEN

Young, Andrew W.
Department of Psychology
University of York
Heslington, York YO1 5DD
ENGLAND
School of Psychology
University of Cardiff, P.O.Box 901
Cardiff CF1 3YG, WALES

We were very sad to hear that Ullin T. Place passed away only a few months before the present volume was published. We greatly appreciated his efforts to finish the chapter that he contributed to this book during a time when he had to struggle with his fatal illness. We would like to dedicate the present volume to the memory of Ullin T.Place.

Acknowledgements

The editors wish to thank Yann Coello, Sandrine Delors, Jonathan Edwards, Edouard Gentaz, Nicolas Georgieff, François Mauguière, Laure Pisella, Mohamed Saoud, and Gilles Rode for their constructive criticism during the reviewing process. Valérie Gaveau has performed an excellent work on the edition of the whole volume, which would never have come out without her outstanding organisation and efficiency. Jean-Louis Borach contributed to the preparation of the illustration proofs. The editorial work of this collective volume was supported by CNRS and INSERM (France) and by the Academy of Finland.

Beyond Dissociations

Reassembling the
mind-brain after all?

Yves Rossetti

Antti Revonsuo

"Comme des bancs de poissons de même espèce, des vols d'oiseaux qui se déplacent d'un même mouvement, des groupements dont les membres ont les mêmes tendances... Leur appliquer un « tu », un « je »... non, nous ne le pouvions plus... il fallait un « nous », un « vous ». Seuls les porte-parole que nous envoyons au dehors continuent à se servir de ces « je », de ces « moi »."

" Just like shoals of fish of the same species, flocks of birds moving together or groups of like-minded people... Apply to them a "tu" or a "je"... no, we couldn't do it any more... a "nous", a "vous" was required. Only the spokes-persons we send outside still use these "je", these "moi". "

Nathalie Sarraute (Tu ne t'aimes pas (you don't like yourself), 1989).

Several important types of dissociation described in science have come to a time to be questioned. For example the contemporary interpretation of the genetics versus epigenesis debate is that there is a complete inter-dependency of the two terms classically opposed. Also, the distinction between matter and space is always becoming fuzzier to physicists. In our field, the debate around the Cartesian dissociation between mind and brain becomes asymptotically closer to the egg and chick question, that is, like Zen koans, producing more silence than wise answers (Suzuki 1971). In many instances, the outcome of the dissociation issue is that the dissociated items constitute the two sides (if not the several) of a single object. In this introduction, we attempt to analyse why so much emphasis has been put on dissociation rather than on integration of the mind-brain components. This debate will justify why the basic question asked throughout the present volume is to know how do diverse systems in the brain co-operate to produce a unified experience and behaviour.

Analysing

"Analysis" is a magic word in science. The breaking up of anything complex into its various simple elements has been the rigorous strategy to oppose to magical and spiritual interpretation of the world. To depart from empiricist or qualitative observation, the usual tool of science and knowledge is decomposition. Alchemy was supposed to produce new substances through the synthesis of ordinary particles, whereas science decomposes compound substances into their primary elements. The determination of the elements or components of anything complex has applied to many different fields including chemistry, mathematics, physics, biology, philosophy and psychology. Separating living from non-living creatures, severing the vegetal and the animal realms, isolating molecules or atoms, distinguishing between genetic and epigenetic, or separating the mind and the body have been proved to promote important steps forward in the understanding of life. The endeavour of what the human is constituted of is indeed very much indebted to the study of dichotomies. As will be further discussed below, the current realm of this dichotomic approach is probably neuropsychology.

Dissociating

Just as "analysis" is a magic word in science in general, "dissociation" is the key word of neuropsychology. The separation of compound psychological functions into their primary elements has proved to be an important source of knowledge and theories about the organisation of the human mind. In this particular discipline, dissociation is viewed as the demonstration that separate systems or separate structures are responsible for two given variables. The study of single cases has provided new directions and improved our understanding of the relationship between the brain and the mental structures and the interpretation of some cases "has proved nothing less than revolutionary" (Code 1996). For most of the important classic cases described in the literature the focus of interest has been the dissociation of function (cf. Code et al. 1996). For example visual agnosia has been regarded as a dissociation of higher (disruption of the cognitive aspects of vision) and lower (intact primary aspects) visual functions (e.g. Teuber 1955).

However the positive and negative behavioural consequences of a given restricted lesion may be partially explained by the reorganisation of surrounding intact brain tissue. Consequently the specificity of the effect of a given single lesion is often questionable. Masterpieces of such demonstrations are thus provided by a "double-dissociation", for which a lesion of structure X will specifically disrupt function A while sparing function B, and a lesion of structure Y will specifically affect function B while function A would remain intact. Teuber (1955) termed this experimental tool 'double dissociation', and used it for both for animal and human studies, arguing that it indicates some specificity of function, e.g. between anterior and posterior brain lesions. Later on Shallice (1979: 260) even stated that "strong neuropsychological evidence for the existence of neurologically distinct functional systems depends on double dissociation of function". Surprisingly, the glossary and the index of Neuropsychology textbooks do not refer to 'dissociation', but only to 'double dissociation' (e.g. Ellis and Young 1988; Kolb and Whishaw 1990; Heilman and Valenstein 1993). Kolb and Whishaw described it as 'an experimental technique whereby two areas of the neocortex are functionally dissociated by two behavioural tests, each test being affected by a lesion to one zone and not the other'. Heilman and Valenstein (1993) present it as an elegant demonstration that the effects being observed cannot be ascribed to non-specific causes, and do not restrict its use to studies of the neocortex. Ellis and Young (1988) provide an interesting discussion on "dissociations and associations". They also describe double dissociations as being more reliable indicators of the separation between two cognitive processes, but they also argue that the search for dissociation should not be regarded "as some sort of Royal road to understanding the structure of the mind" (p. 5). Following Teuber (1955) they point out that: "Having unearthed a double dissociation there is a lot of work to be done in determining just what cognitive processes mediate aspects of tasks 1 and 2 independently". Interestingly, they depart from other authors when they also raise the issue of determining "what processes, if any, the two tasks share in common", raising the question of situating the patients deficit "in the total cognitive system".

Examples of double-dissociation can be found in many different fields of neuropsychology and have been in most cases exported into cognitivist models as separate "boxes" for two isolated functions. Double dissociations have been reported between e.g. conscious perception and sensorimotor transformation (Milner 1995; 1998), between facial expression analysis and facial speech analysis performed during lip-reading (Campbell et al. 1986), between knowing "what" and knowing "where" for vision (Wilson et al. 1997), between motor and semantic implicit memory systems (Heindel et al. 1989), between personal and extra-personal hemispatial neglect (Bisiach et al. 1986), between word finding and syntactic skills (Ellis and Young 1988: 139), or between automatic and propositional speech (review in Ellis and Young 1988: 251). Several of these dissociations can be matched to the general distinction between implicit and explicit processes which constitutes the main theme of this book. Then studies on intact human subjects also attempted to make the case for dissociation, for example between spatial and temporal information processing (Halbig et al. 1998) or between face recognition and facial expression analysis (e.g. Bruce and Young 1986). In addition, neuroimaging studies now provide instances of double dissociation between two functions (e.g. between imagining and actually perceiving colour (Howard et al. 1998) although these recent approaches to human brain functions allow to point to more complex network organisation than just double-dissociation (e.g. Faillenot et al. 1996; Sprengelmeyer et al. 1998). The description of a double dissociation is a necessary condition for cognitive psychologists to identify elementary modules involved in a given function. Although the notion of a modular organisation of cognition can be traced back to the 19th-century phrenology, the modularity of mind is a dominant paradigm in cognitive psychology and neuropsychology (e.g. Fodor 1983).

It may be noticed that the search for double-dissociation is very reminiscent of a dualist attitude. The duality between spirit and matter is in no way compatible, say, with the three natural realms (mineral, vegetal, animal), nor to the four elements (earth, water, fire, air), nor to the 5 or 7 notes of a musical scale, nor to the 7 colours of a rainbow. Nor does it only to unity. The emphasis put on duality has to be connected to the Cartesian heritage, which has been applied to most fields of contemporary science. Other cultures, such as oriental cultures more sensible to the Buddhist tradition, do not naturally follow this thinking habit, and may rather bind together "dissociable substances" (such as death vs. life or body vs. environment) (Motokawa 1989).

The destiny of dissociations

What does science make with a dissociation? As suggested by Teuber (1955), three problems derive from the idea to locate functions in the brain: discovering symptoms of lesion, assigning these symptoms to specific lesions in given areas, analysing the altered performance which underlies the symptom. "All too many studies stop short at discovery and localisation of symptoms, i.e. with the question of "where", and fail to proceed to the analysis of altered functions, i.e. with the question of "what" to localise" (Teuber 1955: 277–78). Thus dissociation observed within an initially presumed single function between two brain areas and/or two symptoms leaves the scientist with two new functions to analyse. At a later stage the initial dissociation becomes obsolete, and looses its interest. Because the aim is to understand how each function is made, no study will be carried out on the mother dissociation after it has been disunited, so that the fate of a dissociation is to disappear. For example no major work is currently being performed on the "old" dissociation described between the anterior and the posterior brain. Nor would it be useful to study a dissociation between sensory and motor functions, between language and vision, or between frontal and occipital areas. The consequence of this is that the analytical thought responsible for producing dissociations will put most emphasis on the last generated dissociation. If one assimilates the several generations of dissociation described in the brain to a genealogical tree, it can be said that the highest focus of attention is directed to the difference between siblings and forgets about the mother dissociation. And in turn the further analysis will give birth to a new generation of functions, which in turn will generate a greater number of functions to analyse.... An outstanding example of this logic has been provided by Felleman and van Essen (1991) in a review article of the connections between the over 30 distinct areas identified within the visual system. Of course the over 300 simple or reciprocal connections described within the visual system do not allow scientists to understand the brain mechanisms underlying vision, nor individuals to find their way to the phenomenological experience of vision. In the same way, the numerous areas involved in the generation of action are extensively interconnected in a way which precludes an overly simplistic description of the visuo-motor organisation as a straightforward dichotomy (Rossetti et al. 2000; see Pisella and Rossetti, this volume: Figure 1).

How far is science going to divide the brain into always-smaller functional units? Luckily enough, there seems to be a natural limitation to the perpetual division of the cerebral matter, so that the dissociating process should not go beyond the level of neurones or of molecules. A growing number of studies suggest that the coding of relevant information is not performed at the level of individual neurones but rather at the level of cell groups. This neuronal population coding is for example better correlated to the direction in space of the movements performed by an animal from which neuronal activity is being recorded, than any individual neurone (ex: Georgopoulos 1995; Sakurai 1996; Kristan 1997). These indications may suggest that the elementary unit of information processing is not out of reach to the current methods used to approach the brain.

Contrasting with the logic of cutting off from association every distinct piece of the mind-brain, one may hope that it has been sufficiently parcellated to initiate a tentative reconstruction. This attitude will provide us with another way of going beyond dissociations. As it has mostly been useful to analyse the different elements of the brain, it becomes even more important to put the puzzle pieces together again. Indeed the interest in dividing the brain in always-smaller parts is not to make the puzzle always more complicated but to understand the global organisation of the nervous system.

To sum up: It can be argued that the destiny of dissociations is to disappear. There are two ways for dissociation to be consumed: they may be deserted or unmade. Firstly, because a dissociation may have heuristic value only when it is not highly predictable, the derivative functions resulting from a dissociation will take its place in the interest of brain researchers and these functions will be further analysed and dissected, giving birth to potential new dissociations. Following this process the former dissociations are just left behind by science, which carries on its parcellation. The second possible destiny of dissociated functions is simply to be re-associated. As mentioned above, making the case for a dissociation is relevant only when two functions are previously considered as a whole. If two functions have been considered as a whole prior to be dissociated, this implies that the resulting dissociated functions must share several characteristics or interact in several ways. Then focusing on the dissociation will emphasise their difference rather than their common features and interrelations.

The basic idea of this book is that, although dissociation has proved to be a very useful heuristic tool for understanding mind-brain functions, studying the way so-called dissociated modules are interacting to contribute to the whole mind-brain function would provide us with even more insight into how consciousness appears. Interestingly the history of re-association may follow that of dissociation. For example the initial distinction made between the anterior and the posterior brain (e.g. Teuber 1955) has first given rise to the study of dissociation within the posterior brain (i.e. dorsal vs. ventral streams of visual processing, Ungerleider and Mishkin 1982). Later only could the study be initiated of how the parietal and temporal cortex work in conjunction to the frontal areas (e.g. Sakata et Taira 1994; Rossetti et al. 2000). The dissociation between the dorsal and the ventral streams itself has been sufficiently explored to allow the study of further dissociation within the dorsal stream (e.g. Milner 1997) or within the ventral stream (e.g. Buckley et al. 1997), and now the study of the interactions between the dorsal and the ventral stream can be developed (e.g. Rossetti 1998).

Implicit and explicit processing

One of the most important steps in reconstructing the unity of the decomposed mind-brain will probably be to understand the relationship between implicit and explicit processes. It is interesting to notice that the seminal work of von Helmoltz or Freud not only emphasised the distinction between conscious and unconscious but also already clearly addressed the issue of the interaction between these two instances of the mental life. Unfortunately for about one century there has been more and more attraction towards the power of unconscious processes as opposed to the conscious mental life and the report of dissociation between the conscious and the unconscious has become more fashionable than it really deserves. For these reasons, we already understand some of the processes underlying for example the interaction between perception and memory or motivation, the intermingling of movement control with several sensory modalities and several cognitive processes, but very little is known about the interaction between implicit and explicit processing. One of the most obvious and important reasons to study these interactions is that the distinction between explicit and implicit processing can apply to all fields of human cognition, ranging from sensory and sensori-motor processing to memory and language (e.g. Kihlstrom 1987). Table 1 shows a non-exhaustive list of several particular fields where the dissociation has been described under various terminologies.

Table 1. Related dissociations?

PERCEPTION		
subcortical vision	cortical vision	Cajal 1909, ...
tectal vision (Where?)	cortical vision (What?)	Schneider 1969
ambient vision	focal vision	Threvarthen 1968
tactile localisation	tactile identification	Paillard 1983
spatial	object	Ungerleider & Mishkin 1982

MEMORY		
procedural	declarative	Cohen & Squire 1980
implicit	explicit	Shacter 1987
sensorimotor	conceptual	Perrig & Hofer 1989

RESPONSE		
action	experiential	Goodale 1983
motor	cognitive	Bridgeman 1981, 1991, 2000, this volume
sensori-motor	cognitive or representational	Paillard 1987, 1991
implicit	explicit	Weiskrantz 1974
action (How?)	perception (What?)	Goodale & Milner 1992, Milner & Goodale 1995
pragmatic	semantic	Jeannerod & Rossetti 1993; Jeannerod 1994
direct parameter specification	conscious representation	Neumann & Klotz 1994
How?	Where?	Rossetti, Rode, Boisson 1994
automatic	voluntary	e.g. Hommel 2000, this volume....

ACTION CORRELATES?		
reflex eye movement	voluntary eye movement	Post & Leibowitz 1985
elicited extension	guided placing	Hein & Held 1967
ballistic movement	terminal guidance	Paillard 1971
feedback	feedforward	Rossetti & Koga 1992
reaching channel	grasping channel	Jeannerod 1981
kinetic visual cues	static visual cues	Paillard & Amblard 1985
automatic	conscious	Goodale, Pélisson, Prablanc 1986
egocentric reference frame	exocentric reference frame	Bridgeman 1991, ...
personal space	extrapersonal space	....

One other reason for the limited number of investigations about implicit-explicit interaction derives from the fact that the dissociation described between implicit and explicit processing is probably one of the highest-level dissociations studied in the field of cognitive science. In addition, the distinction between these two forms can be very difficult to demonstrate, because it seems possible to perform many sophisticated operations in either way. For these two reasons, the need to understand how these dissociable components may interact and co-operate expresses itself more vividly than for other dissociations.

One argument for dissociating implicit and explicit processing is that these two processes are of different nature. A strong argument for this position is that only one of the two process is left in some patients showing blindsight (Jackson, Place) or numbsense (Pisella and Rossetti). In normal subjects a conflict can be produced between the two levels of processing. The contribution of Bhalla and Proffitt, of Bridgeman, and of Pisella and Rossetti clearly show that the implicit processing performed by the action system gives rise to an internal representation of a visual stimulus that qualitatively and quantitatively differs from explicitable representation on several parameters. In addition, Jackson suggests that a patient with blindsight may access some visual information only in an implicit way, whereas another type of information could give rise to visual awareness. Place's model proposes that different neurological structures are responsible for the implicit and explicit processing observed in blindsight. Imanaka and Abernethy provide an interesting series of experiments showing that attended and unattended proprioceptive information may participate in action control in a different way, the implicit contribution having a counter-intuitively stronger weight than the explicit one. The result shown by Hommel (Fig. 5) accordingly demonstrates that the effect of a visual illusion (related to the Roelofs effect described by Bridgeman), can be modulated according to where subjects focus their attention, and thus according to implicit vs. explicit processing of the visual feature responsible for the illusion. In the same vein, Forgas and Ciarrochi show that mood management can depend upon the access of internal states to consciousness.

The discrepancy between implicit and explicit level of sensory processing that is revealed in experimental conditions does however not spontaneously appear in everyday life. Bhalla and Proffitt show that this discrepancy seems to be solved by a biased internal mapping between the two types of representation. If a given stimulus is interpreted as A by a given system (e.g.

verbal) and as A' by another system (e.g. action), then an internal coherence can be maintained if the two systems are referring to the same external object by A and A' respectively. In most of the experimental evidence presented in this volume the discrepancy between implicit and explicit processing is expressed under particular circumstances where a time pressure is applied (e.g. Bridgeman; Pisella and Rossetti). Such time constraints are also crucial for the integration of automatic stimulus-response processing with intentional control (Hommel), and for allowing a visual prime to affect semantic activation of target words (Bar). They may be responsible for the difference found between laboratory exploration of implicit face recognition in prosopagnosic patients and the every day life deficit (Young and Ellis).

Another distinction between implicit and explicit processes emphasises their respective thresholds. A recent article published by Dienes and Perner (1999) proposes an analysis of explicit knowledge based on a progressive transformation of implicit into explicit products, applying this gradient to different aspects of knowledge that can be represented. The ambition of the theory proposed is to bind philosophical conception of knowledge with relevant psychophysical and neuropsychological data. Dienes & Perner propose that the access of a given knowledge to explicit representation is mainly dependent upon the explicitation of the components of this knowledge. Therefore the question arises whether all implicit information can, at least in principle, become explicit, especially in the framework of the dorsal-ventral dissociation that is largely referred to by the authors of this volume. Action offers the opportunity to express implicit knowledge without involving declarative processes and therefore seems to stand in contrast with the views of Millikan (1984) and Dretske (1998). If "sometimes the unconscious and the conscious representations will contradict each other" Dienes and Perner (1999), as is shown in several chapters of the present book, then is there not the need to further refine the theory of accessibility of implicit knowledge to consciousness in order to allow for a possible discrepancy between implicit and explicit processing? This question should be kept in mind because several contributors to the present volume present instances of such contradiction in the field of action. Interestingly studies on implicit and explicit participation to action control are well represented in this book by several stimulating contributions.

The exploration of implicit and explicit processing in unilateral neglect presented by Ladavas also supports the idea of a continuum between these two processes, based on the difference between the thresholds required for their respective activation. Another argument for the threshold view of the relationship between explicit and implicit processing arises from developmental studies. For example Perner and Clements elegantly show that children appear to be progressively shifting from the complete absence of theory of mind (1) to an implicit, and (2) then only to an explicit theory of mind enabling them to attribute conscious states to others.

Despite the dissociation introduced between implicit and explicit processes, some exchange can be described between dissociated systems or subsystems. Most of the present volume contributions show that integration plays a key role in the functional aspects of the specific functions explored. The contribution of Ladavas et al. convincingly demonstrates that explicit and implicit processing of visual information by patients with hemispatial neglect are extremely difficult to disentangle, because unconsciously perceived information can contaminate the explicit responses produced by the patient. The fact that locating an object is largely performed through unconscious processes whereas identifying it spontaneously gives rise to conscious representation may be responsible for this kind of contamination, as is the case for locating one's own hand prior to initiating an action (Imanaka and Abernethy). In addition, Ladavas et al. propose that consciousness implies that object location and intrinsic object properties have to be integrated, which seems to be a converging hypothesis to explain the alteration of consciousness in hemispatial neglect. There is indeed evidence suggesting that location has an essential, primary status with respect to attentional orienting. Although target location can be known in the absence of feature (colour or orientation) information, the reverse does not seem to be true (e.g. Bloem and van der Heijden 1995; Brouwer and van der Heijden 1996).

The tight link that exists between conscious states and the integration of the world complexity is also emphasised by Revonsuo et al. Following Lahav (1993) they argue that unconscious processing has only access to partial information, which is consistent with the experimental data provided in several other chapters (e.g. Bridgeman; Jackson; Pisella and Rossetti). By contrast, conscious processing is necessary to form a meaningful model of the world, which is needed to elaborate, initiate and evaluate integrative, adaptive and flexible behaviour. The question of whether zombies can be found within the human brain can thus be answered positively only in the case of rather simple responses (e.g. pointing to a visual target). Because of their simplicity, these responses can be processed very fast and remain more dependant on the environment than the complex systems responsible for sleep walking (Revonsuo et al.), mood management (Forgas and Ciarrochi) or theory of mind (Perner and Clements). Strong Zombiehood (Revonsuo et al.) seems to be restricted to simple sub-systems whereas the richer both way interaction described in normals between the implicit and explicit processes involved in complex management would leave space only for Weak Zombiehood.

One extremely interesting feature of the dissociation between implicit and explicit processing is that an internal coherence appears to be maintained in the mind-brain, which suggests that under normal circumstances the whole system easily overcomes the divergence between subsystems to produce a unified interpretation of the body and/or the world. This characteristic feature emphasises the gap that has to be filled between the decomposed understanding of the brain provided by cognitive neuroscience and the phenomenological experience of internal states or external perception. It clearly emphasises the need to put together scientific elements so as to build up a more complex whole that would better correlate with subjective experience. The outstanding set of experiments presented by Bhalla and Proffitt further shows that functions related to explicit representation and to action, though dissociated under some circumstances, produce transfer functions from one to the other. Their contribution will suggest that although different internal scales may be used to represent the external world these scales are being put into register in order to preserve this internal coherence. The only limitation to this coherence maintenance system seems to related differences in the temporal constraints attached to the different representations (see also Bridgeman; Pisella and Rossetti). It is interesting to notice that these temporal constraints seem to be distributed along a gradient, which suggests that they are not incompatible with the notion of a continuum between implicit and explicit processing (Hommel; Pisella and Rossetti).

Synthesis

Analysis of the brain has led to an extreme parcellation of the neural matter and of the neuronal processes. However to understand how a brainteaser is built in, one has to be able not only to disassemble but also to recompose its complex 3D structure. In the same way, the major future challenge for consciousness scientists will obviously be to reconstruct the brain after having decomposed it. Let us consider again the famous dissociation between the ventral and the dorsal stream of visual processing. This dissociation can be considered as a first step towards a full decomposition of the visual system into a very sophisticated network of dozens of cortical areas (cf. Felleman and van Essen 1991). On the other hand it may also be regarded as an attempt to make sense of the incredibly complex network of areas and connections forming the visual system. But it remains based on a "dualistic" view of how the brain is organised, which can be challenged in various ways. For example the results described in this book by Bridgeman, by Bhalla and Proffitt, or by Pisella and Rossetti suggest that powerful interactions can take place between the dorsal and the ventral stream of visual processing. These results clearly indicate that dissociating visual functions is not the best way of understanding the complexity of visual processes. After having opposed the two terms of the dissociation between implicit and explicit processing, scientists will then have to follow the Hegelian idea, and initiate the final stage of the triadic progression in which an idea is proposed, then negated, and finally transcended by a new idea that resolves the conflict between the two initial terms. A further step has to be considered to the opposition between two components that are described as a dissociation. In the same vein, Marshall (1996) proposed recently that the future of neuropsychology is made of deconstructing the past. If the past of neuropsychology, as well as other areas of human sciences, is made of dissociations, then future research should be aimed at reconstructing a whole. For example, an alternative view to the dissociation theory would be that vision for action and vision for perception constitute the two extreme terms of a continuum gradient of visual functions (Rossetti, Pisella and Pélisson 2000). For representational level more complex than just visuo-motor behaviour the existence of complex interactions between implicit and explicit processing (among others) is even more obvious (e.g. Young; Forgas and Chiarrochi; Revonsuo et al.).

It is interesting to note that one of the first dissociations heralded between cortical areas dealt with 'association' cortex. More than 100 years ago Flechsig divided the cerebral cortex into three zones: the primary or projection zones on the one hand and the intermediate and terminal zones, together called the *association* cortex (Flechsig 1886, quoted by Gross 1998: 74–75, 183–184). This latter was attributed the function of transforming the sensations into perceptions, and to integrate them together with other sensory modalities. The association cortex has been then considered as the area in charge of 'the process of elaboration and intellectual interpretations...' (Bolton 1900, quoted by Gross 1998). This ironical historical consideration suggests that (1) sensations have to be distinguished from perception, as already argued by the ancient-Greece philosophers following Aristotle (2) perception and elaborated processes require the association of sensation to images and ideas kept in memory, to other sensory modalities, as well as to internal states linked to motivation and emotion. Although the dissociation between the primary and the association areas has been questioned later on (ex: Teuber 1955), these two statements also illustrate the rhetoric of assembling and disassembling the brain. The scientific approach made an extensive use of dissociation, whereas the brain is associating cognitive elements into a person's cognitive life. And the subjective experience is most often that of an individual (*in-dividis*) organism. The putting together of scientifically discovered parts or elements so as to make up a complex mind-brain whole should however not be a simple task. The aim of this book with respect to this project is only to provide the demonstration that combining and unifying the isolated data of science into a cognisable whole is more than just preparing an old alchemist recipe or reheating an old soup to synthesise human consciousness. In no way it constitutes a step backwards in time but rather constitutes the new track that one should follow to make further progresses. The synthesis of implicit and explicit processes is a crucial issue to understanding the organisation and the functions of the mind.

References

Bisiach, E., Perani, D., Vallar, G. & Berti, A. (1986). Unilateral neglect: personal and extra-personal. *Neuropsychologia,* 24, 471–482.

Bloem, W., van der Heijden, A.H.C. (1995). Complete dependence of color identification upon color localization in a single-item task. *Acta Psychologica* 89, 101–120.

Bridgeman, B. (2000). Interactions between vision for perception and vision for behavior. This volume, 17–40.

Brouwer, R.F.T., van der Heijden, A.H.C. (1996). Identity and position: dependence originates from independence. *Acta Psychologica* 95, 215–237.

Bruce, V. & Young, A. (1986). Understanding face recognition. *British Journal of Psychology,* 77, 305–327.

Buckley, M.J., Gaffan, D., Murray, E.A. (1997). Functional double dissociation between two inferior temporal cortical areas: Perirhinal cortex versus middle temporal gyrus.

Journal of Neurophysioly, 77(2):587–98

Campbell, R., Landis, T. & Regard, M. (1986). Face recognition and lipreading: a neurological dissociation. *Brain,* 109, 509–521.

Code, C. (1996). Classic cases: Ancient and modern milestones in the development of neuropsychological science. In C. Code, C-W. Wallesch, Y. Joanette & A. Roch (Eds.) *Classic cases in neuropsychology.* Hove: Psychology Press, 1–10.

Code, C., Wallesch, C-W, Joanette, Y. & Roch, A. (1996). *Classic cases in neuropsychology.* Hove: Psychology Press, pp 385.

Dienes, Z., Perner, J. (1999). A theory of implicit and explicit knowledge. *Behavioral and Brain Sciences,* 22:5, 735–754.

Dretske, F. (1998). *Explaing behavior: reasons in a world of causes.* MIT Press.

Ellis, A.W. & Young, A.W. (1988). *Human cognitive neuropsychology.* Hove and London: LEA, pp 358.

Faillenot, I., Toni, I., Decety, J., Gregoire, M.C. & Jeannerod, M. (1997). Visual pathways for object-oriented action and object recognition: functional anatomy with PET. *Cerebral Cortex,* 7(1), 77–85

Felleman, D.J. & Van Essen, D.C. (1991). Distributed hierarchical processinng in the primate visual cortex. *Cerebral Cortex,* 1, 1–47.

Fodor, J. (1983). *The modularity of mind.* Cambridge MA, MIT Press.

Georgopoulos, A.P. (1995). Current issues in directional motor control. *Trends in Neurosciences.* 11, 506–10.

Gross, C.G. (1998). *Brain, Vision, Memory. Tales in the History of Neuroscience.* Cambridge, MA, MIT Press.

Halbig, T.D., Mecklinger, A., Schriefers, H, Friederici, A.D. (1998). Double dissociation of processing temporal and spatial information in working memory. *Neuropsychologia.* 36, 305–311.

Halligan, P.W. & Marshall, J.C. (1998). Neglect of awareness. *Consciousness and Cognition.* 7(3), 356–380.

Heilman, K.M., Valenstein, E. (1993). Introduction. In *Clinical Neuropsychology* (third edition). K.M. Heilman K.M. & E. Valenstein (Eds). New York: Oxford University Press, 3–16.

Heindel, W.C., Salmon, D.P., Shults, C.W., Walicke, P.A. & Butters, N. (1989). Journal of Neurosciences, 9(2), 582–587.

Hommel, B. (2000). The prepared reflex: automaticity and control in stimulus response translation. In: S. Monsell & J. Driver (eds). *Attention and Performance vol, XVIII.* Cambridge, MA, MIT Press, in press.

Howard, R.J., ffytche, D.H., Barnes, J., McKeefry, D., Ha, Y., Woodruff, P.W., Bullmore, E.T., Simmons, A., Williams, S.C., David, A.S. & Brammer, M. (1998). The functional anatomy of imagining and perceiving colour. *Neuroreport* 9, 1019–1023.

Jones, G.V. (1983). On double dissociation of function. *Neuropsychologia,* 21, 397–400.

Kihlstrom, J. F. (1987). The cognitive unconscious. *Science* 237, 1445–1452.

Kolb, B. & Whishaw, I.Q. (1990) *Fundamentals of human neuropsychology* (third edition). New York: Freeman and Co, pp 910.

Kristan, W.B.Jr, Shaw, B.K. (1997). Population coding and behavioral choice. *Current Opinion in Neurobiology,* 6, 826–31.

Marshall, J.C. (1996). The future of neuropsychology — deconstructing the past. In C. Code, C-W. Wallesch, Y. Joanette & A. Roch (Eds.). *Classic cases in neuropsychology.* Hove: Psychology Press, 363–366.

Milikan, R. (1984). *Language, thought, and other biological categories.* MIT Press.

Milner, A.D. (1995). Cerebral correlates of visual awareness. *Neuropsychologia* 33, 1117–1130.

Milner, A.D. (1997). Neglect, extinction, and the cortical streams of visual processing. In: P. Thier, H.O. Karnath (eds). *Parietal lobe contributions to orientation in 3D space.* Springer-Verlag Berlin, 3–22.

Milner, A.D. (1998). Streams and consciousness: visual awareness and the brain. *Trends in Cognitive Sciences*, 2, 1, 25–30.

Motokawa, T. (1989). Sushi science and Hamburger science. *Perspectives in Biology and Medicine*, 32(4), 489–504.

Pisella, L. & Rossetti, Y. (2000). Interaction between conscious Identification and non-conscious sensory-motor processing: Temporal constraints. This volume, 129–152.

Rossetti, Y. (1998). Implicit short-lived motor representations of space in brain damaged and healthy subjects. *Consciousness and Cognition*, 7, 520–558.

Rossetti, Y., Pisella, L. & Pélisson, P. (2000). Eye blindness and hand sight: temporal aspects of visuo-motor processing. *Visual Cognition*, 7, in press.

Sakata, H. & Taira, M. (1994). Parietal control of hand action. *Current Opinion in Neurobiology*, 4, 847–856.

Sakurai, Y. (1996). Population coding by cell assemblies — what it really is in the brain. *Neuroscience Research*, 1, 1–16

Shallice, T. (1979). *Journal of Clinical Neuropsychology*, 1, 183–211.

Sprengelmeyer, R., Rausch, M., Eysel, U.T. & Przuntek, H. (1998). Neural structures associated with recognition of facial expressions of basic emotions. *Proceedings of the Royal Society of London* ,265, 1927–1931.

Suzuki, D.T. (1971). *Essays in Zen Buddhism* (3d ser.) New-York, Weiser.

Teuber, H.L. (1955). Physiological psychology. *Annual Review of Psychology*, 6, 267–296.

Ungerleider, L.G. & Mishkin, M. (1982). In D.J. Ingle, M.A. Goodale and R.J.W. Mansfield (Eds.), *Analysis of Visual Behavior.* MIT Press, 549–586.

Wilson, B.A., Clare, L., Young, A.W. & Hodges, J.R. (1997). Knowing where and knowing what: a double dissociation. *Cortex*, 33, 529–541.

Interactions between Vision for Perception and Vision for Behavior

Bruce Bridgeman

University of California at Santa Cruz

History of cognitive-sensorimotor dissociations

Saccadic suppression of displacement

Early hints that cognitive and sensorimotor systems are distinct in normal humans came from studies of eye movements. First, human observers are unaware of sizable displacements of the visual world if they occur during saccadic eye movements, implying that information about spatial location is degraded during saccades (Bridgeman et al.1975; Brune & Lücking 1969; Ditchburn 1955; Mack 1970; Wallach & Lewis 1965). Despite this unawareness, however, people do not become disoriented after saccades, implying that spatial information is maintained. Some experimental evidence supports this conclusion, though there is disagreement in the literature and many points remain controversial.

Interest in the conflict between perception and orientation was aroused by a report that the eyes can saccade accurately to a target that is flashed but mislocalized during an earlier saccade (Hallett & Lightstone 1976). The study has been criticized because the subjects might have memorized a few target positions. Some have failed to replicate the result (Dassonville 1992; Honda 1990), while others have found accurate pointing to targets flashed during saccades (Hansen & Skavenski 1977), and hand-eye coordination remains fairly accurate following saccades (Festinger & Cannon 1965; Honda 1985). It would seem on balance that under at least some conditions, accurate behavior can be maintained.

How can loss of perceptual information and maintenance of visually guided behavior exist side by side? A solution to this question begins with the fact that the conflicting observations are based on different response measures. The experiments on saccadic suppression of displacement require a nonspatial verbal report or button press, both symbolic responses. Orienting of the eye or hand, in contrast, requires quantitative spatial information with a one-to-one correspondence between stimulus position and motor output.

Conflict between experiments involving symbolic responses and those involving motor responses might be resolved if the two types of report, which have been labeled "cognitive" and "sensorimotor" (Paillard 1987), could be combined in a single experiment. The saccadic suppression of displacement experiments address only the cognitive system. It is at the cognitive level that symbolic decisions such as button pressing or verbal response are mediated. If two pathways in the visual system process different kinds of information, spatially oriented motor activities might have access to accurate position information even when that information is unavailable at a cognitive level (Goodale et al. 1986; Goodale et al.1991; Goodale et al. 1994b).

Cognitive and sensorimotor systems correspond respectively to the representational and sensorimotor modes of Paillard (1987; 1991), who presents other evidence for a separation of the two modes. An assumption that one system is egocentric and the other exocentric has been suggested (Paillard 1987), but is not a necessary part of the hypothesis. The two conflicting results, saccadic suppression on one hand and accurate motor behavior on the other, were combined by asking subjects to point to the position of a target that had been displaced and then extinguished (Bridgeman, Lewis, Heit & Nagle 1979; Pélisson et al. 1986). Subjects were also asked whether or not the target had been displaced. Extinguishing the target and preventing the subjects from viewing their hands (open-loop pointing) guaranteed that only internally stored spatial information could be used for pointing. The displacement was detected on some trials, while on others it went undetected due to saccadic suppression of displacement. But pointing accuracy was similar whether or not the displacement was detected in the cognitive system (see also Pisella and Rossetti, this volume).

This result implied that control of motor activity was unaffected by the perceptual detectability of target position (Prablanc et al. 1979). Alternatively, it is possible to interpret the result in terms of signal detection theory as reflecting a high response criterion for the report of displacement. That is, a target displacement could go unreported by cognitive measures because of a high criterion or threshold for reporting displacements, even while the displacement affected spatial behavior where a choice of a direction is compulsory.

This possibility was tested with a 2-alternative forced-choice cognitive measure of saccadic suppression of displacement (Bridgeman & Stark 1979). Such a criterion-free measure showed that no information about displacement was available to the cognitive system under conditions where pointing was affected.

Double dissociation of cognitive and sensorimotor modes

A more rigorous method of separating cognitive and motor systems is to introduce a signal only into the motor system in one condition and only into the cognitive system in another. We know that induced motion affects the cognitive system because we experience the effect and because subjects can make verbal judgments of it. But the above experiments imply that the information used for pointing might come from sources unavailable to perception. We inserted a signal selectivity into the cognitive system with stroboscopic induced motion (Bridgeman et al. 1981).

A fixed target was projected in front of a subject, with a frame surrounding it. When the frame was laterally displaced, subjects had the illusion of stroboscopic induced motion (Duncker 1929) — that the target had jumped in the opposite direction. Half of the time the frame jumped to the left, inducing a rightward jump of the target, and half of the time the relationships were reversed. Target and frame were then extinguished, and the subject pointed open-loop to the last target position. Trials where the target had seemed to move to the left were compared with trials where it had seemed to move to the right. Pointing was not significantly different in the two kinds of trials, showing that the induced motion illusion did not affect pointing: the displacement signal was present only in the cognitive system, and the sensorimotor system was insensitive to the visual context.

In another experiment we gave displacement information selectively to the motor system by nulling the cognitive signal. Each subject adjusted the real motion of the target, jumped in phase with the frame, until the target seemed stationary. Thus, the cognitive system specified a stable target. Nevertheless, subjects pointed in significantly different directions when the target was extinguished in the left or the right positions, showing that the difference in real target positions was still available to the motor system. This result suggests that the motor system detected a target displacement that was not available to the cognitive system.

These results meet the requirements of a double dissociation, for in the first experiment the target displacement affected only the cognitive measure, and in the second the target displacement affected only the motor measure. Double dissociation (one case of A and not B, and another case of B and not A) is important because no amount of manipulation of range nonlinearities or threshold differences can explain the results in terms of a single representation of space. Using a similar logic, cognitive and sensorimotor functions have also been dissociated by feeding the two systems opposite signals at the same time (Wong & Mack 1981). The experiment again involved stroboscopic induced motion; a spot jumped in the same direction as a frame, but not far enough to cancel the induced motion. The spot still appeared to jump in the direction opposite the frame, but it actually jumped in the same direction. Saccadic eye movements followed the veridical direction even though subjects perceived stroboscopic motion in the opposite direction. Wong and Mack's subjects fixated a target spot and saw it jump in one direction, but their eyes followed it accurately in the other direction.

If a delay in responding was required, however, eye movements followed the perceptual illusion. This result implies that the motor system has only a short memory, a few hundred msec in this case, and must rely on information from the cognitive system if the motor system's response is delayed.

Dissociating cognitive and sensorimotor modes without motion

The studies reviewed to this point required stimulus motion or displacement, and they reveal the complexity of the dynamics of several distinct control systems and their real-time interactions. They are subject to alternative interpretations, however: the dissociations between cognitive and motor responses might be related in some way to motion systems rather than to representation of visual space per se. Subjects might simply confound motion and position, and the tests for cognitive and sensorimotor information make different demands on motion and position codes respectively. Though such an interpretation is a bit strained, it cannot be logically excluded.

Experiments using stimuli with a potential confound between motion and position do not form the only basis for the two visual systems distinction; others use clinical data from blindsight, where some visually guided motor capability remains despite lack of perception (Weiskrantz et al. 1974; Bridgeman & Staggs 1982), or from other lesions (Goodale et al. 1994a). Recently, another method has been developed that can assess dissociations of cognitive and motor function without motion or displacement of the eye or the stimuli at any time during a trial. The dissociation is based on the Roelofs effect (Roelofs 1935), a tendency to misperceive the position of the edge of a large pattern presented in an unstructured field. The pattern was presented so that one of its edges was in the subject's objective centerline. According to Roelofs, this edge of the pattern is perceived to be deviated to the side opposite the remainder of the pattern. A pattern with its right edge in the center, for instance, is perceived to have that edge somewhat to the right of the center. The pattern as a whole tends to be mislocalized in the direction opposite its spatial bias, as though vision were calibrated on some compromise between the center of gravity of the object and the objective straight ahead.

The principle of the Roelofs effect is elaborated here to measure the misperception of target position in the presence of a surrounding frame presented asymmetrically; this "induced Roelofs effect" will be called a Roelofs effect below. Specifically, locations of targets within the frame tend to be misperceived in the direction opposite the lateral offset of the frame. The effect is similar to stroboscopic induced motion in which only the final positions of the target and frame are presented (Bridgeman & Klassen 1983).

Some experiments

Our first Roelofs experiment had ten subjects: nine undergraduate volunteers and the author. They sat with stabilized heads before a hemicylindrical vertical screen that provided a homogeneous field of view 180° wide x 50° high. A rectangular frame was projected, via a galvanic mirror, either centered on the subject's midline, 5° left, or 5° right of center. Inside the frame, a small "x" could be projected via a second galvanic mirror in one of 5 positions, 2° apart, with the middle "x" on the subject's midline.

To register motor responses, an unseen pointer with its axis attached to a potentiometer was mounted near the center of curvature of the screen, with its tip near the screen (Foley & Held 1972). A simple analog circuit gave a voltage proportional to the tip's position. Subjects held the pointer with the forefinger on its tip, so that their arms were outstretched and most of the rotation came from the shoulder; on pointing trials an 'enter' key was pressed when the pointer reached the desired position. The subject recorded cognitive responses, or perceived target positions, on a keyboard. A key corresponded to each target position, so that subjects performed a 5-alternative forced choice task.

Procedures

In a training session, subjects were shown the 5 possible target positions in sequence, repeated 3 times, on an otherwise blank screen. Each target was visible for 1 sec; the next target followed after a blank interval of 0.5 sec. Then subjects underwent a series of training trials, beginning with a randomly selected target exposed for 1 sec. The subjects estimated the target position with one of the 5 response keys ("judging trials"), and continued with feedback until they were correct in 5 consecutive trials. Next, they were trained on pointing, without feedback, with the same stimuli in a new random sequence ("pointing trials"), until they spontaneously returned the pointer to its rightmost position (as initially instructed) on 5 consecutive trials. Pointing required less practice because there were no positions to memorize; practice served only to familiarize subjects with the apparatus.

In both conditions, subjects were instructed to wait until the offset of the stimulus before responding. Presenting the target alone forced the subjects to use an egocentric judgment, and the long display time reduced the possibility that target onset elicited a spurious neural motion signal that might bias the responses.

For the no delay condition, trials were mixed in a pseudorandom order. On each trial, one of the 5 targets and one of the 3 frames was presented with simultaneous onset, exposed for 1 sec, and simultaneously extinguished. Because they could not respond until the offset of the stimuli, subjects were looking at a blank field at the time of the response. Thus the task was a response to an internally stored representation of the stimulus, not a perceptual task.

Judging and pointing trials appeared in a random sequence, not alternating. Each trial type was repeated 5 times. At stimulus offset, subjects heard a "beep" tone to indicate a judging response or a "squawk" tone to indicate a pointing response. Two separate 2-way ANOVAs were run for each subject and each response mode (assessing target main effect, frame main effect, and interaction). One ANOVA was based on the raw data, and the other on errors (deviations of responses from the actual stimulus positions). The subject with the minimum F is reported below for each condition; F's for other subjects are equally significant or more significant. In general, descriptive statistics are given in the figures and inferential statistics in the text.

Roelofs effects

For the cognitive measure all ten subjects showed a significant main effect of target position in both trial types. This means that when the target was toward the left the subjects judged it to be significantly further to the left than when the target was on the right. There was also a significant main effect of frame position in judging trials (F(2,4) >61.2, p < 0.001 in all subjects). Thus, all subjects showed a Roelofs effect (Figure 1), a tendency to judge the target to be further to the left than its actual position when the frame was on the right, and vice versa. The mean magnitude of the Roelofs effect was a difference of 2.0° between judgments with the frame on the left and judgments with the frame on the right. This is a reliable effect; it is present in all subjects under all conditions and is statistically significant in all subjects. There were no significant interactions, either here or in the subsequent data.

Analyses of the errors in judging target position showed a significant effect of actual target position in all 10 subjects, with the range of position estimates being smaller than the range of target positions. Thus there is a compression of perceived space in the judging mode, with an 8° field represented by estimates less than 8° apart. The same range in the pointing mode, with the same stimuli, usually resulted in pointer positions more than 8° apart: for the pointing measure 6 subjects showed significant overreaching of the target eccentricities, one showed significant underreaching, and 3 had no statistically significant errors. The difference in slopes could yield substantial differences in localization for the pointing and judging modes under some conditions, especially when the frame was offset and the target was at one of its extreme positions. Under these conditions differences between judging and pointing to the same target in the same trial block could amount to more than 5°. With the motor measure, there was a sharp division of the subjects into two groups: 5 subjects showed a highly significant Roelofs effect (F(2,4) >18, p < .01), while the other 5 showed no sign of an effect (F(2,4) <3.16, p > .18). The bimodal distribution shows that two qualitatively different results were obtained; the distribution of significances between subjects is not due to a small, normally distributed effect being significant in some subjects and not in others. That is, each subject showed either a large, robust Roelofs effect or no sign of a frame influence. Thus, responses on pointing trials were qualitatively different from responses on judging trials for half of the subjects; these

Cognitive Measure

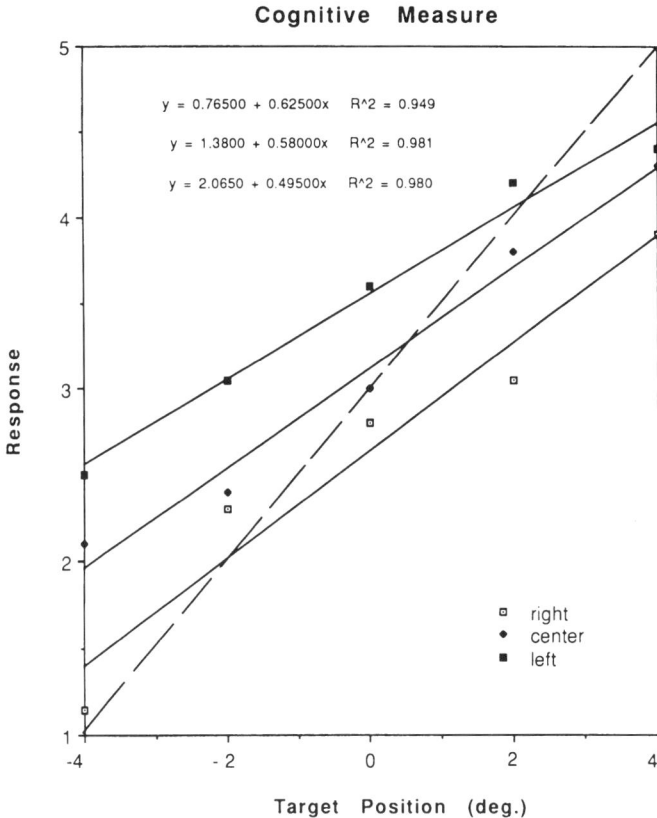

$y = 0.76500 + 0.62500x \quad R^2 = 0.949$

$y = 1.3800 + 0.58000x \quad R^2 = 0.981$

$y = 2.0650 + 0.49500x \quad R^2 = 0.980$

□ right
◆ center
■ left

Target Position (deg.)

Figure 1. Target position estimation in the presence of a rectangle that is offset to the right, centered, or offset to the left. Response is a 5-alternative forced choice to alternatives 2 deg. apart. The 3 solid lines are regression lines for a given frame position through combined data for all subjects. Frame positions are given in the lower right legend. Regression equations and r^2 values are given for each line. The separation of the lines is the Roelofs effect. The dashed line indicates veridical performance. (Original figure, based on data from Bridgeman, Peery & Anand 1997).

subjects showed a Roelofs effect only for judging. The differences in performance among subjects were unrelated to their degree of psychophysical experience or knowledge of the experiment.

Figure 2 illustrates the pointing behavior of one subject (A) who showed no Roelofs effect in pointing, while Figure 3 illustrates another subject (B) ho showed a significant Roelofs effect .

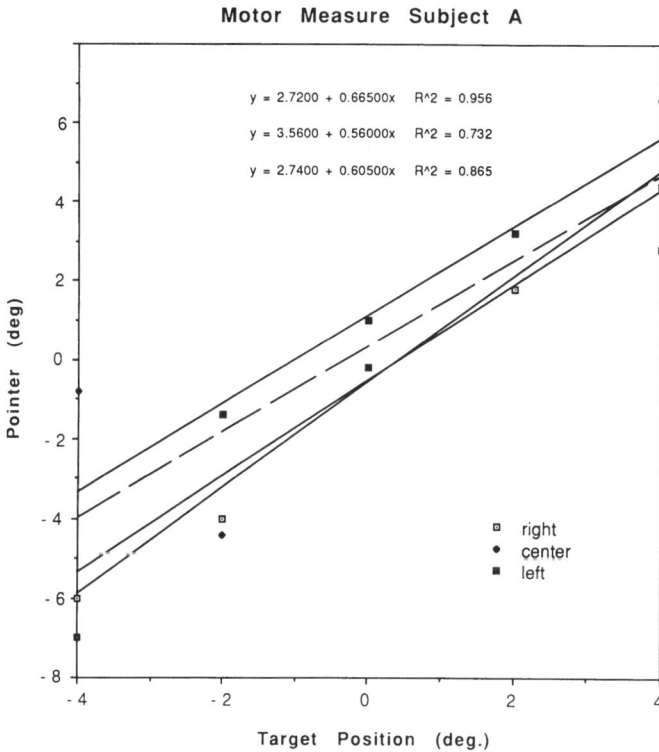

Motor Measure Subject A

$y = 2.7200 + 0.66500x$ $R^2 = 0.956$

$y = 3.5600 + 0.56000x$ $R^2 = 0.732$

$y = 2.7400 + 0.60500x$ $R^2 = 0.865$

□ right
• center
■ left

Pointer (deg)

Target Position (deg.)

Figure 2. Pointing to targets under the same stimulus conditions as in Figure 1, for a single subject. The 3 regression lines are not significantly different, and their intercepts do not vary monotonically with frame position. The dashed line indicates veridical performance. (Original figure, based on data from Bridgeman, Peery & Anand 1997).

Motor Measure Subject B

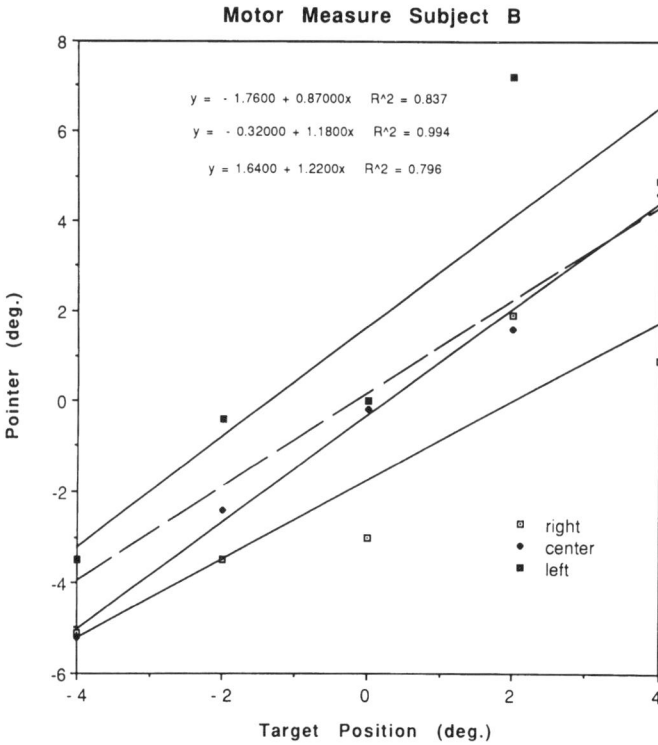

Figure 3. Pointing to targets under the same stimulus conditions as in Figure 2, for a different subject. The dashed line indicates veridical performance. The Roelofs effect is significant for this subject. (Original figure, based on data from Bridgeman, Peery & Anand 1997).

Delaying the response

Procedures were the same as the No Delay condition except that a delay was interposed between stimulus offset and the tone that indicated the type of response that the subject was to make (judging or pointing). Thus the subjects did not know during the delay interval which type of response would be required.

Nine of the 10 subjects were also tested using the cognitive measure with a 4-second delay interposed between display offset and tone. Eight of the 9 showed a significant Roelofs effect for the judging task ($F_{(2,4)} > 18$, $p < 0.01$), with a mean difference of $2.12°$ between perceptual localization when the frame was on the left and when it was on the right. In other words, the localization due to difference in frame position changed by a little more than one target position. This result is comparable to the result in the no-delay condition; results in that condition for the 9 subjects run in the delayed condition were indistinguishable from the data reported above and shown in Figure 1, with a significant and consistent Roelofs effect.

The major difference between the results with the motor measure in this condition and in the no-delay condition was that 7 of the 9 subjects showed a significant Roelofs effect ($F_{(2,4)} > 6.94$, $p < 0.05$ for 2 S's; $F_{(2,4)} > 18$, $p < 0.01$ for 7 S's). One of the two remaining subjects showed no significant effect of frame position for either measure. The other subject whose pointing behavior still showed no effect of the frame was retested with an 8-second delay between display offset and tone. A Roelofs effect was found both for judging trials (similar to the pattern of Figure 1) and pointing trials (similar to the pattern of Figure 3), indicating that after an 8-second delay this subject's pattern of responses corresponded to that of the majority of subjects at the 4-second delay.

Again the analysis of response error showed significant tendencies to underestimate the eccentricities of peripheral targets in the judging task in all subjects, while eccentricity in the pointing task tended to be overestimated.

Judging position with an open-ended scale

The restriction of response alternatives in judging trials may have influenced the observed differences between the pattern of results in judging and pointing, and may have forced the observed compression of visual space in the judging mode. To investigate this possibility, five new subjects were tested with a continuous measure of judged target direction.

Subjects were shown a centimeter ruler on the screen during an orientation session, and they were asked to estimate the position of an 'x' to be displayed in each trial in cm to the left or right of the center. Response was cued immediately after stimulus offset. Pointing trials exactly like those above were interleaved with the judging trials. In judging, variability was somewhat greater with the cm estimation method, resulting in a statistically less reliable Roelofs effect for two of the subjects ($p = 0.064$ and 0.068). The pattern of results was always in the direction of a Roelofs effect with perceived position biased to the side opposite the frame position, however, and the absolute magnitudes of the Roelofs effects in experiments I and II were similar. When asked how many target positions had been presented, the subjects were uncertain but generally guessed 6 or 7 rather than the 5 actually given.

The slopes of the lines describing verbal estimate vs. target position are less than 1 in 4 of the 5 subjects, while slopes in the pointing trials continued to be more than 1, showing that the compression of visual space found in experiment I was not due to the restricted range of alternative responses (not illustrated). Rather, the slope difference seems to represent a more general distinction between the internal representations of 'cognitive' and 'sensorimotor' visual space.

The fact that judging is less accurate than pointing cannot explain the difference in slopes with the two measures, because this interpretation would predict shallower slopes of the pointing functions due to statistical regression to the mean. The pattern of results is the reverse of this: the steeper slope (in pointing) is associated with the larger variability. Another possible explanation for the slope difference is sought in experiment II. Another possible explanation of the lower slope with the judging measure is not that space became compressed, but that the interpretation of the remembered target locations became expanded.

Interpretation in terms of cognitive and sensorimotor systems

Up to this point we had tested 15 subjects. All of them experienced a Roelofs effect in the cognitive measure, showing that the effect is robust and easily obtained. Seven of these subjects showed a Roelofs effect in pointing without a delay, while eight did not. All showed a pointing Roelofs effect after a sufficient delay.

All subjects used pointing information that is biased by the frame position if a long enough delay was imposed before the response cue, even though half of them were not vulnerable to this bias when responding immediately. This implies that the bimodal distribution of Roelofs effects in pointing without delay had been due to the subjects using two different sources of information for pointing. One group had used a motor mode that was not sensitive to visual context, a 'privileged loop' between vision and motor activity. The other group apparently imported spatial information from the cognitive to the sensorimotor representation for use in pointing, and imported the illusion along with it. The results also show a differential decay rate of cognitive responses and pointing responses, along with a steeper slope and greater variability for pointing than for the cognitive measure (see also Rossetti 1998, 2000; Pisella and Rossetti, this volume). In the proprioceptive domain, Rossetti and Régnier (1995) also found a recoding of the reference frame for a pointing task with a delay.

One interpretation of these phenomena is that a single visual representation shows different characteristics when probed with different demands. This interpretation runs into difficulty in explaining effects that are present and robust in one response mode and completely absent in the other, however: No amount of tinkering with differential thresholds and range nonlinearities can account for such effects. An interpretation that is consistent with cortical neurophysiology, as well as with the literature cited in the introduction, is that the two measures access information from different internal maps of visual space.

The two-maps hypothesis also provides a parsimonious language for describing the results. The motor representation is accessed by a pointing measure that requires an isomorphic response, a 1:1 relationship between stimulus position and behavior; a stimulus and a response map directly onto one another. The cognitive representation, in contrast, requires a categorization in which the relationship between target position and behavior is arbitrary.

These results contrast with those of Bacon, Gordon and Schulman (1982), who found a Roelofs effect in a comparable paradigm. In one of their conditions a target oscillated vertically while a background frame oscillated horizontally, resulting in an induced slant in the target's trajectory. Alternatively, the background could be fixed at either its left or right extreme position, and the target at either its highest or lowest point. Pointing to the target yielded a significant horizontal target offset in trials when the frame was on the right compared to trials when it was on the left, a replication of the Roelofs effect.

The effect was significantly smaller than perceptual effects in an induced-motion control, however, indicating again that the pointing measure is significantly closer to veridical than the perceptual measure. The implicit slant between the target's two positions in the Roelofs condition was 30 deg, compared to a veridical slant of 45 deg. Neither they nor we measured response latency, and both experiments used unspeeded pointing that was cued by target offset. But if Bacon et al.'s subjects were not quick about their pointing, a situation similar to our delay condition could have occurred, with a similar result. A similar set of circumstances might account for the similar results of Sugarman and Cohen (1968). We found that most subjects showed a Roelofs effect with a 4-second delay, but the minimum delay may be much shorter; Bacon et al.'s results suggest that it is indeed shorter.

Using both modes at the same time

The work just reviewed leads to the conclusion that the motor representation is short-lived; after a delay subjects relied upon the cognitive map even during motor tasks. But there was a difference in how the subjects reacted to the cognitive and the motor tasks. The cognitive task was perceived to be a difficult problem, and the subjects sometimes expressed some uncertainty about which answer was best. The pointing task, in contrast, seemed much easier, and several subjects reported that as soon as they knew that a pointing response would be required, they could relax and just do what came naturally. It was as though less cognitive effort was required for the motor task. But what would happen if subjects produced both types of response in the same trial (see also Pisella and Rossetti, this volume)?

In this experiment, we asked whether either response modality could affect the other modality when both types of responses are performed. In other words we examined whether use of the accurate motor representation of space on a trial would eliminate the Roelofs effect in the cognitive (judging) task, or alternatively whether accessing the cognitive representation would induce a Roelofs effect in the motor measure. The procedure was the same as above except that subjects both pointed to and judged the target location on every trial. Half of the nine subjects were randomly assigned to point first and half to judge first on each trial. Responses were not delayed.

All subjects showed the same pattern of results for the cognitive measure. ANOVA showed that target location had a significant effect of amplitude 2.2° for all subjects, whether they judged first or pointed first. The results were similar to those of Figure 1.

For the motor measure, the pattern of results was similar. Frame location again had a significant effect (on the pattern of Figure 3) with an amplitude of 4.4° for all subjects, whether they judged first or pointed first. Overall, the average magnitude of the target effect was larger for the pointing responses than for the judging responses ($F(1,1350) = 378.5$, $p<.0001$). That is, as in the earlier experiments, there were steeper slopes for pointing responses than for judging responses.

When both responses occur to a single stimulus they are both biased by a Roelofs effect, in contrast to the situation in which subjects either point to or judge the location of a target surrounded by an offset frame with no delay. This finding is independent of the order in which the responses occur, suggesting that a separate map is not accessed for each response. That is, instead of activating cognitive and motor maps on each trial for the judging and pointing responses respectively, only one representation of visual space is accessed on each trial. This representation appears to be the cognitive map, indicated by the reliable Roelofs effect in the judging responses.

The first experiments showed the motor map to be short-lived, forcing subjects to rely on the cognitive representation when there is a delay before responding. The double-response experiment elaborates on the temporal sequence from cognitive to sensorimotor processing of visual space by showing that motor responses depend on the cognitive map whenever such a map must be used in a given situation.

Normally the motor system is insensitive to context-based biases such as the Roelofs effect. Why, then, did subjects in this experiment show a Roelofs effect during pointing? Our interpretation is that the combined sequential responses of pointing and judging required several seconds, and the subjects knew that the position would have to be remembered during that time. This forced them to store the position internally in the cognitive representation, even when the motor response came first. It is as though the subject said to himself, "I am going to say 'right', so I should point to the right". Each trial was treated as a visual 'event', encoded in one map of visual space. Since the dual response took more time or more complex coding than the motor representation can support, responses were based on the cognitive representation. Rossetti and Régnier (1995) also showed a similar effect in normal subjects: with simultaneous reponses, the motor response followed the perceptual information.

Rossetti et al. (1995) found an analogous result in a patient who has what might be called tactile blindsight or "Numbsense"; the patient could point to the position of a tactile stimulation on his arm, but could not describe the position verbally or point to it on a chart of the arm. The patient lost the ability to point accurately when required to give the location verbally at the same time. And the patient's inability to point to the stimulated position shows that the motor representation is available only for isomorphic responses, not for symbolically reorganized activity, even if the actual motor movement is similar in both cases. This result is consistent with our finding that the subject must actually hit the target, not just hit a button, to access the context-insensitive motor code (see Pisella and Rossetti, this volume).

Theoretical interpretation

Perception of a Roelofs effect is robust, being seen by all subjects under all delays. The Roelofs effect in visually guided behavior, though, depends much more strongly on the subjects and conditions. Half of the subjects showed a strong effect of a surrounding frame on pointing behavior while the other half showed no effect. This bimodal distribution suggests that subjects went about the task in either of two different ways; the data are inconsistent with the hypothesis that subjects varied along a continuum of the amount of influence of the frame.

Since all responses were made in a blank field after the stimuli had been extinguished, these differences may be due to differing strategies of the subjects; some responded in a motor mode, while others switched almost immediately to a cognitive mode, which brought the illusion along with it. All subjects appeared to operate in the cognitive mode when required to both point to and judge the perceived target location on each trial. It is not the case that the two groups of subjects followed different psychological laws, only that they switched from motor to cognitive modes at differing delays after stimulus offset. Differential accuracy and decay rates of cognitive versus motor responses would redescribe the data, but would not explain the source of the differences. Roelofs effects in pointing were universal with a long enough delay between target presentation and response, or when pointing and judging occurred on the same trials; a closer titration of delay times would probably show a unique critical delay for a pointing Roelofs effect in each subject.

Two visual representations in related studies

The results are not comparable to those of studies in which subjects respond while the stimuli are still present (Hansen & Skavenski 1977), or in which responses occur within 400–500 msec of the target event (Hallett & Lightstone 1976; Wong & Mack 1981). All subjects in those studies showed accurate motor behavior, in the present interpretation because the spatial values in the motor representation had not yet been lost. Appearance of a Roelofs effect with a delay between stimulus and motor response is consistent with the results of Wong and Mack (1981), however. They found that saccadic eye movements followed a veridical displacement direction with a short delay but followed a perceived displacement in the opposite direction after a longer delay. Though the delays used here were longer than those of Wong and Mack, the pattern of results is similar.

Thus it appears that the motor representation of space possesses a memory for the positions of stimuli no longer present, but the memory begins to degrade after no more than a few hundred msec; the shift at a 4-sec delay in the present experiments puts an upper bound, but not a lower bound, on the duration of the memory buffer. The duration of this memory and the conditions under which it is degraded are topics for future research. Recent still-unpublished results from our Santa Cruz laboratory suggest that the minimum delay is about 2 sec, and that the influence of the cognitive representation emerges gradually rather than abruptly.

Others have reported data that clarify the contrast between cognitive and sensorimotor streams, though their studies were designed for other purposes and require reinterpretation to relate to the present theoretical interpretation. Abrams and Landgraf (1990) performed an induced-motion experiment with a target and frame similar those described here, and two response measures. In one task, the subject pointed to the final position of the target. Extent of motion was determined in successive trials by pointing to the target in its left and right positions respectively. In the other task, the subject moved a handle, similar to our pointer, through the same distance that the target was perceived to have moved.

These tasks contrast with ours in that the final-position pointing task (which they call a 'location' condition) is egocentric, like our pointing task, but the motion reproduction task (which they call a 'distance' condition) was exocentric; the subject indicated the perceived distance between two target positions, rather than the direction of either target relative to the body. In both of the Roelofs tasks, we took pains to obtain egocentric information. The subjects responded to only one target at a time, and never saw more than one target, even during the training trials. In our theoretical framework, the location task probes the sensorimotor system, because its position is isomorphic to the target position. The distance task probes the cognitive system, because the subject reproduces the perceived extent of movement. The pointer need not coincide with the target's final position. Abrams and Landgraf's first experiment was analogous to our delay condition, while their second experiment was analogous to our no-delay condition, except that in both cases induced motion rather than Roelofs stimuli were used.

The results are consistent with what we found: with no delay, there was a significant interaction between the two tasks. There was an overall induced motion effect, but the significance of the effect is made difficult to interpret by the interaction, and it was not tested statistically for the two conditions separately. The extent of induced motion in their location condition, a sensorimotor measure by the conventions used here, was about 0.5 deg (estimated from their Figure 3). In the delay experiment, however, induced motion was seen with both measures, consistent with our delay condition in which Roelofs effects were seen for both cognitive and sensorimotor systems. There was no statistically significant interaction between their two measures in this experiment.

Our results reinforce the conclusion that the normal human possesses two maps of visual space. One of them holds information used in perception: if a subject is asked what he or she sees, the information in this 'cognitive' map is accessed. This map can achieve great sensitivity to small motions or translations of objects in the visual world by using relative motion or position as a cue. The price that the cognitive system pays for gaining this sensitivity is that it loses absolute egocentric calibration of visual space.

A useful model for the use of relative motion information is the process of differentiation in calculus. In calculating motion dx/dt by differentiation, the constant term (the spatial calibration) drops out of the representation. Such a representation cannot be used to control visually guided behavior, however, and since all mammals have motor control we can assume that the cognitive system evolved after the sensorimotor system. The cognitive system arose later to handle specialized pattern-recognition challenges, but it never had the job of controlling behavior directly.

The other visual map drives visually guided behavior, but its contents are not necessarily available to perception. This map does not have the resolution and sensitivity to fine-grained spatial relationships that the cognitive map has, but it is not required to: a small error in pointing, grasping or looking is of little consequence. The advantage of this map is its robustness; the "motor" map is not subject to illusions such as induced motion and the Roelofs effect. It also has only a short memory, being concerned mainly with the here-and-now correspondence between visual information and motor behavior. If a subject must make motor responses to stimuli no longer present, this system must take its spatial information from the cognitive representation, and brings any cognitively based illusions along with it. This is not to say that a sequence cannot be stored in memory and used to improve motor performance in the future; the current egocentric spatial values are lost, however.

The existence of two parallel visual systems, both carrying spatial information, is also important for interpreting the role of consciousness in human mental life, because the cognitive system is conscious while the sensorimotor system is not. A way of interpreting the relationship between cognitive and sensorimotor representations is in terms of the ability to integrate information from the map with other information. The cognitive map's contents are coded in terms of the entire visual array (both target and frame in our case), while the motor map is generally inaccessible to integration with information from other sources. The difference between cognitive and motor representations in this context is analogous to the distinction between explicit and implicit modes of memory, respectively. The explicit mode is accessible to language and to experiential memory, while the implicit mode may hold information that the subject is unaware of or even that is contradictory to other explicit memory (Roediger et al. 1988). Similarly, in our experiments subjects can hold one position of a stimulus in the cognitive representation and simultaneously hold a different position for the same stimulus in the motor representation. But awareness is always of the information in the system that has an enduring memory, that can be described later and related to other events; and this seems to be the key to consciousness.

More than one motor representation?

Motor behavior can be divided into three components: eye movements, movements of body parts, and locomotion. The first component, eye movements, normally functions without conscious intervention, though some kinds of saccadic eye movements can be initiated voluntarily. As the experiment of Wong and Mack (1981) showed, eye movement control can take advantage of veridical, egocentrically organized spatial information only if that information is used when currently present in the retinal image, or if it is used within a few hundred msec of stimulus offset.

The second component, including arm, hand and head movements, is the subject of most of the empirical work described in this chapter. The evidence cited above shows that information available to this system is available for a few seconds for open-loop control; after that, cognitive information must be imported into the sensorimotor system to control behavior. The work of Milner and Goodale (1995) explicates many of the characteristics of this component (see also Jackson, this volume; Bhalla and Proffitt, this volume; Pisella and Rossetti, this volume).

The final component is for the control of locomotion. It is isolated in studies where subjects can interact with a visual environment only through locomotion, walking or climbing through it. For example, perception of distance on the order of meters, measured by having subjects mark equal-appearing intervals, is non-linear, with large errors. But when subjects were asked to walk to a target, they did so accurately (Loomis et al. 1992). When another target was placed twice as far away, subjects walked twice as far, despite their distorted perceptual judgment. This experiment expands and formalizes a common experience: one can ask a person to judge a distance to a target by any measure (number of body lengths, arm spans, meters, etc.) and receive wildly erroneous estimates. But when asked to throw a ball to the same target, the same person does pretty well.

More recent experiments have shown that the accurate locomotor system's spatial map, like that in the pointing and jabbing experiments above, has a limited memory. Creem and Proffitt (1998) have shown that subjects greatly overestimate the slope of a hill in verbal estimates, but are much more accurate if asked to adjust a tilt board to match the slope. The next day, or a few hours later on the same day, however, the tilt-board estimate is significantly steeper, in the direction of the cognitive overestimate. So again it seems that the cognitive system informs isomorphic motor responses after a delay. Here, however, motor estimates remain accurate for at least a few minutes following termination of exposure to the stimulus situation (see Bhalla and Proffitt, this volume).

The properties of all three of these subsystems, or components of the sensorimotor branch of vision, can be summarized with a few consistent rules that apply to all of them. All three show an initial component that is more veridical than the corresponding cognitive measures, and all three begin to show errors in the direction of cognitive measures after a delay. The critical delay in each system seems to be different, but in each case it corresponds closely to the amount of time required to execute a meaningful interaction with the world in the corresponding motor output modality; on the order of hundreds of msec for saccade control, seconds for arm and head movements (Jakobson & Goodale 1991), and minutes for hill-climbing or other locomotion. Each component seems to hold information long enough to act on it, but no longer. In each case, contradictory cognitive information can coexist in the nervous system without apparent conflict, showing the need for a segregation of cognitive and sensorimotor representations of the relevant information (see Bhalla and Proffitt, this volume; Hommel, this volume; Pisella and Rossetti, this volume, Rossetti 1998, 2000).

Some parts of the story remain incomplete. The most important missing component is that we don't yet know much about the interactions of the two systems. Apparently the cognitive branch can provide the motor branch with spatial information under some conditions, but information cannot flow the other way. The codes used by the two systems seem only partly compatible, resulting in the possibility of cognitive-to-sensorimotor but not sensorimotor-to-cognitive information flow. It is not clear how the cognitive system communicates a particular object as a target, to a system than cannot distinguish different targets. And the temporal lobe / parietal lobe dichotomy is not quite as clean as one would like. The lobes are more convention than anatomical reality in this part of the brain in any case, and nature has not segregated the systems neatly into dorsal and ventral components; things get a bit tangled in the posterior and inferior parietal regions. The distinction between cognitive and sensorimotor, though, has already proved a useful concept in explicating the visual brain.

Acknowledgments

The experiments were partially supported by AFOSR grant #90–0095. I thank Sulekha Anand, Will Aiken, Paul Thiem, Shelley Peery, Andrea Gemmer, Trish Forsman, Denise Caroso and Stephanie Saylor for assistance with executing the experiments.

References

Abrams, R. & Landgraf, J. (1990). Differential use of distance and location information for spatial localization. *Perception and Psychophysics*, 47, 349–359.

Bacon, J., Gordon, A. & Schulman, P. (1982). The effect of two types of induced-motion displays on perceived location of the induced target. *Perception and Psychophysics*, 32, 353–359.

Bhall, M. & Proffitt, D.R. (2000). Geographical slant perception: Dissociation and coordination between explicit awarness and visually guided actions. This volume, 99–128.

Bridgeman, B., Hendry, D. & Stark, L. (1975). Failure to detect displacement of the visual world during saccadic eye movements. *Vision Research*, 15, 719–722.

Bridgeman, B., Lewis, S., Heit, G. & Nagle, M. (1979). Relation between cognitive and motor-oriented systems of visual position perception. *Journal of Experimental Psychology: Human Perception and Performance*, 5, 692–700.

Bridgeman, B., Kirch, M. & Sperling, A. (1981). Segregation of cognitive and motor aspects of visual function using induced motion. *Perception and Psychophysics*, 29, 336–342.

Bridgeman, B. & Klassen, H. (1983). On the origin of stroboscopic induced motion. *Perception and Psychophysics*, 34, 149–154.

Bridgeman, B., Peery, S. & Anand, S. (1997). Interaction of cognitive and sensorimotor maps of visual space. *Perception and Psychophysics*, 59, 456–469.

Bridgeman, B. & Stark, L. (1979). Omnidirectional increase in threshold for image shifts during saccadic eye movements. *Perception and Psychophysics*, 25, 241–243.

Brune, F. & Lücking, C. (1969). Oculomotorik, Bewegungswahrnehmung und Raumkonstanz der Sehdinge. *Der Nervenarzt*, 40, 692–700.

Creem, S.H. & Proffitt, D.R. (1998). Two memories for geographical slant: separation and interdependence of action and awareness. *Psychonomic Bulletin and Review*, 5, 22–36.

Dassonville, P., Schlag J. & Schlag-Rey M. (1992). Oculomotor localization relies on a damped representation of saccadic eye displacement in human and nonhuman primates. *Visual Neuroscience*, 9, 261–269.

Ditchburn, R. (1955). Eye-movements in relation to retinal action. *Optica Acta*, 1, 171–176.

Duncker, D.K. (1929). Über induzierte Bewegung. *Psychologische Forschung* 12, 180–259.

Festinger, L. & Canon, L. K. (1965). Information about spatial location based on knowledge about efference. *Psychological Review*, 72, 373–384.

Foley, J. & Held, R. (1972). Visually directed pointing as a function of target distance, direction, and available cues. *Perception and Psychophysics*, 10, 263–268.

Goodale, M., Pelisson, D. & Prablanc, C. (1986). Large adjustments in visually guided reaching do not depend on vision of the hand or perception of target displacement. *Nature*, 320, 748–750.

Goodale, M.A., Milner, A.D., Jakobson, L.S. & Carey, D.P. (1991). A neurological dissociation between perceiving objects and grasping them. *Nature*, 349, 154–156.

Goodale, M.A., Jakobson, L.S., Milner, A.D., Perrett, D.I., Benson, P.J. & Hietanen, J.K. (1994a). The Nature and limits of orientation and pattern processing supporting visuomotor control in a visual form agnosic. *Journal of Cognitive Neuroscience*, 6, 46–56.

Goodale, M. A., Meenan, J. P., Bülthoff, H. H., Nicolle, D. A., Murphy, K.J. & Racicot, C. I. (1994b). Separate neural pathways for the visual analysis of object shape in perception and prehension. *Current Biology*, 4, 604–610.

Hallett, P. E. & Lightstone, A. D. (1976). Saccadic eye movements towards stimuli triggered during prior saccades. *Vision Research*, 16, 99–106.

Hansen, R. & Skavenski, A. (1977). Accuracy of eye-position information for motor control. *Vision Research*, 17, 919–926.

Hommel, B. (2000). Intentional Control of Automatic Stimulus-Response Translation. This volume, 221–242.

Honda, H. (1985). Spatial localization in saccade and pursuit-eye-movement conditions: A comparison of perceptual and motor measures. *Perception and Psychophysics*, 38, 41–46.

Honda, H. (1990). The extraretinal signal from the pursuit-eye-movement system: Its role in the perceptual and the egocentric localization systems. *Perception and Psychophysics*, 48, 509–515.

Jackson, S.R. (2000). Perception, awareness and action: Insights from blindsight. This volume, 73–98.

Jakobson, L.S., and Goodale, M.A. (1991). Factors affecting higher-order movement planning: A kinematic analysis of human prehension. *Experimental Brain Research*, 86, 199–208.

Loomis, J., DaSilva, J., Fujita, N. and Fukusima, S. (1992). Visual space perception and visually directed action. *Journal of Experimental Psycholology: Human Perception and Performance*, 18, 906–921.

Mack, A. (1970). An investigation of the relationship between eye and retinal image movement in the perception of movement. *Perception and Psychophysics*, 8, 291–298.

Milner, A. D. & Goodale, M. A. (1995). *The Visual Brain in Action*. Oxford: Oxford University Press.

Paillard, J. (1987). Cognitive versus sensorimotor encoding of spatial information. In P. Ellen & C. Thinus-Blanc (Eds.), *Cognitive Processes and Spatial Orientation in Animal and Man*. Dordrecht, Netherlands: Martinus Nijhoff Publishers.

Paillard, J. (1991). Motor and representational framing of space. In J. Paillard (Ed.), *Brain and Space*. Oxford: Oxford University Press.

Pélisson, D., Prablanc, C., Goodale, M.A. & Jeannerod, M. (1986). Visual control of reaching movements without vision of the limb. II. Evidence of fast unconscious processes correcting the trajectory of the hand to the final position of a double-step stimulus. *Experimental Brain Research*, 62, 303–311.

Pisella, L. & Rossetti, Y. (2000). Interaction between conscious Identification and non-conscious sensory-motor processing: Temporal constraints. This volume, 129–152.

Prablanc, C., Echallier, J., Komilis, E. & Jeannerod, M. (1979). Optimal response of eye and hand motor systems in pointing. *Biological Cybernetics*, 45, 113–124.

Roediger, H., Weldon, M. & Challis, B. (1988). Explaining dissociations between implicit and explicit measures of retention: A processing account. In H. L. Roediger & F. I. Craik (Eds.), *Varieties of memory and consciousness*: Essays in honor of Endel Tulving. Hillsdale, New Jersey: Lawrence Erlbaum.

Roelofs, C. (1935). Optische Localisation. *Archiv für Augenheilkunde*, 109, 395–415.

Rossetti, Y. (1998). Implicit short-lived motor representation of space in brain-damaged and healthy subjects. *Consciousness and Cognition*, 7, 520–558.

Rossetti, Y. (2000). Implicit perception in action: short-lived motor representations of space. In: P.G. Grossenbacher (ed.): *Finding consciousness in the brain.* (131–179) Amsterdam/Philadelphia: John Benjamins Publishing Company.

Rossetti, Y. & Régnier, C. (1995). Representations in action: pointing to a target with various representations; in Bardy, B., Bootsma, R. & Guiard, Y. (Eds): *Studies in Perception and Action III* (233–236). Mahwah, NJ: Lawrence Erlbaum.

Rossetti, Y., Rode, G. & Boisson, D. (1995). Implicit processing of somaesthetic information: a dissociation between where and how. *Neuroreport*, 6, 506–510.

Wallach, H. & Lewis, C. (1965). The effect of abnormal displacement of the retinal image during eye movements. *Perception and Psychophysics*, 1, 25–29.

Weiskrantz, L., Warinton, E., Sanders, M. & Marshall, J. (1974). Visual capacity in the hemianopic field following restricted occipital ablation. *Brain*, 97, 709–729.

Wong, E. & Mack, A. (1981). Saccadic programming and perceived location. *Acta Psychologica*, 48, 123–131.

Distance-Location Interference in Movement Reproduction

An Interaction between Conscious and Unconscious Processing?

Kuniyasu Imanaka
Tokyo Metropolitan University, Japan

Bruce Abernethy
The University of Queensland, Australia

Introduction

The process underlying the control and learning of skilled movement have historically been the focus of examinations by researchers from a number of different disciplinary areas but primarily neuroscience and psychology (Prinz & Sanders 1984). Since the pioneering neurophysiological work of Sir Charles Sherrington (e.g., Sherrington 1906) on the integrative action of the nervous system, neuroscientists have investigated the interaction between afferent and efferent neuronal information and the effect of this interaction on movement and position sense at both the spinal and cortical levels. Psychologists, beginning with Woodworth (1899) and others in the late nineteenth century, have long been interested in probing the relationship between perception and action, between cognition and motor acts, and between motor control and learning.

Cognitive and experimental psychology has been dominated since the 1960s by the information-processing approach, which has sought to understand, using a computational analogy, the processes and memory mechanisms underlying verbal, mental and, later, motor aspects of human behaviour. The

basic notion underpinning this approach is that humans behave like a sophisticated information-processing system. In this sophisticated system, input information about both the external environmental conditions and the internal
conditions of the performer is assumed to be processed through a series of
discrete stages, such as stimulus identification, response selection, and response programming stages (Schmidt 1988). The processing at each of these
stages is thought to be mediated, in part, by a short-term memory store in
which movement information is encoded, retained, and re-used for movement
reproduction.

A large amount of research has been conducted to attempt to understand
the encoding, retention, and retrieval of movement information in short-term
memory. Indeed, the role of distance and location information in the short-
term reproduction of arm movement was among the most intensively examined of all motor control topics in the 1970s. While many of the early studies
(Gundry 1975; Jones 1974; Laabs 1973) attempted to separately elucidate the
characteristic nature of information about movement distance and location,
some researchers (e.g., Marteniuk & Roy 1972; Stelmach & Kelso 1973)
recognised that the selective reproduction of either the distance or the end
location of a given criterion (standard) movement appeared to be influenced
by other sources of information available during the criterion movement. The
specific nature of this interference was documented most clearly in the work
of Kerr (1978) and then Walsh and his colleagues (e.g., Walsh & Russell
1979; Walsh & Russell 1980; Walsh et al. 1979). These researchers demonstrated that the reproduction of movement distance is apparently interfered
with by the end location of the criterion movement and, conversely, the
reproduction of movement location is interfered with by criterion movement
distance. Interestingly, the systematic demonstration of the mutual interference between movement distance and location resulted in cessation of the
early enthusiastic debates on the respective coding and retention accuracy
characteristics of distance and location information. After the plethora of
studies on motor short-term memory in the 1970s, there were very few
published studies in this area in the decade that followed.

Another factor leading to a declining research effort on motor short-term
memory issues in the 1980s, especially those relating to linear arm movements, was the rise of alternative approaches to motor control which challenge
many of the implicit assumptions underlying the information-processing approach. The rise of ecological psychology (Gibson 1966; Gibson 1979) chal-

lenged the artificial separation of perception and action in traditional experimental approaches and the emergence of the dynamical systems approach (e.g., Kelso et al. 1981) challenged assumptions about the need for representations of movement through demonstration of the control potential present within the self-organising capabilities of the neuromuscular skeletal system. In line with these paradigmatic challenges by the ecological and dynamical systems approaches, recent findings (e.g., Milner & Goodale 1995; Neumann & Klotz 1994; Rossetti 1998, 2000; Rossetti et al. 1994) concerning dissociation between perception and action have provided strong evidence against the traditional notion of serial information-processing. These recent findings suggest that given stimuli can act directly on the control of movement prior to (or by bypassing) the conscious awareness of the given stimuli. Such findings are difficult to reconcile with an information-processing notion which assumes sequential processing stages and information flow from stimulus identification through response selection to response programming.

Despite both the recent advent of paradigms challenging the traditional information-processing approach and the declining research efforts on motor short-term memory since the early 1980s, we seek to revisit the issue of "distance-location interference in movement reproduction" in this chapter. Our reasons for revisiting the motor short-term memory issues of the 1970s are twofold: first, the available evidence with respect to the cause of the fundamental phenomena of distance-location interference in motor short-term memory is still inconclusive. Second, exploring the cause of the distance-location interference phenomenon, brings us directly to the manipulation of cognitive and attentional factors, such as conscious versus unconscious processing (or explicit vs. implicit use) of movement information. The issue of conscious versus unconscious processing is one of contemporary interest across a broad range of fields in neuroscience and psychology, yet only rarely is this issue brought to focus upon movement encoding and recall. Such issues can be addressed without the need to invoke some of the problematic assumptions of traditional information processing.

This chapter aims to provide both an overview of recent studies which have been conducted to elucidate further the mechanisms underlying the distance-location interference in motor short-term memory and to discuss some alternative perspectives with respect to the interference/integration and dissociation between conscious and unconscious processes in the short-term reproduction of arm movements. The chapter is organized into three major sections. In the first section, we briefly describe the characteristic nature of the distance-location interference phenomenon, giving particular focus to the findings of Walsh and his colleagues and to the typical investigative paradigms which they and others have used. Second, we review a recent series of our own experiments which have been conducted in an attempt to examine whether the distance-location interference phenomenon arises as a consequence of methodological artefacts, kinaesthetic feedback factors, or rather factors related to cognition, strategy, and conscious awareness. In the final section, we discuss the distance-location interference phenomenon from three different theoretical viewpoints with respect to attentional (conscious and unconscious) correlates, namely, (1) the controlled and automatic processing modes perspective (Schneider & Shiffrin 1977), (2) the explicit and implicit perception in action perspective (Milner & Goodale 1995; Rossetti 1998), and (3) a perspective involving a possible biomechanical causal factor ("the centre of mass" of the whole arm used in positioning movement), which is assumed to be unconsciously (implicitly) controlled by the brain (Suzuki et al. 1996; Suzuki et al. 1997).

The original findings on distance-location interference

Demonstration of distance-location interference in motor short-term memory requires the systematic (forward and backward) manipulation of starting position between the criterion and reproduction movement. Such manipulations were first used in a number of motor short-term memory studies appearing in the mid-to-late 1970s. This section provides fundamental information, in turn, about both the manipulation of starting position and the major dependent variables used to illustrate the characteristic features of distance-location interference.

In the manipulation of starting position, blindfolded subjects are asked to reproduce either the movement distance or end location of the preceding criterion movement from a new starting position, i.e., one which is altered from the original criterion starting position (Figure 1). In theory, when subjects are ask to reproduce the end location of a criterion movement they should rely on the end location alone, ignoring completely the (irrelevant) criterion movement distance. Conversely, when they are asked to reproduce movement distance, they should ignore the end location of the criterion movement as this is no longer a reliable source of information. The instruction set should enable subjects to rely on the specific movement cue nominated for accurate movement reproduction and ignore the other (irrelevant) cue. A number of researchers in the 1970s used the starting position manipulation in an attempt to determine the respective roles and utility of distance and location information in the short-term reproduction of arm movement. We have reviewed the major findings of these early studies in detail elsewhere (Imanaka et al. 1998; Imanaka et al. 1996).

Studies on short-term memory for arm movement have typically used three dependent variables to measure movement reproduction performance, namely, constant or algebraic error (CE), which indicates response bias such as undershooting and overshooting; variable error (VE), which indicates the variability (inconsistency) across responses by each subject; and absolute error (AE), which is a composite of both CE and VE reflecting overall accuracy to some degree. The CE measure is the one most relevant to demonstrating distance-location interference, although the AE and, to a lesser extent, VE measures are important in determining the overall accuracy of reproduction using each separate movement cue.

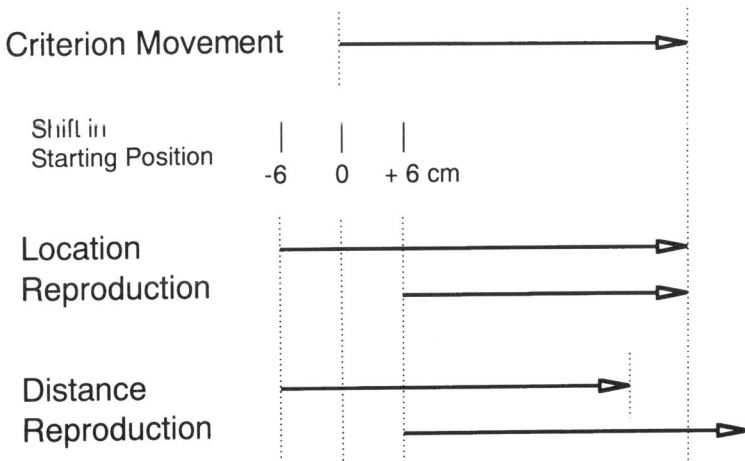

Figure 1. Starting position manipulations as a means of separating the location and distance cues used in the reproduction of a criterion movement. The arrows for both location and distance reproduction indicate perfect reproduction from the altered starting positions.

The distance-location interference phenomenon in motor short-term memory manifests itself in a characteristic pattern of response bias (i.e., overshooting and undershooting, expressed by CEs) which is a function of both the direction and amplitude of the starting position change. Figure 2 shows a typical characteristic pattern of response bias, as reported by Walsh et al. (1979). In Walsh et al.'s experiments, the starting position of the reproduction movement was systematically moved from the original criterion starting position by 0, 2, 4, and 6 cm in either direction. In reproducing the end location of a criterion movement, subjects tended to undershoot the desired location when the starting position of the reproduction movement was moved away from the end location (i.e., negative shifts in starting position; see Figure 1) and tended to overshoot when the starting position was moved relatively closer to the end location than the original criterion starting position (positive shifts). In reproducing movement distance, subjects tended to over-shoot the desired distance when the starting position was moved away from the end location and tended to undershoot when the starting position was moved toward the end location.

Such a systematic pattern of response bias (i.e., undershooting and over-shooting) as a function of the shift in starting position has been interpreted as evidence of the influence of other information from the criterion movement which the subject is supposed to ignore. Information on the end location of the criterion movement appears to bias the reproduction of movement distance toward the criterion movement end location, thereby causing undershooting and overshooting. Similarly, information on distance within the criterion movement appears to cause undershooting and overshooting in reproducing movement end location. It therefore appears likely that subjects cannot re-member either the movement distance or location of the criterion movement independently of the other information available during the criterion move-ment. On the basis of this finding, Walsh et al. (1979) proposed a hypothesis of interference between distance and location information in motor short-term memory: information on distance was hypothesised to interfere with the reproduction of movement location and information on end location was hypothesised to interfere with the reproduction of distance.

The distance-location interference phenomenon is a quite robust effect in short-term memory for arm movement, persisting for both constrained and preselected movements (Walsh et al. 1979), long and short retention intervals (Walsh & Russell 1979), and filled and unfilled retention intervals (Walsh et

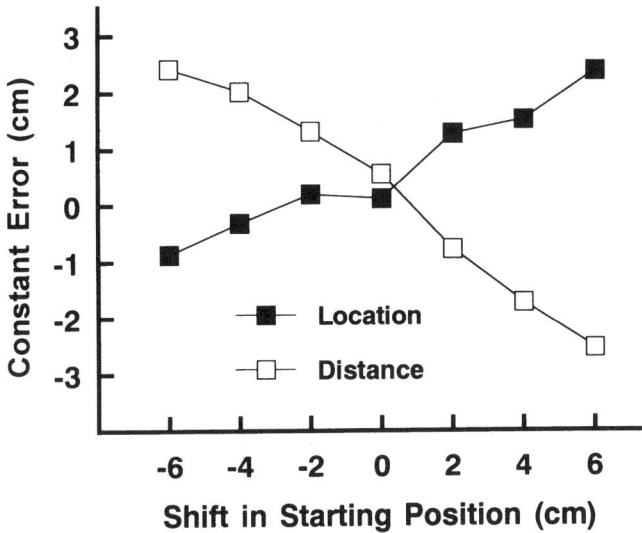

Figure 2. Typical response bias effects in the reproduction of either movement end location or distance from altered starting positions. [Reproduced with permission of the Helen Dwight Reid Educational Foundation from mean error scores calculated on the basis of data on both short and long movement lengths presented in Table 1 in "Memory for constrained and preselected movement location and distance: Effects of starting position and length" by W. D. Walsh, D. G. Russell, K. Imanaka, & B. James. (1979). *Journal of Motor Behavior*, 11, 201–214].

al. 1981b), as well as across differences in the imagery ability of subjects (Walsh et al. 1980), and the angle of approach of the movement (Walsh et al. 1981a). The only major factor that appears to systematically modify the distance-location interference effect appears to be criterion movement length. When the criterion movements are 16 cm or less in length, the reproduction of movement distance does not appear to be affected by changes in starting position (Walsh 1981). In contrast, the reproduction of movement end location appears to be uninfluenced by the shift in starting position when the length of the criterion movement exceeds 40 cm (Wrisberg et al. 1987; Wrisberg & Winter 1985). This observation is consistent with the notion, developed from comparison of AE data, that distance is the pre-eminent information for the reproduction of short movements and location the most reliable information for relatively long movements (e.g., Gundry 1975). The distance-location interference effect is therefore most pronounced for movements ranging in length from about 15 to 40 cm.

Kerr (1978) and Walsh et al. (1979) suggested, on the basis of these findings, that location and distance information may be coded together into memory such that each interferes in reproducing the other. This was postulated to hold true even under conditions where subjects concentrated on a specified movement cue and were allowed to rehearse it during the retention interval. Despite the robustness of the distance-location interference effect and the significance of the explanation advanced by Kerr (1978) and Walsh et al. (1979), the veracity of the explanation and the underlying cause of the interference phenomenon was not subjected to further systematic experimental investigation for more than a decade.

Recent studies on the sources of distance-location interference

We (Imanaka 1989; Imanaka 1991; Imanaka & Abernethy 1990; Imanaka & Abernethy 1991; Imanaka & Abernethy 1992a; Imanaka & Abernethy 1992b) have recently examined, through a series of experiments, three possible causes of the distance-location interference effect. One possibility is that the interference effect (or the systematic undershooting-overshooting pattern in movement reproduction which is a function of starting position shifts) arises simply as a consequence of some artefacts in the methodological approach typically used in the studies of motor short-term memory. A second possibility is that the interference effect arises as a consequence of peripheral factors, such as afferent kinaesthetic inputs from the limb used for movement, and is not an interference between movement information processed at more central, cognitive levels. A third possibility is that it is cognitive or strategic factors, such as the integration of distance and location information in the encoding process as hypothesised by Walsh et al. (1979), which is indeed the root cause of the interference phenomenon. Our studies on these three possibilities were conducted with the global aim of discovering which factors do and, equally importantly, do not affect the systematic undershooting-overshooting pattern of distance-location interference characteristically found in the short-term reproduction of arm movement.

All our experiments used an arm positioning paradigm typical of that employed in the studies by Walsh and his colleagues. Arm abduction movements in the range of 15–25 cm were used in our experiments, with the starting position for the reproduction being moved either 0, ± 2, or ± 4 cm (or in some experiments, 0, ± 3, or ± 6 cm) from the criterion movement starting position. The retention interval was 10 s and unfilled. Blindfolded right-handed subjects were asked to perform a criterion movement by moving, with the right hand, the vertical handle of a linear positioning apparatus in a left-to-right direction to a self-defined stop at a position within the required movement length range. This position was held for approximately 2 s before the subject was instructed to remove their hand from the handle. The handle was then returned by the experimenter (or automatically by software run on a computer) to the starting position for the following reproduction movement. At the completion of the retention interval subjects were required to again move the handle of the positioning apparatus, with their right hand, to reproduce either the distance or the end location of the preceding criterion movement. Instructions as to which movement cue was to be reproduced were given to each subject prior to the beginning of the experiment. To encourage the subjects to rely on the specific movement cue instructed to reproduce, information that the starting position for each reproduction movement might, or might not, alter from the starting position of the preceding criterion movement were also routinely provided to all subjects.

Methodological examinations

In all the previous experiments conducted by Walsh and his colleagues, the systematic undershooting-overshooting pattern was typically observed as a function of the shift in starting position for the reproduction movement, while the criterion movement starting position was always unchanged. The independent variable (i.e., the shift in starting position) was thus always manipulated for the reproduction movement but not for the criterion movement. The question can therefore legitimately be asked as to whether the interference effects characteristically appearing on response bias are in fact due to information available from the criterion movement or rather factors inherent in the set of starting position shifts made for the reproduction movement (Imanaka 1989).

For the reproduction of criterion movement location, the response bias was compared between a typical group (end-location) and a group (target-location) who were not given distance information during the criterion movement. Subjects of the end-location group were asked to make a criterion movement of 15- to 25-cm in length from the usual 0 starting position, and thus had access to movement distance information during the criterion movement. In contrast, subjects assigned to the target-location group did not make a normal criterion movement from the usual 0 starting position. Instead, they grasped the handle, which was located by the experimenter in advance at the mid-point of the criterion target area, and then re-positioned it at their pre-defined (preselected) location within the target area. Thus, distance information was not available during the criterion movement for the target-location group. The reproduction movement which followed was then made in the usual manner as employed by the subjects in the end-location group. The typical undershooting-overshooting pattern in response bias appeared clearly for the end-location group but did not arise for the target-location group (Figure 3). This showed that the interference effect was, in fact, due to distance information available in the criterion movement and was not an artefact derived, per se, from the starting position manipulation used for the reproduction movement.

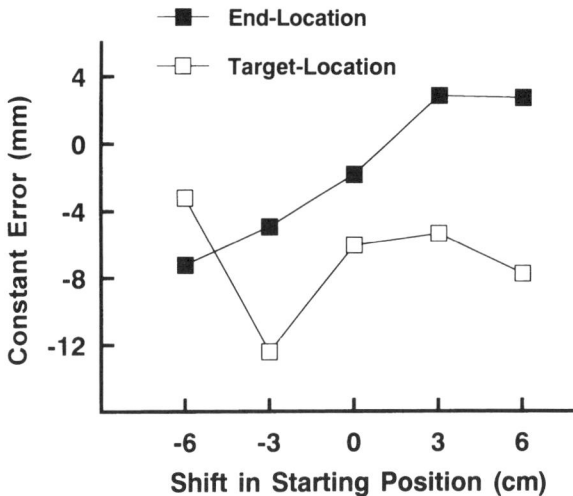

Figure 3. Reproduction of movement location for groups with (end-location group) and without (target-location group) criterion movement distance information. [Reproduced with permission of publisher from data presented in Table 1 in "Effect of starting position on reproduction of movement: Further evidence of interference between location and distance information" by K. Imanaka. (1989). *Perceptual and Motor Skills*, 68, 423–434].

For the reproduction of criterion movement distance, response bias was compared between a typical group (different-start), who were presented with one criterion movement starting position and five different reproduction movement starting positions, and an identical-start group, who were presented with five starting positions for both the criterion and reproduction movement with the starting position being the same for each criterion movement and its subsequent reproduction movement. If the reproduction movement is attracted toward the end location of the criterion movement, then the reproduction performance of the identical-start group should not be biased; rather the reproduction movements made by this group should become much more accurate because of the help of location information available in the criterion movement. In contrast, the typical response bias pattern for the different-start group should appear because of the attracting power of the end location of the criterion movement. This prediction was fulfilled by the experimental data (Figure 4), confirming that the interference effect in distance reproduction is a consequence of the location information available in the criterion movement.

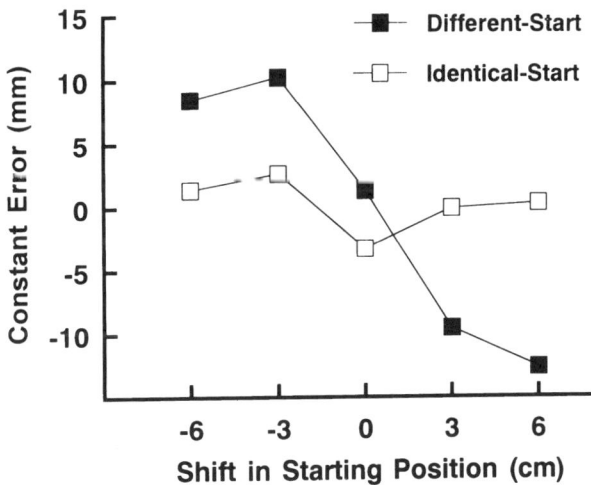

Figure 4. Reproduction of movement distance for groups (different-start group and identical-start group) differing in starting positions between criterion and reproduction movements. [Reproduced with permission of publisher from data presented in Table 2 in "Effect of starting position on reproduction of movement: Further evidence of interference between location and distance information" by K. Imanaka. (1989). *Perceptual and Motor Skills, 68*, 423–434].

We (Imanaka & Abernethy 1991) also examined a further possible meth-odological problem which related to whether the systematic pattern of under-shooting and overshooting in movement reproduction is mediated by learning effects which may occur during the course of the experiment. This examina-tion was motivated by the notion of central tendency effects, which have been suggested by some researchers (Laabs 1973; Poulton 1975) to be a method-ological problem in motor short-term memory research. Laabs suggested that, over the course of an experiment using a number of different within-subject conditions, subjects develop an average "referent" movement based on the distance and location characteristics of all movements experienced during all the experimental conditions and it is this "referent" movement which increas-ingly guides reproduction movements as an experimental series proceeds. If this is the case, the characteristic response bias pattern attributed to distance-location interference could be due simply to the effects of such an average "referent" movement emerging throughout the course of experiment. Our experiments showed that the systematic response bias pattern occurred even in the first (presented) condition after only a single starting position shift was experienced by subjects. Moreover, the pattern of the response bias on the first experienced condition did not differ from the typical response bias pattern arising from data collected across all experimental conditions (i.e., for sub-jects who experienced all five shifts in starting position). This indicated that the systematic undershooting-overshooting pattern in movement reproduction is not an artefact of any simple learning or central tendency effects arising during the course of typical motor short-term memory experiments.

The role of kinaesthetic and neuromuscular factors

Given that the cause of the distance-location interference effect is apparently not a methodological artefact, the next important question that can be posed and addressed experimentally is whether the effect is due to factors related to the specific neuromuscular commands or rather whether the interference effect is mediated by a more abstract, cognitive level of information-processing. Two experiments are summarized here, which attempt to examine whether the systematic response bias pattern varies or remains unchanged when specific neuromuscular aspects of the criterion and reproduction movements are altered. The specific neuromuscular information available from criterion to reproduc-tion movement is manipulated, in the first experiment, by changing the movement speed and, in the second experiment, by changing the limb used in the reproduction movement.

Effects of movement speed. The systematic distance-location response bias phenomenon has typically been examined using slow, self-paced movements (e.g., Kerr 1978; Walsh et al.1979). Under such conditions subjects may rely primarily on feedback information for movement control rather than needing to depend on the preprogramming of efferent commands. The question of interest here is whether the distance-location interference is affected by constraints in the utility of kinaesthetic feedback information available from criterion and reproduction movements. To examine this we (Imanaka & Abernethy 1990) conducted a series of experiments, using all possible combinations of slow and fast movement speeds between the criterion and reproduction movements. For slow movements subjects were instructed to make movements in a slow self-paced speed, resulting in an average duration of 0.93 s (the average movement speed was 30.4 cm/s). For fast movement, subjects were asked to make movements as fast as possible in a ballistic action without any slowing in movement speed during the movement, resulting in an average duration of 0.35 s (the average movement speed was 84.3 cm/s). Mixing slow and fast movement speeds from the criterion to the reproduction movement should alter the availability of conscious feedback[1] information about movement distance (although the availability of end location information may not be altered because subjects were allowed to hold the handle for 2 s at the end of movement execution for both the slow and fast movement speed conditions) These experiments demonstrated that the systematic undershooting-overshooting pattern in movement reproduction is unaffected by the different combinations of slow and fast movement speeds (Figure 5). This suggests that the response bias caused by changing the starting position is not simply a phenomenon observed for slow movement, where there is ample opportunity for using conscious feedback to correct errors, but is characteristic of linear positioning movements of all speed. The robust nature of the effect appears to rule out a feedback-specific or a program-specific parameter as the cause of the typical undershooting-overshooting pattern with respect to the effect of movement distance on the reproduction of end location. The next experiments using a switched-limb paradigm address the feedback-specific or program-specific nature of interference of end location on distance more directly, as well as seeking confirmation of the present conclusion with respect to the interfering effect of movement distance on end location.

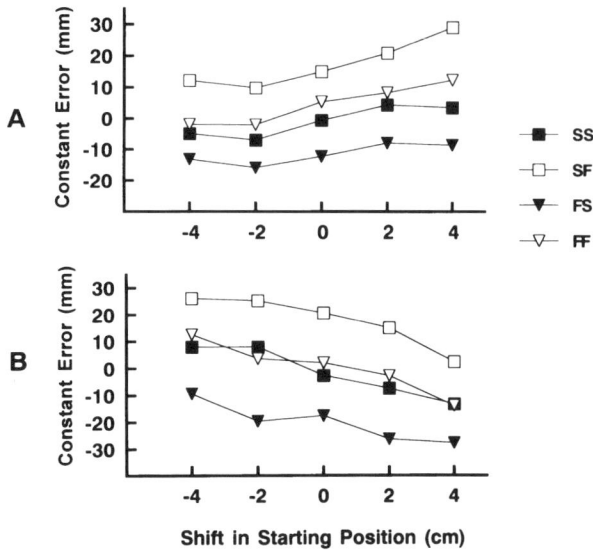

Figure 5. Reproduction of movement location (A) and distance (B) under different combinations of criterion and reproduction movement speeds. SS and FF groups performed both the criterion and reproduction trials at self-paced slow and fast (ballistic) movement speeds, respectively. SF performed slow criterion and fast reproduction and FS performed fast criterion and slow reproduction movements. [Adapted from "Interference between movement location and distance cues in the reproduction of slow and fast movements" by K. Imanaka & B. Abernethy. (1990). *Journal of Human Movement Studies*, 18, 251–268].

Effects of switched-limb manipulations. In the switched-limb manipulation, the reproduction movement is made with the opposite limb (the left hand) to that (the right hand) used for the criterion movement, with both the criterion and reproduction movements being made in the same (left-to-right) direction. We (Imanaka & Abernethy 1992b) compared the systematic undershooting-overshooting pattern in movement reproduction between the same-limb and switched-limb conditions to once again examine whether the locus of the interference was local or central in origin. In the same-limb conditions the subjects used their right hand for both criterion and reproduction movements (both movements were into abduction), while in the switched-limb conditions they used the right hand for the criterion movement (abduction) and the left hand for the reproduction movement (adduction). [Movement performance and response biasing effects had been ascertained in advance to be similar for the right-hand abduction and the left-hand adduction conditions]. If distance-location interference is mediated by abstract information rather than kinaesthetic/neuromuscular information about the criterion movement, then the typical undershooting-overshooting pattern in reproduction should appear similarly for both conditions. Results clearly confirmed this prediction with no differences in the appearance of the systematic pattern in response bias being evident between the same-limb and switched-limb conditions for the reproduction of either movement location (Figure 6A) or distance (Figure 6B).

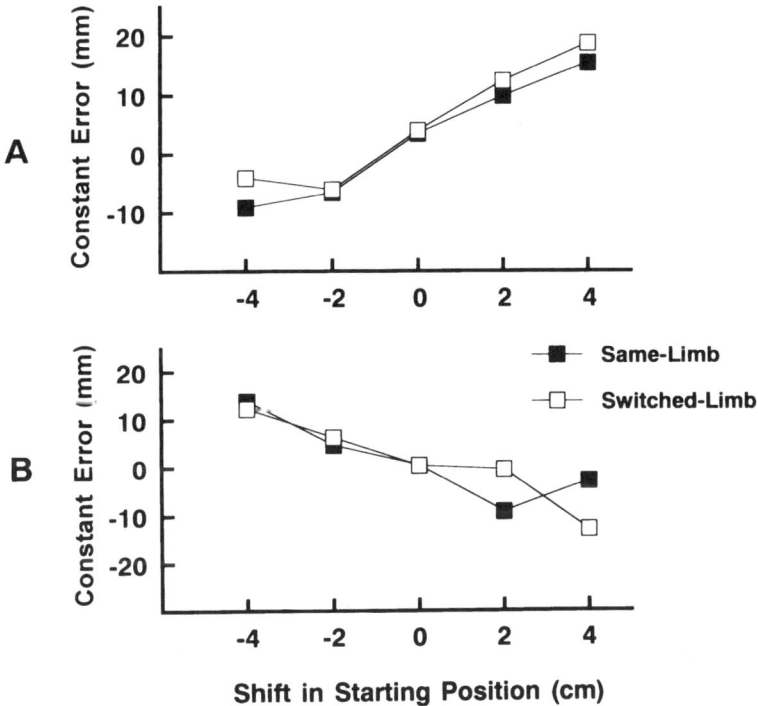

Figure 6. Reproduction of movement location (A) and distance (B) under same-limb and switched-limb conditions. [Adapted with permission of the Helen Dwight Reid Educational Foundation from "Interference between location and distance information in motor short-term memory: The respective roles of direct kinaesthetic signals and abstract codes" by K. Imanaka & B. Abernethy. (1992). *Journal of Motor Behavior, 24,* 274–280].

Collectively, the findings of these two experiments indicate that neither limb-specific kinaesthetic information nor opportunities for using conscious feedback are responsible for the distance-location interference effect. This implies that the interference effect occurs not at the level of local sensorimotor systems, but rather at a more abstract, cognitive level of information-processing, as had been proposed by Walsh and his colleagues (1978–1981).

The role of cognitive and attentional factors

We can tentatively conclude from the experiments described to date that the distance-location interference effect arises, in all probabilities, from factors acting at an abstract, cognitive level rather than at the local level of limb-specific neuromuscular efference or afference. This is the same conclusion proposed by the earlier studies of the 1970–1980s (e.g., Walsh et al.1979) although at that time there was little direct empirical evidence to support it. An important characteristic of the distance-location interference phenomenon observed so far relates to the role of the instructional set in explicitly directing subjects's attention to different source of information (or cues). The reproduction of "attended" movement location from the criterion movement is interfered with by "unattended" movement distance information within the criterion movement and vice versa. The further question this then raises is whether the distance-location interference phenomenon is indeed due to interference between the sources of distance and location information per se or rather, more generally, due to interference between "attended" and "unattended" information. In an attempt to examine this we (Imanaka & Abernethy 1992a) collected empirical data based on direct manipulation of the cognitive strategies used by subjects to remember and reproduce arm movement.

Effects of attended and unattended distance on location reproduction. We first compared the pattern of response bias evident in the reproduction of movement location for two groups (end-only and start-end) which differed in their knowledge of explicit information about the change in the starting position. The end-only group was a typical group in which subjects were given the usual instruction that both the criterion and reproduction starting positions could change and attention should be directed entirely to the reproduction of criterion end location. The start-end group was informed before commencing the experiment that the criterion movements would always be commenced at a fixed position and that the reproduction starting position would be altered 0, 2, or 4 cm in either direction from the criterion starting position. Under such instructions, the starting position (and, in turn, movement distance which is extrapolated from the starting and end positions) may become an attended rather than an unattended source of information. If the distance-location interference effect in the reproduction of movement location occurs between location and distance information per se, then the characteristic response bias pattern should arise for both groups. Conversely, if the interference occurs between the "attended" source of location information and the "unattended" source of distance information, the systematic response bias pattern should disappear for the start-end group, in which both movement distance and location are attention-demanding. Results showed that the previously observed systematic response bias pattern in reproducing movement location disappeared for the start-end group the group for whom explicit information about the starting and end positions, and consequently movement distance, was available (Figure 7). As the distance information is potentially available to both the groups but has attention explicitly drawn to it only for the start-end group, our findings suggest that the systematic undershooting-overshooting pattern is likely caused not by distance information per se but by the unattended nature of the distance information.

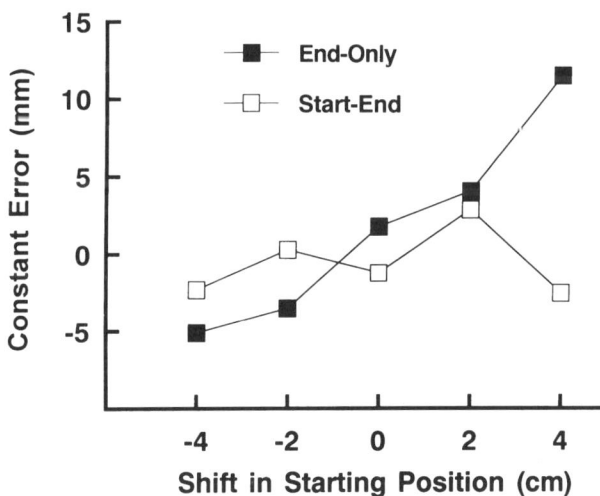

Figure 7. Reproduction of movement location under different strategy conditions. [Adapted with permission of The Experimental Psychology Society from "Cognitive strategies and short-term memory for movement distance and location" by K. Imanaka & B. Abernethy. (1992). Quarterly Journal of Experimental Psychology, 45A, 669–700].

A number of researchers in the 1970s (Diewert & Roy 1978; Keele & Ells 1972; Roy 1977; Roy & Kelso 1977; Stelmach & Kelso 1973; Sullivan & Salmoni 1975) suggested that, in reproducing movement distance, subjects use both the starting and end locations to extrapolate the distance to be reproduced and that, when location information is difficult to use reliably, subjects tend to employ a timing or counting strategy (Diewert & Roy 1978; Laabs 1973; Leuba 1909; Summers, Levey, & Wrigley 1981). We examined the nature of the response bias in distance reproduction for three strategy groups: a group given a location strategy (involving some extrapolation of the starting and end positions), a group given a counting strategy, and a group given a distance sense strategy (in which they were required to use visual imagery of an arm movement or a 20- to 30-cm ruler as the basis for distance reproduction). As shown in Figure 8, the previously observed systematic undershooting-overshooting pattern was diminished for the location strategy group, whereas the typical pattern clearly appeared for the groups using counting and distance sense strategies. As criterion movement location information is potentially available during the criterion movement for all three groups but only the location group attended to it, this would suggest that it is the unattended nature of location information rather than the location information per se that is responsible for the characteristic response bias effects seen in the reproduction of criterion movement distance.

Taken together, these two studies suggest that explicit information about the starting and/or end positions seems to negate the usual effect of change in starting position and therefore that the distance-location interference phenomenon is likely a result of interference between attended and unattended sources of movement information rather than between specific and non-specific cues per se. An important aspect of the interference effect in movement reproduction is therefore whether or not the subjects attend to the non-specific information as well as the specific sources of movement information.

Direct manipulation of subject's attention by post-cueing procedures

In an attempt to confirm the findings of the strategy experiments, a post-cueing technique was employed to directly manipulate the attention of subjects to specific and non-specific sources of movement information. In the post-cueing technique the experimenter gives the subject an instructional signal just before the start of reproduction movement which specifies the cue

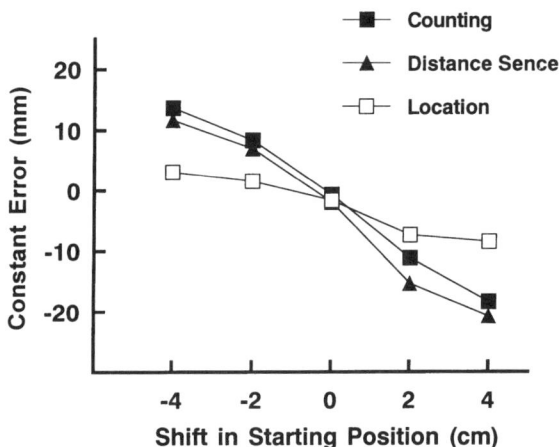

Figure 8. Reproduction of movement distance under different strategy conditions. [Adapted with permission of The Experimental Psychology Society from "Cognitive strategies and short-term memory for movement distance and location" by K. Imanaka & B. Abernethy. (1992). *Quarterly Journal of Experimental Psychology*, 45A, 669–700].

to be reproduced. In such procedures the subjects should necessarily intentionally (or consciously) remember both movement distance and location cues during the preceding criterion movement. Three groups (pre-cued distance, pre-cued location, and post cued) were tested under the usual short-term memory paradigm we have used so far, except for the post cueing procedures. In the two pre-cued groups subjects were required to reproduce either movement distance or end location alone throughout all experimental trials. For the post-cued group, instructional signals about movement cue to be reproduced were presented with equal probability for each of the distance and location cues. The starting positions were altered 0 and 3 cm in either direction from the criterion movement starting position, with the 0 cm starting position being used on the first trial session to familiarise the subjects with the specific presentation probability in the post cueing procedures. As shown in Figure 9, the previously observed interference effects disappeared in reproducing movement distance when movement distance was post-cued for the following reproduction, whereas for the reproduction of location the interference effects persisted even under the post cueing procedures.

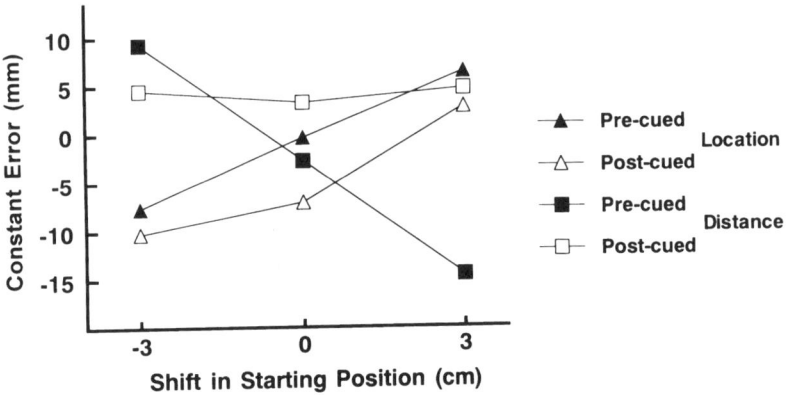

Figure 9. Reproduction of movement location and distance under pre-cued and post-cued conditions.

These results again indicate that the interference phenomenon may arise under conditions in which one source of movement information is processed consciously and the other unconsciously. When both sources of movement information are subject to conscious processing, the interference effects disappear but only for distance reproduction. For the reproduction of end location, the interference effects appear robust even when both cues are subject to conscious processing. Location information possibly persists within the subject's consciousness even after the other cue (distance) is specified as the cue to be reproduced, while distance information is much easier to ignore/forget, quickly fading from consciousness when location becomes the desired cue to be reproduced. In fact, when distance information is maintained within the subject's consciousness during the reproduction of end location, the typical biasing effect of movement distance on the reproduction of end location clearly disappears (see Figure 7). [Remember the subjects in the start-end group, described in the previous section, were attentive to the change in starting position during both the criterion and reproduction movements]. Distance information may well therefore be much more susceptible than location information to withdrawal of subject's attention. It is therefore likely that the mutual attraction power of distance and location information in reproducing arm movement may alter depending on whether each source of information is processed consciously or unconsciously.

Theoretical considerations: Does interaction between conscious and unconscious processing cause distance-location interference?

Our series of experiments has clearly shown that the well-known distance-location interference phenomenon is a result neither of methodological arte-facts in the typical motor short-term memory paradigm nor neuromuscular, kinaesthetic feedback factors which are specific to the limb used for the movement. Rather, it appears that the interference phenomenon is likely a manifestation of the interference/interaction between attended and unattended (or consciously and unconsciously processed) information about movement distance and location. This interaction can be dissociated when both sources of information are subject to conscious processing, necessitating reconsidera-tion of some of the oldest, and most pervasive, issues in all of experimental psychology those that relate to the notions of attention and consciousness. In this final section of our chapter we consider three major concepts/findings which are potentially advantageous in advancing understanding of the atten-tional correlates of the distance-location interference phenomenon. These are: (1) the controlled and automatic processes distinction drawn by Schneider and Shiffrin (1977), (2) the neuropsychological evidence for dissociation between perception and action or between explicit and implicit perception in action (e.g., Milner & Goodale 1995; Rossetti 1998), and (3) the findings of a recent biomechanical study demonstrating the potential control of the centre-of-mass of the whole arm in positioning movements (Suzuki et al. 1996; Suzuki et al. 1997).

Correlates of the controlled and automatic processing modes

A particularly interesting characteristic of the distance-location interference phenomenon is that this interference occurs unavoidably when subjects con-centrate singularly on a given specific cue. In this respect the distance-location interference phenomenon can be interpreted to be a typical manifestation of the interaction of controlled and automatic processing modes proposed by Schneider and Shiffrin (Schneider & Shiffrin 1977; Shiffrin & Schneider 1977). Schneider and Shiffrin have suggested that controlled processing is attention-demanding or effortful, serial, relatively slow, and volitional (under conscious intervention). In contrast, automatic processing is considered as neither attention-demanding nor volitional (i.e., it is impervious to conscious intervention) and can be undertaken in parallel with other operations. This distinction explains well the phenomenon of distance-location interference in movement reproduction. The movement information causing the systematic undershooting-overshooting pattern in movement reproduction may be automatically processed in parallel with the essential information from the specific cues needed for the movement reproduction. Importantly, this additional processing may occur unavoidably and unconsciously, even when subjects are instructed to concentrate on specific cues.

The situation with respect to processing requirements in arm movement reproduction also parallels the uncontrollable and undesirable processing of unattended information which characterises the well-known Stroop effect (Stroop 1935). The classical Stroop effect arises in the perception of colour word stimuli, where subjects are slower to name colours of the given colour-words which conflict with the meaning of the colour-words. A number of variations of the original Stroop effect have also been reported, such as counting the number of stimulus items of numeric digits when the digits presented conflict in meaning with the number to be counted (Morton 1969) and judging speaker gender for the incongruent stimulus words "man" spoken in a female voice and "girl" spoken in a male voice (Green & Barber 1981; Green & Barber 1983).

With respect to the unavoidable and uncontrollable processing modes, the distance-location interference phenomenon parallels these Stroop type phenomena, but with one slight but important difference. As shown in our experiments examining the effects of cognitive strategies (Imanaka & Abernethy 1992a), when subjects are required to attend to non-specific movement cues while reproducing a specified cue (i.e., when subjects attend to the non-specific cues as well as the specific cue, and, as a consequence, the non-specific cues are processed in a controlled, volitional mode), this systematic response bias pattern diminishes or disappears. It is therefore likely that the normally observed distance-location interference/interaction may be caused by the non-specific movement cues which are automatically, unconsciously, and implicitly processed in parallel with the controlled, conscious, and explicit processing of the specified movement cue. Furthermore, as shown in part by our post-cueing experiment presented in the previous section, this interference/interaction can be avoided by shifting the attention of subjects to the non-specific as well as the explicit sources of movement information.

Neuropsychological correlates: Implicit perception in action

With respect to the conscious versus unconscious processes, evidence for implicit, unconscious perception of visual (Berti & Rizzolatti 1992; Desmurget et al. 1997; Goodale et al. 1986; Neumann & Klotz 1994; Pelisson et al. 1986; Rossetti et al. 1994; Taylor & McCloskey 1990), tactile and proprioceptive (Rossetti et al. 1995) stimuli for motor responses has frequently been reported. Rossetti and his colleagues recently demonstrated that finger pointing toward either a visual target (Rossetti et al. 1994) or the unseen fingertip of the other hand (Desmurget et al. 1997) improved in accuracy when the subjects were able to see their hand even for a very short period prior to the onset of the pointing movement, although the subjects were not aware of using such visual information about their hand in completing the pointing task. Furthermore, a number of reaction time studies (e.g., Neumann & Klotz 1994; Taylor & McCloskey 1990) using visual masking procedures have shown that subjects appear to respond to the masked (non-detected) visual stimulus when this stimulus precedes the masking stimulus by some 50 ms. In this situation subjects were not consciously aware of the first stimulus, indicating that it was completely masked by the one that followed. Subjects therefore appear to be able to respond to non-detected, implicitly (unconsciously) perceived stimuli in parallel with explicit perceptual and motor action.

Similar evidence for implicit perception is also available for tactile and proprioceptive modalities. Rossetti et al. (1995) reported that a blindfolded patient with a brain lesion, who was completely anaesthetised on the right side of his body, was able to point with his normal left hand toward the specific site on the right hand where a tactile stimulus was applied by the experimenter. [Since the subject could not feel the stimulation, he was instructed about the application of the stimulus but not the actual stimulation site]. Further, the blindfolded subject was tested in a task where the subject's right (affected side) index finger was placed at a certain location on a tablet to either the left or right side of the subject's sagittal axis and he was then required to point with the left (normal side) index finger underneath the tablet toward the location corresponding to the right index finger position. In this test, again, the pointing performance by the left index finger appeared to be accurate (although with a large variability). These findings provide evidence for the implicit/unconscious use of either visual, tactile or proprioceptive information for motor control. Rossetti et al. (1998, 2000), and also Milner and Goodale

(1995), suggest that the implicit processing of sensory information for action is not restricted to simply some very limited control processes operating at a low level of motor organisation and that both the implicit and explicit sensory representations can interfere at all levels of the nervous system involved in production of motor output.

The distance-location interference phenomenon in short-term reproduction of arm movement can therefore also be interpreted in terms of the mutual interference between explicit and implicit sensorimotor representations available from both the criterion and reproduction movement. In the reproduction tasks we used, subjects usually concentrate on either the movement distance or end location of the criterion movement to remember and re-use this information for the reproduction of the criterion movement. Information about these specific cues is thus processed at an explicit, conscious level whereas the other non-specific movement cue(s) is processed at an implicit, unconscious level. The specific and the non-specific movement cues may well interfere with each other either before or during the execution of the reproduction movement, given that the specific movement cues are processed explicitly while the non-specific cues are processed implicitly. Furthermore, this mutual interference between the explicit (conscious) and implicit (unconscious) sensorimotor representations can be expected to either disappear or diminish when subjects attend to both the specific and non-specific movement cues, as seen in our strategy experiments (Imanaka & Abernethy 1992a). This may well occur because the non-specific movement cues are processed and formed into an explicit representation, thereby eliminating mutual interference between explicit and implicit representations.

Our post-cueing experiment (in which we directly manipulated the subjects's conscious awareness of non-specific movement cues) has shown, however, that the distance-location interference effects disappeared in reproducing movement distance but remained for the reproduction of location (see Figure 9). Both distance and location cues under the post-cueing procedures should be retained in short-term memory as explicit sensorimotor representations so as to be available for use in the reproduction movement. One would predict, if mutual interference indeed arises between explicit and implicit representations, that this should lead to the absence of mutual distance-location interference. Nevertheless, when movement location was post-cued for reproduction, the typical distance-location interference effect still appeared. One possible explanation is that the explicit distance representation may decay (fade) rapidly from consciousness, effectively switching its feature into an implicit form of distance representation, and, through this, causing mutual interference with the explicit movement location information. The interfering power of distance and location information may alter depending on whether each source of information is processed either consciously or unconsciously or changes its nature to be either explicit or implicit, although the precise mechanisms underlying such a difference between movement distance and location under the post-cueing procedures remain unclear.

Biomechanical correlates: Implicit control of the centre-of-mass of the whole arm in positioning movement

Suzuki et al. (1997) have examined invariant kinematic properties of various arm reaching movements, differing in the size and the orientation of the hand stroke. The motion of the individual segments of the forearm and upper arm, as well as the shoulder and elbow joints, appears to be modulated in different ways depending on the size and orientation of the movement that is to be produced. This suggests that there may not be any invariant feature evident within each of these individual segments and joints. The trajectory of the hand is nearly straight for relatively short movements. This is consistent with the predictions of the minimum hand jerk model (Flash & Hogan 1985; Morraso 1981) of nearly straight hand paths and bell-shaped velocity profiles (i.e., the sequence of acceleration and deceleration of the hand movement is temporally symmetric). For large hand strokes, however, the hand path becomes highly curved and its velocity curve appears asymmetry. In contrast, the trajectory of the centre-of-mass (CMt) of the whole arm appears relatively straight toward the target with a smooth, bell-shaped symmetric velocity curve (which implies high efficiency in acceleration and deceleration of the arm movement) over a wide range of movement size and direction. Suzuki et al. suggest that the simple structure in both trajectory and velocity of CMt may reflect a fundamental principle for the planning of point-to-point movements (such as reaching and positioning). These authors also note that the CMt trajectory may be a primary internal representation for this type of movement, although the neural mechanisms underlying the internal representation of CMt are far from clear at the present.

The hand-based (Flash & Hogan 1985; Morraso 1981), rather than CMt-based, planning of arm movement may be effective in determining arm trajectory where the trajectory per se is crucial for accurate execution of the task. This would be true of tasks such as handwriting or drawing, but this is not the case for point-to-point reaching or positioning (Suzuki et al. 1996; Suzuki et al. 1997; Uno et al. 1989). For point-to-point movement tasks, of which linear arm positioning of the type used in motor short-term memory studies are a classical example, a requirement is usually imposed on the accuracy of movement end location but not on the trajectory itself. Subjects can therefore direct their attention to the desired end location of the arm movement. Despite the hand itself needing to ultimately reach the end location and the CMt being a likely candidate for internal representation for the movement, the subjects's attention need not necessarily be directed to the trajectory per se of the hand or the CMt. This implies that the reaching/positioning (or point-to-point) move-ment may possibly be controlled by the brain in such a way as to attain a smooth and efficient CMt trajectory, whereas the subject's concern is more to direct their attention to either the hand movement distance or end location during the planning and execution of the movement. Because the CMt is in fact neither visible nor directly perceived as a single entity (indeed it is usually located out of the arm itself), the reproduction of arm movement, particularly from an altered starting position, is likely to be affected by the representation of the CMt which may be unconsciously processed and stored in memory following the criterion movement. Furthermore, because of the nature of the inertia of the CMt (which is the centre of mass regardless of the mass distribution of the whole arm), the position of the CMt itself should necessar-ily be a most stable biomechanical factor against various external/internal forces imposed on the arm itself during its positioning movement (Suzuki et al. 1996; Suzuki et al. 1997). In this regard, the reproduction of arm position-ing guided by the specific (consciously processed) movement cues is likely affected by unconsciously processed information available from the non-specific movement cues and the usually-unattended CMt for movement. These dual effects may cause the distance-location interference effect to arise.

Conclusions

Since the late 1970s, the locus of distance-location interference in motor short-term memory had been thought to be the integrated storage in (and retrieval from) memory of information about movement distance and location. Our recent series of experiments has provided a more detailed understanding of this distance-location interference effect, indicating that the interference is not caused by any methodological artefacts nor local neuromuscular factors, such as peripheral feedback. Rather, it appears that this interference phenomenon is a result of interference/interaction between implicit and explicit internal representations rather than between the two sources of movement information (distance and location) per se. This interference/interaction can be dissociated, given that the two internal representations are both subject to explicit, conscious processing. These findings lead to further questions which relate to broader issues other than the original motor short-term memory ones issues such as what are processed within or beyond subject's consciousness in positioning movements (that could mediate the characteristic response bias in movement reproduction) and how can cognitive factors, such as conscious/ unconscious processing of movement information, interfere (interact) with some possible biomechanical factor(s). In this respect, the old issue of the distance-location interference in motor short-term memory can now be seen as very much a contemporary issue, concerned centrally with attention and consciousness in perception and action, and its interaction/dissociation with the natural biomechanical dynamics of positioning movements.

Acknowledgement

We wish to express our appreciation to an anonymous reviewer for useful comments on an earlier version of this chapter.

Note

1.   The term "conscious feedback" is used to describe feedback which can be perceived explicitly (i.e., feedback information about which participants are consciously aware). By definition this excludes feedback related to movement execution which occurs below the level of consciousness, such as that from local reflex activity or from efference copy.

References

Berti, A. & Rizzolatti, G. (1992). Visual processing without awareness: Evidence from unilateral neglect. *Journal of Cognitive Neuroscience*, 4, 345–351.

Desmurget, M., Rossetti, Y., Jordan, M., Meckler, C. & Prablanc, C. (1997). Viewing the hand prior to movement improves accuracy of pointing performed toward the unseen contralateral hand. *Experimental Brain Research*, 115, 180–186.

Diewert, G.L. & Roy, E.A. (1978). Coding strategy for movement extent information. *Journal of Experimental Psychology: Human Learning and Memory*, 4, 666–675.

Flash, T. & Hogan, N. (1985). The coordination of arm movements: An experimentally confirmed mathematical model. *Journal of Neuroscience*, 5, 1688–1703.

Gibson, J.J. (1966). *The senses considered as perceptual systems*. Boston: Houghton Mifflin.

Gibson, J.J. (1979). *The ecological approach to visual perception*. Boston: Houghton Mifflin.

Goodale, M.A., Pélisson, D. & Prablanc, C. (1986). Large adjustments in visually guided reaching do not depend on vision of the hand or perception of target displacement. *Nature*, 320, 748–750.

Green, E.J. & Barber, P.J. (1981). An auditory Stroop effect with judgments of speaker gender. *Perception and Psychophysics*, 30, 459–466.

Green, E.J. & Barber, P.J. (1983). Interference effects in an auditory Stroop task: Congruence and correspondence. *Acta Psychologica*, 53, 183–194.

Gundry, J. (1975). The use of location and distance in reproducing different amplitudes of movement. *Journal of Motor Behavior*, 7, 91–100.

Imanaka, K. (1989). Effect of starting position on reproduction of movement: Further evidence of interference between location and distance information. *Perceptual and Motor Skills*, 68, 423–434.

Imanaka, K. & Abernethy, B. (1990). Interference between movement location and distance cues in the reproduction of slow and fast movements. *Journal of Human Movement Studies*, 18, 251–268.

Imanaka, K. (1991). Isolating the sources of the location-distance interference in motor short-term memory. Unpublished doctoral dissertation, University of Queensland, Brisbane, Australia.

Imanaka, K. & Abernethy, B. (1991). The mediating effect of learning on the interference between location and distance recall from motor short-term memory. *Acta Psychologica*, 77, 153–165.

Imanaka, K. & Abernethy, B. (1992a). Cognitive strategies and short-term memory for movement distance and location. *Quarterly Journal of Experimental Psychology*, 45A, 669–700.

Imanaka, K. & Abernethy, B. (1992b). Interference between location and distance information in motor short-term memory: The respective roles of direct kinesthetic signals and abstract codes. *Journal of Motor Behavior*, 24, 274–280.

Imanaka, K., Nishihira, Y., Funase, K. & Abernethy, B. (1996). Interference between location and distance information in the reproduction of arm positioning: Early implications and new directions. *Advances in Exercise and Sports Physiology*, 2, 1–12.

Imanaka, K., Abernethy, B. & Quek, J.-J. (1998). The locus of distance-location interference in movement reproduction: Do we know any more 25 years on? In J. Piek (Ed.), *Motor behavior and human skill: A multidisciplinary approach*. Champaign, IL: Human Kinetics, chap.2, 29–55.

Jones, B. (1974). Role of central monitoring of efference in short-term memory for movements. *Journal of Experimental Psychology*, 102, 37–43.

Keele, S.W. & Ells, J.G. (1972). Memory characteristics of kinesthetic information. *Journal of Motor Behavior*, 4, 127–134.

Kelso, J.A.S., Holt, K.G., Rubin, P. & Kugler, P.N. (1981). Patterns of human interlimb coordination emerge from the properties of non-linear, limit cycle oscillatory processes: Theory and data. *Journal of Motor Behavior*, 13, 226–261.

Kerr, B. (1978). The effect of invalid task parameters on short-term motor memory. *Journal of Motor Behavior*, 10, 261–273.

Laabs, G.J. (1973). Retention characteristics of different reproduction cues in motor short-term memory. *Journal of Experimental Psychology*, 100, 168–177.

Leuba, J.H. (1909). The influence of the duration and of the rate of arm movements upon the judgment of their length. *American Journal of Psychology*, 20, 374–385.

Marteniuk, R.G. & Roy, E.A. (1972). The codability of kinesthetic location and distance information. *Acta Psychologica*, 36, 471–479.

Milner, A.D. & Goodale, M.A. (1995). *The visual brain in action*. Oxford: Oxford University Press.

Morraso, P. (1981). Spatial control of arm movements. *Experimental Brain Research*, 42, 223–227.

Morton, J. (1969). Categories of interference: Verbal mediation and conflict in card sorting. *British Journal of Psychology*, 60, 329–346.

Neumann, O. & Klotz, W. (1994). Motor responses to nonreportable, masked stimuli: Where is the limit of direct parameter specification? In C. Umilta & M. Moscovitch (Eds.), *Attention and performance XV: Conscious and nonconscious information processing*. Cambridge, MA: MIT Press, 123–150

Pélisson, D., Prablanc, C., Goodale, M.A. & Jeannerod, M. (1986). Visual control of reaching movements without vision of the limb. II. Evidence of fast unconscious processes correcting the trajectory of the hand to the final position of a double-step stimulus. *Experimental Brain Research*, 62, 303–311.

Poulton, E.C. (1975). Range effects in experiments on people. *American Journal of Psychology*, 88, 3–32.

Prinz, W. & Sanders, A.F. (1984). *Cognition and motor processes*. New York: Springer-Verlag.

Rossetti, Y. (1998). Implicit short-lived motor representation of space in brain-damaged and healthy subjects. *Consciousness and Cognition*, 7, 520–558.

Rossetti, Y. (2000). Implicit perception in action: short-lived motor representations of space. In: P.G. Grossenbacher (ed.): *Finding consciousness in the brain*. (131–179) Amsterdam/Philadelphia: John Benjamins Publishing Company.

Rossetti, Y., Stelmach, G., Desmurget, M., Prablanc, C. & Jeannerod, M. (1994). The effect of viewing the static hand prior to movement onset on pointing kinematics and variability. *Experimental Brain Research*, 101, 323–330.

Rossetti, Y., Rode, G. & Boisson, D. (1995). Implicit processing of somaesthetic information: a dissociation between where and how? *Neuroreport*, 6, 506–510.

Roy, E.A. (1977). Spatial cues in memory for movement. *Journal of Motor Behavior*, 9, 151–156.

Roy, E.A. & Kelso, J.A.S. (1977). Movement cues in motor memory: Precuing versus postcuing. *Journal of Human Movement Studies*, 3, 232–239.

Schmidt, R.A. (1988). *Motor control and learning: A behavioral emphasis.* (2 ed.). Champaign, Illinois: Human Kinetic Publishers.

Schneider, W. & Shiffrin, R.M. (1977). Controlled and automatic human information processing: I. Detection, search and attention. *Psychological Review*, 84, 1–66.

Sherrington, C.S. (1906). *Integrative action of the nervous system.* New York: Scribner.

Shiffrin, R.M. & Schneider, W. (1977). Controlled and automatic human information processing: II. Perceptual learning, automatic attending, and a general theory. *Psychological Review*, 84, 127–190.

Stelmach, G.E. & Kelso, J.A.S. (1973). Distance and location cues in short-term motor memory. *Perceptual and Motor Skills*, 37, 403–406.

Stroop, J.R. (1935). Studies of interference in serial verbal reactions. *Journal of Experimental Psychology*, 18, 643–662.

Sullivan, S.J. & Salmoni, A.W. (1975). Intersensory integration: A new look at distance and location cues. In D. M. Landers, D. V. Harris, & R. W. Christina (Eds.), *Psychology of motor behavior and sport II* (491–499). University Park, Pa.: Penn State HPER Series No. 10.

Summers, J.J., Levey, A.J. & Wrigley, W.J. (1981). The role of planning and efference in the recall of location and distance cues in short-term motor memory. *Journal of Motor Behavior*, 13, 65–76.

Suzuki, M., Matsunami, K., Yamazaki, Y. & Mizuno, N. (1996). Application of the minimum jerk model to formation of the trajectory of the centre of mass during multijoint limb movements. *Folia Primatol*, 66, 240–252.

Suzuki, M., Yamazaki, Y., Mizuno, N. & Matsunami, K. (1997). Trajectory formation of the center-of-mass of the arm during reaching movements. *Neuroscience*, 76, 597–610.

Taylor, J.L. & McCloskey, D.I. (1990). Triggering of preprogrammed movements as reactions to masked stimuli. *Journal of Neurophysiology*, 63, 439–446.

Uno, Y., Kawato, M. & Suzuki, R. (1989). Formation and control of optimal trajectory in human multijoint arm movement: Minimum torque-change model. *Biological Cybernetics*, 61, 89–101.

Walsh, W.D. & Russell, D.G. (1979). Memory for movement location and distance: Starting position and retention interval effects. *Journal of Human Movement Studies*, 5, 68–76.

Walsh, W.D., Russell, D.G., Imanaka, K. & James, B. (1979). Memory for constrained and preselected movement location and distance: Effects of starting position and length. *Journal of Motor Behavior*, 11, 201–214.

Walsh, W.D. & Russell, D.G. (1980). Memory for preselected slow movements: Evidence for integration of location and distance. *Journal of Human Movement Studies*, 6, 95–105.

Walsh, W.D., Russell, D.G. & Imanaka, K. (1980). Memory for movement: Interaction of location and distance cues and imagery ability. *Acta Psychologica*, 44, 117–130.

Walsh, W.D. (1981). Memory for preselected and constrained short movements. *Research Quarterly for Exercise and Sport*, 52, 368–379.

Walsh, W.D., Russell, D.G. & Boustead, J. (1981a). Memory for movement cues: Angle of approach, terminal location and distance. *Journal of Human Movement Studies*, 7, 108–123.

Walsh, W.D., Russell, D.G. & Crassini, B. (1981b). Interference effects in recalling movements. *British Journal of Psychology*, 72, 287–298.

Woodworth, R.S. (1899). The accuracy of voluntary movement. *Psychological Review*, Monograph Supplement, 3, No.2.

Wrisberg, C.A. & Winter, T.P. (1985). Reproducing the end location of a positioning movement: The long and short of it. *Journal of Motor Behavior*, 17, 242–254.

Wrisberg, C.A., Millslagle, D.G. & Schliesman, E.S. (1987). Reproducing the endpoint of a positioning movement: A further test of the influence of start location. *Journal of Human Movement Studies*, 13, 391–398.

Perception, Awareness and Action

Insights from Blindsight

Stephen R. Jackson

School of Psychology, University of Wales

Introduction

The phenomenon of 'blindsight' has proven to be of considerable interest to neuroscientists because of it's potential implications for delineating the neural correlates of visual awareness. Blindsight is observed when patients who are cortically blind (typically following damage to primary visual cortex) exhibit residual visual processing capabilities for stimuli presented within their scotoma to which they are otherwise unaware. Such residual capabilities can include saccadic and manual localisation of targets, and the discrimination of stimulus orientation and the direction of stimulus motion (Sanders et al. 1974; Weiskrantz 1986).

Demonstrations of spared visual capacity in brain injured patients, including those exhibiting the phenomenon of blindsight, together with psychophysical investigations of visuomotor performance in healthy adults (e.g., Aglioti et al. 1995; Bridgeman et al. 1981; Bridgeman et al. 1997, Bridgeman, this volume; Place, this volume, Rossetti 1998, 2000; Pisella & Rossetti, this volume) have provided evidence for a functional and anatomical dissociation between the visual processes used to guide action and those required for perceptual report. In a series of influential articles, Milner and Goodale have argued for a reconceptualisation of the dorsal and ventral visual processing streams (Ungerleider & Mishkin 1982). They propose a distinction between a ventral stream of visual processing mediating visual perception (object identification and object recognition), and a dorsal stream of visual processing mediating visually guided action (Goodale & Milner 1992; Goodale 1993;

Milner & Goodale 1993; Milner & Goodale 1995). A central tenet of this viewpoint is that visual perception and the visual control of action depend upon functionally distinct and anatomically separable brain systems.

Milner and Goodale have argued that demonstrations of blindsight can be understood as a collection of residual visuomotor responses that depend upon relatively independent neural circuits linking subcortical structures (superior colliculus and pulvinar nucleus) with cortical regions associated with the dorsal visual processing stream (Milner & Goodale 1995). Visual awareness is assumed to be generated separately by processes linked to visual perception and object recognition, which lie within the ventral processing stream (Milner 1995; 1998). They argue that blindsight is not therefore "well characterized as 'unconscious perception', as many writers would have it" (Milner & Goodale 1995, p.75).

While the 'two visual systems' viewpoint of Milner and Goodale can be seen as a useful heuristic, several lines of evidence suggest that there may be more cross-talk between the mechanisms responsible for visual perception and those responsible for visually guided action than is implied by a strong form of the two-systems view. For example, while there have been a number of demonstrations showing that visual illusions can exert a powerful effect upon our perception of objects but have little or no influence on the visuomotor mechanisms used to guide hand action (Aglioti et al. 1995), several recent studies have demonstrated that the calibration of lift (Brenner & Smeets 1996) and grip forces (Jackson and Shaw, 2000) during hand action is significantly influenced by visual illusions affecting the perception of object size. Such demonstrations suggest that the planning and control of hand action depends upon both perceptual mechanisms and object-based knowledge systems. Several studies have also demonstrated that stimuli presented outside of awareness, may nevertheless be processed to a high level of visual description (e.g., Berti & Rizzolatti 1992; Marcel 1998).

Berti and Rizzolatti (1992) reported the results of a category-judgement task in which stimuli (animals vs. fruits) were presented for categorisation within the right hemifield of a group of patients presenting with visuospatial neglect (see also Làdavas et al., this volume). On each trial, the onset of the target stimulus was preceded by the presentation, outside of awareness, of a semantically congruent or non-congruent prime stimulus within the subject's 'neglected' hemifield. The results of this study demonstrated that congruent stimuli presented outside of awareness resulted in speeded RTs on the category judgement task compared to when non-congruent stimuli were presented. Similarly, Marcel (Experiment 4, 1998) demonstrated that the semantic interpretation of an ambiguous word presented within the 'seeing' fields of two hemianopic patients was reliably and consistently biased by the *meaning* of words presented within their 'blind' hemifields of which they were unaware. In both of these instances it is hard to reject the idea that stimuli presented outside of awareness were, nevertheless, analysed to a semantic level of description consistent with object 'identification'.

Pathological visual completion

In each of the above studies, stimuli presented outside of awareness were shown to have influenced how stimuli presented within the subject's 'seeing' field were processed. Many hemianopic patients also show the converse pattern of behaviour, in which stimuli presented within the patient's 'seeing' field influence how a stimulus stimuli presented within the 'blind' hemifield is processed (Marcel 1998). One important example of this pattern of behaviour is the probably mislabelled phenomenon of 'Pathological Visual Completion' in which hemianopic patients report *seeing* a complete visual stimulus (for example a recognisable shape such as a circle or a square) even though part of the stimulus extends into the patient's 'blind' hemifield (Poppelreuter 1917; Fuchs 1921; Torjussen 1978; Marcel 1998; see Walker & Mattingley 1997 for an excellent review of this phenomenon). Early accounts of this phenomenon proposed that completion was based upon an active 'filling-in' process in which the missing components of the figure were inferred from those components presented within the 'seeing' hemifield (Poppelreuter 1917). In contrast, more recent accounts have proposed that 'pathological completion phenomena' reflect the effects of residual visual processing within the supposedly 'blind' hemifield (Marcel 1998; Walker & Mattingley 1997).

Marcel (Experiment 5, 1998) used the after-image technique of Torjussen (1978) to investigate pathological completion in two hemianopic patients (Figure 1A). In his study, subject's viewed a fixation point and were presented with a stimulus for a very brief duration, thereby eliminating the possibility of eye movements. Stimuli were generated using an electronically triggered photographic flash unit which, although having a short duration, produced a relatively long-lasting after-image. Using a variety of stimulus configurations

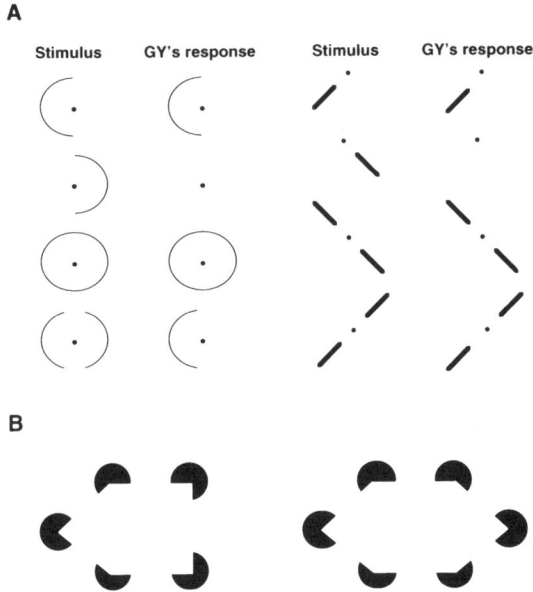

Figure 1. Examples of prior demonstrations of pathological visual completion in the blindsight patient G.Y. **A.** Using the after-image technique pioneered by Torjussen (1978), Marcel showed that G.Y. was unaware of stimuli presented within his blind unless they formed a coherent figural 'gestalt' with stimuli presented within his 'seeing' field (see text for details). **B.** The phenomena of visual completion extends to the completion of 'subjective' figures such as the Kanisza shapes illustrated here. Note that in this case, while G.Y. reported seeing the pentagon and hexagon subjective figures, he reported being unaware of the inducing elements presented within his right hemifield.

(some of which are illustrated in Figure 1A) Marcel showed that stimuli presented completely within the patients' 'blind' hemifield were never consciously seen. However, stimulus configurations which extended from the 'seeing' field into the 'blind' field, and grouped together to make a good gestalt, were accurately reported by both patients. This was the case even where stimuli were asymmetric about the vertical meridian (see Figure 1A for examples). Marcel (Experiment 6, 1998) also demonstrated that hemianopic patients' conscious perception of shapes extending into their blind hemifields included the perception of illusory or subjective figures (illustrated in Figure 1B). Importantly while both patients reliably reported seeing either a pentagon or a hexagon, both patients reported never seeing the inducing elements presented within the 'blind' hemifield.

It is important to note that the phenomenon of 'pathological visual completion' differs from 'blindsight' in several important respects. Most importantly, whereas 'blindsight' refers to the visual processing of a stimulus of which the subject is *unaware*, 'pathological visual completion' refers to the situation in which the subject *becomes aware* of stimuli presented within the supposedly 'blind' hemifield which, under other circumstances would remain outside of awareness. Thus, the area that is 'blind' can be shown to affected by perceptual factors such as spatial grouping. For this reason, the phenomenon of 'pathological visual completion' may be more instructive to neuroscientists interested in understanding the neural correlates of visual consciousness, than the phenomenon of 'blindsight'. In the remaining sections of this chapter I report several experimental studies that we have recently undertaken with the hemianopic patient G.Y. to further investigate his 'pathological visual completion' capabilities.

Selection of Patient G.Y.

At the time of testing, G.Y. was a 40 year old man who had sustained brain injury as a result of road traffic accident when he was an 8 year old child. G.Y.'s accident resulted in damage to the primary visual cortex (V1) of his left hemisphere producing an almost complete hemianopia of the right visual field (he has a small area of macular sparing which extends approximately 3° into his right visual field). G.Y. has been tested on numerous occasions and consistently reports that he cannot 'see' static stimuli presented under normal illumination within his 'blind' field. He does however report having some awareness of high contrast transients, and of stimuli moving in excess of 10–15 degrees per second (Barbur et al. 1994).

Our reasons for choosing to study G.Y. are many. However, two reasons are particular relevant to this chapter. Firstly, the characteristics of G.Y.'s residual vision and his brain pathology have now been investigated over a number of years, using a variety of psychophysical and brain imaging techniques (e.g., Barbur et al. 1980; Barbur et al. 1994; Blythe et al. 1987; ffytch et al. 1996; Zeki & ffytche 1998). Secondly, G.Y. was one of the two patients studied by Marcel (albeit 16 years previously).

Rationale for studies

Physiological investigations in non-human primates (Von der Heydt et al. 1984) together with brain imaging studies in humans (ffytche & Zeki 1996) suggest that visual area V2 within extrastriate cortex is important for the parsing of subjective figures. The demonstration that hemianopic patients such as G.Y. can perceive such subjective figures clearly illustrates that an intact visual area V1 is not a necessary prerequisite for the perception of such figures. However, it remains open to question whether the processing of subjective figures is completed by extrastriate regions independently of 'high-level' visual or attentional mechanisms (as suggested by ffytche & Zeki 1996) or depends upon attentional mechanisms as suggested by Marcel (1998).

While there is now ample evidence to support the view that figure/ground segregation may be carried out preattentively (e.g., Driver et al. 1993; Davis & Driver 1994; Vuilleumier & Landis 1998), it seems likely that whether such figures reach *awareness* may be dependent on higher-level attentional mechanisms. Thus, Marcel (1998) suggests that the potential of stimuli presented within the 'blind' field of hemianopic patients is weakened such that only the figure affording the most economical structural description reaches visual awareness. Therefore patients become aware of the illusory figure, but, remain unaware of the multiple inducing elements which must have been processed in order to construct a representation of the subjective figure (Experiment 6, Marcel 1998; Vuilleumier & Landis 1998). This suggestion is consistent with the Integrated Competition Hypothesis (Duncan *et al.* 1997) which proposes that visual information produces activity within multiple brain systems, within which activations related to different *objects* compete with one another. Such competition is characterised in behavioural terms as a reduction in the efficient processing of each object. It is suggested that mechanisms exist to reduce competition so that "For the sensorimotor network as a whole, the tendency is to settle into a state in which different brain systems have converged to work on the *same dominant object*, analysing its multiple visual properties and implications for action. ... At the neural level, there should be widespread maintenance of the selected object's representation, accompanied by widespread suppression of responses to ignored objects" (p. 255). Support for this suggestion comes from Marcel's demonstration that G.Y.'s awareness of stimuli presented within his 'blind' hemifield is affected by perceptual factors such as spatial grouping, and from studies demonstrating that spatial grouping can ameliorate visual extinction for stimuli presented in the extinguished hemifield of patients with visuospatial hemineglect (Ward et al. 1994).

In summary, the 'two visual systems' theory of Milner and Goodale proposes that independent functional and neural systems exist for visual perception and for the visual analyses which underlie visually guided action (e.g., reach-to-grasp movements). The latter, however, is assumed to lie outside the realm of our conscious visual awareness (Milner 1995; 1998). Thus it is proposed that the visuomotor transformations involved in visually guided action are dissociable from visual mechanisms associated with object identification and visual awareness. In contrast, the phenomenon of 'pathological visual completion' appears to be dependent upon attentional mechanisms, and perceptual factors such as spatial grouping. This suggests that the phenomenon of 'pathological visual completion' should not extend to the domain of visuomotor control.

Study 1: Does 'pathological visual completion' extend to visuomotor responses ?

In a series of experiments we investigated G.Y.'s abilities to execute reach-to-grasp movements toward objects presented within his 'seeing' and 'blind' hemifields (Jackson, 1999). To examine G.Y.'s ability to process object orientation within his 'blind' hemifield, we first required him to reach out and grasp, using a precision grip, wooden blocks randomly presented in one of four orientations (0°, 45°, 90°, and 135°) within either his 'blind' or his 'seeing' hemifields. During each trial G.Y. maintained central fixation and his head movements were minimised using a chinrest. His eye movements were recorded using an infra-red oculomotor tracking system, and his hand movements were recorded throughout the experiment using an electromagnetic recording device. The spatiotemporal pattern of G.Y.'s hand movements were reconstructed off-line. His ability to process object orientation was assessed by measuring the orientation of his grip (i.e., the opposition axis formed by his finger and thumb) immediately *prior to making contact* with the target object. As grip orientation is typically perpendicular to the principal orientation of the target object, we expected G.Y.'s grip orientation to vary systematically with object orientation if his visuomotor system was tacitly processing object orientation. The results of this experiment are shown in Figure 2. As can be seen from Figure 2A, grip orientation for reaches to targets presented in G.Y.'s 'seeing' field varied systematically with target orientation as expected. Grip orientation for reaches directed into G.Y.'s 'blind' field, while considerably more variable (Figure 2A, lower panel). Nevertheless statistical analyses

A.

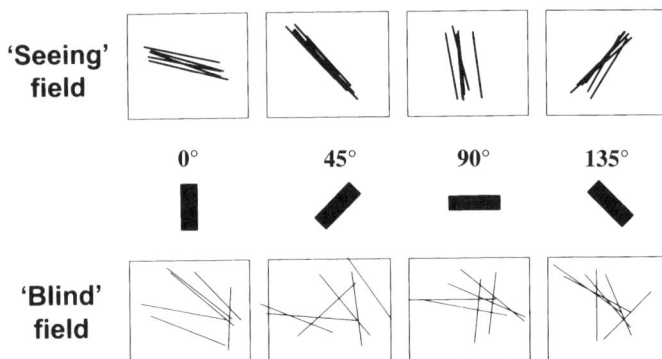

B.

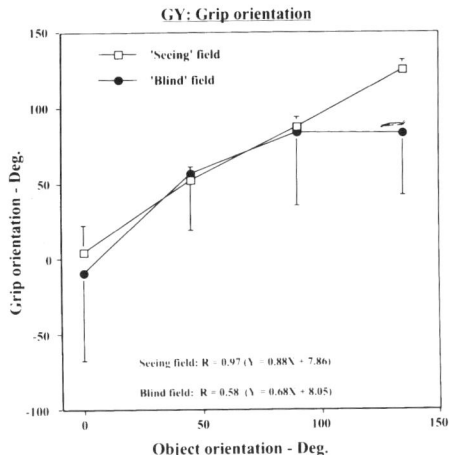

Figure 2. Results of the grip orientation experiment. **A.** The upper panel shows finger-thumb opposition axes for reach-to-grasp movements executed by G.Y. toward objects of different orientations presented in his 'seeing' (upper panels) and 'blind' (lower panels) hemifields. **B.** Shows the correlations between grip orientation (finger-thumb opposition axis) and object orientation for reaches executed by G.Y. into his 'seeing' and 'blind' hemifields.

showed them to be significantly correlated (R = 0.58, p < 0.0001) with target orientation (Figure 2B). These findings confirm previous reports of 'blind-sight' extending to orientation discrimination during reach-to-grasp movements (Perenin & Rossetti 1996; Marcel 1998).

To investigate G.Y.'s ability to process visual information signalling object size, we carried out a further experiment in which we manipulated the width of the wooden block presented in G.Y.'s 'seeing' and 'blind' hemifields. The procedures used were similar to those described above. G.Y. executed reach-to-grasp movements toward three different sized wooden blocks (7.5°, 10°, and 14.7° of visual angle) presented within his 'seeing' or 'blind' hemifields. Maximum grip aperture has been shown over the course of many studies to occur at around 60–80% of the movement duration, and to provide a highly reliable correlate of target object width (see Jeannerod 1988 for a review). To assess G.Y.'s ability to process visual information signalling object width, we therefore measured the maximum grip aperture (separation between finger and thumb) reached on each trial prior to object contact. The results of this experiment are shown in Figure 3.

As can be seen from the figure, for reaches executed by G.Y. toward objects presented into his 'seeing' hemifield, maximum grip aperture de-

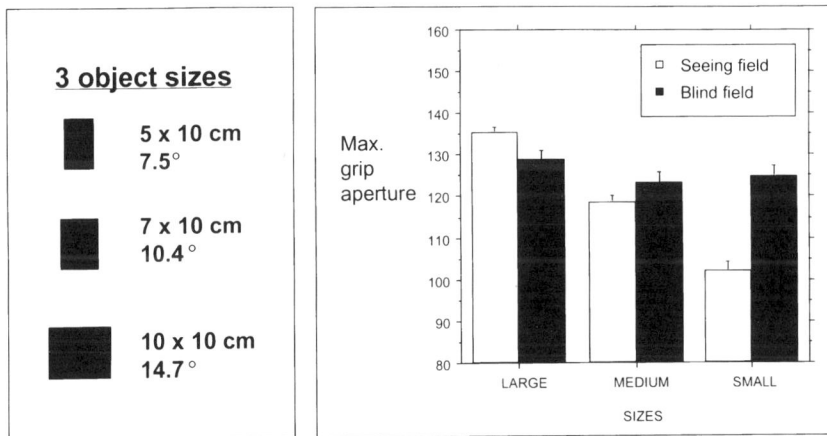

Figure 3. Results of the grip aperture scaling experiment. The left panel shows details of the three different-width objects presented in the study. The right hand panel shows maximum grip apertures (finger-thumb opposition axes) for reach-to-grasp movements executed by G.Y. toward objects of different widths presented in his 'seeing' and 'blind' hemifields.

creased systematically as object size decreased. In contrast, for reaches executed toward objects presented into his 'blind' hemifield, maximum grip
aperture did not vary with changes in object width. Instead, G.Y. appears to
adopt a strategy in which he adopts a wide grip aperture on all trials regardless
of the object's actual width. This result suggests that G.Y. was unable to use
residual visual information signalling object size to scale his grasp aperture
during reach-to-grasp movements directed to objects presented within his
'blind' hemifield.

We acknowledge that this result fails to replicate previous findings that
show: (a) that another 'blindsight' patient can reliably scale his grip aperture for
objects of different widths presented within his 'blind' hemifield of which he is
unaware (Perenin & Rossetti 1996; Rossetti 1998, 2000; Pisella & Rossetti this
volume), and, (6) that G.Y. himself can reliably scale his grip aperture for
objects of different widths presented within his 'blind' hemifield (Marcel 1998).
While this failure to replicate might be considered important by some, we do not
consider it to be of particular theoretical importance. There are many important
methodological differences between our study and those reported previously.
Such experimental parameters may be critical to observing 'blindsight' in G.Y.
and in other patients, as previous studies have demonstrated that even slight
changes in stimulus characteristics can alter G.Y.'s detection performance from
chance to near-normal levels (Weiskrantz 1996).

Walker and Mattingley (1997) argue that methodological factors may be
critical for accounting for reports of pathological visual completion, and that a
key factor is whether evidence of residual vision was adequately assessed.
They argue that an important test of residual vision is whether the subject
responds to stimuli presented entirely within the 'blind' hemifield. For this
reason we do consider it theoretically important however that, while demonstrating 'blindsight' for object orientation, G.Y. was unable to demonstrate
'blindsight' for object size for objects presented, *under identical experimental
conditions*, entirely within his 'blind' hemifield.

To investigate whether pathological visual completion extended to G.Y.'s
visuomotor responses we carried out a further experiment in which we again
manipulated the width of the target objects presented for G.Y. to reach out and
grasp. In this experiment, however, the target objects were presented so that they
spanned the mid-sagittal axis, extending from G.Y.'s 'seeing' field into his
'blind' field. The experimental procedures used were similar to those described
above, and the magnitude of maximum grip aperture was again used to assess

visuomotor processing of object size. G.Y. executed reach-to-grasp movements toward six different wooden blocks (ranging in width from 7.5° to 14.7°). On each trial G.Y. fixated a mark situated at the same position on the left hand edge of each object. Note that in *all* cases the right hand edge of each object extended into G.Y.'s hemianopic field, well beyond his region of macular sparing. Eye movements were recorded throughout the experiment using an infra-red oculo-motor tracking device, and trials were eye movements occurred were rejected. The results of this experiment are shown in Figure 4 which shows the maximum grip aperture for each of the six object widths. Inspection of this figure shows quite clearly that in this experiment G.Y. systematically scaled his grip aperture to the size of the target object ($p < 0.0001$). None of the target objects were ever presented symmetrically across the mid-sagittal axis, and the left hand edge of each object was presented in the same position. For this reason it is unlikely that G.Y. was able to scale his grip aperture based upon some high level perceptual 'filling-in' mechanism. Instead it appears that G.Y.'s ability was most likely based upon residual visual processing in his 'blind' field that somehow benefited from visual analyses carried out simultaneously within his 'seeing'

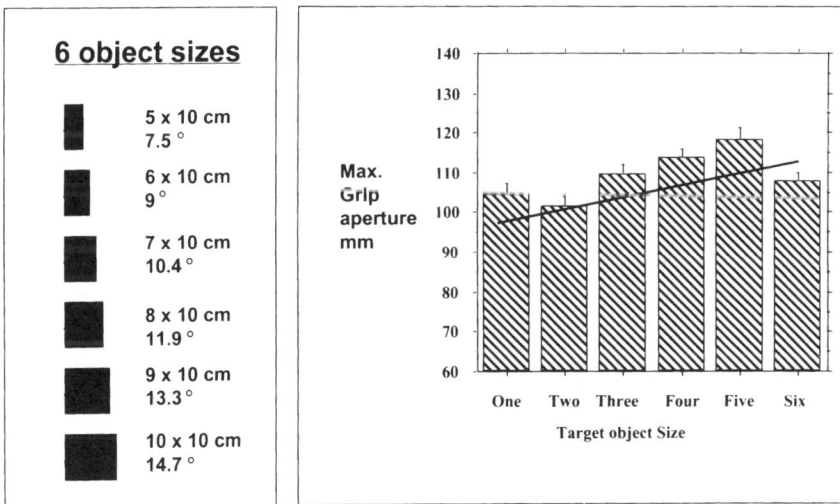

Figure 4. Results of the second grip aperture scaling experiment. The left panel shows details of the six different-width objects presented in the study. The right hand panel shows maximum grip apertures (finger-thumb opposition axes) for reach-to-grasp movements executed by G.Y. toward objects of different widths spanning G.Y.'s mid-saggital axis which extend by different amounts into his 'blind' hemifield.

field. This result suggests that the phenomena of pathological visual completion may extend to visuomotor processing. One interpretation of these data is that when on-line sensorimotor or pragmatic representations are for some reason not available, the visuomotor system uses input from the visual perceptual system. Within this view, the finding that visual completion extends to the control of reach-to-grasp movements for objects presented partially within a hemianopic field, demonstrates the *interaction* of the two visual systems (see also Bridgeman this volume; Pisella & Rossetti this volume).

Does interhemispheric transfer contribute to pathological visual completion?

What mechanisms underlie the phenomenon of pathological visual completion? Given the clear interaction between stimuli presented within the 'seeing' and 'blind' hemifields, an obvious possibility is that residual vision within hemianopic patients' 'blind' hemifield is supported by information transfer from the 'seeing' hemisphere via inter-hemispheric communication channels. Several converging lines of evidence support this suggestion. Here we list just three: Firstly, cells in visual area V2 which represent the vertical meridian in one hemisphere communicate with their counterparts in the opposite hemisphere (Zeki 1993); Secondly, psychophysiological investigations in humans of the visual evoked potentials (VEPs) elicited by a lateralised visual stimulus demonstrate that there is a sequential progression of the contralateral P1 (believed to originate in extrastriate visual cortex) [Mangun & Hillyard 1995] and N1 components to symmetrical sensor locations within the ipsilateral cortex (Lines et al. 1984; Rugg et al. 1984; Tucker et al. 1994). Furthermore, evidence that this contralateral to ipsilateral progression is based upon inter-hemispheric transfer comes from the finding that it is not observed in patients with callosal agenesis (Rugg et al. 1985; Hartry Speiser et al. 1996). In our own studies we have found that this contralateral to ipsilateral progression of the P1 component occurs with a delay of 20–30ms dependent upon stimulus eccentricity (see Figure 6). Finally psychophysical investigations of patient G.Y.'s abilities to detect the direction of motion have shown that when G.Y. is presented with a moving stimulus in his 'seeing' hemifield, he reports not only the veridical stimulus, but also a 'ghost' image moving in a similar fashion at a symmetrical location within his 'blind' hemifield (Finlay et al. 1997).

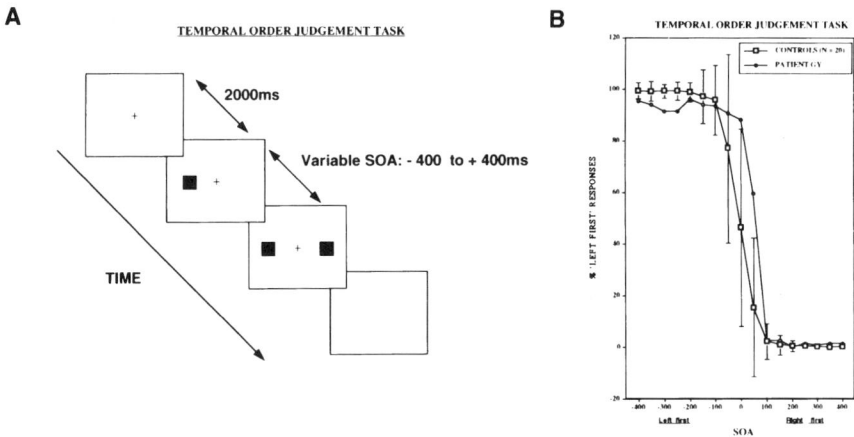

Figure 5. **A.** Details of the temporal-order judgement task. Subjects view a fixation cross which is followed by the abrupt onset a square stimulus at symmetrical locations within each visual hemifield. The stimulus-onset-asynchrony (SOA) between the onset of each stimulus varies between -400ms (the left stimulus precedes the right by 400ms) and 400ms (the right stimulus precedes the left by 400ms). Subjects are required to make an unspeeded judgement of which stimuli was presented first. **B.** Shows the results of the temporal-order judgement task for a group of twenty healthy adult control subjects and for the blindsight patient G.Y. The data presented represent the percentage of 'left-first' responses as a function of the SOA between stimuli. Error bars represent 95% confidence intervals. See text for further details.

To investigate whether interhemispheric communication contributes to the 'pathological visual completion' phenomenon, we have carried out a series of behavioural and psychophysiological (dense-sensor VEP) investigations in G.Y. using a lateralised temporal-order judgement (TOJ) task. One version of this task is illustrated in Figure 5A. Subjects viewed a fixation cross located in the centre of a computer monitor, and, on each trial, after a short delay, two stimuli appear in rapid succession to the left and right of the fixation cross. The subject's task is to report (unspeeded response) which of the two stimuli appeared first. This may seem like a contradiction in terms for a patient with a dense hemianopia, however, it should be noted that, as was outlined above, G.Y. is known to report having some awareness of high contrast transient stimuli presented within his 'blind' hemifield (Barbur et al. 1994). Thus, while he cannot identify the form of a high-contrast transient presented within his hemianopic field, he nevertheless reports that a stimulus has been presented and can, in forced-choice paradigms, report properties of that stimulus such as it's direction of motion. In the TOJ studies outlined below, G.Y. reported experiencing a 'non-visual' awareness of stimuli presented within his 'blind' field. When these stimuli formed a good gestalt he reported experiencing these stimuli as 'more complete' than when they did not form a good gestalt.

In the version of the task shown in Figure 5A, the stimulus onset asynchrony (SOA) between the two stimuli ranged from -400ms (left stimulus first), through 0ms (simultaneous bilateral stimuli), to 400ms (right stimulus first). Healthy adults performing this task respond with a high degree of accuracy until SOAs are reduced to less that 100ms. At SOAs of 50ms or less, healthy adults are impaired at judging which of two stimuli appeared first. Previous studies have also shown that this task is particularly sensitive to brain damage leading to attentional dysfunction. Rorden et al. (Rorden et al. 1997) demonstrated that patients with left-sided visual extinction showed a distinct right-sided bias in their temporal-order judgements. Thus, it was necessary for the left stimulus to appear 200ms *before* the right stimulus in order for the patients to judge the two events as occurring simultaneously. An important implication of this finding is that it appears to demonstrate that disorders of spatial awareness may affect temporal information processing.

The behavioural results of our study are presented in Figure 5B which shows the percentage of 'left first' responses made by a group of twenty control subjects and patient G.Y. as a function of SOA. Inspection of this figure clearly illustrates that control subjects show a high level of accuracy in detecting left-first or right-first trials for SOAs greater than 100ms, but accuracy drops rapidly for SOAs of less than 100ms. Note that for SOAs of 0ms (simultaneous bilateral stimuli) responses are at chance levels (50%). In contrast, patient G.Y. shows a markedly different pattern of results. Firstly, it can be seen that while G.Y. is as accurate as control subjects at detecting right-first stimulation (i.e., stimuli reaching his 'blind' field first) for SOAs of 100ms or greater, his responses are impaired relative to control subjects in detecting left-first stimulation even at long SOAs of -400ms. This finding suggests that G.Y. exhibits an extinction like phenomenon in which stimulation of his 'seeing' field impairs his ability to detect events occurring within his 'blind' field. Secondly, at short SOAs G.Y. exhibits a clear left-sided bias such that on simultaneous bilateral stimulation (0ms SOA) trials he reports the left stimulus as appearing first, and, on trials where the left stimulus is actually preceded by the right stimulus by 50ms, he perceives the left stimulus to have appeared first on a large proportion of trials.

Parietal N200 - LVF target (SOA -400ms)

Patient GY

Controls (N = 20)

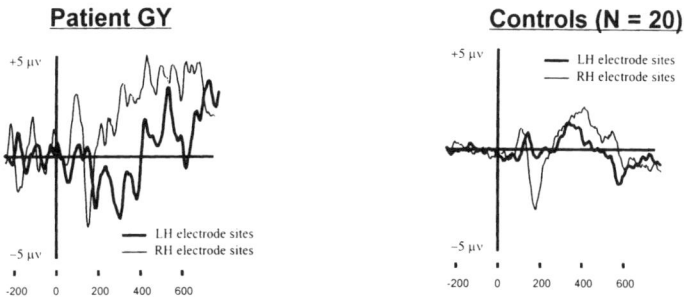

Parietal N200 - RVF target (SOA 400ms)

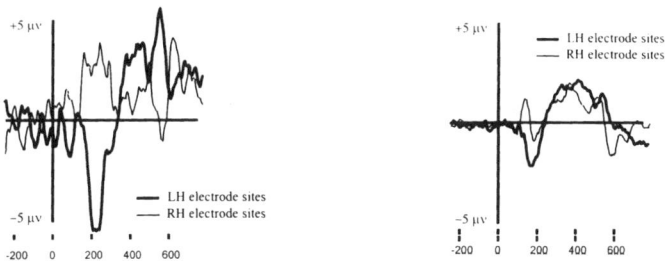

Figure 6. The upper panels illustrate visual evoked potentials (VEPs) for patient G.Y. (left) and a group of twenty health adult control subjects (right) following the presentation of a single lateralised stimulus into the left visual hemifield (G.Y.'s 'seeing' field). In each case, the thicker line represents VEPs recorded at a montage of adjacent electrode sites over the ipsilateral parietal cortex, while the thin line represents VEPs recorded at identical sites over the contralateral parietal cortex. Note in both cases a clear contralateral-to-ipsilateral progression of the P100 / N200 wave. The lower panels illustrate visual evoked potentials (VEPs) following the presentation of a single lateralised stimulus into the right visual hemifield (G.Y.'s 'blind' field). The thicker line now represents VEPs recorded at a montage of adjacent electrode sites over the contralateral parietal cortex, while the thin line represents VEPs recorded at identical sites over the ipsilateral parietal cortex. Note in each case there is still a clear contralateral-to-ipsilateral progression of the P100 / N200 wave.

VEP correlates of G.Y.'s lateralised temporal-order judgements

To better understand the basis of G.Y.'s ability to perform the temporal-order judgement (TOJ) task we have also used dense-sensor EEG recording techniques to study the visual evoked potentials associated with his performance of different versions of the TOJ task. To date we have focused upon examining the time course of the P1 and N1 components recorded over occipital and parietal leads within each hemisphere. We have selected these particular components as we have found that both show a reliable contralateral to ipsilateral progression in healthy adults, and because they are thought to reflect early activity in the ventral (P1) and dorsal (N1) visual processing streams (Mangun & Hillyard 1995). In particular, the parietal N1 component may reflect the activity of motion sensitive areas such as human V5. While a full description of these data is beyond the scope of this chapter, in this section we outline some preliminary findings which suggest something of the mechanisms that might underlie G.Y.'s TOJ abilities.

Relative timing of the parietal and occipital N1 component

While the anatomical basis for 'blindsight' remains highly controversial (see Weiskrantz 1996 for a recent review), functional brain imaging studies suggest that G.Y.'s awareness of stimulus motion is depend upon direct projections to motion-sensitive areas of extrastriate cortex (human V5) which by-pass primary visual cortex [V1] (Barbur et al. 1993; Zeki & ffytche 1998). We have examined the time-course of the visually evoked N1 component at parietal and occipital sensor sites for healthy control subjects and for patient G.Y. on TOJ task trials of SOA -400ms (left first) and SOA 400ms (right first). Note that in both cases, the development of the contralateral N1 component is complete (at 170ms after the onset of the first stimulus) well before the onset of the second stimulus.

It is known that the peak of the visually evoked N1 occurs earlier at more anterior regions than at occipital sensor sites (Mangun & Hillyard 1995), suggesting that these components do not originate from a single neural generator. The data from our control subjects confirm this finding. Our results indicate that the peak of the N1 component, recorded at a montage of adjacent sensor locations over parietal cortex occurs 50ms before it is recorded from a similar montage located over occipital cortex (Figure 6). If, as has been suggested, some portion of the parietal N1 component reflects the activity of motion-sensitive areas in extrastriate cortex (Bach & Ullrich 1994), the later activity seen at occipital sites may reflect a parallel but later developing signal from motion-sensitive regions. These data are consistent with a study reported by Beckers and Zeki (1995) which investigated the effects, on a motion discrimination task, of applying transcranial magnetic stimulation (TMS) to regions of cortex corresponding to V1 and V5. They found that applying TMS over V5 produced an impairment in motion detection at delays of -20ms to +10ms (relative to stimulus onset). In contrast, applying TMS over V1 produced an impairment in motion detection at delays of +60ms to +70ms. We note that the magnitude of the delay observed by Beckers and Zeki (60ms) is in good agreement with our own estimate (50ms) of the delay between the parietal and occipital N1 waveform. Our studies indicate that patient G.Y. also

Occipital N200 - LVF target (SOA -400ms)

Patient GY   Controls (N = 20)

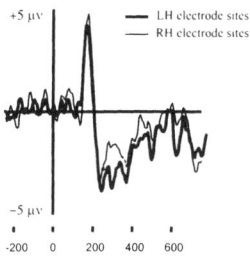
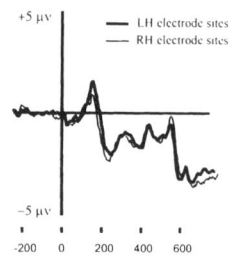

Occipital N200 - RVF target (SOA 400ms)

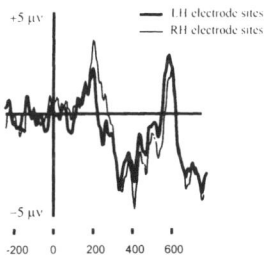
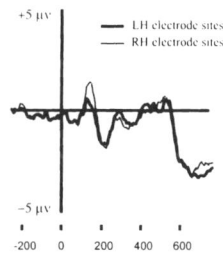

Figure 7. The thicker line now represents VEPs (see Fig.7) recorded at a montage of adjacent electrode sites over the contralateral occipital cortex, while the thin line represents VEPs recorded at identical sites over the ipsilateral occipital cortex. While the time course of the VEPs recorded over G.Y.'s contra- and ipsilesional occipital cortex show similar patterns, the contralateral-to-ipsilateral progression of the P100 / N200 wave observed over parietal cortex is no longer apparent.

shows an observable parietal and occipital N1 component for left ('seeing') and right ('blind') visual field stimuli, in which the peak of the parietal N1 precedes that of the occipital N1.

Interhemispheric transfer and temporal-order judgements

We have speculated that G.Y.'s ability to perform the TOJ task with such high accuracy may result from direct projections to motion-sensitive areas of extrastriate cortex which by-pass primary visual cortex. Consistent with this suggestion we have found that G.Y. shows a similar pattern to control subjects. Specifically, the latency of the P1/N1 components of the VEP recorded from parietal sensor locations precedes that recorded at occipital sensor sites by 40ms or more. In addition, we and others (e.g., Lines et al. 1984; Rugg et al. 1984; Tucker et al. 1994) have found that the parietal P1/N1 components of the VEP show a contralateral to ipsilateral progression with activity at contralateral sensors being reflected at symmetrical ipsilateral sensor locations after a delay which may vary with task conditions. In our own studies we have found this delay to be 10–30ms. G.Y. shows a similar contra-to-ipsilateral progression for both the P1 and N1 components of the VEP (Figure 6), with a delay which ranges from 14–35ms.

Study 3: Do perceptual grouping factors influence temporal-order judgements?

The studies by Torjussen (1978) and Marcel (Experiment 5, 1998) demonstrate that for hemianopic patients, the area that is effectively 'blind' can be influenced by perceptual factors such as grouping. Such patients may exhibit pathological visual completion for figures which are either symmetrical about the midline, or, make a good 'gestalt' around the point of fixation. To further investigate the mechanisms of visual completion, we examined the effects of perceptual grouping on temporal-order judgements (Jackson et al. in prep.). We used a modified version of our previous temporal-order judgement task which we based upon the manipulations reported by Marcel (1998). The stimuli used are illustrated in Figure 8. Bilateral stimulus configurations were either mirror symmetrical about the midline (Figure 8A and 8C) or diagonally opposed (Figure 8B and 8D), and could be of the same orientation (Figure 8A

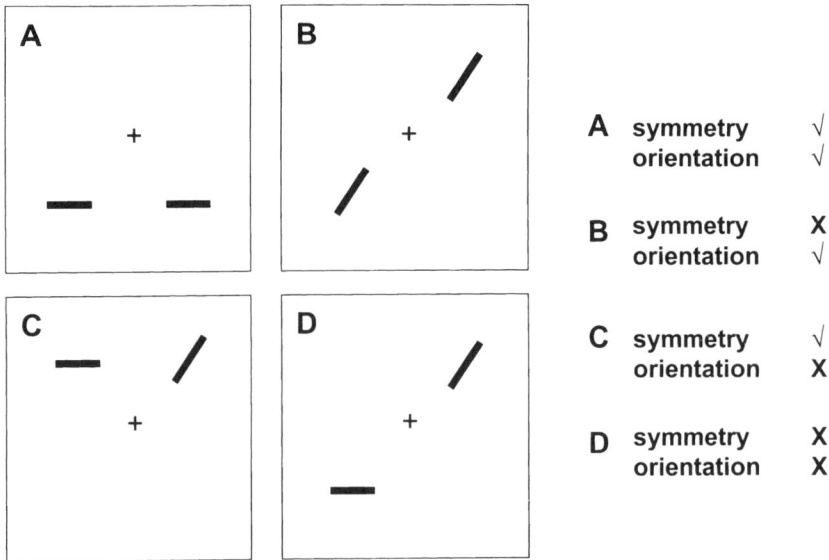

Figure 8. Rationale for second temporal-order judgement experiment. Bilateral stimulus configurations were either mirror symmetrical about the midline (A and C) or diagonally opposed (B and D). Stimuli could be of the same orientation (A and B) or of different orientations (C and D). We classified stimuli of similar orientation as 'grouped' and stimuli of different orientations as 'ungrouped'.

and 8B) or of different orientations (Figure 8C and 8D). The subjects task was, as before, to make an unspeeded judgement as to which stimulus appeared first. Based upon our previous studies we used a restricted set of SOAs (-300ms -100ms -50ms 0ms 50ms 100ms 300ms) in which -300ms signified a trial in which the left visual field stimulus preceded the right visual field stimulus by 300ms. We tested nineteen healthy control subjects on this task as well as patient G.Y. To examine the effects of perceptual grouping, we have assumed that stimuli that are of different orientations form a less coherent gestalt (ungrouped) that stimuli of similar orientations (grouped). The results of this experiment are presented in Figure 9.

The overall results of this study are similar to those seen in the previous task. Control subjects are accurate at making temporal-order judgements for SOAs of 100ms or greater, show a decrease in accuracy as SOAs reduce below 100ms, and drop to chance levels for SOAs of 0ms. Patient G.Y. also

Proportion of
'left-first'
responses

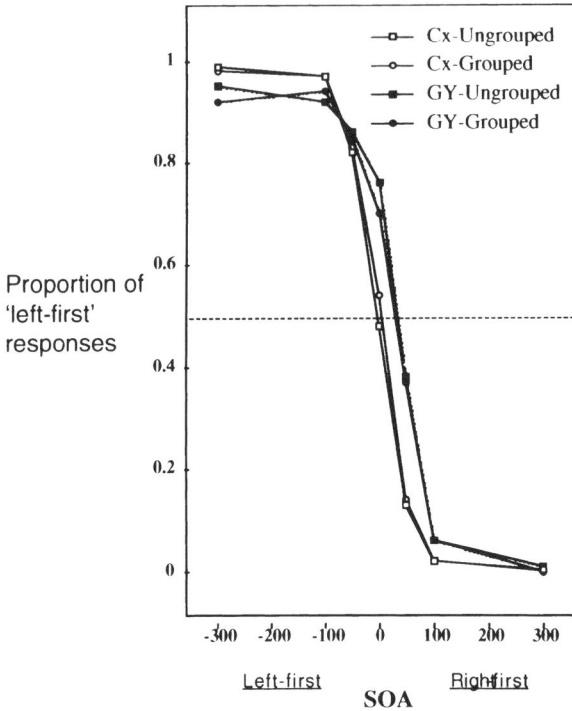

Figure 9. Effects of stimulus grouping on temporal-order judgements for stimuli diagonally opposed across the midline. The graph illustrates the proportion of 'left-first' responses as a function of the SOA between stimuli. Statistical analyses reveal that stimulus grouping (similar orientations) significantly reduces G.Y.'s leftward bias observed at SOAs close to zero.

shows a similar pattern to that seen previously. He again shows a decrease in accuracy, even at long SOAs (-300ms), on trials in which the first stimulus appeared in his 'seeing' field. This decrease in accuracy is not apparent, however, on trials in which the first stimulus appears in his 'blind' hemifield. G.Y. also again shows a left-sided bias, perceiving left stimulus to have arrived first on trials in which bilateral stimulation was simultaneous.

Stimulus grouping was found to have a significant influence on TOJs for control subjects, but only for trials in which left and right visual field stimuli appeared *simultaneously* (0ms SOA) not at all SOAs. For control subjects there was a significant interaction between SOA and Grouping (p < 0.025). While Grouped and Ungrouped trials differed significantly from one another on trials in which stimuli appeared simultaneously (F = 20.1, p < 0.0005), this difference was not significant all other SOAs. For control subjects, grouping led to an increase in the number of TOJ errors. More importantly, stimulus grouping also had a significant effect on patient G.Y.'s temporal-order judgements, interacting with both SOA and stimulus symmetry (p < 0.05). Additional analyses revealed that grouping was strongest for diagonal stimuli of the same orientation (Figure 8B). Means for these trials differed significantly from other trial types for simultaneous bilateral stimulation trials (SOA 0ms, p < 0.01), and for trials with SOAs close to zero (i.e., SOA -50ms, p < 0.05). This difference was not significant at other SOAs. The effects of stimulus grouping on G.Y. was to substantially reduce his left-sided bias.

In summary, the results of these experiments demonstrate that perceptual grouping only influences temporal-order judgements when stimuli are presented simultaneously, or with sufficiently short SOA's that they are likely to be judged as simultaneous. The effects of perceptual grouping on G.Y. were to remove his left-sided bias for stimuli that appeared simultaneously.

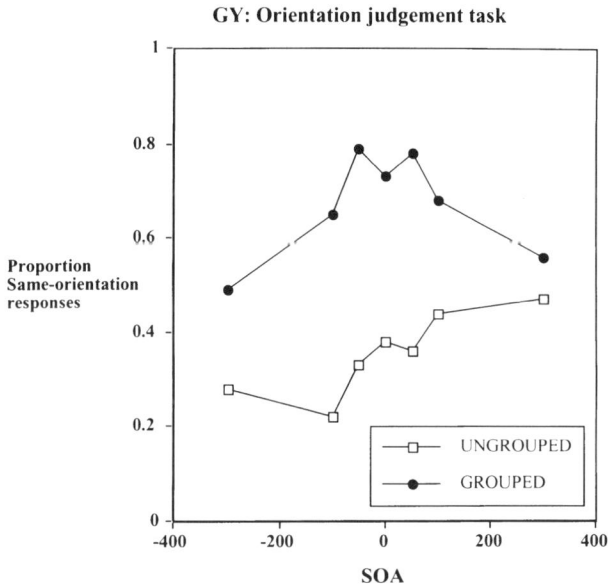

Figure 10. Effects of stimulus grouping on G.Y.'s ability to judge whether bilateral stimuli were the same or different orientation. The graph illustrates the proportion of 'same-orientation' responses as a function of the SOA between stimuli. Note that when SOAs are close to zero, and stimuli group to form a good gestalt, G.Y.'s judgements of same orientation (hit rate) approaches 80% correct.

Study 4: Does perceptual grouping alter G.Y.'s visual awareness during performance of the TOJ task?

To answer this question we carried out a further set of experiments in which we presented G.Y. with *the identical stimuli* that we used to investigate the effects of perceptual grouping on TOJs (Figure 9). However, in these experiments we asked G.Y. to make a different kind of judgement. Instead of having G.Y. judge which of the two stimuli appeared first, we asked him to report whether the orientation of the two stimuli was the same or different. All other aspects of the task were the same. The results of this task are presented in Figure 10 which shows the proportion of 'same-orientation' responses to grouped (hits) and ungrouped stimuli (false alarms) as a function of SOA. Note that chance performance would correspond to hit and false alarm rates of 0.5 while perfect discrimination would correspond to a hit rate of 1.0 and a false alarm rate of 0. Inspection of Figure 10 shows that G.Y.'s false alarm rate is *asymmetrical* for trials in which the left target preceded the right and vice versa. For trials in which the first stimulus appears in G.Y.'s 'seeing' field, (SOAs-300ms to -100ms) G.Y.'s false alarm rate is less than 0.3. In contrast, when the first stimulus appears in G.Y.'s 'blind' field (SOAs 100ms to 300ms), his false alarm rate is much higher, 0.4 or greater. This pattern might be expected if the effects of pathological visual completion were asymmetric, with events occurring within the 'seeing' field influencing *visual awareness* of events within the 'blind' field, but not vice versa. In contrast, G.Y.'s hit rate is both *symmetrical* for trials in which the left target precedes the right and vice versa, and, increases substantially for SOAs of 100ms or less. For very short SOAs (50ms), G.Y.'s hit rate increases to very close to 80% correct. This level of accuracy suggests that at very short SOAs, *and*, when stimuli group together to form a good gestalt, patient G.Y. becomes aware of some aspects of the form of the stimulus presented within his 'blind' hemifield. Thus when questioned regarding his levels of awareness, G.Y. claims that the stimuli feel more 'complete' when they group compared to when they do not group.

Conclusions

In this chapter I have outlined a series of studies that we have carried out with the 'blindsight' patient G.Y. aimed at understanding the phenomenon of 'pathological visual completion'. This phenomenon is observed in circumstances where visual events occurring in a hemianopic patient's 'seeing' hemifield lead to the patient having visual awareness of visual events occurring within the patient's 'blind' hemifield.

The first study I described demonstrated that the perceptual phenomenon of visual completion appears to extend to the execution of visuomotor responses. Thus, while G.Y. was unable to appropriately scale his grip aperture to the width of objects presented entirely within his 'blind' hemifield, he was able to do so when part of the target object extended into his 'seeing' field. This finding would appear to run counter to a simple version of the 'two visual systems' account (Milner & Goodale 1995; Milner 1995; Milner 1998) which proposes that the visuomotor transformations involved in scaling grip aperture "lie outside of the realm of our conscious visual awareness" (p. 25. Milner 1998). Instead, the data from this study is consistent with the view that when on-line sensorimotor representations are unavailable, the visuomotor system uses input from the visual perceptual system (ventral stream). Thus, visual completion in these circumstances appears to demonstrate the interaction of the dorsal and ventral visual processing systems (see also Rossetti 1998, 2000; Pisella and Rossetti this volume; Bridgeman this volume).

In studies 2–4 we attempted to explore the mechanisms which underlie these visual completion phenomena using a lateralised temporal-order completion task together with dense-sensor VEP recording techniques. The findings from these studies, while preliminary, suggest that G.Y.'s preserved ability to be aware of transient stimuli appearing within his 'blind' hemifield may depend upon early signals arriving in motion-sensitive regions located ventrolaterally within extrastriate cortex, which are subsequently communicated across the cortical hemispheres via the corpus callosum.

References

Aglioti, S., DeSouza, J.F.X. & Goodale, M.A. (1995). Size-contrast illusions deceive the eye but not the hand. *Current Biology*, 5, 679–685.

Bach, M. & Ullrich, D. (1994). Motion adaptation governs the shape of motion-evoked cortical potentials. *Vision Research*, 34, 1541–1547.

Barbur, J.L., Ruddock, K.H. & Waterfield, V.A. (1980). Human visual responses in the absence of the geniculo-calcarine projection. *Brain*, 103, 905–928.

Barbur, J.L. Harlow, A.J. & Weiskrantz, L. (1994). Spatial and temporal response properties of residual vision in a case of hemianopia. *Philosophical Transactions of the Royal Society of London* (B), 343, 157–166.

Beckers, G. & Zeki, S. (1995). The consequences of inactivating areas V1 and V5 on visual motion perception. *Brain*, 118, 49–60.

Berti, A. & Rizzolatti, G. (1992). Visual processing without awareness: Evidence from unilateral neglect. *Journal of Cognitive Neuroscience*, 4, 345–351.

Blythe, I.M., Kennard, C. & Ruddock, K.H. (1987). Residual vision in patients with retrogeniculate lesion of the visual pathways. *Brain*, 110, 887–905.

Brenner, E. & Smeets, J.B.J. (1996). Size illusion influences how we lift but not how we grasp an object. *Experimental Brain Research*, 111, 473–476.

Bridgeman, B. (2000). Interactions between vision for perception and vision for behavior. This volume, 17–40.

Bridgeman, B., Kirch, M. & Sperling, A. (1981) Segregation of cognitive and motor aspects of visual function using induced motion. *Perception and Psychophysics*, 29, 336–342.

Bridgeman, B., Peery, S. & Anand, S. (1997). Interaction of cognitive and sensorimotor maps of visual space. *Perception and Psychophysics,* 59 (3), 456–469.

Duncan, J., Humphreys, G. W. & Ward, R. (1997). Competitive brain activity in visual attention. *Current Opinion in Neurobiology*, 7, 255–261.

Ffytche, D.H. & Zeki, S. (1996). Brain activity related to the perception of illusory contours. *Neuroimage*, 3, 104–108.

Ffytche, D.H., Guy, C.N. & Zeki, S. (1996). Motion specific responses from a blind hemifield. *Brain*, 119, 1971–1982.

Finlay, A.L., Jones, S.R., Moreland, A.B., Ogilvie, J.A. & Ruddock, K.H. (1997). Movement in the normal visual hemifield induces a percept in the 'blind' hemifield of a human hemianope. *Proceedings of the Royal Society of London* (B), 264, 267–275.

Fuchs, W. (1921/1938) Completion phenomena in hemianopic vision. Translated by W.D. Ellis. *A source book of gestalt psychology*. London: Kegan Paul, 357–365.

Goodale, M.A. & Milner, A.D. (1992). Separate visual pathways for perception and action. *Trends in the Neurosciences*, 15, 20–25.

Goodale, M.A. (1993). Visual pathways supporting perception and action in the primate cerebral cortex. *Current Opinion in Neurobiology,* 3, 578–585.

Hartry Speiser, A., Tucker, D.M., McDougal, L., Murias, M. & Brown, W. (1996). Absent electrical responses in the unstimulated hemisphere in agenesis of the corpus callosum. In E. Zaidel (Ed.), *The role of the human corpus callosum in sensory motor integration: Anatomy, physiology, and behaviour; individual differences and clinical applications*. NATO.

Jackson, S.R. (1999). Pathological perceptual completion following hemianopia extends to the control of reach-to-grasp movements. *Newsreport* 10(12), 2461–2466.

Jackson S.R. & Shaw, A. (2000). The Ponzo illusion affects grip force but not grip aperture scaling during prehension movements. *Journal of Experimental Psychology: Human Perception and Performance*. 26(1), 418–423.

Jackson, S.R., Ward, R., Owen, V. & Roberts, M. Manuscript in preparation.

Jeannerod, M. (1988). *The neural and behavioural organization of goal-directed movements*. Oxford: Oxford University Press.

Mangun, G.R. & Hillyard, S.A. (1995). Mechanisms and models of selective attention. In M.D. Rugg and M.G.H. Coles (Eds.) *Electrophysiology of mind: Event-related brain potentials and cognition* (40–85). Oxford: Oxford University Press.

Marcel, A.J. (1998). Blindsight and shape perception: deficit of visual consciousness or of visual function? *Brain*, 121, 1565–1588.

Mason, C. & Geffen, G. (1996). Temporal integration of events within and between the cerebral hemispheres. *Cortex*, 32, 97–108.

Milner, A.D. & Goodale, M.A. (1995). *The visual brain in action*. Oxford University Press, Oxford.

Milner, A.D. (1995). Cerebral correlates of visual awareness. *Neuropsychologia*, 33, 1117–1130.

Milner, A.D. (1998). Streams and consciousness: visual awareness and the brain. *Trends in Cognitive Sciences*, 2, 25–30.

Perenin, M.T. & Rossetti, Y. (1996). Grasping without form discrimination in a hemianopic field. *Neuroreport*, 7, 793–797.

Pisella, L. & Rossetti, Y. (2000). Interaction between conscious Identification and non-conscious sensory-motor processing: Temporal constraints. This volume, 129–152.

Place, U.T. 2000. Consciousness and the zombie within: A functional analysis of the blindsight evidence. This volume, 295–330.

Poppelreuter, W. (1917/1990) *Disturbances of lower and higher visual capacities caused by occipital damage: with special reference to the psychopathological, pedagogical, industrial, and social implications*. Translated by J. Zihl: Oxford: Clarendon Press.

Rorden, C.R., Mattingley, J.B., Karnath, H-O & Driver, J. (1997). Visual extinction and prior entry: Impaired perception of temporal order with intact motion perception after unilateral parietal damage. *Neuropsychologia*, 35, 421–433.

Rossetti, Y. (1998). Implicit short-lived motor representation of space in brain-damaged and healthy subjects. *Consciousness and Cognition*, 7, 520–558.

Rossett, Y. (2000). Implicit perception in action: short-lived motor representations of space. In: P.G. Grossenbacher (ed): *Finding consciousness in the brain*. (131–179) Benjamins Amsterdam (in press).

Rugg, M.D., Lines, C.R. & Milner, A.D. (1984). Visual evoked potentials to lateralised visual stimuli and the measurement of interhemispheric transmission time. *Neuropsychologia*, 22, 215–225.

Rugg, M.D., Milner, A.D. & Lines, C.R. (1985). Visual evoked potentials to lateralised visual stimuli in two cases of callosal agenesis. *Journal of Neurology, Neurosurgery, and Psychiatry*, 48, 367–373.

Sanders, M.D., Warrington, E.K., Marshall, J. & Weiskrantz, L. *Lancet* 1, 707–8 (1974).

Torjussen, T. (1978). Visual processing in cortically blind hemifields. *Scandinavian Journal of Psychology*, 16, 15–21.

Tucker, D.M., Liotti, M., Potts, G.F., Russell, G.S. & Posner, M.I. (1994). Spatiotemporal analysis of brain electrical fields. *Human Brain Mapping*, 1, 134–152.

Ungerleider, L.G. & Mishkin, M. (1982). Two cortical systems. In D.J. Ingle, M.A. Goodale & R.J.W. Mansfield (Eds.), *Analysis of visual behaviour*. MIT press, 549–586.

Vuilleumier, P. & Landis, T. (1998). Illusory contours and spatial neglect. *Neuroreport*, 9, 2481–2484.

Walker, R. & Mattingley J.B. Ghosts in the machine? Pathological visual completion phenomena in the damaged brain. *Neurocase*, 3, 313–335.

Ward, R., Goodrich, S.J. & Driver, J. (1994). Grouping reduces visual extinction: neuropsychological evidence for weight-linkage in visual selection. *Visual Cognition*, 1, 101–129.

Weiskrantz, L. (1986). *Blindsight: A case study and implications*. Oxford : Oxford University Press

Weiskrantz, L. (1996). Blindsight revisited. *Current Opinion in Neurobiology*, 6, 215–220.

Zeki, S. (1993). *A vision of the brain*. Oxford: Blackwell..

Zeki, S. & ffytche, D.H. (1998). The Riddoch syndrome: insights into the neurobiology of conscious vision. *Brain*, 121, 25–45.

Geographical Slant Perception

Dissociation and Coordination between Explicit Awareness and Visually Guided Actions

Mukul Bhalla
Loyola University, New Orleans

Dennis R. Proffitt
University of Virginia

Introduction

Common sense argues that vision functions in a unified manner and that actions are directly informed by our awareness of the environment. Although it may seem as if a single, unified system controls all visual functions, there is considerable evidence indicating the existence of a number of specialized subsystems, each responsible for a different set of visually guided functions. The two most distinct subsystems are the explicit awareness and action systems which have been referred to by such names as the "what" and "how" systems (Milner & Goodale 1995), the semantic and pragmatic systems (Jeannerod 1994) and the cognitive and sensorimotor systems (Bridgeman this volume; Bridgeman 1994; Paillard 1987). The primary function of the awareness system is to recognize and identify objects, whereas the action system is responsible for visually guided actions. Although there exists a large body of research showing a clear dissociation of function between the two systems, there is also evidence indicating that the two systems are not completely isolated from one another, but rather are richly interconnected and depend on a mutual exchange of information (see Pisella & Rossetti this volume; Bridgeman this volume; Rossetti 1998, 2000).

This chapter first presents a brief review of the studies — electrophysiological, neuropsychological, and behavioral — that demonstrate both the independence and interdependence of the two streams. We then present our own research on geographical slant perception to further illustrate the dissociation and coordination between explicit awareness and visually guided actions. The latter findings are discussed in terms of a time-dependent coordination between awareness and visually guided actions.

Modularity in the visual system

The idea of modularity in the visual system can be traced back to a proposal by Schneider (1969) that was later developed by Ungerleider and Mishkin (1982). Two broad streams of projections from the striate cortex (V1) had been discovered: A ventral stream projecting to the inferotemporal cortex and a dorsal stream projecting to the posterior parietal cortex. It was proposed that the former system was responsible for the perception of an object's identity (the "what" pathway), whereas the latter was responsible for spatial localization (the "where" pathway).

In the original formulations of this proposal, the two streams were thought to respond to different kinds of information. A more recent formulation (e.g. see Milner 1992; Milner & Goodale 1993; 1995) postulates a functional segregation, in that both streams process similar information about the object, such as size, orientation, position in space, etc., but the purposes toward which this information is used is quite different. The segregation lies not in the input streams, but rather in the different transformations applied to the retinal input so as to promote different functions, explicit perception or action (see also Bridgeman this volume; Pisella & Rossetti this volume).

From this functional perspective, the ventral stream of projections reaching the inferotemporal lobe is mainly concerned with perceptual functions such as visual learning and object recognition, whereas the dorsal stream of projections to the posterior parietal lobe — also having important connections to the premotor and prefrontal cortex — is concerned with the control of motoric actions (Goodale & Milner 1992; Milner & Goodale 1993, 1995). Thus, instead of the "what" and "where" distinction proposed by Ungerleider and Mishkin (1969), Goodale and Milner proposed a "what" (ventral) and "how" (dorsal) distinction in which the former is responsible for the conscious awareness and recognition of objects and the later for visually guided actions.

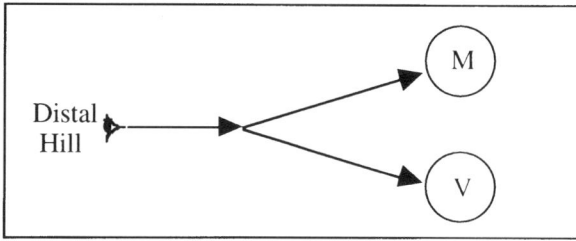

Model A: Complete dissociation

Figure 1. Model A: Complete dissociation between visual awareness and visually guided actions.

A representation of such a formulation is given in Figure 1.

Similar views on this functional segregation have been proposed by other researchers. For example, based on the finding that the parietal and temporal pathways receive mixed inputs from the magno and parvo streams, Ferrara, Nealey and Maunsell (1994) proposed that differences between these streams represent an efficient method for transmitting low-level information about different stimulus dimensions, and that the dorsal and ventral pathways draw on information provided by both the parvo and magno streams according to their particular needs. The parietal pathway thus depends largely on inputs from the magno stream because its spatiotemporal and contrast response properties are necessary to guiding actions (see Pisella & Rossetti this volume). Color and fine detail, inherent in the parvo stream, are of little value to this pathway. Appropriate to its object recognition function, the temporal pathway depends heavily on color, shading and high spatial resolution information carried by the parvo stream; however, it also benefits from the contrast information provided by the magno stream.

Evidence for dissociation

There is considerable evidence indicating a dissociation between the conscious perceptual judgments supported by the ventral stream and the automatic visual guidance of actions supported by the dorsal stream. In the review below, this evidence is divided into three subsections: electrophysiological studies, neuropsychological studies, and behavioral studies with brain-intact participants.

Electrophysiological studies: Single cell recordings from monkeys have revealed that dorsal stream cells are well suited for coding information of relevance for visually guided actions. For example, one of the most striking characteristics of cells in this stream is that they do not respond to visual stimulation when the animal is placed under anesthesia. This is indicative of the fact that most cells in this region fire when the observer is actively interacting with its environment and not passively detecting and storing representations of the world. Another feature of some of the cells in the dorsal stream is that they update information moment to moment with every change of viewpoint, illumination, and head position. For example, Anderson, Asanuma, Essick and Siegel (1990) have found that in area LIP (lateral intraparietal area) and 7a, the amplitude of the cells' response to a visual stimulus in its receptive field is dependent on gaze direction, allowing for the computation of the true (head or body related) coordinates of the stimulus independent of retinal location.

Motion information is especially important for directing visually guided action. Electrophysiological evidence suggests that some parts of area MST (and MT) code for relative motion, size change and rotation of an object in the frontoparallel plane or in depth (Saito et al. 1986). Such information would be essential for the on-line control of limbs as they are directed towards moving targets. In fact, recent kinematic studies of catching in humans by Savelsbergh, Whiting and Bootsma (1991) have shown that the acceleration of the moving limb is controlled by the rate of expansion of the target image on the retina, which is a typical example of the type of change that excites cells in MST.

On the other hand, cells in the ventral stream of projections to the inferotemporal region behave very differently from those in the dorsal stream. Ventral stream cells remaining unaffected by anaesthesia, suggesting that they are not involved in the on-line control of behavior. These cells seem better suited to the coding of detailed object-centered descriptions, being highly selective for the form, pattern and color of objects, maintaining their responsivity over a wide range of these attributes. The work of Ferrera, Nealey and Maunsell (1992, 1994) shows that both the magno and parvo channels provide input to area V4, and thus, the visual information provided to the inferotemporal cortex is very comprehensive in nature.

As information progresses through this pathway — from V1 through V2 and V3 to V4 — more detailed coding of visual features is seen. Upon reaching the inferotemporal cortex, cells show remarkable specificity in their responses to complex visual stimuli, such as hands and faces (Gross et al. 1972; Gross et al. 1985). Further, Tanaka, Saito, Fukada and Moriya (1991) have shown that cells in the anterior region of the inferotemporal cortex are highly selective in their responses to specific object attributes. Other research indicates that cells sensitive to similar stimulus features are clustered together in columns through the depth of the inferotemporal region. (Fujita et al. 1992).

Cells in the inferotemporal region have large receptive fields which almost always include the fovea. This allows the cells to generalize across the visual field and code the specific features of an object independent of location. Moreover, these cells maintain this specificity over different viewpoints, sizes, and colors (Perrett et al. 1984; Perrett et al. 1991). This evidence is in keeping with the view that cells in the inferotemporal region code for object-centered visual descriptions, independent of changes in viewpoint and illuminations.

Motion information is also important for object identification and is conveyed to the ventral stream from area MT to V4. Sary, Vogels and Orban (1993) have found cells in the inferotemporal cortex which respond to a particular shape, even when the contours of the shape are defined by the relative motions of the elements making up the shape and its background, rather than by differences in other features such as luminance and texture.

Neuropsychological studies: Studies of humans with damage to only one projection system provide another opportunity to see this dissociation between explicit perception and action. Damage to the dorsal stream of projections terminating in the parietal region affects the ability to use spatial and object related information to control actions (optic ataxia), even though this information can still be used to identify and describe the object. Such patients exhibit difficulty in reaching out in the right direction and grasping in a manner appropriate to accommodate the size, shape and orientation of the object to be grasped (e.g. Jakobson et al. 1991; Perenin & Vighetto 1983, 1988). In addition, most patients with parietal damage have problems with eye movements, such as slowed saccades in response to visual cues (Pierrot-Deseilligny et al. 1987; Pierrot-Deseilligny et al. 1991), and a failure of pursuit eye movements to keep up with a target moving towards the side of the lesion (Troost & Abel 1982; Morrow & Sharpe 1993).

For example, Perenin and Vighetto (1988) have described the visual and visuomotor capacities of ten patients with unilateral damage, mainly to the parietal lobe (with none to the temporal lobe). They found that these subjects performed above chance at tasks like the spatial localization of targets and perception of line orientations, and were also able to provide accurate estimates of the distance and relative positions of targets in the visual field. This was in stark contrast to the profound difficulties all these patients experienced in reaching towards the same targets and the errors they made in rotating their hands as they reached towards a large slot oriented in different directions over different trials (see Pisella & Rossetti this volume).

A similar problem can be seen when patients with parietal damage attempt to pick up an object. In normal grasping, the hand begins to open as soon as movement to the object is initiated, reaching a maximum about 2/3 of the way to the object. Patients with damage to the parietal lobe, in contrast, do not show this anticipatory grip scaling between their finger and thumb and usually the first contact with the object is made with the palm of the hand, (Jeannerod 1986, 1994; Perenin & Vighetto 1983, 1988), and the grip is corrected after feedback from the object.

Patients with visual agnosia, in contrast, suffer from brain damage to the ventral stream of projections terminating in the inferotemporal region. They often are unable to recognize or describe common objects, faces, or pictures, even though they are able to perform normal everyday actions. Milner et al. (1991) have described the behavior of an agnosia patient, D.F., who suffered damage in the lateral prestriate cortex, affecting areas V2, V3 and V4 (Clarke 1993; Zilles & Schleicher 1993). Most of her primary visual cortex (V1) was spared, as was the tectothalamic pathways to MT and other dorsal stream structures. Hence both the main pathways to the posterior parietal cortex seem to be spared and are capable of conveying the information about orientation, size and shape needed to control visually guided actions. Consequently, her visual system is unable to inform conscious judgments about size or orientation of objects in the world (she is unable to recognize or discriminate between simple geometrical shapes or simple line drawings of everyday objects, or the faces of friends and relatives), but her visuomotor system can control the programming and on-line control of visually guided actions based on these same object characteristics. When presented with a pair of rectangular blocks of the same or different dimensions, she was unable to visually distinguish between them. Even when asked to indicate the width of a single block by using her index finger and thumb, her actions were uncorrelated to the dimensions of the object and varied substantially from trial to trial. In contrast, when she was asked to reach out and pick up the block, the aperture between her index finger and thumb changed systematically with the width of the object, just as in normal subjects. In other words, D.F. scaled her grip to the dimensions of the object she was about to pick up, even though she appeared to be unaware of the magnitudes of these dimensions.

D.F. shows a similar dissociation in her responses to the orientation of stimuli. While she exhibits considerable difficulty in indicating the orientation either verbally or manually (i.e. by rotating her hand or a handheld card), she is as good as normal subjects in reaching out and placing her hand or the card into a slot, rotating her hand in the appropriate direction with the initiation of the movement.

Evidence from "blindsight" patients also provides support for the dissociation between the two systems. Such patients usually report blindness in one visual hemifield following unilateral lesions to the striate cortex. Following this damage, patients are unable to report visual awareness in the region of their scotoma, but exhibit some form of visually guided actions such as blinking, pupillary response, or eye movements (Poppel et al. 1973; Weizkrantz et al. 1974) or even pointing (Weizkrantz et al. 1974), despite a persistent lack of being able to verbally report seeing the very object toward which they can direct their actions (see Jackson this volume; Pisella & Rossetti this volume; Place this volume).

One explanation for "blindsight" phenomena points to the fact that the superior colliculus sends projections to some dorsal stream structures via the pulvinar and it is believed that it is this tectopulvinar route that conveys visual information to the cortex to guide the residual visuomotor abilities observed in the blindsight patients (Weizkrantz et al. 1974; Perry & Cowey 1984). A likely possibility for such a dorsal stream structure that receives input via the tectopulvinar route is area MT. This account is consistent with findings that most blindsight patients show a high sensitivity to object motion, and in fact, show better evidence for blindsight when the stimulus is moving (e.g. Riddoch 1917; Bridgeman & Staggs 1982, etc.).

Behavioral studies: A similar dissociation between perception and action can be observed in brain-intact people. For example, in one of the earliest studies of its kind, Bridgeman, Lewis, Heit and Nagle (1979) found that saccadic suppression could mask target displacement during a saccade; however, accurate reaching for the target still occurred after the saccade. Other studies have also yielded similar results (Goodale et al. 1986; Pelisson et al. 1986; Bridgeman 1987).

Using the Titchner Illusion, Goodale, Aglioti, and DeSouza (1994) showed that while the perception of objects is subject to the illusion, actions directed towards them are not. In the illusion, two target disks of equal size are presented, one surrounded by a set of smaller circles and the other by a set of larger circles. Observers report the target surrounded by the smaller circles as being larger than the target surrounded by the larger set. However, when asked to reach out and pick up the target disks, these same individuals scaled their grip aperture in accordance with the real size of the target disks. Their actions seemed apparently unaffected by the visual illusion (see also Pisella & Rossetti this volume).

Thus, there is substantial evidence for two main visual processing streams, a dorsal stream to the posterior parietal cortex driving visually guided actions and a ventral stream projecting to the inferotemporal cortex that drives conscious visual awareness. However, despite the evidence indicating this dissociation, there is also clear support for their interconnectedness.

Evidence for interconnections

Obvious support for interconnections between the dorsal and ventral streams comes from the harmonious and well coordinated functioning of perception and action in our day-to-day activities. Research shows that this cooperation is also seen in actual anatomical connections between structures belonging to the two streams. As discussed earlier, the input received by both systems is mixed in terms of the parvo and magno channels. Also, Baizer, Ungerleider and Desimone (1991) have shown that while large portions of the area V4 (believed to be part of the ventral stream) project primarily to the inferotemporal cortex, neurons in the more dorsal portions of V4 also project to the posterior parietal cortex. Additionally, there are some areas such as V3A and MT that make major contributions to both the action and perception systems, such that there is even debate about whether these areas belong in one stream or the other.

Interconnections between the ventral and dorsal streams are implicated whenever the visual guidance of actions requires some input from the explicit awareness system. When picking up a rose, for example, the use of a pincer grasp to avoid the thorns would have been prescribed by the "what" system that identified the object as a rose. It has been proposed that a higher level praxic system — with access to the products of ventral stream processing — instructs the relevant visuomotor systems (Milner & Goodale 1995; Jackendoff &

Landau 1994; Jeannerod 1994). In fact, a patient has recently been described by Sirigu, Cohen, Duhamel, Pillon, Dubois and Agid (1995) whose behavior suggests that the damage is to her praxic system. The patient's two cortical visual systems seem to be essentially intact, she suffers neither from visual agnosia nor optic ataxia. She is able to recognize familiar objects and reach for them efficiently. However, when she is shown a familiar object and asked to pick up it up and use it, she will often do so using a grasp that is efficient, but inappropriate for the use of the object. Thus, although the two systems are functioning adequately in isolation for this patient, they appear to be disconnected from each other.

D.F. has also shown similar behavior with everyday objects. Milner and Goodale (1995) reported that if textural or other local information allows her to identify an object, she grasps it appropriately. But when she fails to identify an object, she behaves like Sirigu et al.'s patient — she grasps it efficiently but inappropriately. Based on these results we can assume that information about an object's identity cannot be transferred to D.F.'s praxic and visuomotor systems just as in Sirigu et al.'s patient.

Instances have also been reported where interconnections between the perception and action systems have been manifested in the form of interference between the two. For example, results from experiments with both normal people (Rossetti & Regnier 1995) and brain damaged patients (Rossetti et al. 1995) show that either (1) simultaneously providing a verbal and motoric response or (2) introducing a delay in responding, both result in deterioration of the motoric response. These results indicate that when the representation normally used to drive the motor response cannot be effectively accessed, either because of simultaneous activation of the semantic representation which drives the verbal responses or when the pragmatic representation is longer available because of a time delay, then both the verbal and motor responses are both informed by the semantic representation (see Bridgeman this volume; Pisella & Rossetti this volume; Rosetti 1998, 2000).

Evidence from geographical slant perception

Our studies on geographical slant perception provide evidence for both a dissociation as well as an interconnection between conscious awareness of slant and visually guided actions (Proffitt et al. 1995; Bhalla & Proffitt 1999). These studies show that the dissociation supports the different functions of awareness and motor guidance, whereas the interconnection serves to promote consistency between the two systems over extended periods of time.

Background and basic methodology

All of our experiments employed a similar methodology, which is described below (for further details see Proffitt et al. 1995; Bhalla & Proffitt 1999). Participants viewed the hills binocularly, while standing at the top or the base of hills. They provided estimates of the angle of inclination with respect to the horizontal. Reports were made in three ways: verbally, visually and haptically. The verbal report was simply a numerical estimate (in degrees) of how much the hill was inclined from the horizontal. The visual judgment was made using a disk, which consisted of an adjustable angle representing a cross-section of the inclination of the hill. Haptic judgments were made by using a palm board with a flat palm rest, the tilt of which could be adjusted upward or downward to match the inclination of the hill. The tilt board was placed slightly above waist level and participants adjusted it with their dominant hand, without looking at that hand, keeping their eyes on the hill. See Figure 2 for a representation of the visual and haptic measures. We assume that the verbal and visual reports are informed by conscious awareness, whereas the haptic report taps the visual guidance system.

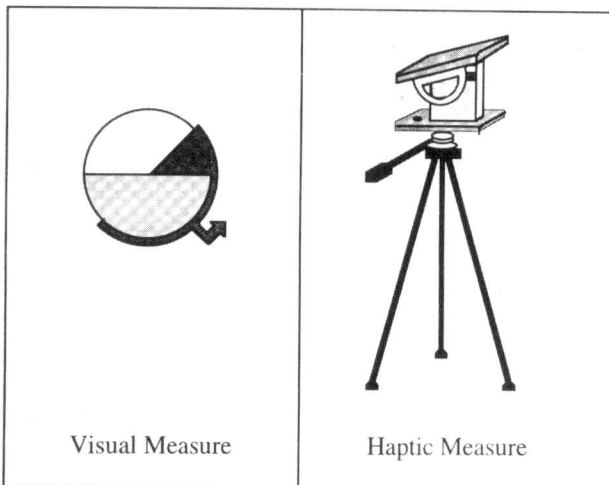

| Visual Measure | Haptic Measure |

Figure 2. The visual and haptic measures used by subjects for reporting geographical slant.

Overall, our findings indicate that conscious awareness of slant is highly exaggerated, in that hills appear to be a good deal steeper than they actually are. Visually guided actions, on the other hand, are far more accurate. For example, when participants look at a 10° hill, on average they verbally judge it to be about 30°, set the visual measure to about 30°, but set the haptic measure to about 10° (see Figure 3).

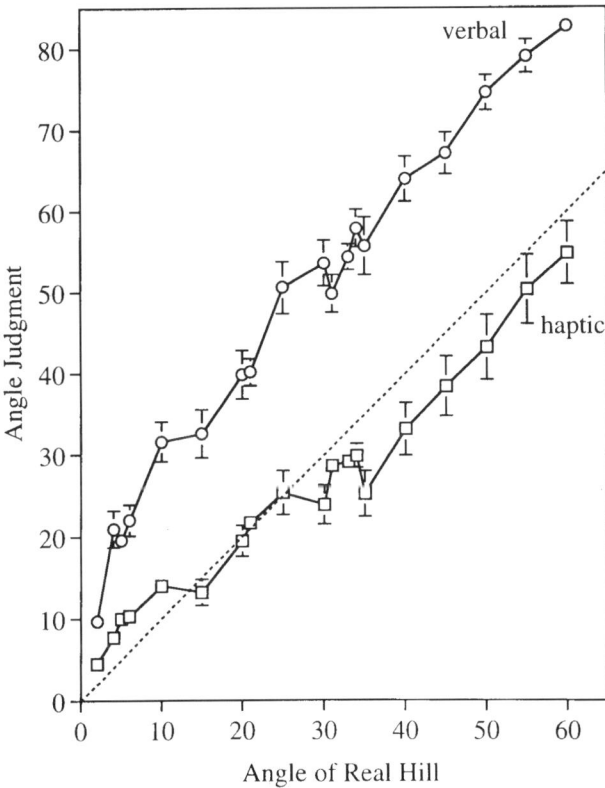

Figure 3. Judgments of geographical slant. Visual reports are not presented because they fall almost on top of the verbal ones. Overestimation in verbal and visual reports contrast with the accuracy of haptic reports (Data from two experiments conducted in real and virtual environments).

We have proposed that this discrepancy between explicit awareness and actions reflects their contrasting functions. Conscious perception is responsible for the representation of spatial layout and the planning of actions, whereas visually guided actions are concerned with the successful implementation of those actions. By this account, the overestimation of slant is an optimal outcome given the function of conscious perception. The reason for this virtue requires some explanation.

Conscious slant overestimation is a symptom of two factors. First, performance on the verbal and visual measures exhibits *response compression*. This means that responses on these measures conform to ratio scales having power-function exponents of less than one. This can be seen in the decelerating functions for these response measures in Figure 3. Similar ratio scaling is found when people make magnitude estimates of such sensory attributes as brightness or loudness. The virtue of response compression is that it affords greater sensitivity to small energy changes at small energy magnitudes at the expense of reduced sensitivity to the same magnitudes of change at larger energy magnitudes. Response compression in conscious slant perception similarly promotes heightened sensitivity to small changes in slant at small slant magnitudes. For example, response compression increases sensitivity to the difference between 5° and 6° hills at the expense of sensitivity to the difference between 65° and 66° hills. Since the slant of terrains that are commonly traversed by people is less than 10°, response compression heightens sensitivity to differences between inclines that are of behavioral relevance. In everyday language, a 5° hill appears to be pretty steep, whereas a 6° one looks much steeper. The legal limit for roads in the state of Virginia is 9°. The difference between 65° and 66° hills is difficult to detect, and moreover, it is of no behavioral significance. Without mountain climbing equipment, one could not ascend either incline.

The second factor responsible for conscious slant overestimation is that responses are anchored at the 0° and 90° values. Horizontal and vertical orientations are special values and are perceived accurately. Given that response compression dictates a decelerating response function and that the function must be anchored at 0° and 90°, overestimation is a necessary outcome. The only way that a decelerating function can be anchored at 0° and 90° is for it to curve above the ideal performance line. Thus, conscious slant overestimation derives from the virtues of response compression and accuracy at the 0° and 90° values.

The function of conscious slant perception is behavioral planning: Perceived steepness is directly related to the effort required to traverse hills, which in turn helps one make conscious decisions about the gait to be adopted. When approaching a hill, explicit decisions must be made about what gait style to employ so as to regulate energy expenditure at a desired rate. For example, if one wants to maintain a relatively constant energy expenditure, then gait will have to be slowed in direct proportion to the steepness of the incline. Response compression — resulting in slant overestimation — promotes the effectiveness of planning within the range of small inclines that are actually encountered. The planning supported by conscious perception is relatively long term since it is concerned with gait regulation over the extent of the hill and beyond.

Visual guidance serves a different function. It directs accurate and efficient actions in the here and now, and requires continuously updated information from moment to moment. Visual guidance entails an on-line control of limbs as they are directed towards the environment, and hence, accuracy is essential. In geographical slant perception, this is reflected in the accuracy of the motoric index of slant. Verbal estimates of 10° hills are 30°, whereas haptic adjustments are about 10°.

Since the explicit awareness of slant relates our physiological potential to the actual incline of hills, it turns out that it is malleable. As the physiological potential to traverse a slope changes, so does the conscious awareness of its slant. We have shown that when subjects judge the inclination of hills after an exhausting run, they verbally overestimate slant more than when they are not tired (Proffitt et al. 1995). In addition, verbal judgments of steep inclines are more exaggerated from the top than from the bottom (Proffitt et al. 1995). Due to biomechanical constraints, it is difficult but possible to walk up a 30° grassy incline; however, it is almost impossible to walk down such a hill without breaking into a run or falling down. Perceived slant informs the planning of ascents and descents by exaggerating slant more from the top of steep hills than from the bottom.

It is important to note, however that this flexibility is seen only for the conscious awareness of slant and not for visually guided actions directed towards the same inclines. Whereas conscious awareness changes with the physiological state of the individual, visually guided actions are unaffected, and remain accurate so as to efficiently guide the on-line control of actions. In the study in which fatigue was induced, only conscious awareness of slant showed an increase in apparent slant; the motoric index was remained accurate and unchanged, in accordance with the functions that each of them serves: the planning of long term actions which changes with the status of the observer, versus the actual execution of actions, which remain unchanged.

One system or two?

The discrepancies between conscious and motoric indices of geographical slant perception suggest a dissociation between visually guided actions and conscious visual awareness, as represented in Figure 1. But it is also possible that the verbal/visual and motor responses tap a single system and are related by a transformation. See Figure 4. This sort of coordination has been suggested in the context of distance perception. For example, Foley (1977, 1980) has proposed that despite differences between the verbal and motoric estimates of distance, the two are related to a single perceptual variable by some output transformations. Similarly for geographical slant estimation, it is possible that the visual control of actions directed towards hills is driven by the same representation as that for visual awareness, but the former compensates for perceived overestimation by constantly calibrating motor programs through feedback.

    In order to test this latter account, we induced a change in visual awareness without allowing an opportunity to recalibrate the transformation relating the two systems. We reasoned that, if the two systems are related by a transformation, then both awareness and visual guidance should also be influenced by the change. On the other hand, if conscious overestimation increased without a change in motoric responses, then since there was no opportunity for recalibration, the two systems must be dissociated. The following experiment compared these alternatives by having subjects judge the inclinations of hills while wearing a heavy backpack.

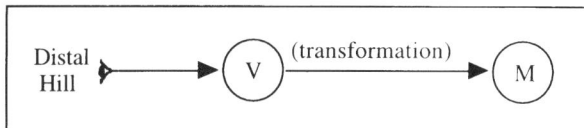

Model B: Constantly recalibrated systems

Figure 4. Model B: Constant recalibration between visual awareness and visually guided actions.

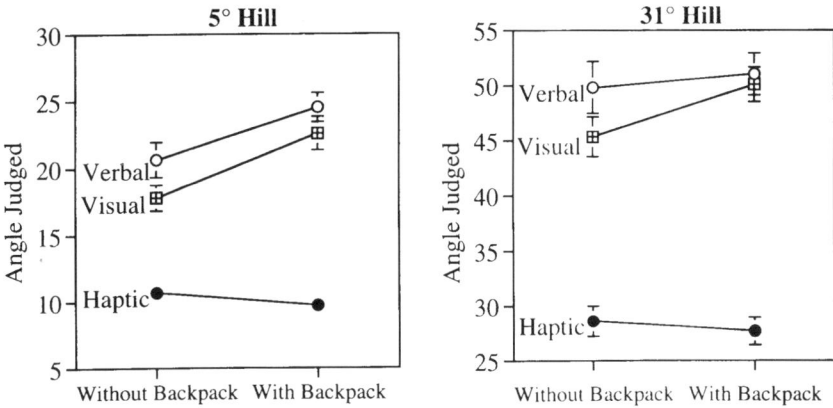

Figure 5. Judgments of geographical slant for the 5° and 31° hill by subject with and without a backpack, on the verbal, visual and haptic measures.

The Backpack Study: Participants judged the inclination of one of two hills (5° and 31°), either without a backpack, or while wearing a one. The backpacks were put on at the testing site and the participants were given no opportunity to walk while wearing them. They reported their judgments on the verbal, visual and haptic measures. Results showed that the participants wearing the heavy backpack overestimated the inclination of the hills more than did the those without backpacks (Figure 5). For instance while participants without back-packs judged a 5° hill to be about 20°, those with backpacks judged the same hill to be about 25°. This increase was seen only for the visual and verbal measures; the haptic measure was unaffected by the backpack manipulation.

Since the haptic reports remained accurate despite a lack of opportunity for recalibration, it can be concluded that the explicit awareness and motor guidance systems function independently over the short duration of the back-pack manipulation. If the two systems were not independent and the haptic response was driven by the same representation that informed the verbal, then the haptic response would have increased along with the verbal since there was no opportunity for recalibration. That the motoric response was unaf-fected by the manipulation implies that over the short term, visually guided actions are not mediated by visual awareness, but are instead modular.

Interconnections between the two systems

Although our studies show that the two visual systems can be dissociated, they also show that these systems are connected in a manner that promotes internal consistency. After having judged the inclination of hills, participants in the Proffitt et al. (1995) studies performed a second task. They were asked to set the haptic measure to a set of verbally given angles, ranging from 5° to 75°. We refer to this task as the *Angle Judgment* task, whereas the hill judgments are called the *Hill Judgment* task. Results revealed good internal consistency in that the haptic response to a hill of a given incline was virtually the same as the haptic response to a verbally given angle that was evoked when viewing that incline. An example is illustrated in Figure 6. There it is shown that when participants view a 5° hill, their verbal estimate is about 20° and their motoric response is 5° (Hill Judgment task). When given a verbal instruction to set the palm board to 20°, they also set it to about 5° (Angle Judgment task). Thus, their haptic responses to visually presented hills as well as to verbal instructions are the same. This shows that although conscious and motoric measures of slant are not the same, they are internally consistent. Haptic judgments are calibrated to the apparent slant overestimations that inform verbal reports.

This calibration of apparent slant to actions is suggestive of sensorimotor learning. Since there is a lawful monotonic relationship between conscious perceptions of slant and the representations that control actions, the co-

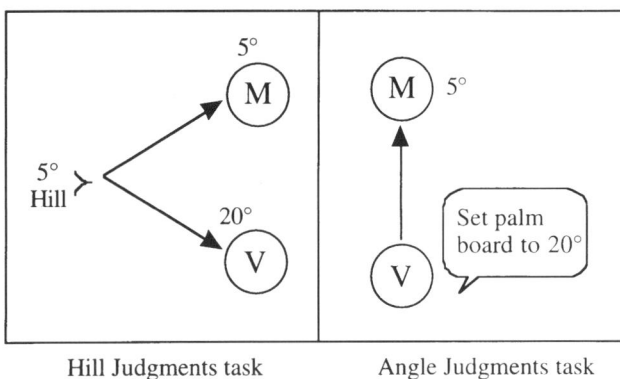

Hill Judgments task   Angle Judgments task

Figure 6. Consistency between direct and indirect influences on motor behavior: Correspondence between the verbal and haptic reports for Hill and Angle Judgments tasks.

occurring states of these two systems could become associated through experience. Should the correspondence between the conscious and motoric responses change (for example, as a result of changes in physiological potential), then the transformations relating visually guided actions to visual awareness would also be modified gradually over time to yield a new mapping.

Nearly decomposable systems

The evidence for both dissociation and interconnectedness between the two visual systems suggests a model such as that shown in Figure 7. By this model, the two visual systems function independently when driven directly by visual information; however, they are also transformationally related in that conscious representations can indirectly inform the action system. Simon (1990) has described such systems as being nearly decomposable, meaning that they function independently over short time intervals; however, they maintain coordination over longer time spans.

The question remains as to the time span over which the awareness and action systems recalibrate their mapping due to changes in the individual's physiological state. The following three studies attempted to answer this question by varying the duration of the change in the participants' physiological potential (short or long term). Participants in the short-term category had a reduced potential due to the induction of fatigue. Participants in the long-term category varied in their level of physical fitness, age or health.

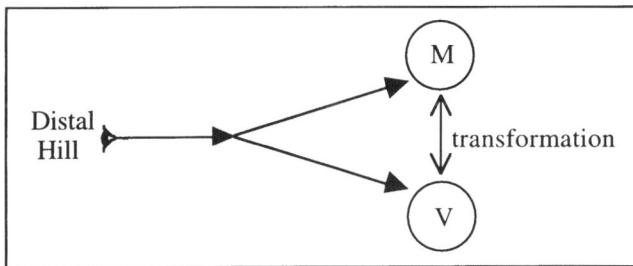

Model C: Nearly decomposable

Figure 7. Model C: Nearly decomposable systems: Visual awareness and visually guided actions are segregated in the short term, but coordinated in the long term.

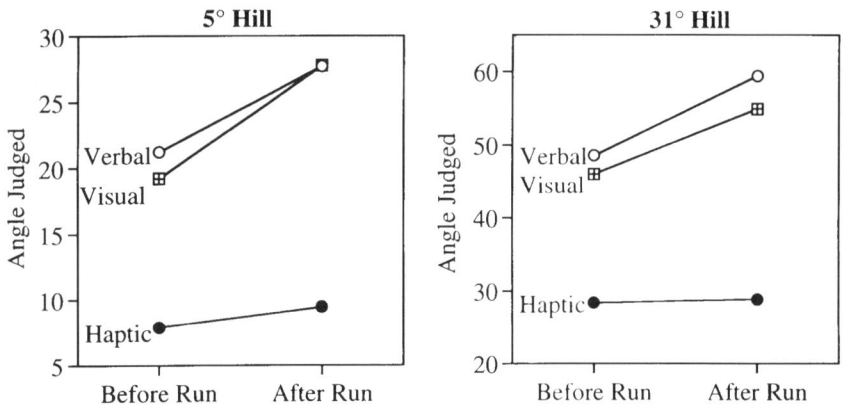

Figure 8. Judgments of geographical slant for the 5° and 31° hill by subjects before and after a tiring run, on the verbal, visual and haptic measures.

The Joggers Study: This experiment looked at whether the time spent during exhausting runs was adequate for the recalibration of the mapping between the visual awareness of slant and visually guided actions. Participants, who were habitual joggers, judged the inclinations of two hills (5° and 31°), one before and one after an exhausting run (Hill Judgments). They also set the visual and haptic measures to a set of verbally given angles twice, once before and once after the run (Angle Judgments).

As shown in Figure 8, the joggers' conscious perception of slant increased in response to fatigue. This increase in overestimation was evidenced for both the verbal and visual reports but not for the haptic measure. For example, when the joggers looked at a 5° hill before their runs, they verbally estimated it to be about 20° while setting the haptic measure to a little over 5°. After their runs, their verbal estimates increased to about 25° while their haptic reports remained unchanged.

Whereas the Hill Judgments given by the joggers after their runs exhibited greater overestimations than those given before their runs, the Angle Judgments were unaffected. See Figure 9. For example, when looking at a 5° hill the fatigued joggers increased their verbal estimate of the hill incline to 25°. But when given a verbal instruction to set the haptic board to 20° they still set it to 5°. Thus, as can be seen in Figure 10, direct and indirect influences on the motor system became less consistent. Hill Judgments had increased in

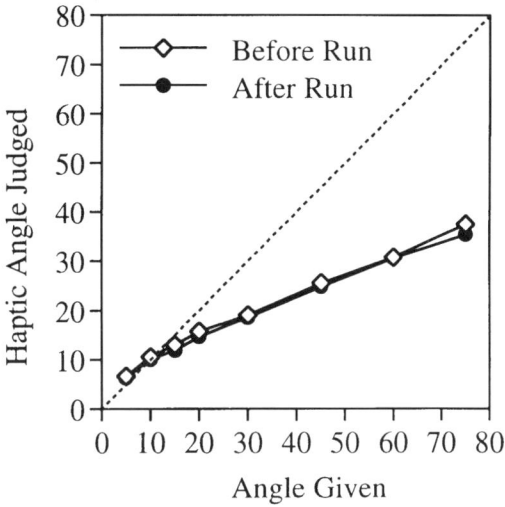

Figure 9. Angle Judgments for the joggers before and after runs, made in response to verbally given angles for the haptic measure.

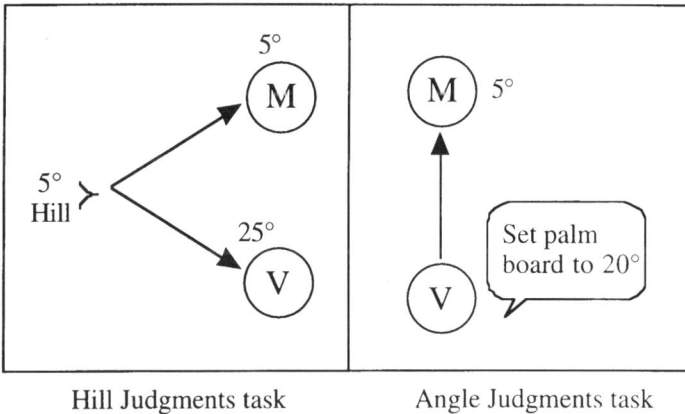

Hill Judgments task   Angle Judgments task

Figure 10. Inconsistency between direct and indirect influences on motor behavior for the joggers: Lack of correspondence between the verbal and haptic reports for Hill and Angle Judgments tasks.

response to fatigue, but Angle Judgments were unchanged, indicating that little or no recalibration had occurred during the duration of the joggers' runs. These results imply that measurable recalibration takes longer than the 45–75 minute duration of the runs.

The following two experiments show that long-term changes in physiological potential do result in a recalibration of the mapping between visually guided actions and conscious visual awareness. As opposed to the fatigue manipulation, in these studies the change in potential was of a more permanent nature.

The Fitness Study: Participants in this study had varying levels of physical fitness. Some were varsity athletes and the rest were regular undergraduates at the University of Virginia. These participants judged the inclinations of four hills (5°, 6°, 21° and 31°) on the three measures (Hill Judgment task) and they set the visual and haptic measures to a set of verbally given angles (Angle Judgment task). Three measures of fitness were obtained using a stationary bicycle assessment procedure. A composite fitness score was assigned to each participant with scores ranging from -2 (low fitness) to 4 (high fitness). (For further details about the fitness assessment, see Bhalla & Proffitt 1999).

The results showed that the verbal and visual judgments of slant were influenced by levels of physical fitness. Participants who were less physically fit judged hills to be steeper on the verbal and visual measures. There was a negative correlation between fitness and overestimation for both of these measures. The haptic responses were unaffected by fitness level. See Figure 11 which plots regression lines for each of the four hills on each of the three measures.

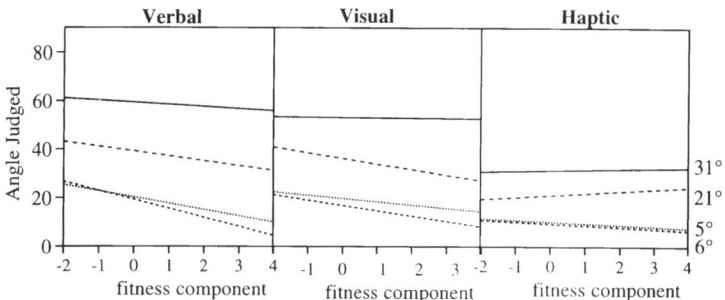

Figure 11. Effect of fitness on mean judgments of geographical slant for four hills by fitness subjects on the verbal, visual and haptic measures.

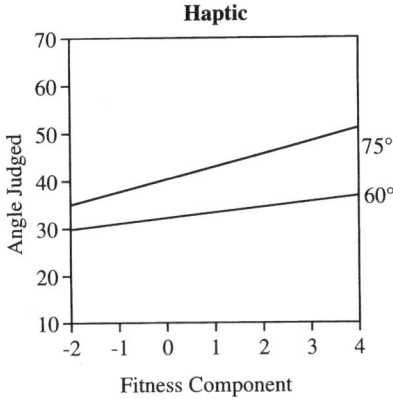

Figure 12. Effect of fitness on Angle Judgments for two angles made by fitness subjects on the haptic measure.

Participants also showed good internal consistency between their Hill and Angle Judgments. Like the Hill Judgments, the Angle Judgments were also affected by fitness level, albeit only for the 60° and 75° angle judgments. As can be seen in Figure 12, there was a positive correlation between fitness and haptic Angle Judgments.

These findings indicate that the awareness and action systems are recalibration over the duration responsible for relatively permanent changes in fitness level. As fitness level declined, people's conscious estimates of hill inclination increased, whereas their motoric responses were unaffected. Consistent with this relationship, people of low physical fitness set the haptic board to lower angles in response to verbal instructions. For example, when participants at a high level of fitness looked at a 30° hill, they verbally estimated it to be 50°, and set the palm board accurately to 30°. Accordingly, for the Angle Judgment task, when asked to set the palm board to 50°, they set it to 30°. Participants at low fitness levels, on the other hand, called a 30° hill 60° and set the palm board to 30°. In the Angle Judgment task, when verbally given an angle of 50°, they set the palm board to 25°, and when given a 60° angle, they set it to 30°. This consistency is illustrated in Figure 13. Thus, regardless of whether participants were at a low or high level of fitness, they maintained internally consistent in their responses.

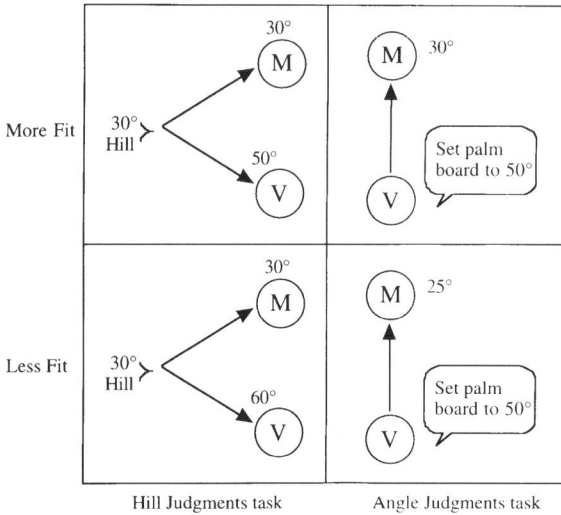

Figure 13. Consistency between direct and indirect influences on motor behavior in more fit and less fit subjects: Correspondence between the verbal and haptic reports for Hill and Angle Judgments tasks.

The Elderly Study: Participants for this study were aged 60 years and over, and like the joggers, backpackers and the minimally fit, represented a group that had seen a reduction in physiological potential, but the reduction was of a different nature, arising out of old age, one that was probably the most gradual of all. Like other participants they performed the Hill and Angle Judgment tasks. Two sets of fours slopes each (2°, 3°, 4° and 25° and 3°, 5° 10° and 29°) were used in this study with each participant judging one set of slopes. All participants were given a brief self-report questionnaire about their health and general physical fitness, in which they rated their health and fitness on 10 questions using a five-point rating scale, with 5 indicating excellent health/ physical fitness and 1 indicating poor health/physical fitness.

The results show that judgments of inclination are indeed affected by a reduction in physiological potential brought about by a decline in health and levels of physical fitness associated with old age. The older and less healthy subjects tended to overestimate the slants of hills on the verbal and visual measures more than those who were younger and more healthy among their own elderly peer group and also as compared to young adults. These results

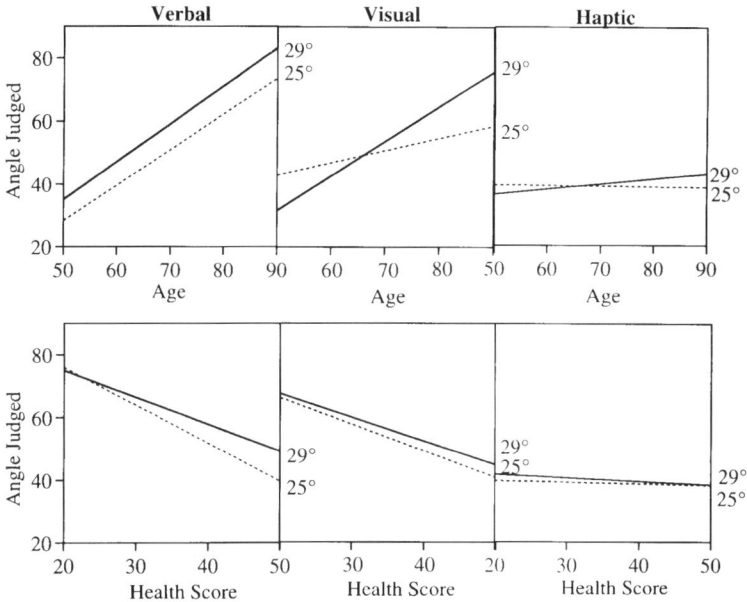

Figure 14. Effect of age and health on mean judgments of geographical slant by elderly subjects on the verbal, visual and haptic measures for steep hills.

were obtained only for steep (25° and 29°) but not for shallow (2°, 3° , 4°, 5° and 10°) hills. The haptic adjustments of the elderly were not different from the young on any of the hills. The age and health of the elderly participants were good predictors of their verbal and visual slant judgments for the steep (25° and 29°) hills: the older and less healthy the individual, the greater were their verbal and visual estimates of geographical slant for these hills. See Figure 14.

Importantly, Angle Judgments made by the elderly were also significantly different from those made by young people. This change in Angle Judgments was consistent with the increase in their verbal estimates of slant. As shown in Figure 15, the elderly set the palm board to smaller angles than did the young in response to the largest angles. To see how this relates to the maintenance of internal consistency, consider an example illustrated in Figure 16. When young people looked at a 30° hill, they verbally judged it to be 50° and set the palm board accurately to 30°. Accordingly, for the Angle

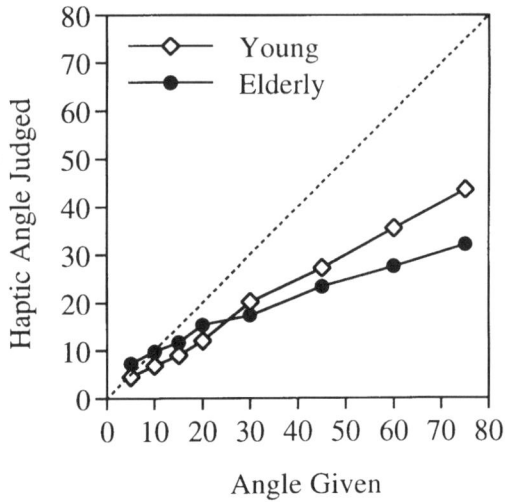

Figure 15. Angle Judgments for the elderly and young subjects in response to verbally given angles for the haptic measure.

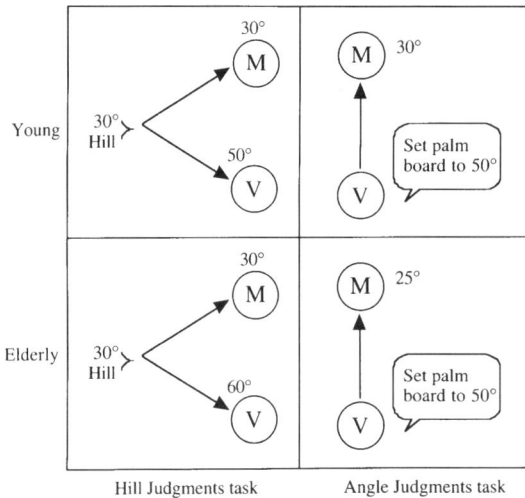

Figure 16. Consistency between direct and indirect influences on motor behavior in elderly subjects: Correspondence between the verbal and haptic reports for Hill and Angle Judgments tasks.

Judgment task, they set the palm board to 30° when instructed to set it to 50°. In contrast, elderly people verbally judged a 30° hill to be 60° and set the palm board to 30°. In keeping with their judgments for hill inclines, these subjects set the palm board to 30° on being asked verbally to set it to 60° and to 25° for an angle of 50°. The responses of both age groups are different but are equally consistent. This shows that the reduction in physiological potential associated with old age and/or poor health leads to an increased overestimation of slant, and since this change is relatively permanent, the mapping between conscious awareness and visually guided actions is recalibrated as well.

Discussion

People's explicit awareness of slant can be dissociated from their motoric actions directed towards inclines. Whereas explicit awareness increases with load, fatigue, lack of physical fitness, old age and declining health, motoric adjustments remain accurate and unaffected by these factors. Despite this dissociations, the two systems are interconnected. The awareness and action systems maintain an internal consistency over time. The transformation that relates the two systems recalibrates slowly. We observed no evidence of recalibration over the course of 1 to 1 1/2 hours (joggers study); however recalibration was observed in the studies where changes in physiological potential were more permanent (fitness and elderly studies) (see also Pisella & Rossetti this volume).

Indices of explicit awareness and visually guided actions yield different estimates of "perceived" slant, moreover the former is influenced by changes in physiological potential whereas the latter is not. These differences arise from the different functions that each system subserves. Explicitly perceived steepness provides information about the affordances of hills which include the possibility and effort entailed in traversing them. An important function of conscious awareness of slant is to inform the planning and modulation of gait with respect to the hills that are to be traversed so as to expend energy at a desired rate. Slant overestimation serves this purpose by exaggerating the apparent steepness of hills, and thereby, increasing sensitivity to small inclines that are within the range of our physiological potential. Changes in apparent slant brought about by changes in physiological potential serves to directly relate inclines to people's changing abilities to traverse them. In contrast, the task of visually guiding one's feet over inclines is not dependent on such factors and instead requires the veridical evaluation of surface layout for effective interaction with the environment.

This account can be well assimilated into Milner and Goodale's (1995) theoretical framework. For them, the distinction between the two visual systems is rooted in a functional rather than an informational dissociation. The information supporting the explicit perception of slants and the actions directed at them is similar, but the use to which this information is put differs considerably.

Despite the dissociation seen between explicit perception and action, there is also evidence for a connection between them. This is seen in the good internal consistency between the various measures of perceived geographical slant. When a person's physiological potential changes, his or her conscious awareness of slant also changes. When the change in potential is long term, this change is also accompanied by a change in the mapping between conscious awareness and visually guided actions. Not only do judgments of hill incline change, but also haptic responses to a set of verbally given angles change in a manner that is consistent with the changes seen in the verbal hill judgments. Such changes in the mapping between awareness and actions are seen only with long term changes in physiological potential and not for temporary change in physiological state.

This notion of separable systems that accommodate to each other gradually is consistent with Simon's (1990) discussion of "nearly decomposable systems". Simon pointed out that, for most natural hierarchical systems, the interactions between subsystems are usually "weak but not negligible" (see also Hommel this volume). A system is said to be nearly decomposable when the behavior of one of its elements or subsystems is independent of the behavior of other subsystems over short but not long durations. In the long run, subsystems are dependent on the aggregate behavior of the other elements that make up the system (More thorough discussions of this issue can be found in Bhalla & Proffitt (1999)).

Our findings indicate that the two visual systems can function independently over short durations. Conscious awareness of slant is subject to short term influences, such as fatigue, that affect physiological potential, whereas visually guided actions are accurate and unchanged by such factors. Over the long run, these systems maintain an internal consistency with each other, and the mapping between them gets modified as a result of long term or irreversible changes in the individual, such as a relatively permanent change in physiological potential due to declining health and fitness in old age.

References

Anderson, R.A., Asanuma, C., Essick, G. & Siegel, R.M. (1990b). Corticocortical connections of anatomically and physiologically defined subdivisions within the inferior parietal lobule. *Journal of Computational Neurology*, 296, 65–113.

Baizer, J.S., Ungerleider, L.G. & Desimone, R. (1991). Organization of visual inputs to the inferior temporal and posterior parietal cortex in macaques. *Journal of Neuroscience*, 11, 168–190.

Bhalla , M. & Proffitt, D.R.P. (1999). Visual-motor recalibration in geographical slant perception. *Journal of Experimental Psychology: Human Perception and Performance*, 25, 1076–1097.

Bridgeman, B. (2000). Interactions between vision for perception and vision for behavior. This volume, 17–40.

Bridgeman, B., Lewis, S., Heit, G. & Nagle, M. (1979). Relationship between cognitive and motor systems of visual position perception. *Journal of Experimental Psychology: Human Perception and Performance*, 5, 692–700.

Bridgeman, B. & Staggs, D. (1982). Plasticity in human blindsight. *Vision Research*, 22, 1199–1203.

Bridgeman, B. (1987) Separate visual representations for perception and for visually guided behavior. *In Spatial Displays and Spatial Instruments*. N.A.S.A. Conference Publication # 10032.

Bridgeman, B.(1994). Spatial and cognitive vision differentiate at low levels, but not in language, *Behavioral and Brain Sciences*, 16, 240.

Clarke, S. (1993). Callosal connections and functional subdivision of the human occipital cortex. In B. Gulyas, D. Ottoson and P. E. Roland (Eds.), *Functional Organization of the Human Visual Cortex*. Pergamon Press, Oxford, 137–149

Ferrera, V.P., Nealey, T.A. & Maunsell, J.H.R. (1992). Mixed parvocellular and magnocellular geniculate signals in visual area V4. *Nature*, 358, 756–758.

Ferrera, V.P., Nealey, T.A. & Maunsell, J.H.R. (1994). Responses in Macaque visual area V4 following inactivation of the parvocellular and magnocellular LGN pathways. *Journal of Neuroscience*, 14, 2080–2088.

Foley, J.M. (1977). Effect of distance information and range on two indices of visually perceived distance. *Perception*, 7, 449–460.

Foley, J.M. (1980). Binocular distance perception. *Psychological Review*, 87, 411–434.

Fujita, I., Tanaka, K., Ito, M. & Cheng, K. (1992). Columns for visual features of objects in monkey inferotemporal cortex. *Nature*, 360, 343–346.

Goodale, M.A,. Pelisson, D. & Prablanc, C. (1986). Large adjustments in visually guided reaching do not depend on vision of the hand or perception of target displacement. *Nature*, 320, 748–750.

Goodale, M.A. & Milner, A.D. (1992). Separate visual pathways for perception and action. Trends in Neurosciences, 15(1–163), 20–25.

Goodale, M.A., Aglioti, S. & DeSouza, J.F.X. (1994). Size illusions affect perception but not prehension. Society of Neuroscience Abstracts, 20, 1666.

Gross, C.G., Rocha-Miranda, C.E. & Bender, D.B. (1972) Visual properties of neurons in the inferotemporal cortex of the macaque. Journal of Neurophysiology, 35, 96–111.

Gross, C.G., Desimone, R., Albright, T.D. & Schwartz, E.L. (1985). Inferior temporal cortex and pattern recognition. In C. Chagas, R. Gattass & C. Gross (Eds.), Pattern Recognition Mechanisms. Springer-Verlag, Berlin, 179–201.

Jackendoff, R. & Landau, B. (1994). What is coded in parietal representations? In The representing brain: Neural correlates of motor intention and imagery. Behavioral and Brain Sciences, 17, 187–245.

Jackson, S.R. (2000). Perception, awareness and action: Insights from blindsight. This volume, 73–98.

Jakobson, L.S., Archibald, Y.M., Carey, D.P. & Goodale, M.A. (1991). A kinematic analysis of reaching and grasping in a patient recovering from optic ataxia. Neuropsychologia, 29, 803–809.

Jeannerod, M. (1986). The formation of finger grip during prehension: A cortically mediated visuomotor pattern. Behavior and Brain Research, 19, 99–116.

Jeannerod, M. (1994). The representing brain: Neural correlates of motor intention and imagery. Behavioral and Brain Sciences, 17, 187–245.

Milner & M. D. Rugg (Eds.). pp 139–158.

Milner, A.D., Perrett, D.I., Johnston, R.S., Benson, P.J., Jordan, T.R. & Heeley, D.W. (1991). Perception and action in "visual form agnosia". Brain, 114, 405–428.

Milner, A.D. (1992). Disorders of perceptual awareness — commentary. In The Neuropsychology of Consciousness, A. D.

Milner, A.D. & Goodale, M.A. (1993). Visual pathways to perception and action. In T. P. Hicks, S. Molotchnikoff & T. Ono (Eds.), Progress in Brain Research. Amsterdam: Elsevier, Vol.95, 317–337

Milner, A.D. & Goodale, M.A. (1995) The Visual Brain in Action. Oxford: Oxford University Press.

Morrow, M.J. & Sharpe, J.A. (1993). Retinotopic and directional deficits of smooth pursuit initiation after posterior cerebral lesions. Neurology, 43, 595–603.

Paillard, J. (1987) Cognitive versus sensorimotor encoding of spatial information. In P. Ellen & C. Thinus-Blanc (Eds.) , Cognitive Processes and Spatial Orientation in Animal and Man, Martinus Nijhoff.

Pelisson, D.M., Prablanc, C., Goodale, M. & Jeannerod, M. (1986). Visual control of reaching movements without vision of the limb II. Evidence for fast unconscious process correcting the trajectory of the hand to the final position of a double-step stimulus. Experimental Brain Research, 62, 303–311.

Perenin, M.T. & Vighetto, A. (1983). Optic ataxia: A specific disorder in visuomotor coordination. In A. Hein & M Jeannerod (Eds.), Spatially Oriented Behavior. New York: Springer-Verlag, 305–326

Perenin, M.T. & Vighetto, A. (1988). Optic ataxia: A specific disruption in visuomotor mechanisms I. Different aspects of the deficit in reaching for objects. Brain, 111, 643–674.

Perrett, D.I., Smith, P.A.J., Potter, D.D., Mistlin, A.J., Head, A.S., Milner, A.D. & Jeeves, M.A. (1984). Neurones responsive to faces in the temporal cortex: Studies of functional organization, sensitivity to identity and relation to perception. *Human Neurobiology*, 3, 197–208.

Perrett, D.I., Oram, M.W., Harries, M.H., Bevan, R., Hietanen, J.K., Benson, P.J. & Thomas, S. (1991). Viewer-centered and object-centered coding of heads in the macaque temporal cortex. *Experimental Brain Research*, 86, 159–173.

Perry, V.H. & Cowey, A. (1984). Retinal ganglion cells that project to the superior colliculus and pretectum in the macaque monkey. *Neuroscience*, 12, 1125–1137.

Pierrot-Deseilligny, C., Rivaud, S., Penet, C. & Rigolet, M.H. (1987). Latencies of visually guided saccades in unilateral hemispheric cerebral lesions. *Annals of Neurology*, 21, 138–148.

Pierrot-Deseilligny, C., Rivaud, S., Gaymard, B. & Agid, Y. (1991). Cortical control of reflexive visually guided saccades. *Brain*, 114, 1473–1485.

Pisella, L. & Rossetti, Y. (2000). Interaction between conscious Identification and non-conscious sensory-motor processing: Temporal constraints. This volume, 129–152.

Place, U.T. 2000. Consciousness and the zombie within: A functional analysis of the blindsight evidence. This volume, 295–330.

Poppel, E., Held, R. & Frost, D. (1973) Residual visual function after brain wounds involving the central visual pathways in man. *Nature*, 243, 295–296.

Proffitt, D.R., Bhalla, M., Gossweiler, R. & Midgett, J. (1995). Perceiving geographical slant. *Psychonomic Bulletin and Review*, 2, 409–428.

Riddoch, G. (1917). Dissociation of visual perceptions due to occipital injuries, with especial reference to appreciation of movement. *Brain*, 40, 15–57.

Rossetti, Y. & Regnier, C. (1995). Representations in action: Pointing to a target with various representations. In B. G. Bardy, R.J. Boutsma & Y. Guiard (Eds.) *Studies in perception and Action III*: Lawrence Erlbaum Associates, Inc.

Rossett, Y. (1998). Implicit short-lived motor representation of space in brain-damaged and healthy subjects. *Consciousness and Cognition*, 7, 520–558.

Rossett, Y. (2000). Implicit perception in action: short-lived motor representations of space, In: P.G. Grossenbacher (ed): *Finding consciousness in the brain*. (131–179) Benjamins Amsterdam (in press).

Rossetti, Y., Rode, G. & Boisson, D. (1995). Implicit processing of somaesthetic information: A dissociation between where and how *? Cognitive Neuroscience and Neuropsychology, Neuroreport* 6, 506–510.

Saito, H., Yukie, M., Tanaka, K., Hikosaka, K., FukadaY., & Iwai, E. (1986). Integration of direction signals of image motion in the superior temporal sulcus of the

Sary, G., Vogels, R. & Orban, G.A. (1993). Cue-invariant shape selectivity of macaque inferior temporal neurons. *Science*, 260, 995–997.

Savelsbergh, G.J.P., Whiting, H.T.A. & Bootsma, R.J. (1991). Grasping tau. Journal of Experimental Psychology: Human Perception and Performance, 17, 315–322.

Schneider, G.E. (1969). Two visual systems. *Science*, 163, 895–902.

Simon, H.A. (1990). *The Sciences of the Artificial*. MIT Press, 209–217.

Sirigu, A., Cohen, L., Duhamel, J.R., Pillon, B., Dubois, B. & Agid, Y. (1995) A selective impairment of hand posture for object utilization in apraxia. Cortex.

Tanaka, K., Saito, H.A., Fukada, Y. & Moriya, M. (1991). Coding visual images of objects in the inferotemporal cortex of the macaque monkey. *Journal of Neurophysiology*, 66, 170–189.

Troost, B.T. & Abel, L.A. (1982). Pursuit disorders. In G. Lennerstrand, D.S. Zee & E.L. Keller (Eds.) , *Functional Basis Ocular Motility Disorders*. Oxford: Pergomon Press, 511–515.

Ungerleider, L.G. & Mishkin, M. (1982). In D.J. Ingle, M.A. Goodale and R.J.W. Mansfield (Eds.), *Analysis of Visual Behavior*. MIT Press, 549–586.

Weizkrantz, L., Warrington, E.K., Sanders, M.D. & Marshall, J. (1974) Visual capacity in the hemianopic field following a restricted occipital ablation, *Brain*, 97, 709–728.

Zilles, K. & Schleicher, A. (1993). Cyto- and myloarchitecture of human visual cortex and the periodical GABAa receptor distribution. In B. Gulyas, D. Ottoson & P. E. Roland (Eds.), *Functional Organization of the Human Visual Cortex*. Oxford: Pergamon Press, 111–122.

Interaction between Conscious Identification and Non-Conscious Sensori-Motor Processing

Temporal Constraints

Laure Pisella & Yves Rossetti

Institut National de la Santé et de la Recherche Médicale

Introduction

Vision is not a single and unified process. There have been numerous demonstrations that the visual system can be broken up into several sub-systems. Within the complex network formed by these subsystems, a few major information processing streams can be isolated. A great deal of convergence can be observed between neuroanatomical, electrophysiological, behavioral, and neuropsychological studies to argue for a clear dissociation between a visual system devoted to perception and perceptual awareness and another visual system specialized for controlling goal-directed actions (Goodale and Milner 1992, reviews in: Milner and Goodale 1993; Jeannerod and Rossetti 1993; Milner and Goodale 1995; Rossetti et al 2000). This dichotomy is exemplified by the double dissociation observed between optic ataxia (which follows a lesion of the posterior parietal cortex) and visual agnosia (which follows a lesion of the inferior temporal cortex). Neuropsychological studies have provided key arguments for building up the notion that a specific area of the parietal cortex is specialized for producing motor representations of space that are used for controlling goal-directed movements (e.g. Goodale et al. 1991, 1994; Milner et al. 1997; Perenin and Rossetti 1996; Rossetti 1998).

The dissociation between "perceptual" and "sensory-motor" processing has been exemplified and discussed in many aspects. For vision, evidence for this dissociation arises from many different fields, ranging from neuroanatomy and neuropsychology to psychophysics and functional brain imaging (review in Milner and Goodale 1995). A similar dissociation can be also observed for the somesthetic modalities (review in Rossetti 1998).

The main aims of this chapter are (1) to demonstrate that the two main systems observed for several sensory modalities can interact; (2) to report the necessary conditions for such interaction to develop; (3) to explore the temporal constraints imposed to potential interactions between the "dissociated" sensory systems. A review emphasizing the dissociation between sensory subsystems considered here can be found elsewhere (Rossetti et al. 1998), and the present chapter will rather focus on interactions.

Explicit → implicit interference in brain-damaged patients

Dissociation between visual processing for action and for perceptual identification has been well supported by neurological cases of patients with occipito-parietal (dorsal) and occipito-temporal (ventral stream) lesions (review in Milner and Goodale 1995). In addition to optic ataxia and visual agnosia, mentioned above, blindsight is another neurological deficit that is interesting to consider in the framework of the dissociation between implicit and explicit sensori-motor processing. Early studies on patients with lesion of the primary visual area (V1), considered to be amputed from the half of their visual field, showed that they remained able to orient eyes and/or the hand to visual stimuli briefly presented within their blind field (see Weiskrantz 1989). It has been recently shown that such patient could orient his hand and size his finger grip appropriately when reaching out to unseen visual objects (Perenin and Rossetti 1996). The neuroanatomical substrate proposed to explain this residual ability was the projection from the colliculus superior to the posterior parietal cortex via the putamen (Bullier et al. 1994; Girard 1995). Therefore this fascinating non-conscious vision emerging during a goal-directed action was considered to provide one more instance of dissociation between the dorsal and the ventral streams of the visual system (e.g. Perenin and Rossetti 1996).

There are however a number of possible interconnections between the dorsal stream and the ventral stream. First, neuroanatomical direct and indirect cross connections between these two streams have been identified, in particular through the superior temporal sulcus (e.g. Morel and Bullier 1990). Second, the anterior ends of the two pathways converge onto neighboring areas of the prefrontal and premotor cortex (e.g. Schwartz 1994). Experiments were specifically designed to search for functional interactions between cognitive and sensori-motor representations. The logic of this paradigm, contrasting with that of experiments aimed at demonstrating a dissociation between the two visual streams, consisted of co-activating the two types of representation and then looking for effects on the patient's performance. In this experimental condition, patients were instructed to simultaneously produce a movement toward the stimulus and a verbal forced-choice response about the same stimulus. This task could be performed easily after little training, and the verbal response generally occurred during the second half of the arm movement. Three predictions could be put forward: (1) if there is a complete independence of the sensori-motor and the cognitive systems, then the verbal and motor responses will be performed without any modification of their respective performances. (2) if a transfer of information is possible from the sensori-motor to the cognitive system, then the verbal response will become more accurate. (3) if a transfer of information is possible from the cognitive to the sensori-motor system, then the previously accurate performance observed for the arm movement will disappear.

Patient N.S., with a lesion of the right occipital lobe, presented a complete hemianopia for the left visual field. Nevertheless, as other blindsight patients, she could introduce a postcard in a slot (from which she could not perceive orientation) (see Perenin and Rossetti 1996; Rossetti 1998). When required to perform again the same reaching task, and at the same time to guess aloud the orientation of the target slot during her hand movement, verbal and motor responses were always congruent (Rossetti et al. 1995). In this particular condition, her motor performance dropped down to chance level. Therefore no facilitation of the verbal response by the simultaneous pointing movement was observed. An observation possibly related to the competition between the two representations was also reported by Weiskrantz about blindsight (1989: 379): "...it was actually better to use less salient stimuli to improve performance by switching the subject into an 'implicit' rather than an 'explicit' mode, in which [the patient] depended upon his real but non-veridical experiences".

The effect of cognitive- sensori-motor co-activation was also investigated for touch and proprioception, in a patient with a lesion of the somesthetic relays of the left thalamus (VL and VPL). This patient, J.A. was shown to present a somesthetic analog to blindsight, that is "numb-sense". Under normal conditions, he was able to point to an undetected tactile stimuli delivered to his right arm, although he failed to demonstrate any ability to consciously locate these stimuli. In separate sessions, in which he was asked to make verbally guesses or to locate the stimuli through pointing on an arm drawing, he could not produce above chance performance. When he was required to produce the motor and the verbal responses at the same time, J.A.'s pointing responses were at chance. As for blindsight, there was a congruency between the pointing and the verbal responses in this condition. In addition, the mean distance between the stimulus and the response increased up to a similar value as when pointing on the arm drawing (Rossetti, Rode, Boisson 1995).

The same patient was tested for proprioception in the same way as described above for touch. J.A. demonstrated an ability to locate his right unfelt finger with a pointing response, but consistently failed to guess its location verbally (among 2 or 6 possible positions). When asked to produce the verbal and the pointing responses simultaneously, these responses were always congruent, but the pointing performance was reduced to random. This was confirmed by the mean locations reached for the two locations explored: the mean pointing toward the left location was located right of the mean pointing to the right location. As for touch, activation of a semantic representation of where the target finger was (required for the verbal response) disrupted J.A.'s ability to point to this finger. We will see later in this chapter that such interference effect does not appear when the verbal response produced by normal subjects is not specific to the representation of the goal.

The literature provides several examples of interaction between sensorimotor and cognitive framing of space, which suggests that elaborating a categorial representation of the action goal prevents the expression of the short-lived sensori-motor representations, and also that immediate action is not mediated by the same sensory system as delayed action (Rossetti 1998). Interesting observations were obtained in brain-lesioned patients when immediate and delayed responses were compared.

Delayed responses were studied in a patient (DF) with a bilateral lesion of the occipito-temporal cortex, exhibiting a strong visual agnosia (Goodale et al. 1994). DF was not able to recognize objects or to identify shapes or orientations. Although she was able to preshape her hand in-flight when performing immediate responses to visual objects, her grip size was no longer related to object size when a delay between object viewing and movement initiation was imposed.

A related observation was made on a blindsight patient (N.S.) performing a motor task at different paces (Rossetti et al. 1995). It was observed that N.S. performance was at chance level as she was reacting slowly to the stimuli. Performance improved significantly under speed constraints, when movement latency decreased from about 500 ms to about 300 ms. This result suggests that sensory information responsible for blindsight in action is available only during a short period following stimulus presentation. An inverse relationship between the latency of the response and performance was also reported in another blindsight patient (G.Y.) in an experiment comparing several types of response with several delays (Marcel 1993). It was found that the several detection reports made to identical trials could be dissociated. An eye blink response (latency about 290 ms) provided more accurate detection than button press (latency about 365 ms). In addition, a speeded condition produced better performance in both motor responses.

The same effect of time was also observed for touch and proprioception (Rossetti and Rode 1996). Patient J.A. demonstrated that latencies up to 1 s for tactile stimuli and up to about 4 s for proprioceptive stimuli were compatible with above-chance performance in motor tasks, but longer delays completely disrupted his performance.

There is thus converging evidence arising from three sensory modalities that the pragmatic representation can only be expressed within a short delay following stimulus presentation. These results may lead to a reinterpretation of the data obtained in the verbal and the matching tasks. In spite of encouragement to perform faster, it took more time to subjects to respond in the verbal task or in the matching task (in some trials between 1 and 2 s) than it took for the reaching and grasping tasks (see Perenin and Rossetti 1996). It could therefore be argued that time is the decisive variable for explaining the difference between the fast reaching and the matching task. However, results obtained with numb-sense are not compatible with this interpretation. Indeed, J.A. performed at chance level when asked to point on the arm drawing, although the latencies observed in these cases were shorter than 2 s. This result suggests that the failure to perform above chance in semantic tasks cannot be specifically attributed to a problem with time but should be, at least partly, attributed to the nature of the response made to the stimulus. Rapid aiming movements directly performed toward the stimulus therefore seem to be of particular status.

Conclusion

The deleterious effect of time on motor representations suggests that delayed action may be based on more cognitive representations than immediate action. When pointing was delayed or associated with a verbal response about the target (either visual, tactile or proprioceptive stimulus), the motor performance dropped to random. These findings first suggest that the implicit processing observed in these patients is specifically observed during aiming movements rapidly and directly oriented toward the stimulus. They also confirm that attempts to elaborate a semantic representation of the stimulus location can have detrimental effects on the relatively intact sensori-motor processing. Whether this may be due to interconnections between the dorsal and the ventral streams or to convergence of their ends in the pre-motor cortex remains to be further investigated.

The above ideas lead to a clear prediction. As described above, a patient with visual agnosia has been shown to perform accurately immediate actions whereas she was impaired for delayed responses (Goodale et al 1994). Reciprocally, patients with a lesion of the posterior parietal cortex responsible for optic ataxia (dorsal stream), shown to be impaired for the production and control of visually guided aiming movements, should be able to produce accurate actions in the delay condition (via the ventral stream). We have recently tested specifically such patient in a simple pointing task to visual stimuli. When several stimulus-response delays were tested (0, 2, and 8 s), only a slight increase in variability was observed along time, as compared to normals. However, no improvement was observed for the two delays as compared to the 0 s condition, which did not comply with the above prediction.

Because optic ataxia patients are primarily impaired for reaching performed in the peripheral visual field (Perenin & Vighetto 1988), the same experiment should be performed in peripheral vision by restraining eye movements (so that an error reduction may be observed after a delay). But this lack of effect in central vision is contrasting with results observed when the target location was unexpectedly modified during the patients reaching movement. Whereas normals can update the direction of their movement without significantly increasing its duration, optic ataxia patients are clearly deprived of such automatic visuo-motor processing, even without constraints imposed on eye movements (Pisella et al. 1999, 2000; Gréa et al. in preparation). The apparent contradiction between these two lines of results indicates that the implication of the posterior parietal cortex in immediate vs. delayed action remains to be further investigated before we can draw an accurate picture of how the continuum of responses ranging from fully automatic sensori-motor transformation to fully conscious verbal reports are handled by the nervous system (Figure 1).

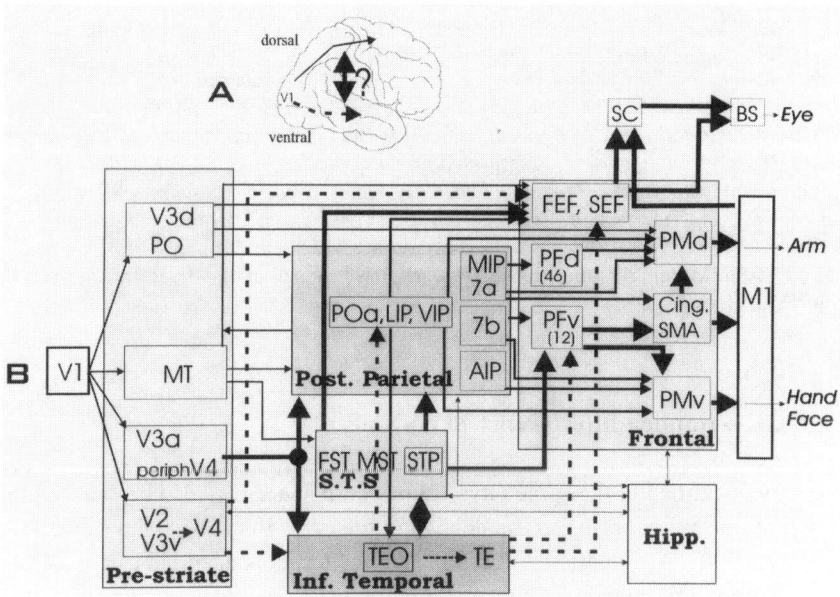

Figure 1. Neuroanatomical basis for dissociated perception and action systems
A: Schematic drawing of the two main neural pathways in the visual system. From the main visual input to area 17, two segregated streams of processing have been described projecting respectively to the posterior parietal cortex (dorsal pathway) and to the inferotemporal cortex (ventral pathway). While the ventral pathway is specialized in processing colour and form, and is assumed to play a key role in object identification ('What'), the dorsal pathway is known to be primarily involved in the computation of places ('Where') and in the sensori-motor processing of the object metrics ('How').
B: Cortical neuronal networks allowing visual inputs to be transformed into motor output. Although the dorsal and the ventral streams can be individuated from this network, this illustration emphasises the reductionism presented on Figure 1A, and displays possible

substrate for interactions between these two main pathways driving information from V1 to M1. The dorsal and the ventral projections are depicted here in plain and dotted lines respectively. Bold arrows arise from areas receiving convergent dorsal and ventral inputs, either directly or indirectly. Further projections from areas receiving these mixed convergent inputs have also been represented in bold lines. Even though the posterior parietal cortex and the inferior temporal cortex receive a single direct projection from each other, they were not considered as mixed recipient areas. By contrast, areas in the frontal lobe receive parallel dorsal, ventral, and mixed projections. Interestingly, M1 receives only pure dorsal projections and mixed projections, but no pure ventral projections. Since recent reviews have focused on the role of sub-cortical areas in visuo-motor processing, such as the projections from the superior colliculus via the pulvinar to the posterior parietal lobe and the inferior temporal lobe (e.g. Milner and Goodale 1995; Rossetti 1998), this figure primarily depicts cortical networks.

Abbreviations: AIP: anterior intraparietal area; BS: brainstem; Cing.: Cingulate motor areas; d: dorsal; FEF: frontal eye field; FST: floor of the superior temporal sulcus; Hipp.: Hippocampus; LIP: lateral intraparietal area; M1: primary motor cortex; MIP: mesial intraparietal area; MST: medial superior temporal area; MT: medio-temporal area; PF: prefrontal cortex; PM: premotor cortex; SC: superior colliculus; SEF: supplementary eye field; SMA: supplementary motor area; STS: superior temporal sulcus, STP: superior temporal polysensory area, TE: temporal area; TEO: temporo-occipital area; v: ventral; V1: primary visual cortex, VIP: ventral intraparietal area.
(derived from Morel & Bullier, 1990; Schwarz, 1994; Schall et al., 1995; Tanné et al., 1995; Van Hoesen, 1982).

Explicit → implicit interference in normals

Movements aimed to the same physical target in space can also be affected by different biases according to the delay and the experimental set-up (review in Rossetti 1998). As in patients, it seems that the target is encoded as part of the visual context in the delay condition. Several experiments have confirmed the dissociation between sensori-motor sub-systems on the basis of temporal variables.

For example, Goodale et al. (1994) applied the delay paradigm used with their patient D.F. to a group of healthy subjects. They reported that many kinematic landmarks of the grasping movement were affected by a 2 s delay introduced between stimulus viewing and movement onset. In particular, the opening and closure of the finger grip was altered and maximal grip size was reduced as compared to normal movements. Strikingly, movements delayed by 30 s and pantomimed movements performed beside the object were similar to those observed after 2 s. Allowing a good comparison with experiments performed on patients, this study further supported the view that brain mechanisms underlying perceptual representations are quite independent of those activated during action, and stressed the necessity for motor representations to have an on-line access to target parameters.

This and other experiments strongly support the existence of two distinct ways of encoding spatial information for action. As has been suggested earlier by Bridgeman (1991), an immediate sensori-motor system would depend on an egocentric frame of reference, whereas a second, slower system would represent the target within an external context. As a function of the delay between target encoding and the motor response, the result of the action would exclusively reflect one type of organization. Alternatively, and according to Gentilucci et al. (1996), responses observed for intermediate delays suggest that the two systems can gradually interact. The experiment reported below attempted to explore reference frames of the two types of representations on the one hand, and to co-activate them in order to test for their interactions on the other hand.

Dissociation of semantic and pragmatic representations, previously explored in brain-damaged patients, was also investigated in healthy subjects pointing to memorized proprioceptive targets (Rossetti and Régnier 1995). In these experiments, subjects were required to point with the right hand to a location previously encoded by a displacement of the left hand, guided by the investigator. Subject's response was randomly triggered as immediate (0 s) or delayed response (8 s). Pointing scatters produced for each target position were analyzed separately for the two delays. The orientation of these pointing scatters was the most sensitive parameter in this experiment. As expected, the scatter surface systematically increased with the response delay. This experimental paradigm allowed us to demonstrate a dissociation between immediate and delayed responses in terms of the reference frame used to produce the action (Rossetti and Régnier 1995; Rossetti et al. 1996; Rossetti and Procyk 1997). Specifically, scatter orientations obtained for the delayed response were aligned with the target array used during the experiment (arc, horizontal or vertical lines), whereas it tended to be circular for single target sessions. In the immediate condition, this alignment was never observed. It was concluded that delayed responses were computed in an external frame of reference whereas immediate actions would be prepared in an egocentric reference (see Rossetti 1998).

Later experiments were aimed at testing interactions between the two action systems at work for the two delays studied, using again a simultaneous activation of semantic and pragmatic representations. Prior to the test session, subjects were taught a number associated with each of the six target positions from an arc array. As in patients, they were then required to speak aloud the number corresponding to the pointed target during each movement (target number condition). In a control condition, subjects were required to count backward aloud (from 6 to 1 and so forth), so that an utterance (without spatial content) would accompany each movement (number condition). Distributions of scatter orientations are shown on Figure 2. It can be seen that the "target number condition" modified the distribution obtained for the 0 s delay, so that it became similar to the 8 s pattern. Results of the "number condition" were comparable to those previously obtained without verbal response or with a less specific verbal response (Rossetti and Régnier 1995), suggesting that producing an arbitrary number had no effect on the reference frame used for action. This finding suggests that activation of a semantic representation of target position had the same effect as the memory delay. Indeed similar distributions were observed (1) after a delay but without verbalization and (2) without delay but with verbalization of target position. In other words, it is likely that the specific verbalization forced the motor system to immediately use the same frame of reference as was normally used after the delay, namely an external frame dependent on the target array (Pisella et al. 1996).

Conclusion

Experiments performed on healthy subjects were aimed at replicating the situations found to activate sequentially or simultaneously a motor and a more cognitive representation of the goal in patients. A great convergence is found between these two lines of results. Patients could perform accurately only in the "natural" condition, in which they neither delayed the response, nor attempted to represent the stimulus at a higher cognitive level (matching, pantomiming, verbalizing). The performance observed in healthy subjects in the same "natural" condition may also suggest that a motor representation was used, whereas the representation used after the delay or the verbalization became contingent upon the external context. The effect of the simultaneous verbalization was crucial to demonstrate that segregation of the two representations is based not only on the response delay.

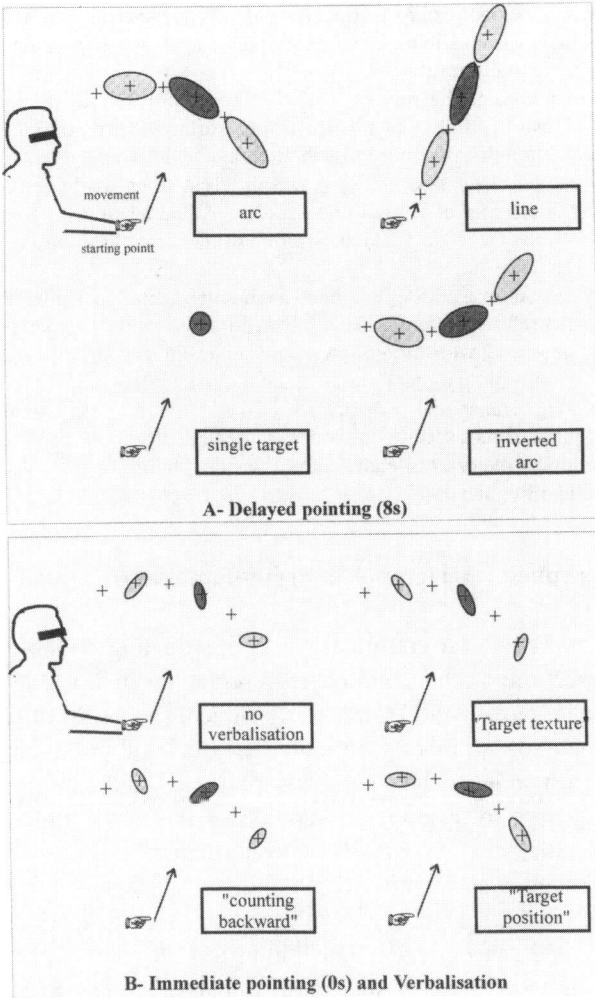

Figure 2. Immediate vs. delayed action
Blindfolded healthy subjects were required to point to proprioceptive targets presented along various arrays. For each trial the target fingertip was briefly placed on one location and the subject was instructed by a computer-generated tone when to point at it with the other hand. Confidence ellipses were calculated for the pointing distributions obtained for each target location and each delay. For the sake of clarity, only one confidence ellipse was represented out of two target locations. As expected, these confidence ellipses were larger for the 8 s delay (lower panel) than for the 0 s delay (upper panel). The most interesting

observation was made on the ellipse orientation: delayed responses were influenced by the target array, whereas immediate responses did not. Panel A and B provide a schematic representation of the main results:

A: For delayed pointing, the influence of the target array on ellipse orientation was demonstrated by testing different target arrays: three different arrays of 6 locations and one single target condition. The pointing distribution obtained for one given target (the same absolute point in space across conditions) was different when it was presented as single target or among three types of arrays of 6 targets, such that the ellipse's major axes tended to be aligned with the target array. Memorization of the target location therefore used the target array as reference frame.

B: For immediate pointing, ellipses exhibited a random orientation, showing that the target array is not used as reference frame. The effect of different types of verbalization on ellipse orientation is illustrated with targets presented along an arc array. Verbalization of a "texture number" or arbitrary "backward counting" do not affect the ellipse orientation for immediate pointing. The spatial verbalization of the "target number" simultaneous to the immediate pointing exerts a specific influence on the reference frame used for the pointing, such that the ellipse's major axes tended to be aligned with the arc as for delayed pointing. (From Rossetti and Régnier 1995).

Implicit → explicit interference in brain-damaged patients

We have reviewed so far empirical work investigating possible interactions between sensori-motor and cognitive representations involved in action at the level of a single movement. However, dynamical properties of sensori-motor representation allow to modify not only the course of an ongoing action but also the correspondence between sensory inputs and motor outputs. For example, exposure to an optical alteration of the visual field is known to produce an initial disorganization of visuo-motor behavior, which can be corrected through visuo-motor adaptation. Such adaptation has been used widely to demonstrate the plasticity of coordinate transformations involved in multisensory and sensori-motor integration (e.g. Rossetti et al. 1993). One major compensatory effect of short-term wedge-prism exposure is a shift of proprioceptive representations, which can be demonstrated by requiring subjects to point straight-ahead in the dark (e.g. Redding and Wallace 1992, 1996). After adaptation, this finger straight-ahead demonstration is shifted in a direction opposite to the optical deviation, indicating that internal visual and proprioceptive 'maps' have been realigned.

Interestingly, this after-effect resembles one of the consequences of parietal lesions in human. Hemispatial neglect is a neurological deficit of perception, representation, and/or performing actions within the left-sided space. The frequent parietal locus of the lesion producing neglect reflects the impairment of coordinate transformation used by the nervous system to represent extrapersonal space. Given that prism adaptation can be considered as a way to stimulate neural structures responsible for the transformation of sensori-motor coordinates, the effect of prism adaptation were explored on various neglect symptoms, including the pathological shift of the subjective straight-ahead to the right.

In a first experiment, we measured the adaptability of neglect patients to a lateral shift of the visual field. Manual body-midline demonstration was used to evaluate adaptation to base-left wedge prisms (inducing a 10° shift of the visual field to the right) by a simple target-pointing task. A group of eight neglect patients and a group of five control subjects produced 10 straight-ahead pointing trials before and after a short period of adaptation. The patient's mean straight-ahead was initially shifted to the right. Following the adaptation, straight-ahead were shifted to the left in both groups, and thus the patient's pathological deviation was greatly improved. This first result demonstrated that neglect patients can easily adapt to a lateral shift of the visual field to the right. A second experiment investigated whether prism adaptation could also improve the main clinical manifestations of neglect. Twelve neglect patients were randomly assigned to the prism group and the control group. All patients underwent a similar procedure. A series of traditional neuropsychological tests (Halligan and Marshall 1989) was performed on three sessions. After the first session (Pre-test), patients had to perform the elementary pointing task with the prismatic goggles used in experiment 1, in order to adapt to the visual-proprioceptive discrepancy. Patients in the Prism group were exposed to the optical deviation to the right. Patients in the Control group wore neutral goggles with thick flat glasses. Immediately after removing the goggles, a second session was performed with the same battery of tests (Post-test). Patients were again tested after a delay of about two hours following the goggle exposure (Late-test). The standard neuropsychological procedure included: line bisection, line cancellation, copying a simple drawing, drawing of a daisy from memory, and reading a simple text.

All patients in the Prism group exhibited a clear improvement following prism exposure. A dramatic improvement was observed for all tests following prism exposure and was fully maintained two hours later. By contrast, there was no significant improvement in the Control group. Figure 3A shows results obtained for the copying test (Gainotti et al. 1972) by one representative patient of each group.

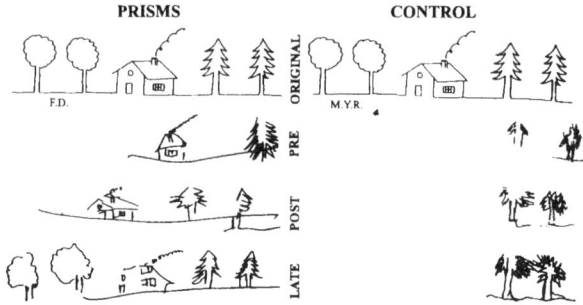

Figure 3A: Copying test

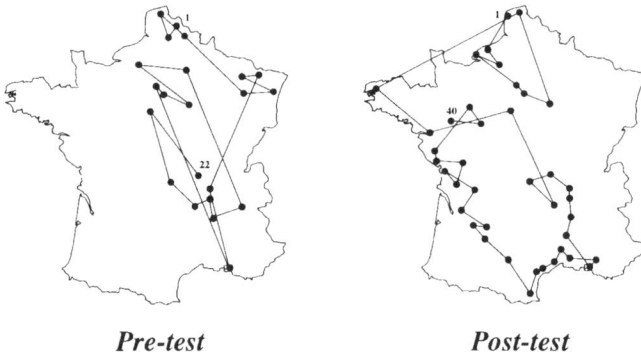

Pre-test　　　　　　*Post-test*

Figure 3B: Mental imagery

Figure 3. Effect of visuo-motor adaptation on space representation in unilateral neglect.
A: One of the most classical tests used to assess hemispatial neglect referred to as the Gainotti test, in which the patient is required to copy a drawing made of five items. In the representative example of one patient of Prisms group (left panel), the drawing made prior to prism exposure (Pre-test) demonstrates complete neglect of three items. In the Post-test (on prism removal) one item is added to the patient's drawing, and in the Late-test (after 2 hours) all items are drawn. Please note that no decrease of performance was observed between the Post-test and the Late-test in this particular test, as well as in others. In the Control group (right panel), patients wearing neutral goggles did not significantly improved. (From Rossetti et al. 1998).
B: Towns evoked during the mental evocation of the maps of France in two conditions: prior to a prism exposure (Pre-test), and immediately after removing the goggles (Post-test). The filled circles indicate the geographical loci of the different responses and the numbers indicate the first (1) and the last (22 and 40) town given in 2 minutes. It is obvious that towns from the western part of France are evoked only after prism adaptation. (From Rossetti et al. 1999; Rode et al. 2000).

Recent experiments have focused on the exploration of other levels of space representation, ranging from postural control and wheel-chair driving (Jacquin et al. 1998) to mental representations of space (Rossetti et al. 1999; Rode et al. 2000). Our preliminary results suggest that various other levels of space representation can be altered by prism adaptation in patients. Figure 3B shows the effect of adaptation on mental representation of a geographic space. The patient was asked to mentally visualize the map of France, and was then given 2 minutes to name as many towns of France as possible. A clear neglect of the western part of the map was initially observed (see Rode and Perenin 1994). After adaptation, the map was more extensively explored, and the western part was normally described (Rode et al. 2000).

Conclusion

Alteration of the perception-action loop can affect in deep functions participating in space representation, so that higher level spatial function may be modified following sensori-motor adaptation procedures. It is interesting to stress that performing a single action does not seem to affect perceptual experience in blindsight and numbsense patients, and that the explicit system was affecting the implicit motor function in that case. For a reverse interaction to appear between from the sensori-motor to the perceptual system, a deeper modification is required, which implies changes to occur over a much longer time scale. The same conclusion is reached by Bhalla and Proffitt (2000: This volume), when they show that long-term changes in sensori-motor coordination due to aging also affect the cognitive processing of another type of spatial information, that is slope perception. This idea is in accordance with the notion that action, and its sensory correlates such as reafference, is the basis for many aspects of sensory organization. It is also to be emphasized that this type of implicit → explicit interaction is worth considering with respect to the claim that interaction between sensori-motor and cognitive framing of space can occur only in the explicit → implicit direction (Rossetti 1998; Bridgeman 2000: this volume).

Implicit → explicit interference in normals ?

We have reviewed experimental data suggesting that a communication can be observed from the explicit to the implicit action processing system at the level of a single action in both brain-lesioned and healthy subjects. We have also shown that a modification of implicit sensori-motor representations can affect cognitive space representation in neglect patients. The question now arises whether similar implicit → explicit interference can be observed in normal subjects in the field of perception and action. In the same way as double-dissociations have been reported between the two levels of sensory processing, it would be extremely interesting and informative to test whether double-interactions can occur between them. It should be reminded that despite 100 years of active research on wedge prism adaptation, shown to be very active on the neglect patients cognitive framing of space, no such cognitive after-effect seem to be available in the literature on healthy subjects. We have therefore initiated a series of experiments aimed at investigating possible effects of prism adaptation on cognitive space representations in normals. Preliminary results suggest that no significant after-effect can be observed on the highest level of space representation, that is mental imagery. Normal subjects do not seem to be affected by prism adaptation when they perform a mental evocation of the map of France, as already tested in hemispatial neglect. However, lower level perceptual responses could be affected. In a preliminary experiment, we have shown that a significant proportion of subjects exhibited an effect of prism adaptation on simple reaction-time (key press) to visual stimuli (Farné et al. unpublished). It is noteworthy that although the level of these responses is rather low in the hierarchy of cognitive space representation, they do not pertain to the category of direct sensori-motor transformations involved in goal-directed actions which are spared in blindsight and numbsense. More extensive testing is now required to explain why some subjects did not show any after effects on this simple reaction time task, and to explore other cognitive responses independent from direct sensori-motor transformations. A first experiment has already shown that prism adaptation can affect a perceptual line bisection task in normals, by inducing a bias in the same direction as observed in hemispatial neglect (Colent et al. 2000).

Discussion

The data reviewed here demonstrate that implicit and explicit sensory representations involved in action, which have been shown to be clearly dissociated in numerous instances on the basis of temporal parameters, can interact in several ways which are also dependent on temporal factors. It has been previously proposed that interaction between sensori-motor and cognitive processing of spatial information can occur only from the cognitive to the sensori-motor system (Rossetti 1998; Bridgeman 1999). More recent experiments have shown that the reverse pattern of interaction can be observed on a longer time scale, through adaptative changes (Rossetti et al. 1998; Bhalla and Proffitt 1999: this volume). To synthesize these data, several stages of sensori-motor control have to be emphasized. Before to initiate a possible synthesis, let us first consider recent experiments exploring the temporal constraints of interaction between motor and cognitive functions.

All experiments reported above investigated explicit → implicit interference on response production. Effect of time was explored by comparing between immediate and delayed responses. The co-activation of cognitive and sensori-motor representations seems to affect response production in an "all or none" pattern, the semantic representation of the target overwhelming the sensori-motor representation. However, some reaction time inevitably pertain to the production of motor responses, whether produced immediately or delayed. Although reaction times may be short (about 250 ms in normals), one cannot exclude that this period of time is likely to favor an early effect of delay and/or of early semantic representations on sensori-motor processes. In order to explore possible interactions within a shorter range of time following the stimulus onset, we made use of specific target perturbations during ongoing aiming actions. To co-activate the direct sensori-motor representation of the target responsible for automatic on-line motor control and higher level cognitive representation of the same stimulus, we designed an experimental device producing double-perturbations of a visual target. These double perturbations were made of a change in location, mainly processed in the dorsal stream and known to trigger a fast updating of the ongoing action, and a simultaneous change in color, known to be mainly processed in the ventral stream and implying a categorization process. The change in color could be associated with an instruction to immediately stop the ongoing movement. Unperturbed trials (80%), simple perturbations in either location or color and double perturbations were intermixed in each session (Pisella & Rossetti, 1998; Rossetti & Pisella 1998). The purpose of the double-perturbation was to explore the interplay between intentional and automatic motor control during the execution of an overt action.

Because of the expected faster processing obtained for the location attribute as compared to the color attribute (Pisella et al. 1998), it can be predicted that this double-perturbation will create a conflict between the fast correction response to the location perturbation, and the instructed stop response to the color change. Analysis of the performance of six subjects showed that for pointings which duration was shorter than about 200 ms, no effect of the perturbation was observed (cf. Pisella et al. 1998). Surprisingly, for movement times ranging from 200 to about 280 ms, subjects actually pointed to the forbidden, displaced and turned red target and reached this secondary target as frequently as for the simple location perturbation (Pisella et al. 1999). Movement interruptions began to progressively appear only for slower movements. This shows that on-line motor corrections can be produced even when subjects are explicitly instructed to block their motor response in response to this perturbation (Figure 4).

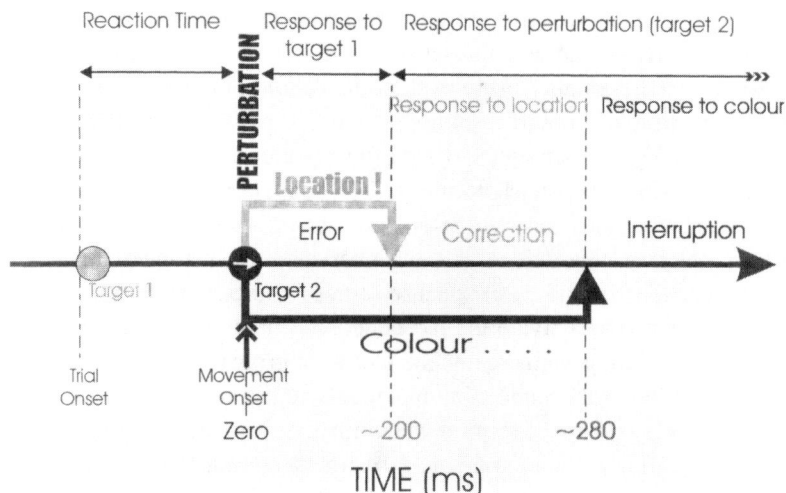

Figure 4. Time constraints on implicit and explicit sensori-motor processing
The three phases of responses to the double-perturbation (target location and colour simultaneously changed) are represented along a time axis. Subjects planned their movement to target 1. Double perturbation was triggered unexpectedly by movement onset. Subjects had to modify their programmed movement in response to the perturbation. Trajectory correction was associated to the location perturbation and initiated for movement times as short as 200 ms (upper arrow). Movement interruption was instructed in response to the colour change and was possible only for slower movements lasted about 280 ms (lower arrow). Movements ranging between these two durations were guided by an automatic pilot without upper control. Movements produced in this temporal window led to correction responses instead of the instructed response of movement interruption. (From Pisella et al. 1999)

However, because the instructions given to the subjects delineated two stimulus/response combinations (location/correction and color/interruption), the fact that automatic motor corrections were initiated more quickly than the movement interruption can be related to either the different stimulus attributes (location vs color change) and/or to the requested responses (correction vs. interruption).

To investigate whether a single stimulus could also produce a conflict between an automatic and an instructed response, we performed a further experiment with a simple perturbation (Pisella & Rossetti 1997; Pisella et al. 2000). Two groups of subjects received different instructions: in a location-stop condition, interruption was requested in response to a target change in location. In a location-go condition, a third group of subjects was instructed to reach the secondary target. As expected, errors were close to 100% in the fastest sessions (100% touch to initial target), and close to 0% in the slowest sessions (i.e. about 100% of pointings redirected to the new target location or interrupted, according respectively to the 'go' or to the 'stop' instruction). But a surprising result was obtained in the intermediate range of movement time: corrections made towards the second target were as numerous in the go and the stop condition between about 200 and 250 ms, which revealed that corrections can be observed even by subjects who have never been required to produce corrections (Pisella et al. 2000). Then only the instructed interruption began to progressively take over the automatic corrections.

These recent results and the experimental work described in the previous sections suggest that several time ranges have to be considered in the discussion of interactions between sensori-motor and cognitive processing of spatial information, that is respectively between mostly implicit and explicit spatial representations. Figure 5 attempts to describe these time ranges. Let us first consider the level of a single action. For the shorter reaction time, and for tasks performed without delay, we have seen that at the implicit processing provides the only representation, which can affect the motor outcome. This exclusive influence of sensori-motor representation might be sustained by the dorsal stream of visual processing. Then the voluntary control, which is activated more slowly, can influence the motor response, and gradually supplant the pure sensori-motor system. This influence might be supported by the ventral stream, probably through indirect projections made to the motor cortex via the prefrontal and premotor cortex. Then let us consider a much larger time scale, which allows slow adaptative processes to take place through sensori-motor plasticity. Both visuo-motor adaptation in neglect patients (Rossetti et al. 1998, 1999) and aging (Bhalla and Proffitt 1999) have been shown to affect the elaboration of explicit cognitive representation of spatial information. It is likely that the cerebellum is involved in this type of deep modification of the several levels of space representation, because this brain structure is the best candidate for the neurological substrate of adaptation (Jeannerod and Rossetti 1993 for a review, Desmurget et al. 1998 for a recent account).

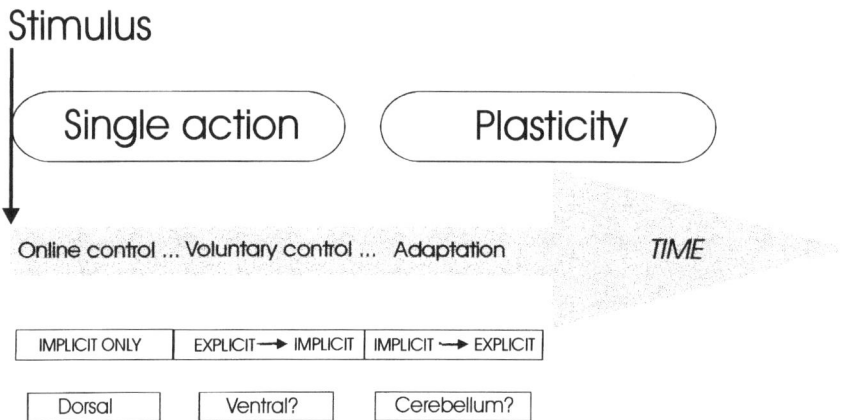

Stimulus

(Single action)   (Plasticity)

Online control ... Voluntary control ... Adaptation   *TIME*

| IMPLICIT ONLY | EXPLICIT → IMPLICIT | IMPLICIT → EXPLICIT |

| Dorsal | Ventral? | Cerebellum? |

Figure 5. Time constraints and implicit-explicit processing.
Tentative synthesis of the temporal constraints impinging on the relationship between implicit and explicit processing. As reviewed in the present chapter, implicit processing can be performed faster than explicit processing, which is particularly useful for on-line motor control. The plausible neural substrate for this particular speed seems to be the dorsal pathway. Slower action can be supervised by the voluntary control, which implies a transfer from the explicit to the implicit system. For example the verbalization of the movement goal location during the action induces a loss of the implicit residual abilities observed in blindsight and numbsense patients and a change in the reference frame used to control the action. Interestingly these effects are similar to the effect of a delay between the stimulus delivery and the action. Several other chapters provide examples of such interaction (Bridgeman, Hommel, Bhalla and Proffitt). These interactions might involve the posterior or the anterior portion of the ventral pathway. To evoke a transfer from the implicit to the explicit mode of sensory processing, one has to study a more extended time scale. This time scale allows for plasticity to gradually develop and thus implies that several movements are involved. Prism adaptation provides an example of such transfer from an implicit sensori-motor level to an explicit space representation.

At the end of this tentative synthesis, it appears that explicit and implicit processing of space representations involved in action are not completely dissociated and that there are multiple interferences between them. Following several reports of simple interaction between implicit and explicit sensory processing in the context of action (review in Rossetti et al. 1998; Bridgeman, this volume), we demonstrate here that a double-interaction is possible between an implicit sensori-motor level of processing and an explicit cognitive level of space representation. The relationship between these two main systems that can give rise to action is more complex than it has been thought previously, and its precise understanding constitutes a real challenge for the understanding of how the whole brain is able to deal with multiple subsystems specialized for processing specific aspects of the interplay between the environment and the body in action. Therefore we propose that the concept of double-interaction should play a complementary role to that of double-dissociation in the understanding of the complex brain networks involved in the generation of consciousness.

Acknowledgements

This work was supported by the Center for Consciousness Studies (Tucson, Arizona), Région Rhône-Alpes and ELYPSES (France). The authors wish to thank Jean-Louis Borach for his help with the illustrations.

References

Bhalla, M. & Proffitt, D.R. (2000). Geographical slant perception: dissociation and coordination between explicit awareness and visually guided actions. This volume, 99–128.

Bridgeman, B. (1991). Complementary cognitive and motor image processing. In G. Obrecht & L. W. Stark (Eds.), *Presbyopsia Research. From molecular Biology to Visual Adaptation*. New York: Plenum Press, 189–198.

Bridgeman, B. (2000). Interactions between vision for perception and vision for behavior. This volume, 17–40.

Bullier, J., Girard, P., Salin, P.A. (1994). The role of area 17 in the transfer of information to extrastriate visual cortex. In A. Peters and K.S. Rockland (Eds.), *Primary visual cortex in primates. Cerebral Cortex* 10, 301–330.

Colent, C., Pisella, L., Bernier, C., Rode, G., Rossetti, Y. (2000). Cognitive bias induced by visuo-motor adaptation to prisms: A simulation of unilateral neglect in normals? *Neuroreport* 11,9: in press.

Desmurget, M., Pelisson, D., Urquizar, C., Prablanc, C., Alexander, G.E., Grafton, S.T. (1998). Functional anatomy of saccadic adaptation in humans. *Nature Neuroscience*, 1, 524–528.

Gainotti, G., Messerli, P. & Tissot, R. (1972). Qualitative analysis of unilateral spatial neglect in relation to laterality of cerebral lesions. *Journal of Neurology and Neurosurgery.Psychiatry*, 35, 545–550.

Gentilucci, M., Chieffi, S., Daprati, E., Saetti, M.C., & Toni, I. (1996). Visual illusion and action. *Neuropsychologia*, 34(6), 369–376.

Girard, P. (1995). Anatomic and physiologic basis of residual vision after damage to the primary visual area. *Revue Neurologique*. (Paris), 151:8–9, 457–465.

Goodale, M.A., Milner, A.D., Jakobson, L.S. & Carey, D.P. (1991). A neurological dissociation between perceiving objects and grasping them. *Nature*, 349, 154–156.

Goodale, M.A. & Milner, A.D. (1992). Separate visual pathways for perception and action. *Trends in Neurosciences*, 15(1), 20–25.

Goodale, M.A., Jakobson, L.S. & Keillor, J.M. (1994). Differences in the visual control of pantomimed and natural grasping movements. *Neuropsychologia*, 32, 1159–1178.

Gréa, H., Pisella, L., Desmurget, M., Tilikete, C., Vighetto, A., Rossetti, Y., Prablanc, C. (2000). The posterior parietal cortex mediates hand path adjustment during goal-directed movements, submitted.

Halligan, P.W., Marshall, J.C. & Wade, D.T. (1989). Visuospatial neglect: underlying factors and test sensitivity. *Lancet*, 2(8668), 908–911.

Hommel, B. (2000). Intentional control of automatic stimulus-response translation. This volume, 221–242.

Jacquin, S., Luauté, J., Li, L., Rode G., Rossetti, Y., & Boisson, D. (1998). Amélioration de la conduite en fauteuil roulant après adaptation prismatique chez le patient héminégligent. *Annales de Réadaptation et Médecine Physique*, 41, 320–321.

Jeannerod, M. & Rossetti, Y. (1993). Visuomotor coordination as a dissociable visual function : experimental and clinical evidence. In C. Kennard (Ed.), *Visual perceptual defects*. London: Ballière Tindall, 439–460.

Marcel A. (1993). Slippage in the unity of consciousness. In *experimental and theoretical studies of consciousness* (Ciba Foundation symposium 74). Ed. Wiley, 168–186.

Milner, A.D. & Goodale, M.A. (1993). Visual pathways to perception and action . In T. P. Hicks, S. Molotchnikoff & T. Ono (Eds.), *Progress in Brain Research*, 317–337.

Milner, A.D. & Goodale, M.A. (1995). *The visual brain in action*. New York: Oxford University Press.

Milner, A.D. (1997). Vision without knowledge. *Philos.Trans.R.Soc.Lond.B.Biol.Sci.*, 352(1358), 1249–1256.

Morel, A., & Bullier, J. (1990). Anatomical segregation of two cortical visual pathways in the macaque monkey. *Visual Neuroscience*, 4, 555–578.

Perenin, M.-T. & Rossetti, Y. (1996). Grasping in an hemianopic field. Another instance of dissociation between perception and action. *Neuroreport*, 7(3), 793–797.

Perenin, M.T., & Vighetto, A. (1988). Optic ataxia: a specific disruption in visuomotor mechanisms. I. Different aspects of the deficit in reaching for objects. *Brain*, 111(Pt 3), 643–674.

Pisella, L., Rossetti, Y. & Arzi, M. (1997). Dorsal versus Ventral parameters of fast pointing: effects of stimulus and of response type [Abstract]. *International Conference on Vision and Action,* Toronto.

Pisella, L. & Rossetti, Y. (1997). Stimulus location is processed faster than stimulus color. *Perception,* 26: 100.

Pisella, L., Arzi, M. & Rossetti, Y. (1998). The timing of color and location processing in the motor context. *Experimental Brain Research,* 121(3), 270–276.

Pisella, L., Gréa, H., Tilikete, C., Vighetto, A., Desmurget, M., Rode, G., Boisson, D., Rossetti, Y. (2000). An automatic pilot for the hand in the Posterior Parietal Cortex: toward a reinter pretation of Optic Ataxia. *Nature Neuroscience,* 3 (7), in press.

Pisella, L., Attali, M., Frange, H., Régnier, C., Gaunet, F., Rossetti, Y. (1996). Representations en action: une même representation spatiale pour la memorisation et al verbalisation? *Actes du 6e Colloque de l'Association pour la Recherche Cognitive,* Villeneuve d'Ascq.

Pisella, L., Tiliket, C., Rode, G., Boisson, D., Vighetto, A., & Rossetti, Y. (1999). Automatic corrections prevail in spite of an instructed stopping response. In M. Grealy & J.A. Thomson (Eds.), *Studies in Perception and Action V.* Erlbaum Associates, Mahwah, New Jersey, London: 275–279.

Redding, G.M., & Wallace, B. (1992). Adaptative eye-hand coordination: implication of prism adaptation for perceptual-motor organization. In L. Proteau & D. Elliott (Eds.). *Vision and motor control.* Amsterdam: Elsevier Science Publishers, 105–127

Redding, G.M. & Wallace, B. (1996). Adaptive spatial alignment and strategic perceptual-motor control. *Journal of Experimental Psychology in Human Perception and Performance.,* 22(2), 379–394.

Rode, G., Rossetti, Y., Li, L., Boisson, D. (2000). The effect of prism adaptation on neglect for visual imagery. *Behavioral Neurology,* in press.

Rode, G. & Perenin, M.T. (1994). Temporary remission of representational hemineglect through vestibular stimulation. *Neuroreport,* 5, 869–872.

Rossetti, Y., Koga, K. & Mano, T. (1993). Prismatic displacement of vision induces transient changes in the timing of eye-hand coordination. *Perception & Psychophysics,* 54(3), 355–364.

Rossetti, Y., & Régnier, C. (1995). Representations in action : pointing to a target with various representations. In B. G. Bardy, R. J. Bootsma, & Y. Guiard (Eds.), *Studies in Perception and Action* III. Mahwah, NJ: Lawrence Erlbaum Associates, Inc, 233–236

Rossetti, Y., Rode, G. & Boisson, D. (1995). Implicit processing of somaesthetic information: a dissociation between where and how? *Neuroreport,* 6(3), 506–510.

Rossetti, Y. & Rode, G. (1996). In search of nonvisual motor images. *Behavioral and Brain Sciences,* 17, 762–763.

Rossetti, Y. & Procyk, E. (1997). What memory is for action: the gap between percepts and concepts. *Behavioral and Brain Sciences,* 20(1), 34–36.

Rossetti, Y. (1998). Implicit short-lived motor representations of space in brain damaged and healthy subjects. *Consciousness and Cognition,* 7, 520–558.

Rossetti, Y. & Pisella, L. (1998). Temporal asynchrony between sensory and between motor components of visuo-motor response: a time-grounded dissociation between implicit and explicit processing? *Toward a science of Consciousness,* Tucson.

Rossetti, Y., Rode, G., Pisella, L., Farne, A., Ling, L., Boisson, D. & Perenin, M.T. (1998). Hemispatial neglect and prism adaptation: when adaptation to rightward optical deviation rehabilitates the neglected left side. *Nature,* 395, 166–169.

Rossetti, Y. (1999). In search of immaculate perception: evidence from motor representations of space. In S. Hameroff, A. Kaszniak, & A. Scott (Eds.), *Towards a Science of Consciousness.* Cambridge MA: MIT Press, 141–148.

Rossetti Y., Rode G., Pisella L., Farne A., Ling L., Boisson D. (1999). Sensorimotor plasticity and cognition: prism adaptation can affect various levels of space representation. In M. Grealy & J.A. Thomson (Eds.), *Studies in Perception and Action V.* Lawrence Erlbaum Associates, 265–269

Rossetti, Y., Pisella, L., & Pélisson, D. (2000). Eye blindness and handsight: temporal aspects of visuo-motor processing. *Visual Cognition,* in press.

Schwartz, A.,B. (1994) Distributed motor processing in cerebral cortex. *Current Opinion in Neurobiology* 4, 840–846.

Weiskrantz (1989). *Blindsight: a case study and implications.* Oxford University Press.

Conscious and Nonconscious Processing of Visual Object Identity

Moshe Bar

Department of Psychology, Harvard University

NMR center — Massachusetts General Hospital

Priming as implicit memory

Recognizing a perceptual stimulus improves with familiarity. This experience-specific facilitation is termed *priming*. In a typical priming experiment, subjects are initially exposed to a set of briefly presented stimuli in the prime block and their performance in naming, for example, is recorded (usually reaction times and correct responses). In a subsequent test block, subjects are presented with either the same stimuli or stimuli that have some defined relationship to the prime stimuli. Any improvement that is specific to the stimulus is taken as a measure of priming.

Priming is considered an implicit type of memory because it does not involve explicit recollection of previous experience. It is believed to exist as an independent mechanism, while closely interacting with other memory systems (Tulving & Schacter 1990). Amnesic patients, for example, can show almost intact priming while their explicit recognition memory (as measured in an old/new judgment task) has been severely impaired (Weiskrantz & Warrington 1970; Warrington & Weiskrantz 1974; Cave & Squire 1992). In other types of experiments, it has been shown that elaborating the study material improved explicit memory (e.g., measured by a cued recall of stem completions),[1] but not priming (Graf & Mandler 1984). Priming and explicit memory have also been suggested to have different retention time courses (Jacoby 1983). Priming of object naming can last 48 weeks after a single exposure to a picture (Cave 1997), and priming of word completions can even last as long as 16 months (Sloman, Hayman, Ohta, Law & Tulving 1988).

Although the contribution of priming is implicit, it has been shown to facilitate tasks that require explicit knowledge, such as object naming[2] (Bartram 1974; Biederman & Cooper 1991; Schacter, Delaney & Merikle 1990). The mechanisms subserving the interaction between priming and explicit reports, as manifested in object recognition, will be the focus of this chapter.

Working definitions

The terms *subliminal* and *visual awareness* are being used extensively. The following are working definitions for these concepts.

Subliminal is taken here in its literal meaning: below-threshold. The threshold is defined by the task. Therefore, if subjects are required to detect the presence or absence of a certain stimulus on the screen and they cannot do it above chance, this detection is considered to be below their threshold, and therefore subliminal. However, if the task is naming briefly presented objects, the threshold is identification. A trial in a naming task is then considered subliminal if subjects cannot name the objects, even if they are above chance in detecting their presence. The tasks of detection and naming differ largely in the information that they require for successful performance, and the thresholds are expected to be different. In addition, in light of the priming phenomenon, this threshold should not be considered as fixed but rather as a measure that can vary with experience. As demonstrated by the experimental work reviewed here, subjects could gain from subliminal presentations information that can render the same stimuli supraliminal in subsequent trials.

Work on signal detection theory (Swets 1961; Green & Swets 1966) challenges the existence of a sensory threshold. The threshold is described instead by a bell-shaped curve representing the distribution of the probability for correct performance. In the present context, "subliminal" is used to describe success (or, rather, failure) in performing the task at hand, and in that sense it is a binary concept. "Visual awareness," on the other hand, is taken to be more like a continuum, and therefore closer to the threshold definition of signal detection theory.[3] If a presentation of an object is too brief for identification, it is subliminal in that subjects cannot identify it, and therefore they are unaware of the name. At the same time, however, they might be aware of other aspects of the identity, such as orientation and texture. In that sense, awareness is a set of dimensions on which a threshold may be defined.

Such "intermediate-awareness" of the identity is often hard to infer from subjects' reports. In trying to estimate the awareness of subjects with regard to different aspects of the stimulus, the experiment should be designed so that the report will be minimally affected by subjective factors. When subjects cannot name the stimulus, intermediate reports can vary significantly, and they are likely to depend on individual differences in verbal articulation, visual memory, etc. In addition, subjects can make accurate discriminations even when they believe that their knowledge is insufficient for a correct judgment (reported as early as Sidis, 1898, and more recently, Kolb & Braun 1995). Indeed, Cheesman and Merikle (1984) distinguish between "subjective-threshold," when subjects believe they are guessing while their performance is above chance, and an "objective-threshold," which is chance-level perfor-mance. Self-judgments of awareness and confidence are thus highly subjec-tive, and should be augmented with objective measures of performance.

Subliminal perception and visual awareness

Direct tests such as recognition are likely to involve effects of both explicit and implicit processes. To distinguish their contribution, Jacoby (1991) devel-oped the process dissociation task. He assumed that "implicit" and "nonintentional" are representing unconscious processes, and that "explicit" and "intentional" are representing conscious processes. The rationale behind Jacoby's task is that the contribution of intentional and nonintentional pro-cesses can be inferred by comparing performance between conditions in which they are acting together and conditions in which they are competing. For example, after studying a list of words, subjects were required to complete stems of words with either words from the study list (*inclusion* condition), or with words not from the study list (*exclusion* condition) (Jacoby, Toth, Yonelinas 1993). The difference in performance between the two conditions was taken to indicate an intentional retrieval, and any study items that are provided in the exclusion condition to indicate nonintentional use of memory. The results show that study words that were presented very briefly (Debner & Jacoby 1994), or in a divided attention task[4] (Jacoby *et al.* 1993) were given equally often on inclusion and exclusion conditions, and at a rate that was significantly higher than baseline.[5] Therefore, under these conditions, all the priming was nonintentional.

This technique has been proven useful and is extensively used for similar assessments of conscious and unconscious effects. Other demonstrations, using various paradigms, have shown that the effect of subliminal presentations might range from the bias of judgment and affect to the facilitation of visual object recognition.

In one type of such studies (Marcel 1983; Merikle, Joordens & Stolz 1995), subjects were required to name the color of a target patch that was presented on the screen until they responded. The patch was preceded by a subliminal (individually determined for each subject) color name (e.g., 'GREEN'). Performance was affected by the congruency between the name and the color patch (Stroop effect) such that color-congruent words shortened reaction times (RTs), and color-incongruent words delayed RTs. Therefore, although the prime was not recognizable it affected responses in the subsequent naming task.

Another example is the effect of subliminal presentations on subsequent liking judgments (Zajonc 1968). In one such study (Kunst-Wilson & Zajonc 1980), subjects were first presented with irregular octagons for a very brief duration (1 ms). Then, pairs of such octagons — one new and one from the set that had been presented previously — were displayed on the screen for 1 sec. Subjects were required to: (a) choose which octagon they liked more, and (b) judge which of the two octagons they had seen before (old/new judgment). Although they were at chance in the old/new judgment task, they tended to like the old stimuli more than the new ones. Consequently, the authors concluded that the subliminal presentations only affected judgments of liking. Experiments reviewed here show that subliminal presentations can also facilitate object identification (Bar & Biederman 1998; 1999). An implication of these results is that priming of perception may be more affected by a subliminal stimulus than the explicit measure of old/new judgments.

Finally, in a recent study of subliminal semantic activation (Greenwald, Draine Abrams 1996), a prime word was presented very briefly before the presentation of above-threshold target words. Subjects were required to judge whether the target was a pleasant or unpleasant word, or whether it represented a male or female name. Their judgments were biased by the subliminal prime. For example, a prime word "kill" biased judgments of a target word "bomb" towards unpleasantness, while a prime word "happy" biased the judgment of the same word towards pleasantness. This subliminal priming, which was purely semantic (as the prime and the target were different words that could only be semantically related), has been found to be very short-lived: the target word had to be presented within 100 ms following the prime in order to obtain the effect. Subliminal visual priming, on the other hand, is suggested later to persist for longer durations. Therefore, this ephemeral nature might be unique to subliminal semantic priming.

We turn now from studies of subliminal priming to consider the related issue of visual awareness. While studying visual awareness in general has a long history, the underlying neural mechanisms have been addressed only recently. Two related phenomena that have been studied extensively are *blindsight* and *binocular rivalry*.

Blindsight is the ability of patients with a damaged primary visual cortex (or the projections to it) to report aspects of a stimulus that is presented to the blind area of their visual field (Weiskrantz 1986). Such patients perform reliably above chance (typically in localization tasks), often despite their low confidence in their response. Blindsight may thus be considered as an example of perception without awareness.

Experimental methods have been devised to induce behavior similar to blindsight in healthy human observers (Meeres & Graves 1990; Kolb & Braun 1995). For example, when subjects had to locate an open circle that was presented very briefly in one of six possible positions (Meeres & Graves 1990), they were significantly better than chance in guessing its location, even when they reported that the circle was absent. In such studies, however, the relation between subjective confidence judgments and awareness is not completely defined.

The capacity of blindsight is likely mediated by alternative connections to other areas. Hypotheses regarding the anatomical basis of blindsight include the retinocollicular pathway (i.e., the pathway from the retina to the superior colliculus), the direct projections from the thalamus to extrastriate cortex, and residual projections that survived the damage (Stoerig 1993). Each patient might have a different type of damage, and therefore blindsight might have different substrates in each instance. The important common aspect is subjects' ability to perform successfully in spite of their low confidence.

Findings from studies of form-agnosia further extend the blindsight phenomenon. One striking example is patient D. F. (Milner & Goodale 1995), who has suffered damage to her visual cortex following carbon monoxide intoxication. While visual areas V2, V3 were severely damaged, area V1 remained mostly intact. D.F. is unable to recognize familiar faces, line drawings of objects, or even simple geometric shapes. She also cannot discriminate between objects that differ in size or orientation. Her basic visual abilities (e.g., contrast sensitivity, visual field), however, are relatively intact. In one study (Goodale, Meenan, Bülthoff, Nicolle, Murphy & Racicot 1994), D.F. was required both to discriminate between blob-like wooden objects (same/ different task), and grasp them using shape information. Although she failed to discriminate between the shapes, she had no difficulty in choosing stable grasping points on the circumference of the object. These results suggest that D.F. could match her grasping points to the specific object form without being aware of its shape.

Another class of studies related to visual awareness is binocular rivalry. When the two eyes are presented with conflicting information, our perception alternates between the two interpretations rather than combining them into one percept.[6] This phenomenon turned out to be an excellent tool for correlating neuronal activity with subjective experience. In a series of experiments, Logothetis and his collaborators (Logothetis & Schall 1989; Logothetis & Leopold 1996) presented monkeys with motions in different directions in each eye while recording from area MT (medial temporal cortex; believed to process primarily visual motion). Many neurons fired as a response to the retinal stimulus (i.e., they fired whenever their preferred direction of motion was presented to either eye, regardless of the perception of the monkey). However, the activity of other neurons reflected the reports of the monkey (i.e., fired to their preferred direction of motion only if it was presented to the "active" eye). These neurons are likely to reflect the subjective rather than sensory experience. Similar findings were obtained from cells in V4 (Leopold & Logothetis 1996), when the conflicting stimuli were gratings in different orientations. Because these neurons reside in the deeper layers of the cortex, this activity is likely to be projected to other areas. Tracking the destination of these projections has a good potential of revealing areas that are more closely involved in visual awareness (Koch & Braun 1996).

Subliminal visual priming — The basic phenomenon

Priming is often used as a tool for studying representations, but it can also be considered as a mediating phenomenon that allows the study of visual awareness during the different stages of object recognition. While recognizing objects is often immediate and unambiguous, it is not clear at what stage do we become aware of the interpretation of the visual input. Studies addressing this and related questions will be reviewed here, as well as speculations regarding mechanisms and cortical localization.

In typical demonstrations of visual priming (Bartram 1974; Biederman & Cooper 1991; Schacter, Delaney & Merikle 1990), observers are generally able to name the stimulus on its first presentation. Priming is then manifested by improved performance in subsequent encounters with this stimulus (i.e., supraliminal priming). Can visual priming be evidenced even if the observer cannot recognize the prime, or even guess its name from among a few alternatives? As will become clearer in this section, priming of object recognition is possible although subjects are not aware of the identity of the prime, and a considerable amount of time and intervening information buffer between the prime and the test images.

In a study by Bar & Biederman (1998), line-drawing images of objects and animals were flashed very briefly (at an average of 48 ms), and were followed by a highly effective mask. Following each stimulus presentation, subjects were required to identify the object by name, even if they had to guess, and then to choose from four object names in a 4-alternative forced-choice (4AFC) test. The subsequent 4AFC task was used in order to assess the information extracted from unidentified presentations.[7] The experiment included two blocks of pictures of objects. The objects in the second block had the same names as the objects in the first, and were presented in one of four possible conditions relative to the image with that name on block 1: either at the same or different position, and either with the same shape or as a different exemplar of the same object (Figure 1). Changes in position were incorporated to study translation invariance[8] in subliminal priming, and to compare it with the complete translation invariance reported for supraliminal priming (Biederman & Cooper 1991). Different exemplars were used to assess a possible semantic component in the priming (Bartram 1974). (Stimulus-specific improvement can stem from either visual or semantic priming. Subtracting the priming of different-exemplar conditions from same-exemplar priming provide an assessment of visual and semantic priming.) Two control blocks were incorporated: one before the first experimental block, and the other after the second experimental block. The images of the second control block had different names than those in the first control block. Any improvement in naming objects in the second control block, compared with the first control block, would represent general improvement that cannot be attributed to priming. Twenty images and fifteen minutes, on average, intervened between the first and second presentations of the same object.

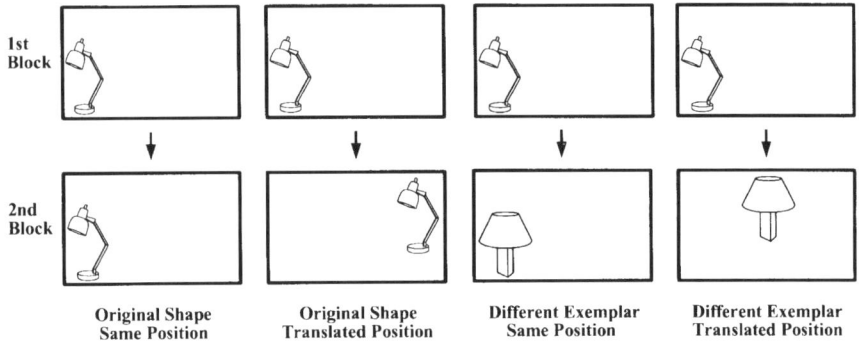

Figure 1: Each object from the first block repeated on the second block in one of four possible conditions. Shift in position was used to study translation invariance in subliminal priming, and different exemplars were used to estimate the semantic component in the priming.

Most of the experimental objects (86.5%) could not be identified on their first presentation (Figure 2). Accuracy increased substantially (21%) for naming objects of the same shape (i.e., same exemplars) when they repeated at the same location on the second block. The 4% increase in accuracy of naming the control objects over the course of the experiment reflects general improvement that is not attributable to priming. The 17% advantage of the same shape, same position objects over the second block control objects is therefore a manifestation of priming. When the same shape was repeated at a different position, the magnitude of priming was reduced to 8%. No priming was evident for the different exemplar conditions. Therefore, all the priming of the same-shape objects was visual; none could be attributed to verbal or semantic factors.[9]

Performance in the 4AFC test on the first block for objects that could not be named was at chance (25%). Consequently, we can assume that subjects were not aware of the identity of the objects that they could not name. Therefore, the priming was subliminal. This is the first demonstration of

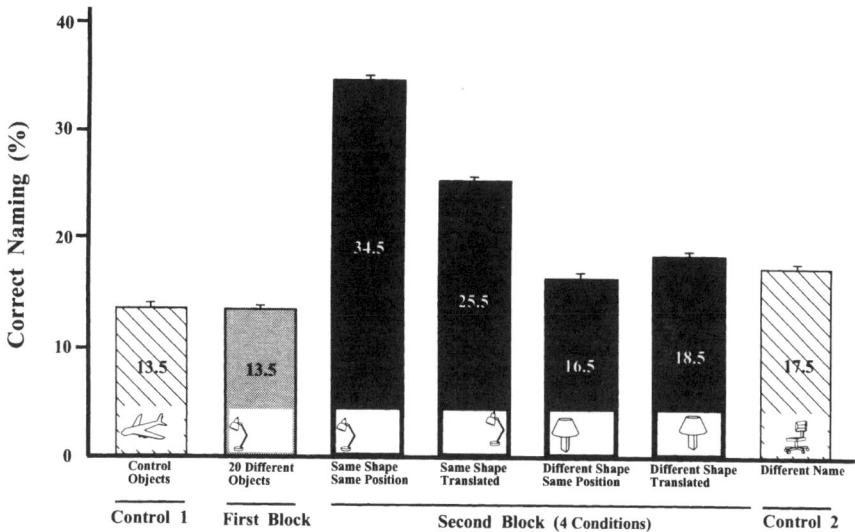

Figure 2: Percent correct in the naming task. Repeating the same image in the same position improved identification markedly. Translating the second presentation of the same image reduced but did not eliminate the priming. Objects with the same name but different shape (i.e., different exemplars) demonstrated no significant priming. (After Bar & Biederman 1998, with permission.)

facilitatory visual recognition priming by unidentified pictures when the subject could not anticipate if, when, or where the previously unidentified picture was to be shown again.

It is always possible to argue that subjects experienced a fleeting awareness (Crick & Koch 1990) during a subliminal presentation but could not report it. The *attentional blink* is one such example. In a rapid serial visual presentation (RSVP) of words, it has been demonstrated that subjects are "blind" to stimuli appearing during the first 400–600 ms following the target they have to detect (Shapiro, Raymond & Arnell 1994). For example, if the sequence of images includes A – B – F – G – H – K – J – Y – T (where different letters here represent different stimuli in the experiment), and subjects have to detect both H and K, the K would be detectable only if it is separated by more than 500 ms (on average) from the H. Using event-related potentials (ERP), it was later shown that subjects can, in fact, recognize the stimuli presented during the attentional blink (Luck, Vogel & Shapiro 1996), but fail to report it. This result suggests that subjects were aware of the identity for some time but could not report it when asked. Further experiments are required in order to determine whether the backward masking used with the brief presentations of stimuli in the Bar & Biederman (1998) study interfered with processing or reporting.

Cortical regions mediating awareness of object identity

Little is known about the neural mechanisms underlying visual priming. Nevertheless, the studies reviewed above allow for several conjectures and speculations that will be described here, following a brief introduction on the functional organization of visual cortex.

From the primary visual cortex, V1, information is propagated along two main pathways: the ventral and the dorsal (Ungerleider & Mishkin 1982). The dorsal pathway processes information such as object position, size, and orientation, that is typically used for motor interactions. The ventral pathway, V1→ V2 → V4 → inferior temporal (IT), is believed to be responsible for the processing of shape and other cues of identity, and is largely invariant to transformations in position, size, and (to a certain extent) depth rotation. The anterior part of IT (area TE) is the last solely visual area. It is thus considered the "output" of the ventral visual pathway, and is the main source of projection to areas outside the visual cortex such as the hippocampus, prefrontal cortex, amygdala, and basal ganglia. Lesion studies suggest that while area IT serves short-term memory for shape, the projections to the hippocampus are vital for long-term coding (Miyashita 1993).

Neurons of the temporal visual cortex in the macaque are ordered in a rough hierarchy along two dimensions: cells in anterior areas have larger receptive fields (RFs), and they prefer more complex features than cells in posterior areas. Therefore, cells in the primary visual cortex (V1) have small RFs (typically < 1°; Roe & Ts'o 1995), and are sensitive to simple stimuli (e.g., oriented lines). On the other hand, cells in IT are sensitive to complex stimuli (e.g., faces), and have large RFs (averaging 26°; Desimone & Gross 1979). RFs in IT, however, vary largely within its subdivisions: RFs in its posterior part (area TEO) are similar to those of cells in V4 (Boussaoud, Desimone & Ungerleider 1991), whereas RFs in its anterior part, area TE, can be as large as 60° (Desimone & Gross 1979). Lesion studies in the subdivisions of IT indicate that TEO is important for pattern discrimination while TE is vital for object memory (Iwai & Mishkin 1968; Iwai & Mishkin 1969). Furthermore, stimulus familiarization affects the tuning of IT cells (Ringo 1996), and object naming produces enhanced activation in that area (Martin, Wiggs, Ungerleider & Haxby 1996). Consequently, area IT is believed to have a fundamental role in visual object recognition (Kobatake & Tanaka 1994; Miyashita 1993).

In light of this cortical organization, Bar and Biederman (1998) proposed that one possible interpretation of their results is that the first presentations that were not identified did not affect a sufficient number of the cells representing that object in TE. Therefore, it is possible that the subliminal priming is a consequence of a change in intermediate areas prior to TE. These intermediate representations might not be available for conscious report such as naming, but, when combined with the activity of a second presentation of the same stimulus, the resultant activity might be sufficient for identification.

Bar and Biederman (1998) noted that this hypothesis is consistent with the size of RFs of cells in the ventral visual pathway, and the effect of translation on subliminal visual priming.[10] Cells with larger RFs have a greater chance of being activated by translated presentations, and cells in different visual areas have RFs of different sizes. Therefore, priming that is mediated by different areas will result in different degrees of position invariance. For example, when most of the objects were recognizable also on the first block (i.e., supraliminal), priming has been shown to be completely translation invariant for a translation extent of 4.8° (Biederman & Cooper 1991). Supraliminal visual priming is therefore likely to affect an area with RFs large enough to accommodate such translation (e.g., TE).

The 4.9° shift that was used in the Bar & Biederman (1998) experiment cannot be accommodated at all by the small RFs of cells in early areas such as V1/V2, but would be fully accommodated by the large RFs of most cells in TE, resulting in a complete translation invariance. Therefore, we proposed that partial translation cost indicates that the effect of subliminal visual priming may be concentrated in a cortical area where cells have RFs of intermediate size. Likely candidates are the human homologues of areas V4, where the RFs size, 0.7° — 10° (Tanaka, Weber & Creutzfeldt 1986)[11] would straddle the 4.9° shift, and TEO in which cells have RFs similar to those of V4.

This hypothesis was later tested (Bar & Biederman 1999) by comparing the properties of subliminal visual priming with known physiological characteristics of cells in intermediate visual areas. Namely, using the propensity of cells in V4 and TEO to have RFs that are confined to a single quadrant of the visual field (Boussaoud, Desimone, & Ungerleider 1991). Cells in area TE, on the other hand, have RFs that often cover multiple quadrants. In this experiment, images were translated either between different quadrants or within the same quadrant. Subliminal priming was obtained only for images that remained within the same quadrant in both prime and test trials. In other words, although the extent of translation and eccentricity were identical in both conditions, crossing a midline of the visual field eliminated the priming. Therefore, subliminal visual priming is likely mediated by cortical areas in which cells have RFs large enough to respond to both presentations of a stimulus shifted 4.8°, but at the same time are confined to a single quadrant (e.g., V4, and TEO). Consequently, visual awareness of object identity might be associated exclusively with activity at area TE or beyond.

A recent functional Magnetic Resonance Imaging (fMRI) study was designed to address the cortical mechanisms associated exclusively with conscious object recognition (Bar *et al.* 1999), using subliminal visual priming as a tool. The specific goal was to image the cortical activity elicited by trials in which participants were able to recognize pictures of familiar objects, and to compare it with the activity elicited by trials in which they could not recognize the same set of objects. The visual stimulation and the task requirements were identical in both cases; the only difference was subjects' ability to identify the objects. Consequently, any resulting differential activity should reveal the cortical focus and dynamics directly associated with the moment when subjects can first recognize an object explicitly.

Participants were scanned while they performed an object recognition task. In this task, pictures of familiar objects were presented very briefly, interposed between two masks. Participants were required to recognize each of the objects and to respond by pressing one of four buttons, indicating their level of confidence as to the identity of the object. The same object image was repeated, intermixed with the presentation of the other objects, for up to five times. As demonstrated by reports of subliminal visual priming (Bar & Biederman 1998, 1999), presenting the same objects repeatedly provides participants with multiple opportunities for successful recognition of those objects.

A visual cortical focus in the anterior fusiform gyrus was identified that was modulated exclusively by the ability to recognize objects. As subjects gained more information regarding an object's identity, activity in the temporal lobe intensified and propagated anteriorly and laterally. These findings support reports of single-unit studies in monkeys that revealed a cortical hierarchy of object representation in the temporal lobe. We suggested that information about objects is also represented in the fusiform in a hierarchical manner, such that shape properties and appearance-related information are represented in the posterior parts of the fusiform, whereas knowledge about object name and meaning is represented in the anterior parts.

Furthermore, these results suggest that the frontal cortex may have a special role in coping with difficult tasks such as recognition of briefly presented objects. Because the activity in the frontal lobe was more substantial in the masked presentations, it may reflect a general increased effort during the recognition attempt, or the manifestation of feedback signals and top-down processes, which may have had a more central role in the masked trials. This activation is possibly related to the semantic analysis involved in recognition. At the moment, it cannot be determined whether this frontal activity started only after recognition has been accomplished, or already before that moment. However, it is conceivable that when recognition is difficult (e.g., brief and masked presentations), top-down processes could facilitate successful recognition (Ullman 1995), and therefore may be expected to be active even before recognition has been accomplished.

Dissociation and cooperation in visual cognition

Priming in general, and subliminal visual priming in particular, can be seen as empirical support for the possibility that processes of which subjects are unaware can nevertheless facilitate performance. Before turning to describe more examples of facilitatory nonconscious contribution, two exceptions will be mentioned. The first is *negative priming*. In a typical study of negative priming (Tipper 1985; DeSchepper & Treisman 1996), two superimposed shapes, in different colors, are presented on each trial. Subjects are required to ignore one of them (e.g., the red) and attend the other (e.g., the green). If the stimuli are pictures of familiar objects, the task is often to name the attended object as fast as possible. If the stimuli are novel unfamiliar shapes, a typical task is a match-to-sample. The general finding is that when a previously ignored object becomes the relevant object in another trial (by switching its color to green), response time is significantly slower. Although the increase is often modest (tens of ms), the effect has been found to be robust. Therefore, in negative priming, implicit knowledge from the priming stage interferes with subsequent performance without subjects' intention.

A second exception is the inclusion-exclusion dissociation task of Jacoby (1991). As reviewed earlier, Jacoby and his colleagues (Jacoby *et al.* 1993; Debner & Jacoby 1994) found that subliminally presented words were given equally often in inclusion and exclusion tasks, suggesting a nonintentional use of memory. Both instances are taken to reflect involuntary processing that degrades, rather than facilitates performance.

In addition to visual priming of object recognition, in which subjects gain information of which they are not aware, there are other examples of sub-threshold stimuli that affect performance in a way that supports a "dissociation but cooperation" principle. Two studies that will be reviewed in this context represent two extremes: one involves cognitive judgments of liking, and the other includes low-level perceptual tasks such as orientation detection of basic spatial cues.

In the first study (Murphy & Zajonc 1993), non-Chinese speakers were required to rank their liking of Chinese ideographs. The ideographs were preceded by a prime stimulus: a face with either an angry or a happy expression. The primes were presented half of the time above threshold and half of the time subliminally (such that subjects could not even detect that there was a prime on those trials). The affective prime biased the judgment so that priming with a happy face resulted in an increased liking of the ideographs, and priming with an angry face resulted in a decreased liking of the ideographs. While the influence of subliminal priming on affective judgments has been demonstrated in the past (Zajonc 1968), it is interesting that in the study of Murphy & Zajonc the prime itself is a highly complex stimulus and is likely to be analyzed by cells in IT (Rolls & Tovee 1994). Therefore, durations that were too fast for detecting the presence of the prime were nevertheless sufficient for interpreting the face expression.

In another study (Tanaka & Sagi 1998), subjects had to detect oriented gratings (a Gabor signal in this case) that were presented for 90 ms, and that were preceded by a prime stimulus that had the same spatial frequency but a different contrast. The contrast of the prime could be either very low (near-threshold), or high enough to be detectable. Priming the target with a subliminal prime facilitated detection by 40%. This priming effect could persist for as long as 16 seconds. High contrast primes (supraliminal) did not facilitate the detection of the target. Therefore, a sub-threshold stimulus may facilitate performance with targets of different complexity, and in various tasks.

Stimuli such as gratings are usually analyzed and resolved by earlier visual areas (e.g., V1/V2). On the other hand, subliminal visual priming in object recognition has been suggested by Bar and Biederman (1998; 1999) to take place higher along the ventral pathway (e.g., V4 or TEO), whereas supraliminal priming is likely to affect even higher areas such as TE. In spite of the different loci, these different types of priming all seem to manifest similar cooperation between nonconscious gain and subsequent explicit reports.

Correlating visual awareness with cortical activity

If we could measure all the activity elicited by a brief presentation, and could define the visual properties to which this activity corresponds, then we could compare it with subjects' report. Any difference is likely to represent activity, and possibly knowledge, of which subjects were not aware. For example, if we know that a certain stimulus elicited activity in an (imaginary) area that is dedicated to, say, "circles-processing," and at the same time the subject cannot report seeing circles, we can say that the subject is unaware of the activity in that area. Using picture naming and 4AFC tests provided one end of this contrast: an assessment of subjective awareness of object identity. A comparison will now be made between this behavioral assessment and physiological data obtained in similar experimental designs.

In an imaging study of the cortical activity during object classification, subjects had to judge if there was an animal in a briefly presented picture (Thorpe, Fize & Marlot 1996). The stimuli were color photographs of natural scenes that were presented for 20 ms. An ERP signal in the frontal cortex was found to be discriminative even for such brief exposure durations. Therefore, 20 ms presentations were sufficient for processing the visual information required for performing this detection task. However, the images in this study were not masked. It might be that the same discriminative activity would not develop when a mask follows the stimuli.

In another study (Rolls & Tovee 1994), pictures of faces were presented for 16 ms, and were either followed by a mask or not. Activity of single cells in the visual temporal cortex of macaques (superior temporal sulcus; STS) was recorded while the animals viewed these brief presentations. When there was no mask, the response of the cells lasted for 200–300 ms, perhaps to allow memory consolidation (Potter 1976; Biederman, Subramaniam & Madigan 1994). However, this prolonged activity was reduced by masking, such that cells fired for 20–30 ms before the mask interrupted their activity. Analysis using techniques from information theory (Tovee, Rolls, Treves & Bellis 1993) suggested that the first 20 ms of activity contained 64.9% of the information available from the total prolonged response of the cell, and 50 ms contained 87%.[12] Therefore, (a) masked presentations in the range of 20–40 ms can be sufficient for performing high-level visual tasks (though it is not clear that these durations would suffice for more complicated tasks such as object naming), (b) the response of cells in IT to a brief stimulus is sustained for much longer than is required for certain discrimination tasks, and (c) this response is gradually more diagnostic of the object.

The stimuli in those experiments were faces, rather than objects. Faces differ from other objects in many respects (e.g., frequency of occurrence, social and ecological importance, and class-similarity), and they thus might have different cortical substrates and underlying mechanisms. The next study that will be described in this context, then, is a study where the stimuli were masked line drawings, and thus more similar to the stimuli of Bar and Biederman (1998).

In studying the cortical correlates of visual masking in IT, Kovács, Vogels, and Orban (1995) demonstrated that the mask does not reduce the response of cells in TEO and TE to the target, but rather shortens it. Before the effect of the mask, the activity during the first 20 ms was shape-specific. In addition, the average number of spikes in the first 20 ms period of the response was not significantly different in the masked and unmasked conditions. However, when a mask did not follow the 20 ms presentation, the shape-selective response persisted much longer. Therefore, these results extend those of Rolls and his colleagues to masked line drawings.

It seems that during the initial response the cells "know" more than the monkey can report. One possible, though speculative, account is the following: Assume that it takes cells in area TE (or an area to which TE is projecting) some time to reach the "final decision" as to the identity of the stimulus, such that eventually only the population that represents the specific object continues to fire. This interval is likely to stem from a need for integration of incoming information over time, for binding complex features, or for selecting the correct identity from among multiple possible interpretations of the input, and is often very short. Indeed, recent physiological evidence (Tamura & Tanaka 1997) suggests that the response of cells in the visual cortex to an image of an object is initially broad and less selective, and gradually reduces while becoming more stimulus-specific.

A similar fine-tuning process is assumed to take place in all areas of the visual ventral pathway such that each area processes over time the information that is projected to it from other areas, and gradually (though within a short interval) projects information that is more and more accurate. We may consider the initial, coarse activity as a set of multiple hypotheses regarding the identity (see also Ullman 1995). For example, if the initial (possibly crude) information will be first interpreted as a "circle," the cells that represent a ball, a coin, and a plate will all be active because they all have the "circular" property. As the incoming information is becoming more accurate (or fine-tuned), only one representation will remain active, the one that best corresponds to the specific object, while the others will be suppressed.

Projecting these results, analysis, and proposal to the findings of Bar & Biederman (1998), it seems that the brief presentation durations are capable of activating cells probably even in TE. This activity might have contained sufficient information to specify the identity of the object. The reason subjects could not report the stimulus might be that they were not aware of this activity as it was not sufficiently "fine-tuned," and that the mask interfered before the fine-tuning has been completed (Bar, submitted).

Summary

In the studies reviewed here, performance was often improved in spite of the dissociation between the implicit gain and explicit reports. The phenomenon of subliminal visual priming was reviewed here as an instance of such nonconscious interaction that promotes conscious knowledge.

The effect of a primed image, even if it is unidentified, is robust over time and intervening information. It is therefore likely to be accompanied by long lasting synaptic modifications. A hypothesis as to the cortical localization of subliminal visual priming suggests that the locus of this interaction be in an intermediate site along the visual cortex (Bar & Biederman 1998; 1999). Nevertheless, priming demonstrated in different tasks might affect different cortical areas, and therefore such interaction might take place in several possible loci along the visual cortex. The level at which subjects are aware of the prime stimulus likely depends on the area in which priming has concentrated. Consequently, the information subjects can report explicitly is determined by the complexity of the visual information that is processed by the primed area.

In addition, it was also suggested that observers become aware of certain visual aspects of the input only after their analysis have been accomplished to a certain degree. This can be achieved via a gating mechanism that projects information to areas such as the prefrontal cortex only after the sensory information has been fine-tuned sufficiently to allow an unequivocal interpretation of the input. Such gating mechanism should exist in conjunction with other mechanisms that permit quick and coarse analysis of the input to facilitate processes that aid survival (e.g., fight-or-flight).

Acknowledgments

I would like to thank I. Biederman for collaborating and inspiring, to A. Revonsuo, P. Merikle, and an anonymous reviewer for helpful comments and to J. Bichsel for proofreading. Most of this work was completed while MB was at the Psychology department, University of Southern California. Partially supported by the McDonnell-Pew Cognitive Neuroscience Award, 99–6 CNS-QUA.05. Address correspondence to: bar@nmr.mgh.harvard.edu

Notes

1. In word stem completion tests, the task is usually to complete a stem with the first word that comes to mind. This test might be preceded by a study phase in which subjects are presented with a list of words.

2. Object *naming, identification,* and *recognition* are all considered equivalent here. In all three, subjects have to recognize the identity of an object by providing its name.

3. The discussion here is limited to visual awareness, which is narrower than self-awareness.

4. In the divided attention condition, subjects were also required to add two digits that flank the study word.

5. Baseline performance was defined as the frequency of providing a word from the study list as a completion in a non-match trial.

6. The conflicting information is initially fused, and the alterations begin only after a few seconds.

7.   In one of the most comprehensive critiques of subliminal (semantic) perception, Holender (1986) asserted that forced-choice tests are exclusive measures of awareness. Tasks such as forced-choice are optimal as they rule out effects of intention, and by this are likely to "filter" the subjective component of the response.

8.   Translation invariance is the invariance in the magnitude of priming to changes in position between prime and test presentations.

9.   The subjective impression, occasionally volunteered by the participants, was that the primed images (those that were recognized correctly only on the second block) were presented for a longer duration. Interestingly, Witherspoon & Allan (1985) have found that when subjects had to judge temporal durations of briefly presented words, they tended to overestimate the duration of words that were presented before, compared with their judgment of novel words.

10. It is assumed that priming requires reactivation of the same cells that were initially activated by the prime. Consequently, translation invariance is obtained when the new stimulus position allows activation of the previously activated cells.

11. Assuming that the size of RFs of humans are similar to those of monkeys.

12. In this regard, it is interesting that it is difficult to associate the 87% knowledge contained in the first 50 ms of activity reported by Tovee *et al.* (1993) with subjects' performance. For example, does 87% include figural detail? Global shape? Aspect-ratio? Being able to name the object might require exactly 100%.

References

Bar, M. & Biederman, I. (1998). Subliminal visual priming. *Psychological Science*, 9. 464–469.

Bar, M. & Biederman, I. (1999). Localizing the cortical region mediating visual awareness of object identity. *Proceedings of The National Academy of Sciences*, USA, 96, 1790–1793.

Bar M., Tootell R., Schacter D., Greve D., Mendola J., Rosen B. and Dale A. (1999). Where in the cortex do we associate visual shape with object identity? *Soc. Neurosci. Abstr.*, 25, 529.

Bar, M. Efficient and deficient coding in visual memory. Submitted.

Bartram, D. (1974). The role of visual and semantic codes in object naming. *Cognitive Psychology*, 6, 325–356.

Biederman, I. & Cooper, E.E. (1991). Evidence for complete translational and reflective invariance in visual object priming. *Perception*, 20, 585–593.

Biederman, I., Subramaniam, S. & Madigan, S. (1994). Chance forced choice recognition memory for identifiable RSVP object pictures. In the *35th Annual meetings of the Psycholomics Society. St. Louis, MO.*

Boussaoud, D., Desimone, R. & Ungerleider, L. (1991). Visual topographyof area TEO in the macaque. *J. Comparative Neurology, 306*, 554–575.

Cave, C. B. (1997). Very long-lasting priming in picture naming. *Psychological Science, 8*, 322–325.

Cave, C.B. & Squire, L.R. (1992). Intact and long-lasting repetition priming in amnesia. *Journal of Experimental Psychology: Learning, Memory and Cognition, 18*, 509- 520.

Cheesman, J. & Merikle, P. (1984). Priming with and without awareness. *Perception & Psychonophysics, 36*, 387–395.

Crick, F. & Koch, C. (1990). Towards a neurobiological theory of consciousness. *Seminars in the Neursciences, 2*, 263–275.

Debner, J. & Jacoby, L. (1994). Unconscious perception: Attention, awareness, and control. *Journal of Experimental Psychology: Learning, Memory and Cognition, 20*, 304–317.

DeSchepper, B. & Treisman, A. (1996). Visual memory for novel shapes: Implicit coding without attention. *Journal of Experimental Psychology: Learning, Memory and Cognition, 22*, 27–47.

Desimone, R. & Gross, C. G. (1979). Visual areas in the temporal cortex of the macaque. *Brain Research, 178*, 363–380.

Dow, B.M., Snyder, A.Z., Vautin, R. G. & Bauer, R. (1981). Magnification factor and receptive field size in foveal striate cortex of the monkey. *Experimental Brain Research, 44*, 213–228.

Goodale, M., Meenan, J., Bülthoff, H., Nicolle, D., Murphy, K. & Racicot, C. (1994). Separate neural pathways for the visual analysis of object shape in perception and prehension. *Current Biology, 4*, 604–610.

Graf, P. & Mandler, G. (1984). Activation makes words more accessible, but not necessarily more retrievable. *Journal of Verbal Learning and Verbal Behavior, 23*, 553–568.

Green, D.M. & Swets, J.A. (1996). *Signal detection theory and psychophysics.* New York: Wiley.

Greenwald, A. G., Draine, S. C. & Abrams, R. L. (1996). Three cognitive markers of unconscious semantic activation. *Science, 273*, 1699–1702.

Holender, D. (1986). Semantic activation without conscious identification in dichotic listening. parafoveal vision, and visual masking: A survey and appraisal. *Behavioral and Brain Sciences, 9*, 1–66.

Iwai, E. & Mishkin, M. (1968). Two visual foci in the temporal lobe of monkeys. In N. Yoshii & N. Buchwald (Eds.), Neurophysiological basis of learning and behavior (pp. 1–8). Osaka: Osaka University Press.

Iwai, E. & Mishkin, M. (1969). Further evidence on the locus of the visual area in the temporal lobe of the monkey. Experimental Neurology, 25, 585–594.

Jacoby, L. L. (1983). Perceptual enhancement: Persistent effects of an experience. *Journal of Experimental Psychology: Learning, Memory and Cognition, 9*, 21–38.

Jacoby, L. L. (1991). A process dissociation framework: Separating automatic from intentional uses of memory. *J. of Memory and Language, 30*, 513–541.

Jacoby. L.L., Toth, J. & Yonelinas, A. (1993). Separating conscious and unconscious influences of memory: Measuring recollection. *Journal of Experimental Psychology: General, 122*, 139–154.

Kobatake, E. & Tanaka, K. (1994). Neuronal selectivities to complex object features in the ventral visual pathway of the macaque cerebral cortex. *Journal of europhysiology, 71*, 856–857.

Koch, C. & Braun, J. (1996). Towards the neuronal correlate of visual awareness. *Current opinion in neurobiology* (pp. 158–164).

Kolb, F. & Braun, J. (1995). Blindsight in normal observers. *Nature, 377,* 336–338.

Kovács, G., Vogels, R. & Orban, G. (1995). Cortical correlate of pattern backward masking. *Proceedings of the National Academy of Science, 92,* 5587–5591.

Kunst-Wilson, W.R. & Zajonc, R.B. (1980). Affective discrimination of stimuli that cannot be recognized. *Science, 207,* 557–558.

Leopold, D. & Logothetis, N.K. (1996). Activity changes in early visual cortex reflect monkeys' percepts during binocular rivalry. *Nature, 379,* 549–553.

Logothetis, N.K. & Leopold, D. (1996). What is rivaling during binocular rivalry? *Nature, 380,* 621–624.

Logothetis, N.K. & Schall, J. (1989). Neuronal correlates of subjective visual perception. *Science, 245,* 761–763.

Luck, S., Vogel, E. & Shapiro, K.L. (1996). Word meanings can be accessed but not reported during the attentional blink. *Nature, 383,* 616–618.

Marcel, A. (1983). Conscious and unconscious perception: Experiments on visual masking and work recognition. *Cognitive Psychology, 15,* 197–237.

Martin, A., Wiggs, C. L., Ungerleider, L. G. & Haxby, J. V. (1996). Neural correlates of category-specific knowledge. *Nature, 379,* 649–652.

Meeres, S. & Graves, R. (1990). Localization of unseen visual stimuli by humans with normal vision. *Neuropsychologia, 28,* 1231–1237.

Merikle, P., Joordens, S. & Stolz, J. (1995). Measuring the relative magnitude of unconscious influences. *Consciousness & Cognition, 4,* 422–439.

Milner, A. & Goodale, M. (1995). *The visual brain in action.* New York: Oxford University Press.

Miyashita, Y. (1993). Inferior temporal cortex: Where visual perception meets memory. *Ann. Rev. Neurosci., 16,* 245–263.

Murphy, S. T. & Zajonc, R. B. (1993). Affect, cognition, and awareness: Affective priming with optimal and suboptimal exposures. *Journal of Personality and Social Psychology, 64,* 723–739.

Potter, M. C. (1976). Short-term conceptual memory for pictures. *Journal of Experimental Psychology: Human Learning and Memory, 2.* 509–522.

Ringo, J. L. (1996). Stimulus specific adaptation in inferior temporal and medial temporal cortex of the monkey. *Behavioral Brain Research, 76,* 191–197.

Roe, A. W. & Ts'o, D.Y. (1995). Visual topography in primate V2: Multiple epresentation across functional stripes. *Journal of Neuroscience, 5,* 3689–3715.

Rolls, E. T. & Tovee, M. (1994). Processing speed in the cerebral cortex and the neurophsiology of visual masking. *Proceedings of the Royal Society of London B, 257,* 9–15.

Schacter, D. L., Dulaney, S. M. & Merikle, E. P. (1990). Priming of nonverbal information and the nature of implicit memory. In G. H. Bower (Ed.), *The Psychology of Learning and Motivation,* Volume 26 (pp. 83–123). New York: Academic Press.

Shapiro, K., Raymond, J. & Arnell, K. (1994). Attention to visual pattern information produces the attentional blink in rapid serial visual presentation. *Journal of Experimental Psychology: Human Perception and Performance, 20,* 357–371.

Sidis, B. (1898). *The psychology of suggestion.* New York: D. Appleton and Company.

Sloman, S. A., Hayman, C. A. G., Ohta, N., Law, J. & Tulving, E. (1998). Forgetting in primed fragment completion. *Journal of Experimental Psychology: Learning, Memory and Cognition, 14*, 223–239.

Stoerig, P. (1993). Sources of blindsight. *Science, 261*, 493–496.

Swets, J. (1961). Is there a sensory threshold? *Science, 134*, 168–177.

Tamura, H. & Tanaka, K. (1997). Recurrent circuits contribute to the formation of stimulus selectivity in the inferotemporal cortex. *Soc. Neurosci. Abstr., 23*, 2063.

Tanaka, M., Weber, H. & Creutzfeldt, O. D. (1986). Visual properties and spatial distribution of neurons in the visual association area on the prelunate gyrus of the awake monkey. *Experimental Brain Research, 65*, 11–37.

Tanaka, Y. & Sagi, D. (1998). A perceptual memory for low contrast visual signals. *Proceeding of the national Academy of Sciences*, USA. 95, 12729–12733.

Thorpe, S., Fize, D. & Marlot, C. (1996). Speed of processing in the human visual system. *Nature, 381*, 520–522.

Tipper, S. (1985). The negative priming effect: inhibitory priming by ignored objects. *Quarterly Journal of Experimental Psychology, 37A*, 571–590.

Tovee, M., Rolls, E., Treves, A. & Bellis, R. (1993). Information encoding and the responses of single neurons in the primate temporal visual cortex. *J. Neurophsiology, 70*, 640–654.

Tulving, E. & Schacter, D. L. (1900). Priming and human memory systems. *Science, 247*, 301–306.

Ullman, S. (1995). Sequence seeking and counter streams: A computational model for bidirectional information flow in the visual cortex. *Cerebral Cortex, 1*, 1–11.

Ungerleider, L. G. & Mishkin, M. (1982). Two cortical visual systems. In D. J. Ingle, M. A. Goodale & R. J. W. Mansfield (Eds.), *Analysis of visual behavior* (pp. 549- 586). MA: MIT.

Warrington, E. K. & Weiskrantz, L. (1974). The effect of prior learning on subsequent retention in amnesic patients. *Neuropsychologia, 12*, 419–428.

Weiskrantz, L. (1986). *Blindsight: A case study and implications*. Oxford: Clarendon Press.

Weiskrantz, L. & Warrington, E. K. (1970). A study of forgetting in amnesic patients. *Neoropsychologia, 8*, 281–288.

Witherspoon, D. & Allan, L. (1985). The effect of a prior presentation on temporal judgments in a perceptual identification task. *Memory & Cognition, 13*, 101–111.

Zajonc, R. B. (1968). Attitudinal effects of mere exposure. *Journal of Personality and Social Psychology Monograph Supplement, 9*, 1–27.

Dissociation between Conscious and Non-conscious Processing in Neglect

Elisabetta Làdavas
University of Bologna

Anna Berti
University of Padua

Alessandro Farnè
University of Bologna

Full dissociation between conscious and non-conscious processing

Stimulus awareness is considered to be the subjective or phenomenal experience of the existence of the stimulus and consequently of the recognition of its
physical and semantic properties.

Awareness of a stimulus is usually inferred from the subject's overt
behaviour or verbal report, consequent to stimulus presentation. If the subject
is aware of the stimulus then he or she can act upon it. As a consequence, in the
neuropsychological domain, the lack of any action upon stimulus presentation
has been taken as evidence of the patients' unawareness of the event. For
instance, patients with visual neglect who miss objects on the left side of the
environment, who do not interact with people when they are on the left side of
the room, and do not even eat the part of meal on the left side of the plate, have
been considered to lack phenomenal experience of left presented stimuli.
Many experimental studies confirmed, through formal testing of left space
events, that patients with neglect may not be able to overtly detect any kind of
left stimulus characteristic. The same pattern of results has been found in the
extinction phenomenon, in which the patient fails to detect a contralesional

stimulus (as in neglect) but only when another stimulus is concurrently presented at a more ispilesional location (Critchley 1949; De Renzi 1982). When an isolated contralesional stimulus is presented, detection is normal or close to normal (Làdavas et al. 1990).

An assumption that was initially made in the neglect literature is that, since the patient does not show any phenomenal experience of the neglected stimulus *then* the stimulus is not processed by the brain. This assumption was *neither logically* nor *experimentally* justified and prevented a better approach to the comprehension of the mechanisms of space representation for many years. Recently, the assumption has been, in fact, falsified by many evidences showing that both extinguished and neglected stimuli can be processed up to a high level.

Volpe, LeDoux and Gazzaniga (1979) asked four patients with right-parietal lesion and visual extinction to report whether or not two words or two line-drawings of objects, one on each side of the fixation point, were the same or different. Not only did two patients show extinction (i.e. they did not name any stimulus on the left side when presented simultaneously with another one on the right side), but they even claimed that the test was 'silly', since there was *no stimulus* on the left with which to compare the right stimulus. Nonetheless, the patients, asked to guess, gave almost perfect correct same/different judgements. This was interpreted as the presence of non-conscious processing of left side extinguished stimuli. Since in the study referred to when the stimuli were "the same" they were actually identical and when they were "different" they were by all means different, the implicit processing originating the correct judgement might have occurred at a very low level. In other words, patients implicit processing might have been based only on the computation of the physical characteristics of the stimuli. However, Berti and colleagues (1992) replicated the observation made by Volpe et al. (1979) by using stimuli with a different degree of complexity. Their study showed how correct same/different judgement could be achieved also when stimuli were physically different in the "same" condition and physically similar in the "different" condition. In other words, in order to give correct same/different judgements to such a complex comparing task, the implicit processing had to be carried out at the level of stimulus category.

In the neglect domain, Marshall and Halligan (1988), using a different experimental paradigm, also suggested that neglect patients can process the neglected stimuli beyond the perceptual level. They described the results of a patient with severe left neglect to whom they repeatedly presented two draw-ings of a house. The drawings were identical but for the presence of bright red flames appearing from a window on the left-hand side of one house. The patient denied any differences between the houses, but when asked which house she would have preferred to live in she tended to choose the one without flames. In other words, despite her inability to detect the difference between the two stimuli, the patient showed a consistent preference for a picture of a normal house over a picture of the same house with flames coming from its left side. According to the authors, the patient implicitly recognised the left salient features of the stimuli, but the outcome of such semantic processing did not reach the conscious level. However, the authors did not carried out any control test (i.e., direct questions, association tasks) in order to verify the presumed semantic elaboration. It is possible that the patient's choices were perceptually and not semantically based. Since the traced "flames" were graphical features which altered the canonical shape of the house, the patient may have rejected the "burning" house because it was physically anomalous and not because it was dangerous to live in.

After the seminal paper of Marshall and Halligan (1988) a number of studies have been published confirming the possibility of implicit processing in neglect patients. Berti and Rizzolatti (1992) showed that five patients with severe neglect always denied the presence of line drawing of objects tachisto-scopically presented to the left visual field. Presentation of left stimuli was followed by the presentation of a stimulus to the right visual field. Patients had to decide whether right-side stimuli belonged to the animal or fruit category. The authors found that reaction times to stimuli presented to the right visual field were influenced by the kind of relation existing between the right and the left stimulus. A facilitatory priming effect was observed when the two stimuli were either physically identical or, although not identical, they belonged to the same category of objects (fruit or animal). This result was interpreted as an evidence that, despite the lack of awareness of the presence of left stimuli, patients were able to extract enough information for their correct categorisa-tion. A similar priming effect of left-side stimuli on centrally presented pictures was shown by McGlinchey-Berroth and collaborators (1993) on four patients with visual neglect.

Làdavas, Paladini and Cubelli (1993) described a patient with neglect who was not able to detect the presence, to read aloud or to judge the lexical status and semantic content of left sided words. Nevertheless, this patient showed an associative priming effect from the neglected stimulus. Indeed, reaction times to words presented to the right visual field were influenced by the stimulus presented to the left visual field. When the word presented on the left was semantically associated with the word on the right, patients were faster in judging the lexical status of the words presented to the right visual field. The fact that reaction times were influenced by the relation between the meaning of the right and the left visual stimulus clearly shows that the left visual field stimuli were processed up to the semantic level.

Berti, Frassinetti and Umiltà' (1994) showed that a patient with neglect dyslexia made omission errors on the left side in reading regular words and colour words. For instance, he read the Italian word for brown, 'MARRONE', as 'ONE', which has no meaning in this language. Forced to say what word it might be, the patient said that it had some relation with power energy, a word like 'NEUTRONE' or 'PROTONE'. However, when asked to name the colour in which colour words were written (Stroop 1935), naming time was found to be longer when the meaning of the word was non congruent with the colour in which the word was written (e.g. the word 'MARRONE' written in red). In other words, the meaning of those words he was not able to read influenced his naming performance, showing that even though he did not seem to be aware of the existence of the left part of the words, the left side was processed up to the level of meaning.

The above reviewed studies show that a patient with a brain damage that prevents an overt detection and recognition of contralesional stimuli can nevertheless carry out many cognitive processes on stimuli which have been neglected. Not only can low-level physical characteristics be extracted, but even the level of meaning can be achieved *without stimuli reaching the threshold of awareness*. A tentative explanation of how it is possible to achieve a semantic representation of an object without being aware of it will be given in the following paragraphs.

Dissociation between the 'What' and the 'Where' of conscious experience

The findings discussed in the previous paragraph clearly demonstrate a *full* dissociation between conscious and non-conscious processing in the neglected field. Patients are unable to overtly identify *any* attribute of the stimuli, in spite of being able to covertly perform a post-perceptual processing of neglected stimuli. However, there are cases in which the dissociation between conscious and non-conscious processes can be drawn with respect to the representation of the "what" and the "where" of the stimulus attributes. It is well known that neglect patients may report contralesional sensory information as being perceived on the ipsilesional side and usually in a mirror-symmetrical location. This phenomenon has been termed 'allochiria' by Obersteiner (1982). Although it had formerly been known to occur only with respect to very elementary stimuli in the extra somatic domain, two recent observations have shown that allochiria may also manifest itself with complex visual stimuli. Halligan, Marshall and Wade (1992) described a patient who in copying a figure of a butterfly, although omitting the left wing, transposed some details of the missing wing to the right side of the drawing.

Similar results were found by Vallar et al. (1994) with asymmetrical chimeric figures. RG, a patient with left visual neglect, remarked that the animal depicted on the unidentified left side of the chimera could have been traced on its right side. While tracing the head of a kangaroo on a deer-left/kangaroo-right chimera, the patient said: "Here one could draw a deer". Likewise, while tracing the head of a swan on a shark-left/swan-right chimera, he said: "Here one could draw a shark". In both cases the patient had not recognised the chimeric nature of the drawing.

In a recent study (Làdavas, Bisiach, Perini & Bosinelli, in preparation), the previous observation has been confirmed by showing that information in the neglected field may be consciously processed up to the level of meaning attribution, even though localisation of the information is not consciously available. In other words, in this study the authors report a further example of a dissociation between the 'what' and the 'where' of conscious experience. The Rorschach cards were presented to right brain-damaged patients with left visual neglect without directional limb hypokinesia. The patients were required to tell what the picture looked like (interpretation task), to point to (pointing task) and to outline the contour of the whole configuration appearing on each card (outlining task).

The results showed that, in the interpretation task, patients provided responses based on the perception of the whole card. In contrast, when patients were required to point at, or outline, the configuration of which they had given an interpretation, they confined the manual responses to the right side of the configuration. It is worth noting that patients had visual neglect without directional limb hypokinesia and that information on the right side of the card was not sufficient to support recognition of the total configuration. When patients were presented with the half right-side of the card only and they were asked to give an interpretation, this was confined to elements located on the far right of the half card and, accordingly, the responses were qualitatively different from those given in the full card condition. In the pointing and outlining tasks, responses were limited to the far right of the half card, as it was found for the full card condition. It can therefore be concluded that whole responses given by the patient in the full card condition were based on the perception of the left half of the card and not on a phenomenological completion (Kaniza 1980), or on the information available on the right side of the card.

The overt processing of the left side of the original card can be explained considering the perceptual structure of the stimuli. Stimuli in the full card condition were perceptually very well structured because symmetry is a strong organisation factor. It has been shown in normal subjects that symmetry about the vertical axis exerts powerful effects on figure-ground segregation (Rock 1983). Therefore, sensitivity to symmetry in our patients can be considered as evidence of the representation of both left and right sides of the figures.

Of special interest were responses (double responses) suggesting allochiric-type phenomena whereby the content of the 'neglected' side of the picture is localised on the opposite (ipsilesional) side. These type of responses can (also) be considered as evidence of overt processing of the left objects presented in the neglected space. This would suggest that symmetry is not a necessary condition for overt processing of the neglected side.

We can conclude that in all these studies patients were able to *overtly* process left side stimuli even though the localisation of the information was not consciously available. In other words, patients were able to perceive objects located in the impaired spatial representation, but, due to the impairment of this representation, they could not locate the perceived object in that space. As a consequence, they located the objects in the intact space representation. This phenomenon corresponds to a dissociation between the 'what' and the 'where' of the conscious experience.

The issue of *implicit processing* of neglected stimuli and the finding of complex *allochiric phenomena* in neglect patients are important for they have, for the first time, raised the problem of how a full conscious experience of extrapersonal visual events may depend on the interaction between different cognitive representations. In the studies reviewed in the first paragraph (e.g.

Marshall & Halligan 1988; Berti & Rizzolatti 1993; McGlinchey-Berroth et al. 1993; Làdavas et al. 1993; Berti et al. 1994), the overt behaviour of neglect patients suggests the absence of stimulus awareness, whereas the implicit processing of left-side stimuli up to semantic level suggests that *object recognition* is intact or quasi-intact. The notion that object recognition may be unimpaired is dramatically shown in the studies reviewed in the present paragraph ((Vallar et al. 1994) and Làdavas et al. (in preparation)), in which patients showed an *explicit knowledge* of objects presented in the neglected field, although they were not aware of *where* the stimuli have been presented.

The extensive preserved object processing in neglect can be understood in terms of the known organization of the primate visual system. Two streams of cortical visual processing can be distinguished (Miskin et al. 1983; Milner & Goodale 1995): a 'dorsal' stream, which projects from the primary visual cortex via extra-striate regions into the upper regions of the parietal lobe, is thought to be involved in the spatial control of action. A more 'ventral' stream, which projects from the striate cortex via extra-striate regions into the temporal lobe, is concerned with object recognition. Damage to primary visual cortex (as in blind-sight cases) will disrupt the ventral object-recognition stream. As a consequence, blindsight patients are not able to recognize objects presented in the impaired portion of the visual field, although they can overtly localize the object that has been presented (Corbetta et al. 1990). By contrast, damage to the 'dorsal' stream leaves much of the ventral object-recognition stream intact, and, as a consequence, a preserved object recognition is found for the neglected objects.

The challenge for current neuropsychological studies is in explaining the dramatic loss of awareness despite the considerable processing that the neglected stimuli received within the ventral object-recognition system. A possible interpretation of the phenomenon of implicit knowledge of left-presented objects is that coding of space is a necessary prerequisite for conscious perception of the objects located in that space. In order to have conscious experience of spatially presented events, one needs a full activation of at least two representations: space representation and object representation. If the representation of space is impaired (as it is in neglect patients and patients with extinction) the activation of only one representation (object representation) is not enough to give the subjects the awareness of left-side presented stimuli. Object representation, carried out by brain areas which are different from those that carry out space processing, may be activated by the left stimulus and may be sufficient to accomplish unconscious processing of left presented stimuli but not conscious processing, and the patient remains unaware of what has been presented.

If the activation of left object representation is sufficient to gain *explicit knowledge* of the stimulus, the absence of a synergetic activation of left space representation induces the allochiric phenomenon. In this case, the patient has a full knowledge of what is presented but the impaired space representation does not allow a correct localisation of the stimulus. The synergy between the operation of different brain representations is therefore fundamental to achieve the ideal level of awareness of the external world for the subject's action.

How can overt responses be elicited in the neglected field

If awareness is strictly linked to the impairment of space representation, then stimulus awareness in neglect patients can be obtained by the activation of different spatial maps whose level of activation were diminished by the brain lesion. It is well known that stimulus awareness in neglect patients can be obtained through neurophysiological manipulation. If we induce caloric stimulation in patients with severe visual neglect, we may obtain a temporary remission of the symptomatology, during which the patients become aware of left presented stimuli (e.g. Cappa et al. 1987). One possible interpretation of this phenomenon is that central vestibular projections activate different spatial maps whose level of activation were diminished by the brain lesion. In this case the activation of these spatial maps is a direct consequence of a *physiological reflex*. However, phenomenal experience of the contralesional stimuli can be also *behaviourally* induced by specific manipulation of the experimental tasks, aimed at producing an activation of the damaged space representation.

Space perception is strictly related to the joint activity of multiple brain maps, which co-operate through mutual excitation or inhibition . If we conceive neglect as a representational deficit due to the competition between left and right space representations (Ward et al. 1994; di Pellegrino et al. 1997; Cohen et al. 1994; Làdavas et al. 1997), it becomes clear how the competition might operate on a number of different topographically mapped brain areas encoding both the input and output components of responses, each of them contributing to the construction of the perceived space representation. The unilateral damage of a brain area with a contralateral field representation results in a reduction of competitive weights in the affected field. After a right brain damage, the activation of the representation of contralateral sectors of space is weak and, as a consequence, the competition with intact ipsilesional space representations induces neglect in that sector of space. The antagonism between left and right space representation may be reduced (a) by the activation of an intact left space representation mapped in another right brain structure, which co-operates, through mutual excitation, with the damaged representation, (b) by the activation of an intact left representation of space integrated with the damaged one at the level of a single neuron, and (c) by an attentional strategic control of space coding. The reduction of this antagonism will produce a better level of activation of the left side representation of the space and, as a consequence, it will increase the level of awareness for stimuli presented in that portion of space.

Interaction between different space representations coded in different areas

As previously said, the antagonism between left and right space representation may be reduced by the activation of an intact left space representation mapped in another right brain structure, which co-operates, through mutual excitation, with the damaged representation. For example, the level of awareness of left-sided stimuli presented in the extrapersonal space can be increased by the activation of an intact left spatial representation, like the proprioceptive signals specifying the current hand positions. But, this can occur only if the two spatial maps are parts of an integrated system, i.e. the intact map is functionally linked to the damaged one. An example of this integrated system is given in recent studies by Halligan, Manning and Marshall (1991), Robertson and North (1992) and Làdavas, Berti, Ruozzi and Barboni (1997).

Halligan, Manning and Marshall (1991) showed that neglect in a line-bisection test was less severe when the left hand was used, although the effect disappeared when the subject was required to begin the task with his/her left hand positioned in the right space. Therefore, it seems that the spatial position of the hand, more than the responding hand, be the crucial factor in determining the modulation of neglect. However, this conclusion has been contradicted by Robertson and North (1992). Indeed, when patients with neglect were asked to make minimal finger movements in the left hemispace with either hand, a reduction of neglect was found *only* in the condition in which the left hand was making little movements in the left hemispace. This means that, in order to obtain a reduction of neglect, the hand (left) and the spatial position of the hand (left) have to be combined: neither right hand responses in the left hemispace nor left hand responses in the right hemispace produced an amelioration of neglect.

The amelioration of neglect under these circumstances (Robertson & North 1992) may be due to proprioceptive or visual aspects of spatial cueing. The left hand located in the left space may act as a powerful visual cue for the enhancement of the left visuo-spatial representation, in the same way as a visual stimulus presented in the periphery of the visual field (Làdavas et al. 1994; Posner et al. 1987; Posner & Rafal 1988). Alternatively, it is possible that the perceived hand location (due to the activation of the proprioceptive system) acts as an attentional field able to enhance the representation of the left space. In a recent study (Làdavas et al. 1997), in order to disentangle these two hypotheses, a sheet of paper, on which 42 line drawings of objects were printed, was positioned on a table in front of a mirror, and one patient's hand at a time, located on the table on the left or on the right side of the page, was passively moved by the experimenter. The direct view of the hand and of the stimuli was prevented by the use of a board placed above the hand. In this way, the hand, as well as the stimuli, could be seen only by looking at a 90° angle mirror (see Tégner & Levander 1991): the objects on the left side of the display were seen on the right half of the mirror, whereas the objects on the right side of the display were seen on the left half of the mirror. The patient's task was to name the objects projected on the mirror. In this study, the authors found that neglect patients were more accurate in naming left side objects when the left hand located in the left space was passively moved in comparison with the condition in which the left hand was located in the centre or in the right space. Since the stimuli and the hand were reflected in a mirror that inverted right and left space and the direct view of the stimuli and of the stimulated hand was prevented by a board, the better performance was clearly due to the proprioceptive information related to the limb position and not to visual cueing. This study clearly shows that the activation of *the intact proprioceptive information related to the position of the limb* was able to modulate the impaired representation related to extrapersonal space. Thus, the antagonism between left and right extrapersonal space was reduced in this study by the activation of one intact representation of the space, which co-operates through mutual excitation with the damaged representation, and, as a consequence, patients were able to detect the previously ignored left-sided stimuli.

As already said, in this study the effect was due to the interaction between two different spatial representations, each coded in separate brain areas. However, the modulatory effect of one intact representation on a damaged one can also be achieved at the level of a single neuron.

Interaction between different space representations coded at a level of a single neuron

In a study by Làdavas, di Pellegrino, Farnè and Zeloni (1998a, see also di Pellegrino et al. 1997 and Làdavas et al. 1998b), the authors addressed the question of whether the competition between left and right representations of space in one sensory modality (i.e., touch) can be reduced or exacerbated by the activation of an intact spatial representation in a different modality, function-ally linked to the damaged representation (i.e., vision). This hypothesis was tested in ten right-hemisphere lesioned patients who suffered from reliable tactile extinction. The authors found that a visual stimulus presented near the patient's *ipsilesional hand (or face)* (i.e., visual peripersonal space) inhibited the processing of a tactile stimulus delivered on the contralesional hand (or face) (cross-modal visuo-tactile extinction) to the same extent as an ipsile-sional tactile stimulation (unimodal tactile extinction). Moreover, and more important to the aim of the present paragraph, it was also found that a visual stimulus presented near the *contralesional hand (or face)* improved the detec-tion of a tactile stimulus applied to the same hand (or face). In striking contrast, only very week modulatory effects of vision on touch perception were ob-served when a visual stimulus was presented far from the space immediately surrounding the patient's hand (or face) (i.e., extrapersonal space).

This study clearly demonstrates the existence of an integrated visuo-tactile system for coding visual peripersonal space, centred on the hand or the face, which is responsible for the modulatory effects of visual spatial informa-tion on tactile perception.

Results from animal research help to illuminate the nature of the mecha-nism underlying the inhibitory and facilitatory effects of vision on touch perception reported here, and to clarify how such a mechanism operates to co-ordinate visual and tactile representations of space. Single-cell recording studies in monkeys show that the ventral intra-parietal area (VIP area), the premotor area 6, and the putamen, a large subcortical nucleus forming part of the basal ganglia, appear to represent visual space near the body (Duhamel et al. 1991; Gentilucci et al. 1988; Graziano & Gross 1994; Graziano & Gross 1993). These areas have tactile neurons that respond also to visual stimuli: their bimodal cells have visual receptive fields which match in space the location of the tactile receptive fields, and are confined in depth to a region near the animal. Since the tactile fields are arranged somatotopically, the associated visual receptive fields form a map of the visual space immediately around the body, which is thus coded in body-part-centred co-ordinates and not in retinal or other egocentric reference systems. Therefore, these areas provide an integrated (visuo-tactile) system for coding peripersonal space. As a consequence of this sensory integration, the activation of these bimodal neurons by a visual stimulus presented near the hand also activates the corresponding somesthesic representation of the hand.

Since extinction, as well as neglect, become manifest when there is a competition between two (Ward et al. 1994; di Pellegrino et al. 1997; Cohen et al. 1994) or more spatial representations (Làdavas et al. 1997), the simulta-neous activation of the somatosensory representation of the left hand (or face) by a tactile stimulus, and of the right hand (or face) by a visual stimulus produces an extinction of the stimuli presented in the weaker representation, i.e. the left hand (or face). Likewise, the stimulation of the visual space near the left hand (or face) results in the enhancement of the damaged (and hence weak) somatosensory representation of the left hand (or face). This stimula-tion is thus able to correct the abnormal bias towards the ipsilesional hand (or face) representation and, as a consequence, left tactile extinction improves substantially.

Single-neurons studies also showed that visuo-tactile bimodal cells are less active when visual stimuli are administered far from the hand (or face), i.e., in the extrapersonal space (Gentilucci et al. 1988; Graziano & Gross 1994). This neurophysiological evidence is consistent with the impressive reduction of cross modal extinction and the absence of visuo-tactile facilita-tion, found in the study by Làdavas et al. when the visual stimulus was presented far from the hand (or face). Visual events presented far from the ipsilesional hand (or face) (extrapersonal space) did not compete with left tactile stimuli, as did visual events presented near the hand (or face). Thus, this study suggests the existence of a unified attentional system that controls both visual and tactile inputs within peripersonal space, and it shows how this system is functionally separated from the one which controls visual informa-tion in the extrapersonal space.

Due to the existence of this integrated visuo-tactile system, the antagonism between left and right space representations may be reduced, and, as a consequence, the level of awareness of tactile stimuli presented in the contralesional side is increased, and patients are able to detect the previously ignored left sided tactile stimuli. In contrast, due to the fact that tactile and visual extrapersonal space are not functionally linked, and, therefore, they do not interact, no changes in the level of awareness for tactile stimuli are observable by activating the intact extrapersonal visual map.

Strategically different attentional control of stimulus processing

As previously said, the antagonism between left and right space representation may be reduced by using a strategic attentional control, on the basis of which a stimulus might be perceived as a single perceptual input instead of multiple perceptual units.

In neglect patients one manifestation of the lack of responsiveness to contralesional stimuli can be the failure to read verbal material that appears in the space opposite to the damaged hemisphere. This phenomenon is termed neglect dyslexia. Patients with neglect dyslexia usually make errors in reading the left part of the written word and non-word (i.e., the beginning in Western scripts). They may omit some of the letters (e.g., table → "able") or insert letters that are not present (e.g., love → "glove"). They may also substitute some or all of the letters on the left side (e.g., bear → "pear").

Interestingly, the number of erroneously substituted letters often matches the number of letters actually present in the letter string (Ellis et al. 1987; Warrington 1991). This finding shows that the patient has some knowledge about the letters presented on the left side. Perhaps, on the left there is an impaired visuo-spatial representation that, however, conveys sufficient information about the word length. The fact that errors tend to be more numerous for non-words than for words (Behrmann et al. 1990; 1991) seems to suggest that lexical information too may in part be preserved in neglect dyslexia.

These suggestions have been verified in recent studies (Làdavas et al. 1997; Làdavas, Umiltà and Mapelli 1997) showing in neglect patients a preserved lexical and semantic access for words they are not able to read. When patients were required to judge the lexical status and to make semantic judgement of the letter string they were not able to read, their performance was as good as in *the condition in which the pair of words as well as the target were read aloud by the experimenter.* Moreover, patients were able to read words immediately following a semantic decision at a far higher level than in the simple reading task. In other words, immediately after the semantic task, patients were able to read the letter string on which they had made the semantic judgement. This improvement, however, was not maintained in the final reading task and it was confined to words. Non-words showed only a minor improvement.

One way to explain the results is to consider a possible interaction between the attentional system and the classical dual-route model of reading aloud (e.g., Coltheart 1985; Seidenberg & McClelland 1989). According to this model, a written letter string can be read by a non-lexical phonological route that implies grapheme-to-phoneme conversion (i.e., the compiled or assembled phonology), and by a lexical and semantic routes (addressed phonology), that imply direct access to the mental lexicon through the visual representation of words. The better performance of neglect patients in reading words after the semantic task in comparison with the normal reading task can be interpreted in terms of an interaction between the attentional system and the different reading routes, and provides evidence that lexical/semantic routes are less affected by neglect.

In the basic reading task, the responses of the patients were generally non-words indicating that a non-lexical phonological procedure was used. In the semantic tasks *and also in* the semantic+reading task the semantic route was presumably used. It seems plausible that the use of the semantic route requires, but also leads to, a broadening of the attentional focus, while the use of non-lexical phonological correspondences involves a narrower attentional focus. As far as a broader attentional focus being involved when the semantic route is used, this is compatible with the way that latency for semantic category decisions is unaffected by word length even when multi-syllabic words are used (Green & Shallice 1976). In contrast, it seems plausible that the use of the non-lexical phonological route would be linked to a narrower attentional focus, if we assume that the transmission of information about the relevant level of units — sub-syllabic or syllabic — is at least partially serial and results in achieving the so-called "assembled" phonological representations. Therefore, the existence of multiple perceptual units of the relevant level within the same display could well lead to a greater bias on the right in comparison with the single perceptual unit, that is the input to the addressed phonology route. The existence of multiple perceptual units in a display has been shown to lead to severe neglect in many other perceptual tasks (Làdavas et al. 1990; Làdavas et al. 1993).

The notion that the assembled phonological route has much more difficulties than the addressed phonological route in dealing with a spatial attentional deficit can also be applied to the lexicality effect. Words suffer little from neglect because they can be coded as a single lexical object, whereas non-words may only be coded using sub-string segment (letters and letter clusters), each of which must be attended in sequence (see Riddoch et al. 1990, for a similar argument). Thus spatial attentional deficit will have more serious consequences for non-words. This also explains why most patients manifest neglect dyslexia for non-words, and only a few patients manifest it for words (see Làdavas et al. 1997b). This notion is also compatible with the distinction between object-based and location-based attentional effects (Humphreys & Riddoch 1993; Farah 1994), whereby object representations to which attention can be allocated may include such abstract objects as words, that is the input to the lexical routes.

In conclusion, these studies show how patients with neglect dyslexia may be able to report the previously ignored left side stimuli by using a strategic attentional control, on the basis of which the letter string is perceived as a single perceptual input instead of multiple perceptual units.

Conclusions

In 1986 Smith-Churchland wrote: 'So long as the brain functions normally, the inadequacies of the common-sense framework can be hidden from view, but with the damaged brain the inadequacies of theory are unmasked'. From this point of view, the studies of implicit processing in neglect patients reviewed above have challenged the traditional assumption on what being aware of something means. We have seen that subjects who are not aware of stimuli, or of some of their characteristics, can nonetheless use, under certain conditions, the same stimuli for purposeful behaviour (giving, for instance, correct same/different judgements). It has been assumed very often that behaviour at this level of sophistication implies subject awareness and that if a subject can systematically give correct answers to the same/different tasks then he/she must have a full visual experience of the stimulus. This has turned out to be not the case.

The study of implicit processing in neglect, not only has induced a rethinking of the idea of awareness, but has also stimulated the proposal of new models of space coding, dealing with the counterintuitive aspects of patients behaviour. The model we outlined to explain implicit processing and allochiric phenomena in neglect is also able to predict that awareness at a given moment, and in the same patient, can vary according to different ways of testing, which in turn activate different brain maps in a competitive manner. As a result, visual awareness, after a brain lesion, cannot be considered as a definite state of the mind but, instead, it would be better conceived as a result of a dynamic process involving different space maps interacting with one another to offer the subject a representation of the external world which represents the 'winner' view emerging from the competition (see Crick & Koch 1995, for a similar view).

References

Behrmann, M., Moscovitch, M., Black, S.E. & Mozer, M. (1990). Perceptual and conceptual mechanisms in neglect: two contrasting case studies. *Brain,* 113, 1163–1183.

Behrmann, M., Moscovitch, M. & Mozer, M. (1991). Directing attention to words and non words in normal subjects and in a computational model: implications for neglect dyslexia. *Cognitive Neuropsychologia,* 8, 213–248.

Berti, A., Allport, A., Driver, J., Dienes, Z., Oxbury, J. & Oxbury, S. (1992). Levels of processing for visual stimuli in an "extinguished" field. *Neuropsychologia,* 30, 403–415.

Berti, A. & Rizzolatti, G. (1992). Visual processing without awareness: evidence from unilateral neglect. *Journal of Cognitive Neuroscience,* 4, 346–351.

Berti, A., Frassinetti, F. & Umiltà, C.A. (1994). Nonconscious reading? Evidence from neglect dyslexia. *Cortex,* 30, 181–197.

Berti, A., Oxbury, S., Oxbury, J., Affanni, P., Umiltà, C. & Orlandi, L. Somatosensory extinction for meaningful objects in a patient with right hemisphere stroke. (submitted)

Cappa, S.F., Sterzi, R., Vallar, G. & Bisiach, E. (1987). Remission of hemineglect and anosognosia during vestibular stimulation. *Neuropsychologia,* 25, 775–782.

Cohen, J.D., Romero, R.D., Farah, M.J. & Servan-Schreiber, D. (1994). Mechanisms of spatial attention: The relation of macrostructure to microstructure in parietal neglect. *Journal of Cogntitive Neuroscience,* 6, 377–387.

Coltheart, M. (1985). Cognitive neuropsychology and the study of reading. In: M.I. Posner & O.S.M. Marin (Eds.), *Attention and Performance XI.* Hillsdale, New Jersey: Lawrence Erlbaum, 3–37.

Corbetta, M., Marzi, C.A., Tassinari, G. & Aglioti, S. (1990). Effectiveness of different task paradigms in revealing blind sight. *Brain,* 113, 603–616.

Crick, F. & Koch, C. (1995). Are we aware of the neural activity in primary visual cortex? *Nature,* 375, 121–123.

di Pellegrino, G., Basso, G. & Frassinetti, F. (1997). Spatial extinction to double asynchronous stimulation. *Neuropsychologia,* 35, 1215–1223.

di Pellegrino, G., Làdavas, E. & Farnè, A. (1997). Seeing where your hands are. *Nature,* 338: 730.

Duhamel, J.R., Colby, C.L. & Goldberg, M.E. (1991). Congruent representation of visual and somatosensory space in single neurons of monkey ventral intra-parietal area (area VIP). In: J. Paillard J (Ed.), *Brain and Space.* Oxford: Oxford University Press, 223–236.

Ellis, A.W., Flude, B.M. & Young, A.W. (1987). "Neglect Dyslexia" and the early visual processing of letters in words and non words. *Cognitive Neuropsychologia,* 4, 439–464.

Farah, M. (1994). Visual perception and visual awareness after brain damage: a tutorial overview. In C. Umiltà & M. Moscovitch (Eds.), *Attention and Performance XV.* Cambridge : MIT Press, 37–75

Gentilucci, M., Fogassi, L., Luppino, G., Matelli, M., Camarda, R.M. & Rizzolatti, G. (1988). Functional organisation of inferior area 6 in the macaque monkey. I. Somatotopy and the control of proximal movements. *Experimental Brain Research,* 71, 475–490.

Graziano, M.S.A. & Gross, C.G. (1993). A bimodal map of space: tactile receptive fields in the macaque putamen with corresponding visual receptive fields. *Experimental Brain Research,* 97, 96–109.

Graziano, M.S.A. & Gross, C.G. (1994). Mapping space with neurons. *Curr Directions Psychol Science,* 3, 164–167.

Green, D. & Shallice, T. (1976). Direct visual access in reading for meaning. *Memory Cognition,* 41, 753–758.

Halligan, P.W., Manning, L. & Marshall, J.C. (1991). Hemispheric activation vs spatiomotor cueing in visual neglect: a case study. *Neuropsychologia,* 29, 165–176.

Halligan, P.W., Marshall, J.C. & Wade, D.T. (1992). Left on the right: allochiria in a case of left visuo-spatial neglect. *Journal Neurology Neurosurgery Psychiatry,* 55, 717–719.

Humphreys, G.W. & Riddoch, M.J. (1993). Interactive attentional systems and unilateral visual neglect. In: I.H. Robertson & J.C. Marshall (Eds.), *Unilateral neglect: clinical and experimental studies.* Hillsdale, New Jersey: Lawrence Erlbaum, 123–136.

Kaniza, G. (1980). La grammatica del vedere. Saggi su percezione e gestalt. Il Mulino: Bologna

Làdavas, E., Petronio, A. & Umiltà, C. (1990). The deployment of attention in the intact field of hemineglect patients. *Cortex,* 26, 307–317.

Làdavas, E., Paladini, R. & Cubelli, R. (1993). Implicit associative priming in a patient with left visual neglect. *Neuropsychologia,* 31, 1307–1320.

Làdavas, E., Umiltà, C., Ziani, P., Brogi, A. & Minarini, M. (1993). The role of right-side objects in left-side neglect: a dissociation between perceptual and directional motor neglect. *Neuropsychologia,* 31, 761–773.

Làdavas, E., Carletti, M. & Gori, G. (1994). Automatic and voluntary orienting of attention in patients with visual neglect: horizontal and vertical dimension. *Neuropsychologia,* 32, 1195–1208.

Làdavas, E., Berti, A., Ruozzi, E. & Barboni, F. (1997). Neglect as a deficit determined by an imbalance between multiple spatial representations. *Experimental Brain Research*, 116, 493–500.

Làdavas, E., Shallice, T. & Zanella, T. (1997a). Preserved semantic access in neglect dyslexia. *Neuropsychologia*, 35, 257–270.

Làdavas, E., Umiltà, C. & Mapelli, D. (1997b). Lexical and semantic processing in the absence of word reading: evidence from neglect dyslexia. *Neuropsychologia*, 35, 1075–1085.

Làdavas, E., di Pellegrino, G., Farnè, A. & Zeloni, G. (1998a). Neuropsychological evidence of an integrated visuo-tactile representation of peripersonal space in humans. *Journal of Cognitive Neuroscience*, 10, 581–589.

Làdavas, E., Zeloni, G. & Farnè, A. (1998b). Visual peripersonal space centred on the face in humans. *Brain*, 121, 2317–2326.

Làdavas, E., Bisiach, E., Perini, P. & Bosinelli, M.A dissociation between the "what" and the "where" of conscious experience in a patient with visual neglect. (In preparation).

Marshall, J.C. & Halligan, P.W. (1988). Blindsight and insight in visuospatial neglect. *Nature*, 336, 766–767.

McGlinchey-Berroth, R., Milberg, W.P., Verfaellie, M., Alexander, M. & Kilduff, P.T. (1993). Semantic processing in the neglected field: evidence from a lexical decision task. *Cognitive Neuropsychology*, 10, 79–108.

Milner, A.D. & Goodale, M.A. (1995). *The visual brain in action*. Oxford: Oxford University Press.

Miskin, M., Unerleider, L.G. & Macko, K.A. (1983). Object vision and spatial vision. *Trends in Neuroscience*, 6, 414–417.

Obersteiner, H. (1982). On allochiria. A peculiar sensory disorder. *Brain*, 4, 153–163.

Posner, M.I., Walker, J.A., Friederich, F.A. & Rafal, R.D. (1987). How do parietal lobes direct covert attention? *Neuropsychologia*, 25, 135–145.

Posner, M.I. & Rafal, R.D. (1988). Cognitive theories of attention and the rehabilitation of attentional deficits. In: M.J. Meier, A. Benton & L. Diller (Eds.), *Neuropsychological rehabilitation*. New York: Guilford, 182–201.

Riddoch, J. (1990). Neglect and peripheral dyslexia. *Cognitive Neuroscience*, 7, 479–517.

Robertson, I. & North, N. (1992). Spatio-motor cueing in unilateral left neglect: the role of hemispace, hand and motor activation. *Neuropsychologia*, 30, 553–563.

Rock, I. (1983). *The logic of perception*. Cambridge: MIT Press

Seidenberg, M.S. & McClelland, J.L. (1989). A distributed, developmental model of word recognition and naming. *Psychological Review*, 96, 523–568.

Stroop, J.R. (1935). Studies of interference in serial verbal reactions. *Journal of Experimental Psychology*, 18, 643–662.

Tégner, R. & Levander M. (1991). Through a looking glass: a new technique to demonstrate directional hypokinesia in unilateral neglect. *Brain*, 114, 1943–1951.

Vallar, G., Rusconi, M.L. & Bisiach, E. (1994). Awareness of contralesional information in unilateral neglect. Effects of verbal cueing, tracing and vestibular stimulation. In M. Moscovitch & C. Umiltà (Eds.), *Attention and Performance XV*. Cambridge: MIT Press.

Volpe, B.T., LeDoux, J.E. & Gazzaniga, M.S. (1979). Information processing of visual stimuli in an "extinguished" field. *Nature*, 282: 722–724.

Ward, R., Goodrich, S. & Driver, J. (1994). Grouping reduces visual extinction: neuropsychological evidence for weight linkage in visual selection. *Visual Cognition*, 1, 101–129.

Warrington, E.K. (1991). Right neglect dyslexia: a single case study. *Cognitive Neuropsychology*, 8, 193–212.

Overt and Covert Face Recognition

Andrew W. Young and Hadyn D. Ellis
University of Cardiff

Introduction

The human face carries an exquisite range of social signals — informing among other things about the age sex, identity and feelings of its bearer (Bruce & Young 1998). The use of these different types of facial information probably has a long evolutionary history, but until recently the possibility that regions of the human brain might play specialised roles in face perception was widely resisted. However, striking findings have demonstrated localised neural responses to faces (Kanwisher et al. 1997), interest in faces by newborn infants (Johnson et al. 1991), highly selective deficits of face recognition after brain injury (De Renzi 1986; McNeil & Warrington 1993), and the existence of several regions of face-selective cells in primate temporal cortex (Gross 1992; Perrett et al. 1992). Taken together, such results make a persuasive case that, even though there are undeniable and important contributions of learning and experience, there is something special about human face perception (Ellis & Young 1989).

Without the ability to recognise other individuals, the members of any primate species would be severely handicapped — unable to modify their behaviour according to whom they are interacting with. Since the face forms an especially important source of information for human recognition, studies of face recognition present an interesting opportunity to try to tease apart conscious and non-conscious contributions to this fundamental social task.

Here, we discuss a number of pertinent lines of evidence, including studies of covert recognition in prosopagnosia, simulations of covert recognition, autonomic responses to faces, and our account of the Capgras delusion. We use these to explore how overt and covert systems might interact in normal cognition.

Prosopagnosia

Prosopagnosia is a neuropsychological condition in which a brain-injured person loses the ability to recognise familiar faces. The recognition deficit can be very severe, encompassing famous faces, friends, family, and even the patient's own face when they look in the mirror. The loss of any sense of recognising the face is usually complete — with not even a feeling of familiarity. Even the simplest of overt face recognition tasks is failed — even just deciding which of two faces (one highly familiar, one unfamiliar) you have ever seen before. For example, case PH was shown a photograph of a famous face and a photograph of an unknown person, both presented together, and given as long as he wanted to decide which one was the familiar person. Across 128 such trials, he scored 65/128 correct — a perfectly chance-level performance (Young & de Haan 1988).

Face recognition is a capacity most of us take for granted, and it is hard to imagine what life must be like without it — how disconcerting it must be not to recognise people you have known all your life, or to stand before a mirror and shave or put make-up on the face of an apparent stranger. The recent creation of a number of internet support groups for prosopagnosics shows the level of distress.

The potentially devastating impact of this loss is mitigated by the fact that recognition from non-facial cues remains possible — acquaintances can still be recognised from their voice, their name, sometimes by the way they are dressed, or even (though the evidence here is anecdotal only) the way they walk. In other words, prosopagnosia does not involve any severe loss of non-facial forms of knowledge of familiar people. It is therefore usual to draw a distinction between the domain-specific recognition failure that characterises prosopagnosia and the kind of problem which involves failure to recognise familiar people from all input domains — i.e. from face, name or voice (Ellis et al. 1989; Hanley et al. 1989; Young 1992).

Prosopagnosia is by no means common, but it is sufficiently striking that it has received a lot of attention from neurologists and neuropsychologists. There are now hundreds of case reports in the literature, ranging from very sketchy descriptions to incredibly thorough and painstaking investigations. Although there are many details which can vary, it is quite easy to identify recurrent themes and findings.

Before the mid-1980s, four questions were regularly addressed in studies

of prosopagnosia. These concerned:
1. whether it forms a distinct neuropsychological condition;
2. the location of the underlying brain lesions;
3. whether it can be reduced to a more general visual deficit; and
4. whether only faces are affected.

There was (and still is) less consensus as to the correct answer as one moves down this list, and the same issues are with us today. At present, the balance of neuropsychological opinion is strongly inclined to accept prosopagnosia as a distinct condition whose aetiology usually involves lesions of mesial occipito-temporal regions, especially in the right hemisphere. Left upper quadrant visual field defects and achromatopsia (loss of colour vision) are fairly frequently found to accompany prosopagnosia, but these visual deficits are usually considered to reflect damage to contiguous anatomical regions rather than to have any primary causal role (Meadows 1974). This is because both types of visual deficit can occur without prosopagnosia, because vision is sometimes remarkably good in the unaffected parts of the visual field (Rizzo et al. 1986), and because there is no reason to think that colour (unlike shading) is particularly important in face recognition (Bruce & Young 1998). There are as yet no consistent reports of any visual deficit which might have a causal role in prosopagnosia, but the issue is complicated by the fact that many people think that a distinction can be drawn between prosopagnosias which are of apperceptive origin and those which are more like a loss of the stored memories for the appearances of familiar faces (De Renzi et al. 1991; Young et al. 1994a). The possibility of a common perceptual deficit for the apperceptive cases should certainly not be overlooked, and ingenious hypotheses continue to be suggested (Kosslyn et al. 1995).

The question of whether only faces are affected in prosopagnosia has proved particularly tricky. In the opinion of many neuropsychologists, loss of ability to recognise faces is simply the most obvious manifestation of a more general problem in recognising the members of perceptual categories which contain many items of similar appearance. To bolster this argument, they point out that when recognition of items from categories such as cars or flowers is tested in cases of prosopagnosia, it is very often noted to be defective. The prosopagnosic person can know that a face is a face, or a car is a car, but has no idea *whose* face it is, *which type* of car, and so on (Damasio et al. 1982). Moreover, there are a number of reports indicating that people with expert recognition abilities can lose these together with their ability to recognise faces — bird species are not recognised by prosopagnosic bird watchers, or livestock by prosopagnosic farmers (Bornstein 1963; Bornstein et al. 1969).

The main limitation of this line of reasoning is that it relies on an inference from associated deficits — the fact that loss of ability to recognise faces is highly correlated with problems in recognising members of other visually homogeneous categories is taken to imply that there is a common underlying cause. However, although such deficits do frequently co-occur, they can dissociate in some (very rare) cases. Examples include De Renzi's (1986) description of a person with prosopagnosia who could recognise individual items from all categories tested except faces, Sergent and Signoret's (1992b) prosopagnosic patient who was exceptionally good at recognising cars, and a prosopagnosic farmer who was able to recognise individual sheep from their faces (McNeil & Warrington 1993). These remarkable dissociations show that face recognition and other forms of within-category recognition are not inextricably intertwined.

We think that there is in any case a need to rethink what the more common co-occurrence of face recognition and within-category recognition deficits might imply. The question whether prosopagnosia is really specific to faces is usually seen as a way of exploring whether there is an evolved neural substrate for face recognition, and as we have noted it actually forms only one of a number of lines of evidence relevant to this question (Ellis & Young 1989). The starting assumption tends to be that if a specialised neural system has evolved for the important social purpose of face recognition, then that system will deal with faces *and no other stimuli*. We think this assumption need not be correct. Any specialised system which could underpin the learning of face recognition must be highly plastic — we are continually learning new faces, or having to update our representations of existing faces as people age and change in appearance. There is no reason why a plastic system which originally evolved in response to the demands of face recognition should not be utilised for related purposes when there are strong environmental influences, and in fact there is good evidence that the acquisition of significant expertise at recognising stimuli from other visual categories leads to the creation of a recognition system with face-like properties (Diamond & Carey 1986) and which draws on the activity of neurons in regions of the cortex which contain other cells responses to faces (Logothetis & Pauls 1995). From this perspective, the co-occurrence of face recognition and within-category recognition deficits may simply point to the extent to which within-category recognition can be achieved by parasitising on to a highly-evolved but plastic neural substrate.

Covert recognition in prosopagnosia

In the 1980s, the agenda for research on prosopagnosia was broadened by important papers by Bruyer and his colleagues (Bruyer et al. 1983) and by Bauer (1984). Bruyer et al. (1983) reported a very thorough investigation of prosopagnosic patient Mr.W., documenting that many of his face perception skills remained intact — he could recognise facial expressions, match the identities of unfamiliar faces, and correctly state whether they were male or female, even though he failed to recognise many familiar faces. Part of their study involved comparing Mr. W's ability to learn to associate names with various types of stimuli, and it was found that Mr. W was better able to learn to pair correct names than incorrect names with photographs of familiar faces he no longer recognised. This led Bruyer et al. (1983) to conclude that Mr. W. showed some 'covert remembrance' of the familiar faces he no longer recognised.

Bauer's (1984) results were more dramatic. He showed patient LF slides of famous faces, and read out five alternative names for each, one of which was the correct choice. As would be expected for a person with prosopagnosia, LF was unable to choose which name belonged with each face. However, Bauer also measured LF's skin conductance response (SCR) to each face-name combination. The SCR is a measure of autonomic nervous system activity. It is usually recorded by measuring electrical conductivity from the finger or the palm of the hand. When we have an emotional response to something, the secretions from sweat glands caused by activity of the autonomic nervous system alter skin conductance; even very small degrees of emotional arousal can be measured in this way. Remarkably, LF's SCRs tended to show the greatest change when the name matched the face presented. In other words, although LF could not consciously choose which name went with which face, his autonomic responses were sensitive to the correctness of the pairings.

The technique used by Bauer (1984) is the same as that of the 'guilty knowledge' test employed in lie detection — a guilty person will often show an autonomic nervous system response to material pertaining to the crime, even if they deny committing it. Of course, no-one is suggesting that people with prosopagnosia are lying when they say that they cannot recognise familiar faces — it is just that Bauer's (1984) research exploited the same principle that autonomic responses are to some extent independent of conscious control, using it to demonstrate some form of non-conscious, covert recognition.

A number of subsequent studies have reported findings of covert recognition of familiar faces in prosopagnosia, across a wide range of tasks. These are summarised in Table 1, which lists appropriate references. The methods first used to demonstrate the phenomenon are still employed. Bruyer et al.'s (1983) technique of exploiting *savings in relearning* by comparing learning rates for correct and incorrect pairings of faces with names has become the most commonly used procedure (because it is so easy to carry out). Bauer's use of the guilty knowledge rationale has been developed by Tranel and his co-workers into a simpler procedure which compares *SCR*s to familiar and unfamiliar faces.

Other methods which rely on comparisons of responses to familiar and unfamiliar faces have also been introduced; further findings include differences in *evoked potentials* and *eye movements* between familiar and unfamiliar faces, and better performance with familiar faces for *face matching* tasks.

Several methods make use of the fact that prosopagnosic patients can still recognise names of familiar people, by examining the influence of 'unrecognised' faces on name recognition using *interference* (a face can interfere with the semantic classification of a simultaneously presented name), *self priming* (a face can facilitate recognition of the subsequently presented name of the same person), and *associative priming* (a face can facilitate recognition of the subsequently presented name of a closely associated person). In all of these tasks, the face exerts its influence indirectly, since the instruction is generally to ignore it and concentrate on recognising the name. For neurologically-normal people, however, the identity of the distractor face cannot be completely ignored, and it influences the performance of the name recognition task. Remarkably, the same pattern is found in prosopagnosia — even though the person with prosopagnosia does not consciously recognise the distractor faces, they affect his or her ability to recognise names.

A different variant of face-name interaction paradigms involves *cued recognition*, in which a person with prosopagnosia is asked which of two names belongs to a familiar face — for example, whether the face of John Lennon is John Lennon or Paul McCartney. Performance is not perfect, but it

Table 1. Examples of findings indicating covert recognition of familiar faces reported in cases of prosopagnosia

Effect	Brief description	Reported by
SCR	Skin conductance response to familiar faces, or to face paired with correct name.	(Bauer, 1984; Bauer, 1986; Tranel & Damasio, 1985; Tranel & Damasio, 1988; Tranel, Damasio & Damasio, 1995).
Evoked potentials	Difference between familiar and unfamiliar faces.	(Renault, Signoret, Debruille, Breton & Bolgert, 1989).
Eye movements	Difference between familiar and unfamiliar faces.	(Rizzo, Hurtig & Damasio, 1987).
'Mere exposure' effect	Preference for faces seen previously in judging which of two faces is 'more likeable'.	(Greve & Bauer, 1990).
Face matching	Better performance at matching photographs of familiar than unfamiliar faces.	(de Haan, Young & Newcombe, 1987a; Sergent & Poncet, 1990; Sergent & Signoret, 1992)
Savings in relearning	Faster learning of correct than incorrect face+name or face+occupation pairings.	(Bruyer, Laterre, Seron, Feyereisen, Strypstein, Pierrard, et al., 1983; de Haan et al., 1987a; 1991; Diamond, Valentine, Mayes & Sandel, 1994; McNeil & Warrington, 1991; Schweinberger, Klos & Sommer, 1995; Sergent & Poncet, 1990; Sergent & Signoret, 1992; Young & de Haan, 1988)
Interference	Faces can interfere with semantic classification of simultaneously presented names.	(de Haan, Bauer & Greve, 1992; de Haan et al., 1987a; de Haan, Young & Newcombe, 1987b; Sergent & Signoret, 1992)
Self priming	A face can facilitate recognition of the subsequently presented name of the same person.	(de Haan et al., 1992).
Associative ('semantic') priming	A face can facilitate recognition of the subsequently presented name of a closely associated person.	(Schweinberger et al., 1995; Young, Hellawell & de Haan, 1988).
Cued recognition	Above-chance performance at guessing which of two names is correct for a familiar face.	(de Haan et al., 1991; Diamond et al., 1994; Sergent & Poncet, 1990; Sergent & Signoret, 1992)

has consistently been found to be above chance-level for people who show other phenomena indicating covert recognition — usually there are around 70% correct responses, in contrast to the expected chance rate of 50%. Despite their above-chance performance, the patients maintain that they are guessing (de Haan et al. 1991; Sergent & Poncet 1990) — they express no more confidence in their correct than their incorrect choices, and are just as willing to choose when both names are incorrect (e.g. if asked whether John Lennon's face is Paul McCartney or George Harrison).

One of the interesting things about cued recognition is that it forms a parallel with some of the procedures used to investigate blindsight, which also rely on forced-choice and encouraging 'guessing' (Weiskrantz 1986). However, this parallel needs to be approached cautiously. As we have already noted, the same prosopagnosic patients perform at chance level when asked to choose between a simultaneously presented famous and unfamiliar face, even if encouraged to guess. Hence, it is not simply the combination of forced-choice procedure and guessing which leads to above-chance performance in the cued recognition task, but more likely the possibility of some form of interaction between information derived from faces and names (Young 1994).

Even so, there are some circumstances in which responses to faces alone can be shown in forced-choice. To demonstrate this, Greve and Bauer (1990) used the *'mere exposure'* phenomenon, in which people develop preferences for things simply by virtue of their having been seen before (Bornstein 1989; Zajonc 1980). Prosopagnosic patient LF (the person who had participated in Bauer's original SCR study) was shown faces of unfamiliar people for 500 ms each, interspersed among a task which involved rating verbal personality descriptors for how much he would like to meet a person with that attribute. Later, LF was shown these faces again, and each was paired with a new unfamiliar face which had been rated as of similar 'likeability' by neurologically-normal controls who had not seen the faces before. When LF was asked which member of each pair of faces he had seen before, he performed at chance-level (choosing the face he had seen before on 53% of trials), but when asked which face he 'liked' the best, LF tended to choose the face he had seen before (choosing this face on 70% of trials). This instructive study both showed clearly the contrast between LF's performance of a direct test ("which face have you seen before?") and an indirect test ("which face do you like better") of recognition, but also established that he was able to create new representations of faces — all of the faces were unfamiliar to LF when the experiment began.

Understanding covert recognition

We have seen that a wide range of procedures can be used to demonstrate covert recognition of familiar faces in cases of prosopagnosia. The existence of the phenomenon of covert recognition therefore is no longer disputed — what remains controversial is how best to interpret it.

Two important pointers come from aspects of the literature we have not yet introduced. First, not all people with prosopagnosia show covert recognition effects. Findings of lack of covert recognition by some patients have been reported with SCR (Bauer 1986; Etcoff et al. 1991), associative priming (Newcombe et al. 1989), and learning tasks (Etcoff et al. 1991; Humphreys et al. 1992; McNeil & Warrington 1991; Newcombe et al. 1989; Sergent & Villemure 1989; Young & Ellis 1989). The fact that some prosopagnosic patients show covert recognition and some do not fits with a point we made earlier, that there is probably more than one form of prosopagnosia. In general, the patients who do not show covert recognition seem to have the more 'apperceptive' types of deficit. Presence or absence of covert recognition may thus be used alongside other methods (Young et al. 1994a) to determine the nature of the functional impairment in each case.

Second, most covert recognition effects seem to reflect the same underlying cause. In a number of the case studies reported in the literature, multiple measures of covert recognition were used. When this has been done, dissociations between different measures of covert recognition have not been found. In other words, it seems that a prosopagnosic patient who shows associative priming from unrecognised faces will also show interference, savings in relearning, cued recognition, better matching for familiar than unfamiliar faces, and so on. The implication is that these various effects may have a common source — although there are different forms of prosopagnosia, there do not (yet) seem to be different forms of prosopagnosia with covert recognition.

A possible caveat concerns the relation between autonomic measures of recognition (in this context, SCR) and the more behavioural techniques such as associative priming, interference, and savings in relearning. These tend to belong to different laboratory traditions, and have only once been tested together. In an enterprising international collaboration, de Haan, Bauer and Greve (1992) assessed patient LF (from Bauer's 1984 SCR study) with some of the behavioural tests developed by de Haan and his colleagues (specifically, interference and self priming). LF was found to show covert recognition for these tasks, showing a clear parallel to the previously reported SCR findings (Bauer 1984). This is an important finding, but whether this parallelism of autonomic and behavioural indices of covert recognition holds more generally, or was simply coincidental in the case of LF, remains a question of central theoretical importance.

The reason why this particular issue is so important is that are two main accounts of covert recognition, one of which focuses on SCR (Bauer 1984), whilst the other focuses on behavioural measures (Burton et al. 1991). These theories have important differences, and better understanding of the empirical relation between autonomic and behavioural indices of covert recognition would assist in deciding whether each account is valid for its own domain or whether a more integrated theory is needed.

Bauer's (1984) theory was linked to his original insight of using the guilty knowledge technique to examine non-conscious responses to familiar faces in prosopagnosia. He viewed SCR and other autonomic measures as reflecting orienting responses to stimuli of high social and biological significance. Although non-conscious, these orienting responses prepare the person for what is likely to happen next whereas overt, conscious recognition is required for intentional, non-automatic reactions. In Bauer's (1984) account, orienting responses and conscious recognition are mediated through distinct neurological pathways — orienting responses via a dorsal cortico-limbic pathway, and conscious recognition via a more ventral pathway. Each pathway can be dissociably impaired, giving rise to the phenomenon of orienting responses (and hence SCR changes) without overt recognition when the ventral pathway is especially affected.

In discussing Bauer's model, it is important to keep separate his general conception that autonomic and conscious recognition involve dissociable pathways and his specific proposals concerning the underlying neurology. The neurology of Bauer's (1984) proposals has been questioned by other experts (Hirstein & Ramachandran 1997; Tranel & Damasio 1988; Tranel et al. 1995) who have none the less accepted what we think is the more important proposition that autonomic and overt indices of recognition effectively tap different neural systems.

Bauer's dual-route approach to the SCR findings contrasts with the dominant account of the behavioural effects, which involves demonstrating how they can be simulated by damaging a connectionist model of normal face recognition. Two such simulations have been offered, first by Burton and his colleagues (Burton et al. 1991), then by Farah and her co-workers (Farah et al. 1993). Although the techniques used to create these simulations are very different, they have in common the aim of showing how a network which (because of damage) no longer 'recognises' face inputs can still pass activation or tap into residual function in ways which closely mimic the patterns of behaviour found in studies of covert recognition in prosopagnosia. Because of the common underlying purpose, and the fact that we consider it to be the more successful, we will only discuss Burton's model here — a full discussion of the differences between these models, their successes and limitations, can be found elsewhere (Burton & Young 1999; Young & Burton 1999).

Figure 1 shows the central architecture of the model used by Burton et al. (1991). The system uses interactive activation and competition (IAC) principles. It has pools of units corresponding to the appearances of known faces (face recognition units, or FRUs), the orthography of familiar names (name

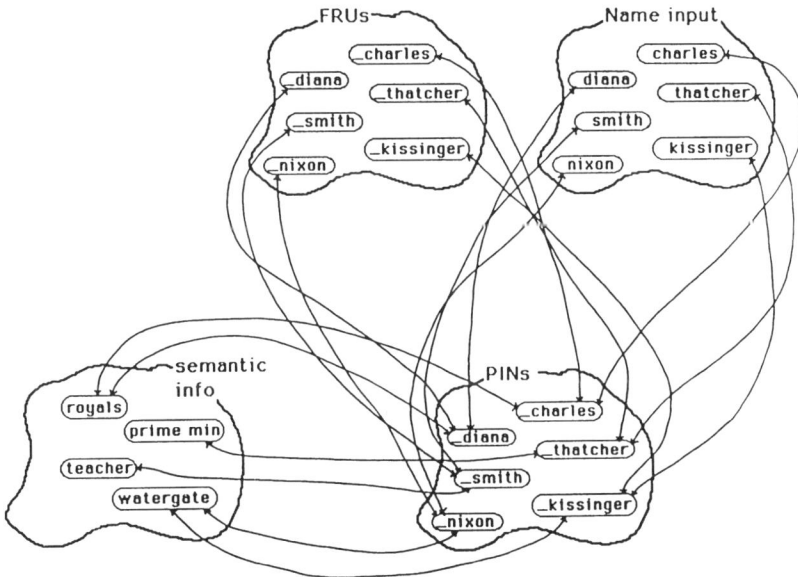

Figure 1. Central architecture of the interactive activation and competition (IAC) model developed by Burton and his colleagues (Burton et al., 1990, 1991). Reproduced by kind permission of Professor A.M. Burton and the British Psychological Society.

recognition units, or NRUs), and stored knowledge about these people (semantic information units, or SIUs). In addition, a pool of person identity nodes (PINs) acts as an amodal interface between the input pools (FRUs and NRUs) and semantic information (the SIUs). Within each pool, units are interconnected and inhibit each other, whereas the connections between units in different pools are excitatory. The weights of these excitatory and inhibitory connections are determined by a set of rules, and the extent to which a unit will try to excite units in adjacent pools and inhibit other units in the same pool is proportional to its own activation.

This IAC model was developed by Burton and his colleagues to account for some of the properties of normal face recognition (Burton et al. 1990), using an implementation which was as close as possible to the theoretical proposals of Bruce and Young (1986). The IAC model has undergone further development since — the most important change is that the original 'hand-wired' version has been replaced by a version which incorporates a learning rule (Burton 1994). However, Burton has taken care to show that each revised version of his IAC model retains the properties of the original alongside whatever new capabilities have been added, so for present purposes we do not need to concern ourselves too much with this point.

To get a clearer idea of how this system works, we will look at how it generates associative priming effects. Recall that in associative priming, seeing the face of (say) Paul McCartney will facilitate recognising the name of John Lennon. Suppose, then, that we ask a person to decide whether or not a series of names are those of familiar people, and precede each name with a face prime. Responses to familiar target names will be faster if the face prime was a close associate (e.g. when Paul McCartney's face precedes John Lennon's name) than if the prime face and target name are unrelated (e.g. when Paul McCartney's face precedes Tony Blair's name).

In the IAC model, recognition of an item's familiarity is modelled by its being able to generate sufficient activation at its corresponding PIN. When the FRU for Paul McCartney is activated (which corresponds to presenting Paul McCartney's face) it starts to inhibit the other FRUs and to pass activation to the PIN for Paul McCartney. As Paul McCartney's PIN becomes active, it in turn inhibits the other PINs and passes activation back to Paul McCartney's FRU and forward to the SIU for Beatles. As it gains in activation, the Beatles SIU inhibits other SIUs, but passes activation back to other PINs to which it is linked — Paul McCartney, John Lennon, George Harrison, Ringo Starr. The consequence of this is that, although only Paul McCartney's PIN accumulates sufficient activation to cross the threshold for the input's being deemed familiar, the PINs for the other Beatles are gaining some activation from the associated Beatles SIU even though they are simultaneously being inhibited by each other (and especially by the more active PIN for Paul McCartney). As a result, when John Lennon's NIU is activated (corresponding to the subsequent presentation of John Lennon's name), the John Lennon PIN is already above its resting level of activation, and it is correspondingly easy for the John Lennon NIU to raise the Lennon PIN's activation across the threshold for recognition as familiar. In contrast, if Tony Blair's NIU was activated after presentation of Paul McCartney's face, the Blair PIN would at the time be receiving no supporting semantic activation from Paul McCartney, and therefore maximally inhibited by its PIN competitors, making it correspondingly slow to gain sufficient activation for recognition as familiar.

Although Burton and his colleagues developed the IAC model as a simulation of properties of the normal face recognition system, it turns out that a simple modification produces a plausible account of some of the main features of prosopagnosia (Burton et al. 1991). This modification involves reducing the strengths of the excitatory connections between FRUs and PINs — reducing these connection strengths is in line with the obvious hypothesis that prosopagnosia involves some kind of malfunction on the input side of the face recognition system.

For example, consider what happens when the strengths of the FRU-PIN connections are halved. When a face's FRU is activated, the reduced FRU-PIN connection strength means it can no longer pass sufficient to raise the excitation of its corresponding PIN above threshold. Overt recognition of the input face therefore does not occur. Yet sufficient activation is passed to raise the activation of the PIN above its resting level, as are also the activation levels of PINs associated via common SIUs. In consequence, associative priming can be found even though there is no overt recognition (Burton et al. 1991).

Several other effects found in the covert recognition research literature can be modelled in the same way. Of the list given in Table 1, Young and Burton (1998) showed that *face matching, savings in relearning, interference, self priming, associative priming*, and *cued recognition* were all amenable to an account in terms of reduced FRU-PIN connectivity.

Mirror images of prosopagnosia

Although Burton's IAC model provides a plausible account of a number of covert recognition effects, it achieves this in a different way from Bauer's 'dual-route' approach. The obvious difference is that from Bauer's perspective double dissociations are possible between deficits affecting overt and covert recognition, whereas from Burton's account there can be covert without overt recognition, but overt recognition without covert recognition could not arise.

We suspect that both positions are correct, with respect to the phenomena they are interested in. That is, we think that Burton's account is valid for the more obviously 'behavioural' effects (associative priming, etc.), whereas the dual-route approach has much to commend it for SCR.

There is certainly evidence of double dissociations between overt recognition and SCRs. Tranel and his colleagues have documented this for people with brain injuries (Tranel et al. 1995), and we have studied what we think is an equivalent dissociation in people who have experienced the Capgras delusion.

The Capgras delusion is an unusual but striking neuropsychiatric symptom (Enoch & Trethowan 1991), named after the psychiatrist who first brought it to widespread attention (Capgras & Reboul-Lachaux 1923). People who experience the Capgras delusion claim that one or more of their close relatives is an impostor who is a near-perfect look-alike.

We chose the Capgras delusion as a focus of interest for a number of reasons. It was manifestly bizarre, many cases had been described in the literature without any convincing explanation, some of these reports linked the delusion to brain injury, and it had been suggested that it might be related to prosopagnosia. Since we were actively researching prosopagnosia, it seemed like a reasonable first step to explore the possibility that face processing impairments might be involved in the Capgras delusion.

During the last 12 years, we have had the opportunity to meet and carry out tests with people who have experienced the Capgras delusion (Ellis et al. 1997; Young 1998; Young et al. 1994b; Young et al. 1993). From this work, a constellation of features has stood out, and these are also evident in other published case reports. People who experience the Capgras delusion usually claim that they can see that their relative is an impostor, though they have great difficulty explaining just what this visible difference entails. On tests of face perception, they tend to perform less well than normal controls, but seldom at chance level. When questioned carefully, they report a more wide-spread feeling that things have changed in a way that makes them seem not quite right — strange, somehow unfamiliar, almost unreal. Their mood is often one of some suspiciousness.

This pattern does not form a close parallel to what is found in cases of prosopagnosia. For people with prosopagnosia the impairment of familiar face recognition can be very severe (affecting the recognition of faces as familiar as their spouse's face or their own face when seen in the mirror), but other aspects of face perception (such as recognition of emotion from facial expression), may remain relatively spared. In Capgras delusion, recognition of familiar faces is much less severely compromised in absolute terms (sufferers can recognise their spouse's face, even if they maintain it is not the real person), and it does not seem to be any more affected than other aspects of face perception, most of which are somewhat abnormal.

A more promising approach seemed to us to think of Capgras delusion as something akin to a mirror-image of prosopagnosia (Ellis & Young 1990). In prosopagnosia, overt recognition of familiar faces is severely affected but, as we have discussed, some non-conscious forms of response to familiar faces can still be demonstrated (Bruyer 1991; Young 1998; Young & Burton 1999). In particular, autonomic nervous system responses to familiar faces can be shown (Bauer 1984; Tranel & Damasio 1985) by measuring changes in skin conductance. These autonomic responses are usually interpreted as reflecting some form of emotional orienting to stimuli which have personal significance. If one lost these autonomic responses, it seemed to us conceivable that familiar faces would seem strange, unusual, not quite right.

In prosopagnosia, then, overt recognition of familiar faces is profoundly impaired, whereas autonomic responses to the same faces can be relatively spared. We hypothesised that in Capgras delusion the opposite pattern applies — autonomic responses to familiar faces are lost, whereas overt recognition is relatively preserved (Ellis & Young 1990). The delusion that relatives have been replaced by impostors then is an attempt to make sense of the fact that they no longer generate appropriate emotional responses, i.e. a form of confabulation.

This account explains why the Capgras delusion is mainly found for close relatives, since these are the people who would normally produce the greatest autonomic response, and hence for whom the absence of this response is the most noticeable and disconcerting. It also explains why the delusion occurs in a background of more pervasive feelings that things are not as they should be. More importantly, it made the prediction that people who experience the Capgras delusion will not show differential skin conductance responses to familiar compared to unfamiliar faces. Since this prediction did not follow from any other theory as to what might cause the Capgras delusion, it was non-trivial.

Two recent studies have demonstrated the predicted loss of differential skin conductance response (Ellis et al. 1997; Hirstein & Ramachandran 1997) in Capgras delusion. Hirstein and Ramachandran (1997) investigated a person who developed the Capgras delusion after sustaining a head injury in a traffic accident; across 3 separate test sessions he showed no difference in SCR between familiar and unfamiliar faces. Ellis et al. (1997) investigated 5 people who had experienced the Capgras delusion and had received psychiatric diagnoses, comparing their SCRs to those of 5 other psychiatric patients taking similar anti-psychotic medication and a group of 5 psychiatrically-normal controls. The Capgras delusion cases showed low overall SCRs to faces, and no differential SCR to familiar faces. In contrast, their SCRs to a loud tone were normal in magnitude and rate of habituation, showing that the loss of responsiveness to faces was to some extent circumscribed.

These findings are exactly as would be predicted from Ellis and Young's (1990) account of Capgras delusion. In addition, Hirstein and Ramachandran (1997) also noted that their patient claimed his parents were impostors when he was looking at them, but treated them as his real parents when talking to them on the telephone — as might be expected if the cause of the delusion is a discrepant response to visual information.

A plausible hypothesis which has received empirical support is therefore that the basis of the Capgras delusion lies in a loss of appropriate emotional orienting responses to familiar visual stimuli. However, there seems to be something missing.

A minor discrepancy is that people who suffer the Capgras delusion also tend to be poor on a range of face perception tasks — it is not just their autonomic responses to faces that are impaired. It is the loss of autonomic responses, however, which is the most severe problem, and it is possible that the other defects of face perception simply reflect anatomical proximity between the pathways involved in the different aspects of face perception — it would be unusual for brain malfunction to compromise one of these pathways without affecting the others to some extent.

The more serious issue concerns why people with Capgras delusion should arrive at such an unlikely account of their experiences as to think that relatives have been replaced. Why, for instance, don't they just accept that other people seem a bit strange for reasons they can't figure out? Two points seem pertinent here. First, it seems likely that many people who suffer this type of anomalous perceptual experience may well generate more plausible explanations of what has happened to them — but those who do will not attract as much interest from psychiatrists or neurologists. Second, the suspiciousness noted in people with Capgras delusion may be one of the factors which limits the possibilities they consider to those which involve changes in other people rather than changes in themselves and disposes them to think they are the victims of some kind of trick (Ellis & Young 1996).

We think therefore that the Capgras delusion reflects an unfortunate interaction of impairments involving anomalous perceptual experience and reasoning biases of the type noted in other people with delusions, and paranoid delusions in particular (Dudley et al. 1997a; Dudley et al. 1997b; Huq et al. 1988; Kaney & Bentall 1989). The relative balance of these differing contributory factors may vary according to the aetiology underlying the delusion, as has been noted by Fleminger and Burns (1993). We think that the Capgras delusion represents just one among a number of ways in which people might try to explain similar anomalous perceptual experiences to themselves, and that to understand this delusion properly we need to understand not just the perceptual anomaly but also the factors which create and sustain the relatively bizarre impostor explanation.

The Capgras delusion may have important implications for modelling face recognition processes, as has been pointed out by Ellis (1998). Recall that we drew attention earlier to the difference between Bauer's dual-route model of overt face recognition and SCRs, and Burton's IAC model of the more behavioural forms of covert recognition. Burton's model, in common with certain other proposals (Farah et al. 1993), tries to account for covert recognition in some prosopagnosics by arguing that the system, though damaged at some stage, may still yield sufficient information to elicit covert activity. This type of model, however, cannot accommodate the finding of overt face recognition coupled with the absence of covert signs, as is observed in the SCRs of people with Capgras delusion. The issue of whether all indices of covert face recognition may stem from the same source is therefore of interest. We noted that LF showed both autonomic and cognitive signs of covert recognition (de Haan et al. 1992), and so a crucial empirical question yet to be tested is whether patients with Capgras delusion who do not evince differential skin-conductance responses to familiar compared with unfamiliar faces also fail to show covert recognition effects with behavioural measures. Preliminary data that we have collected in fact do reveal such effects — our results indicate that although they lack SCRs to familiar faces, people who experience the Capgras delusion still show priming, interference, etc. — suggesting that it may be necessary to distinguish among the various signs of covert face recognition. If substantiated by further work, this will have some interesting theoretical ramifications.

Interaction of overt and covert recognition abilities

Face recognition usually proceeds automatically. We cannot look at a familiar face and decide not to recognise it; the processes involved are not open to introspection or conscious intervention. We are only aware of the outcome of the recognition process.

Even so, there are findings that show differences between overt and covert recognition for normal people. Consider, for example, the implications of the fact that repetition priming effects do not cross stimulus domains (Ellis 1992). Repetition priming refers to the facilitation in recognising an item due to having encountered it before. It turns out that recognising a particular face is made easier if that face has been previously seen, but is unaffected by having seen the person's name or even her or his (clothed) body (Bruce & Valentine 1985; Ellis et al. 1987). It follows that repetition priming is not due to participants' deliberately remembering which people have been encountered in the experiment. Explicit memory would be little different across faces, names, or bodies, yet it is only seeing faces that affects subsequent face recognition. Thus there is an independence between repetition priming and explicit memory for the items that have been seen, which is consistent with the idea that the priming effects have a relatively automatic, non-conscious origin. This claim is borne out by findings of preserved face repetition effects in amnesic patients (Paller et al. 1992).

What seems to be involved in repetition priming are those aspects of recognition whose operation is relatively automatic and does not require conscious initiation; there is a clear parallel between the findings for normal and prosopagnosic participants (Young 1988). Another example of this parallel comes from Greve and Bauer's (1990) use of the 'mere exposure' paradigm with LF, described earlier (see Table 1). Recall that LF performed at chance-level when asked which member of a pair of faces he had seen before, but tended to choose the face he had seen before when asked which face he 'liked' the best. An equivalent phenomenon of preference for briefly presented stimuli (including faces) without overt recognition of which stimuli have been seen before can be demonstrated in neurologically-normal people (Bornstein 1989; Bornstein et al. 1987; Kunst-Wilson & Zajonc 1980; Zajonc 1980).

This parallel between prosopagnosia and phenomena found when neurologically-normal people fail to recognise familiar faces overtly is also found for SCRs. Ellis, Young and Koenken (1993) adapted the method used in Tranel and Damasio's (1985) study of prosopagnosia to demonstrate differential SCRs to familiar as compared to unfamiliar faces for neurologically-normal participants when the faces were masked to prevent overt recognition.

There are thus a number of grounds for thinking that covert recognition phenomena happen in everyday life — they are not unique consequences of prosopagnosia. In daily life, though, the integration of covert and overt abilities is relatively seamless — in prosopagnosia, it is much easier to see the join. This is dramatically apparent from the failure of people with prosopagnosia to act on the covert abilities so readily demonstrated in the laboratory. In everyday life, they just do not seem to recognise familiar faces at all.

Of course, the relative preservation of non-facial forms of recognition often allows the person with prosopagnosia to avoid excessive social embarrassment with a modicum of luck, strategy, and ingenuity. We have noticed that some of the people who participate in our own studies are quite good at keeping an affable but open-ended conversation going until they have figured out who you are, and De Renzi (1986) remarked that one of his patients was able to continue to work as a public notary because his secretary introduced clients by name. But such techniques do not always work. There are equally striking instances where face recognition failure has obvious and sometimes very distressing consequences — including people who have stood aside to let themselves pass when seeing a reflection in a shop window, people who have introduced strangers as their spouses at parties, and a particularly disconcerting incident in which someone lost his court case after discussing its details with his opponent's lawyer because he could not tell these similarly-dressed individuals apart (Pevzner et al. 1962).

In such cases, whatever covert recognition contributes did not influence intentional actions. This is slightly surprising in that a remarkable discovery by Sergent has shown that the boundary between covert and overt recognition in prosopagnosia can be surmounted under certain conditions in the laboratory.

Sergent and Poncet (1990) found that their prosopagnosic patient, PV, could achieve overt recognition of some faces if several members of the same semantic category were presented together. This only happened for some semantic categories, and it reflected genuine recognition rather than laborious deduction. It wasn't due to PV thinking things like 'if they're film stars, I guess the blonde one could be Marilyn Monroe', because when PV could not identify the category herself she continued to fail to recognise the faces even when the occupational category was pointed out to her. This observation of overt recognition provoked by simultaneously presenting multiple exemplars of a semantic category has since been replicated with cases PH (de Haan et al. 1991), PC (Sergent & Signoret 1992a), and ET (Diamond et al. 1994). The phenomenon is very striking; the patients themselves tend to be highly surprised at being able to recognise faces overtly.

Such findings in prosopagnosia show that the boundary between awareness and lack of awareness is not as completely impassable as it seems to the patients' everyday experience. Sergent and Poncet (1990) suggested that their demonstration shows that 'neither the facial representations nor the semantic information were critically disturbed in PV, and her prosopagnosia may thus reflect faulty connections between faces and their memories'. They thought that the simultaneous presentation of several members of the same category may have temporarily raised the activation level above the appropriate threshold. This account bears a striking resemblance to the Burton et al. (1991) account of prosopagnosia with covert recognition, but at present the Burton model has not proved able to reproduce these results (Young & Burton 1998). The reasons for the Burton IAC model's current lack of success in this respect are to be found in the fact that interactive activation and competition networks use within-pool inhibitory links to help stabilise activation in each pool. The advantage which accrues through sharing semantic information (SIUs) with other stimuli presented at the same time is therefore balanced, or even outweighed, by the disadvantage which accrues from within-pool inhibition. It remains to be seen whether further work on the IAC account can rectify this problem.

Although it is clear that there are many outstanding questions to be resolved, research on face recognition has produced findings which are certainly of interest with respect to covert and overt abilities, and which may have wider implications for issues in philosophy (Stone & Young 1997; Young & Block 1996). The advantages of using the face as a tool for investigating these questions lie in its long evolutionary history, the wide range of social signals it can carry, and our incredible expertise in interpreting them. This may be a unique combination, offering potentially privileged insights.

References

Bauer, R.M. (1984). Autonomic recognition of names and faces in prosopagnosia: a neuropsychological application of the guilty knowledge test. *Neuropsychologia*, 22, 457–469.

Bauer, R.M. (1986). The cognitive psychophysiology of prosopagnosia. In H.D. Ellis, M.A. Jeeves, F. Newcombe & A. Young (Eds.), *Aspects of face processing*. Dordrecht: Martinus Nijhoff, 253–267.

Bornstein, B. (1963). Prosopagnosia. In L. Halpern (Eds.), *Problems of dynamic neurology*. Jerusalem: Hadassah Medical School, 283–318.

Bornstein, B., Sroka, H. & Munitz, H. (1969). Prosopagnosia with animal face agnosia. *Cortex*, 5, 164–169.

Bornstein, R.F., Leone, D.R. & Galley, D.J. (1987). The generalizability of subliminal mere exposure effects: influence of stimuli perceived without awareness on social behavior. *Journal of Personality and Social Psychology*, 53, 1070–1079.

Bornstein, R.F. (1989). Exposure and affect: overview and meta-analysis of research, 1968–1987. *Psychological Bulletin*, 106, 265–289.

Bruce, V. & Valentine, T. (1985). Identity priming in the recognition of familiar faces. *British Journal of Psychology*, 76, 363–383.

Bruce, V. & Young, A. (1986). Understanding face recognition. *British Journal of Psychology*, 77, 305–327.

Bruce, V. & Young, A.W. (1998). *In the eye of the beholder: the science of face perception*. Oxford: Oxford University Press.

Bruyer, R., Laterre, C., Seron, X., Feyereisen, P., Strypstein, E., Pierrard, E. & Rectem, D. (1983). A case of prosopagnosia with some preserved covert remembrance of familiar faces. *Brain and Cognition*, 2, 257–284.

Bruyer, R. (1991). Covert face recognition in prosopagnosia: a review. *Brain and Cognition*, 15, 223–235.

Burton, A.M., Bruce, V. & Johnston, R.A. (1990). Understanding face recognition with an interactive activation model. *British Journal of Psychology*, 81, 361–380.

Burton, A.M., Young, A.W., Bruce, V., Johnston, R. & Ellis, A.W. (1991). Understanding covert recognition. *Cognition*, 39, 129–166.

Burton, A.M. (1994). Learning new faces in an interactive activation and competition model. *Visual Cognition*, 1, 313–348.

Burton, A.M. & Young, A.W. (1999). Simulation and explanation: some harmony and some discord. *Cognitive Neuropsychology,* 16, 73–79.

Capgras, J. & Reboul-Lachaux, J. (1923). L'illusion des "sosies" dans un délire systématisé chronique. *Bulletin de la Société Clinique de Médicine Mentale,* 11, 6–16.

Damasio, A.R., Damasio, H. & Van Hoesen, G.W. (1982). Prosopagnosia: anatomic basis and behavioral mechanisms. *Neurology,* 32, 331–341.

de Haan, E.H.F., Young, A. & Newcombe, F. (1987a). Face recognition without awareness. *Cognitive Neuropsychology,* 4, 385–415.

de Haan, E.H.F., Young, A. & Newcombe, F. (1987b). Faces interfere with name classification in a prosopagnosic patient. *Cortex,* 23, 309–316.

de Haan, E.H.F., Young, A.W. & Newcombe, F. (1991). Covert and overt recognition in prosopagnosia. *Brain,* 114, 2575–2591.

de Haan, E.H.F., Bauer, R.M. & Greve, K.W. (1992). Behavioural and physiological evidence for covert face recognition in a prosopagnosic patient. *Cortex,* 28, 77–95.

De Renzi, E. (1986). Current issues in prosopagnosia. In H.D. Ellis, M.A. Jeeves, F. Newcombe & A. Young (Eds.), *Aspects of face processing.* Dordrecht: Martinus Nijhoff, 243–252.

De Renzi, E., Faglioni, P., Grossi, D. & Nichelli, P. (1991). Apperceptive and associative forms of prosopagnosia. *Cortex,* 27, 213–221.

Diamond, R. & Carey, S. (1986). Why faces are and are not special: an effect of expertise. *Journal of Experimental Psychology: General,* 115, 107–117.

Diamond, B.J., Valentine, T., Mayes, A.R. & Sandel, M.E. (1994). Evidence of covert recognition in a prosopagnosic patient. *Cortex,* 30, 377–393.

Dudley, R.E.J., John, C.H., Young, A.W. & Over, D.E. (1997a). The effect of self-referent material on the reasoning of people with delusions. *British Journal of Clinical Psychology,* 36, 575–584.

Dudley, R.E.J., John, C.H., Young, A.W. & Over, D.E. (1997b). Normal and abnormal reasoning in people with delusions. *British Journal of Clinical Psychology,* 36, 243–258.

Ellis, A.W., Young, A.W., Flude, B.M. & Hay, D.C. (1987). Repetition priming of face recognition. *Quarterly Journal of Experimental Psychology,* 39A, 193–210.

Ellis, A.W., Young, A.W. & Critchley, E.M.R. (1989). Loss of memory for people following temporal lobe damage. *Brain,* 112, 1469–1483.

Ellis, H.D. & Young, A.W. (1989). Are faces special? In A.W. Young & H.D. Ellis (Eds.), *Handbook of research on face processing.* Amsterdam: North Holland, 1–26.

Ellis, H.D. & Young, A.W. (1990). Accounting for delusional misidentifications. *British Journal of Psychiatry,* 157, 239–248.

Ellis, A.W. (1992). Cognitive mechanisms of face processing. *Philosophical Transactions of the Royal Society,* London, B335, 113–119.

Ellis, H.D., Young, A.W. & Koenken, G. (1993). Covert face recognition without prosopagnosia. *Behavioural Neurology,* 6, 27–32.

Ellis, H.D. & Young, A.W. (1996). Problems of person perception in schizophrenia. In C. Pantelis, H.E. Nelson & T.R.E. Barnes (Eds.), *Schizophrenia: a neuropsychological perspective.* Chichester: Wiley, 397–416.

Ellis, H.D., Young, A.W., Quayle, A.H. & de Pauw, K.W. (1997). Reduced autonomic responses to faces in Capgras delusion. *Proceedings of the Royal Society: Biological Sciences*, B264, 1085–1092.

Ellis, H.D. (1998). Cognitive neuropsychiatry and delusional misidentification syndromes: an exemplary vindication of the new discipline. *Cognitive Neuropsychiatry*, 3, 81–89.

Enoch, M.D. & Trethowan, W.H. (1991). *Uncommon psychiatric syndromes* (3 ed.). Oxford: Butterworth-Heinemann.

Etcoff, N.L., Freeman, R. & Cave, K.R. (1991). Can we lose memories of faces? Content specificity and awareness in a prosopagnosic. *Journal of Cognitive Neuroscience*, 3, 25–41.

Farah, M.J., O'Reilly, R.C. & Vecera, S.P. (1993). Dissociated overt and covert recognition as an emergent property of a lesioned neural network. *Psychological Review*, 100, 571–588.

Fleminger, S. & Burns, A. (1993). The delusional misidentification syndromes in patients with and without evidence of organic cerebral disorder: a structured review of case reports. *Biological Psychiatry*, 33, 22–32.

Greve, K.W. & Bauer, R.M. (1990). Implicit learning of new faces in prosopagnosia: an application of the mere-exposure paradigm. *Neuropsychologia*, 28, 1035–1041.

Gross, C.G. (1992). Representation of visual stimuli in inferior temporal cortex. *Philosophical Transactions of the Royal Society*, London, B335, 3–10.

Hanley, J.R., Young, A.W. & Pearson, N. (1989). Defective recognition of familiar people. *Cognitive Neuropsychology*, 6, 179–210.

Hirstein, W. & Ramachandran, V.S. (1997). Capgras syndrome: a novel probe for understanding the neural representation of the identity and familiarity of persons. *Proceedings of the Royal Society: Biological Sciences*, B264, 437–444.

Humphreys, G.W., Troscianko, T., Riddoch, M.J., Boucart, M., Donnelly, N. & Harding, G.F.A. (1992). Covert processing in different visual recognition systems. In A.D. Milner & M.D. Rugg (Eds.), *The neuropsychology of consciousness*. London: Academic Press, 39–68.

Huq, S.F., Garety, P.A. & Hemsley, D.R. (1988). Probabilistic judgements in deluded and non-deluded subjects. *Quarterly Journal of Experimental Psychology*, 40A, 801–812.

Johnson, M.H., Dziurawiec, S., Ellis, H. & Morton, J. (1991). Newborns' preferential tracking of face-like stimuli and its subsequent decline. *Cognition*, 40, 1–19.

Kaney, S. & Bentall, R.P. (1989). Persecutory delusions and attributional style. *British Journal of Medical Psychology*, 62, 191–198.

Kanwisher, N., McDermott, J. & Chun, M.M. (1997). The fusiform face area: a module in human extrastriate cortex specialized for face perception. *Journal of Neuroscience*, 17, 4302–4311.

Kosslyn, S.M., Hamilton, S.E. & Bernstein, J.H. (1995). The perception of curvature can be selectively disrupted in prosopagnosia. *Brain and Cognition*, 27, 36–58.

Kunst-Wilson, W.R. & Zajonc, R.B. (1980). Affective discrimination of stimuli that cannot be recognized. *Science*, 207, 557–558.

Logothetis, N.K. & Pauls, J. (1995). Psychophysical and physiological evidence for viewer-centred object representations in the primate. *Cerebral Cortex*, 5, 270–288.

McNeil, J.E. & Warrington, E.K. (1991). Prosopagnosia: a reclassification. *Quarterly Journal of Experimental Psychology*, 43A, 267–287.

McNeil, J.E. & Warrington, E.K. (1993). Prosopagnosia: a face specific disorder. *Quarterly Journal of Experimental Psychology*, 46A, 1–10.

Meadows, J.C. (1974). The anatomical basis of prosopagnosia. *Journal of Neurology, Neurosurgery, and Psychiatry*, 37, 489–501.

Newcombe, F., Young, A.W. & de Haan, E.H.F. (1989). Prosopagnosia and object agnosia without covert recognition. *Neuropsychologia*, 27, 179–191.

Paller, K.A., Mayes, A.R., Thompson, K.M., Young, A.W., Roberts, J. & Meudell, P.R. (1992). Priming of face matching in amnesia. *Brain and Cognition*, 18, 46–59.

Perrett, D.I., Hietanen, J.K., Oram, M.W. & Benson, P.J. (1992). Organization and functions of cells responsive to faces in the temporal cortex. *Philosophical Transactions of the Royal Society*, London, B335, 23–30.

Pevzner, S., Bornstein, B. & Loewenthal, M. (1962). Prosopagnosia. *Journal of Neurology, Neurosurgery, and Psychiatry*, 25, 336–338.

Renault, B., Signoret, J.L., Debruille, B., Breton, F. & Bolgert, F. (1989). Brain potentials reveal covert facial recognition in prosopagnosia. *Neuropsychologia*, 27, 905–912.

Rizzo, M., Corbett, J.J., Thompson, S. & Damasio, A.R. (1986). Spatial contrast sensitivity in facial recognition. *Neurology*, 36, 1254–1256.

Rizzo, M., Hurtig, R. & Damasio, A.R. (1987). The role of scanpaths in facial recognition and learning. *Annals of Neurology*, 22, 41–45.

Schweinberger, S.R., Klos, T. & Sommer, W. (1995). Covert face recognition in prosopagnosia: a dissociable function? *Cortex*, 31, 517–529.

Sergent, J. & Villemure, J.-G. (1989). Prosopagnosia in a right hemispherectomized patient. *Brain*, 112, 975–995.

Sergent, J. & Poncet, M. (1990). From covert to overt recognition of faces in a prosopagnosic patient. *Brain*, 113, 989–1004.

Sergent, J. & Signoret, J.-L. (1992a). Implicit access to knowledge derived from unrecognized faces in prosopagnosia. *Cerebral Cortex*, 2, 389–400.

Sergent, J. & Signoret, J.-L. (1992b). Varieties of functional deficits in prosopagnosia. *Cerebral Cortex*, 2, 375–388.

Stone, T. & Young, A.W. (1997). Delusions and brain injury: the philosophy and psychology of belief. *Mind & Language*, 12, 327–364.

Tranel, D. & Damasio, A.R. (1985). Knowledge without awareness: an autonomic index of facial recognition by prosopagnosics. *Science*, 228, 1453–1454.

Tranel, D. & Damasio, A.R. (1988). Non-conscious face recognition in patients with face agnosia. *Behavioural Brain Research*, 30, 235–249.

Tranel, D., Damasio, H. & Damasio, A.R. (1995). Double dissociation between overt and covert recognition. *Journal of Cognitive Neuroscience*, 7, 425–432.

Weiskrantz, L. (1986). *Blindsight: a case study and implications*. Oxford Psychology Series, 12. Oxford: Oxford University Press.

Young, A.W. (1988). Functional organization of visual recognition. In L. Weiskrantz (Eds.), *Thought without language*. Oxford: Oxford University Press, 78–107.

Young, A.W. & de Haan, E.H.F. (1988). Boundaries of covert recognition in prosopagnosia. *Cognitive Neuropsychology*, 5, 317–336.

Young, A.W., Hellawell, D. & de Haan, E.H.F. (1988). Cross-domain semantic priming in normal subjects and a prosopagnosic patient. *Quarterly Journal of Experimental Psy-*

chology, 40A, 561–580.

Young, A.W. & Ellis, H.D. (1989). Childhood prosopagnosia. *Brain and Cognition*, 9, 16–47.

Young, A.W. (1992). Face recognition impairments. *Philosophical Transactions of the Royal Society*, London, B335, 47–54.

Young, A.W., Reid, I., Wright, S. & Hellawell, D.J. (1993). Face-processing impairments and the Capgras delusion. *British Journal of Psychiatry,* 162, 695–698.

Young, A.W. (1994). Covert recognition. In M.J. Farah & G. Ratcliff (Eds.), *The neuropsychology of high-level vision: collected tutorial essays.* Hillsdale, New Jersey: Lawrence Erlbaum, 331–358.

Young, A.W., Humphreys, G.W., Riddoch, M.J., Hellawell, D.J. & de Haan, E.H.F. (1994a). Recognition impairments and face imagery. *Neuropsychologia*, 32, 693–702.

Young, A.W., Leafhead, K.M. & Szulecka, T.K. (1994b). The Capgras and Cotard delusions. *Psychopathology*, 27, 226–231.

Young, A.W. & Block, N. (1996). Consciousness. In V. Bruce (Eds.), *Unsolved mysteries of the mind: tutorial essays in cognition.* Hove, East Sussex: Erlbaum (UK) Taylor & Francis, 149–179.

Young, A.W. (1998). *Face and mind.* Oxford: Oxford University Press.

Young, A.W. & Burton, A.M. (1999). Simulating face recognition: implications for modelling cognition. *Cognitive Neuropsychology,* 16, 1–48.

Zajonc, R.B. (1980). Feeling and thinking: preferences need no inferences. *American Psychologist*, 35, 151–175.

Intentional Control of Automatic Stimulus-Response Translation

Bernhard Hommel

Faculty of Social Sciences, University of Leiden

Introduction

Human behavior is not so much driven by immediate stimulation from the environment, but steered by intentional states representing short- and long-term goals. Of course, this does not imply that environmental information is irrelevant for action control. In fact, adaptive action does not only require intentions to take into account the environmental conditions for and the context adequacy of action, it also heavily relies on the availability of environmental information for on-line control. That is, to successfully tailor an action to a given situation there must be a whole wealth of interactions between internal and external states, presumably on many different levels at the same time.

Although intentional action is almost by definition bound to the conscious representation of the action goal(s), many processes subserving the realization of this goal are not. In fact, authors such as Lotze (1852) or James (1890) have claimed that *only* action goals can be consciously represented, while the remaining processes are more or less automatic consequences of the assumed intentional state — processes that are not accessible to consciousness and, thus, not under its direct control (for an elaboration of this theme, see Baars 1987). Meanwhile, it has become less fashionable to speak of phenomenal experience and subjective states, and so the functional aspects of what was previously discussed under the heading of conscious versus unconscious states was translated into the dichotomy of intentional (or controlled) versus automatic processes.

This chapter deals with the relationship and the interplay between intentional and automatic processes in the translation of environmental information into overt action. In everyday action, this interplay produces perfect outcomes most of the time: Actions typically come out as wanted, and they do so very efficiently. Although this is certainly a great achievement of (not only) human evolution, failures of this interplay are of greater theoretical interest as they tell us something about the structure and the modes of operation of the underlying cognitive mechanisms. The most obvious expressions of such failures are action errors, and there is an increasing literature on which kinds of action errors are likely to occur under which circumstances (e.g., Heckhausen & Beckmann 1990; Reason 1990). Milder forms show up as hesitations in reaction time experiments in the face of ambivalent stimuli. A well-known example is the Stroop task, where subjects are to name the ink of color words (Stroop 1935). As one may imagine, responding is much easier in terms of reaction times and errors if the meaning of the word is congruent with the to-be-named color and the required response (e.g., the word RED written in red ink) than if it is not (e.g., the word GREEN written in red ink). Obviously, presenting an incongruous word leads to a conflict between the intended translation of stimulus color into the appropriate color-naming response and the unintended, but highly overlearned and automatized translation of the word into the corresponding color name. Although conflicts of this sort are rarely observed in everyday life, where intentional and automatic processes usually complement each other, they are highly interesting for the study of intentional and automatic processes. If it were possible to selectively influence the intentional or the automatic part of such a conflict, we would be able to experimentally dissociate and study them — or at least their relative contribution — in isolation.

I will describe two paradigms that turned out to be very helpful in separating and dissociating intentional and automatic processes of S-R translation. The first is a rather old and unknown one — the so-called combined method, developed by Narziß Ach, which requires subjects to overcome overlearned, automatic response tendencies. The second is more recent and better known — the Simon effect and its variants, which makes use of people's automatic tendency to respond to stimuli in a spatially corresponding manner. I will show that and how both paradigms are well suited to analytically dissociate intentional and automatic processes of S-R translation, so that their characteristics can be studied more or less independently. Eventually, however, I will also point out that the relationship between intentional and automatic translation processes is much more intricate than available approaches seem to admit, and I will sketch how a more realistic approach may look like.

Dissociating intentional and automatic stimulus-response translation

Ach's combined method and the interplay of will and habit

Recent reviews dealing with the relationship and interactions between intentional and automatic S-R translation processes (e.g., Allport et al. 1994; Ouellette & Wood 1998; Monsell 1996; Shallice 1994) typically assume that the systematic treatment of this issue began somewhere in the seventies, motivated by the classical papers of Atkinson and Shiffrin (1968), Posner and Snyder (1975), and Shiffrin and Schneider (1977). In fact, however, the question of how "will" and "habit" (the terms preferred in the earlier days) interact launched extensive experimental research and theoretical work between 1910 and 1935 already, with Narziß Ach and Kurt Lewin being the main opponents in a furious debate (for a less selective English overview of this German literature, see Gibson 1941).

The debate was initiated by a book of Ach (1910), in which the author proposed what he called the *combined method* ("kombiniertes Verfahren") as a means to experimentally investigate intentional processes (i.e., the will). These processes can be studied best, so he argues, if the intention to act is opposed to an overlearned habit that calls for another, conflicting action — not unlike the Stroop task. Consequently, the combined method was designed to induce a habit in a practice phase, which then had to be overcome in a test phase. A typical practice phase required subjects to read lists of consonant-vowel-consonant nonsense syllables that were structured in particular ways. Some lists consisted of rhymed syllable pairs (e.g., "zup, tup, tel, mel, …"), some of pairs with the first and second consonant exchanged (e.g., "dus, sud, rol, lor, …"), and some were unstructured. Reading those lists again and again was assumed to form increasingly strong associations between succeeding list members, so that seeing and reacting to the syllable "zup" from the rhymed list, say, would automatically evoke the next response "tup", and so forth. After several days of practice subjects were presented with, for instance, the

first, third, fifth, ..., syllable from the learned lists (i.e., the first members of
the syllable pairs in the rhymed and rearranged lists), or with new syllables,
and were asked, in separate blocks, to respond to that stimulus with either a
rhymed word, the syllable with the two consonants exchanged, or any word
(so-called "reproduction task").

Figure 1 shows typical results from four subjects working on a restricted
version of the combined method. First look at the findings obtained with little
practice in list reading before (and during) the test phase (20 repetitions
overall, see dark bars). Although syllables from rhymed lists yield better
performance than those from unstructured lists, this is true for both the
reproduction task and for the rhyming task, hence there is no specific effect of
learning on performance. Things are different, however, if practice increases
(110 repetitions overall, see bright bars). In the reproduction task, practice has
improved performance for both kinds of syllables, but more so for those from
the unstructured list. The opposite pattern is obtained in the rhyming task,
where performance improved with practice only with syllables from rhymed
lists but was impaired for syllables from unstructured lists.

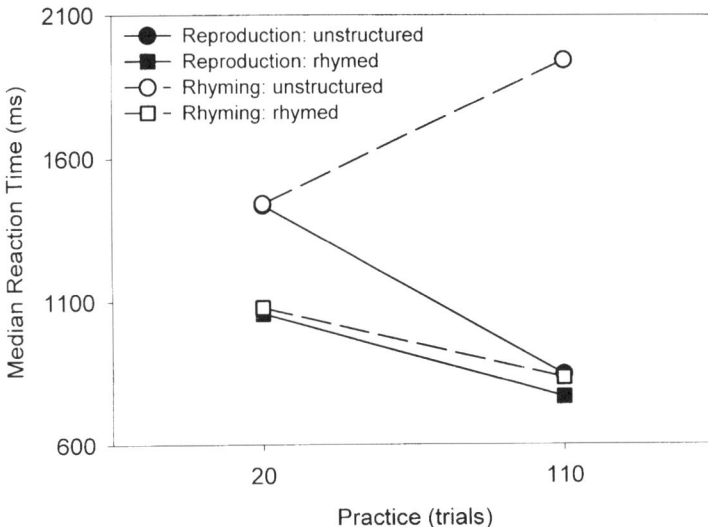

Figure 1. Median reaction times for syllable reproduction (free association) and syllable
rhyming in Ach (1910, Designs I and II), as a function of the syllables' previous list
membership (rhymed vs. unstructured list) and practice (20 vs. 110 repetitions of list
reading). Data are taken from, and averaged across, subjects B-E.

According to Ach, this outcome pattern reflects the conflict between will and habit. Practice in pairing particular stimuli with particular responses should strengthen the associations between the corresponding stimulus and response representations, so that presenting the stimulus another time will automatically induce the tendency to repeat the associated response. To overcome this habit, some amount of "will power" is required, the more the stronger the respective S-R association is. As applying will power arguably takes time, reaction time should in fact increase with increasing conflict between willed and automatically activated response, hence the better practiced a conflicting response to a given stimulus (or the underlying S-R association) is. High degrees of practice should also call up habit-related errors — a prediction that is also nicely confirmed by Ach's findings.

Following the pioneer study of Ach (1910), the combined method was continuously improved and refined, mostly by Ach's students (for a review, see Ach 1935). For instance, Glässner (1912) showed that syllables from a previously learned fixed-order list (i.e., items which are presumably highly associated) facilitate performance in a reproduction task ("name any associate") but impair performance in a rhyming task, as compared to syllables from a varied-order list (i.e., weakly associated items). Müller (1932) manipulated the strength of S-R associations by varying the type of interitem relationship, ranging from arbitrary pairings (e.g., "pin-jor", "wad-tim") to identical syllables combining to a legal word (e.g., "bon-bon", "dum-dum"). As expected, reproduction performance monotonously increased with hypothesized association strength, whereas performance in a task requiring a novel response to each item ("replace vowel by 'au'") showed the opposite effect.

The theoretical considerations of Ach and his students did not go without challenge, however. In his dissertation work, Lewin (1917, 1922a, 1922b) not only made a (rather unsuccessful) attempt to replicate Ach's findings with the original combined method, he also investigated the impact of practicing the rhyming and rearranging of syllables on their later practice-consistent versus inconsistent use in rhyming and rearranging tasks. Whereas the original method required subjects to read through structured or unstructured syllable lists in order to induce associations between succeeding list members, Lewin attempted to induce those associations by having subjects actually perform rhyming and rearranging tasks on syllables. So, instead of presenting his subjects with pairs of rhymed or rearranged syllables, he presented only one syllable and asked the subjects to produce the rhyme or rearranged member themselves. There were several blocks of practice for the rhyming and the rearranging task. Some syllables only appeared under the rhyming instruction, some only under the rearranging instruction, and some under both instructions (control items). After nine days of practice, all syllables were tested under either instruction. However, there was hardly any difference between reaction times and error rates for practice-consistent and practice-inconsistent task instructions, suggesting that S-R associations were not formed or not operative under these circumstances (Lewin 1922a). Interestingly, though, practice consistency did have the predicted effect if during practice the control items were not presented among the consistent items (Lewin 1922b).

Lewin (1922b) attributed his findings to different task sets, presumably induced by the occurrence versus non-occurrence of control items. Note that, in the practice phase, consistent items always validly specified the corresponding task and, therefore, the correct response. In contrast, control items can occur under either instruction, so that each of these items becomes associated with two tasks and two responses. Consequently, Lewin argues, if no control items appear during practice subjects can rely on the automatic retrieval of responses through stimulus presentation, that is, they can follow where their habits lead them. If they adopt this kind of automatic mode, the presentation of inconsistent items in the experimental test phase is likely to result in the automatic retrieval of the practiced, but incorrect responses, this leading to many errors and/or considerably prolonged reaction times — the outcome predicted by Ach's theory. However, if ambivalent control items do occur during practice, subjects are unable to rely on automatic retrieval, because this would produce too many errors. Therefore, they adopt a more controlled S-R translation mode, which is much less susceptible to the presentation of inconsistent stimuli. If so, automatic S-R translation processes would not be as independent from intentional processes as Ach's original approach suggests. In fact, it may be exactly those intentional processes that actually set the stage for automatic translation.

It should be noted that the empirical basis for Lewin's arguments is not watertight. Simoneit (1926) and Ach (1935) pointed out that having people not read through pairs of syllables but practice a particular task is likely to call up task-specific strategies that may work against strong interitem associations. For instance, practicing the rhyming task might lead one to focus onto the rhyming-relevant letter position only and to ignore the remaining letters, which may not allow for strong associations between the whole stimulus syllable and the response. In fact, Simoneit (1926) demonstrated pronounced practice-consistency effects even in Lewin's original design by only increasing the frequency of task switching, that is, by introducing a condition that is likely to counteract the development of task-specific strategies. So, it would be premature to settle the Ach-Lewin debate without further systematic experimenting, the more so as the original findings are based on very few (often single) subjects without any formal statistical testing. However, we will also see that the figures of thought that arose in this debate are still topical today, after having been rediscovered, if not reinvented, several times already. Moreover, the available studies also demonstrate that S-R translation is not only determined by intentional processes, but strongly affected by overlearned, automatic translation processes as well. Obviously, these automatic processes can be experimentally manipulated and even induced independently from intentional processes. Nevertheless, whether their behavioral effects are also independent from intentions remains to be seen.

The Simon effect and the rediscovery of dual routes

Ach's combined method was designed to bring intentional and automatic processes into conflict, so that their relative contribution to action control can be determined, compared, and investigated. A very similar method was discovered accidentally by Simon and Rudell (1967). While exploring the role of handedness and left-vs.-right-hemispheric processing in man-machine interactions, they presented the words "left" and "right" to signal left- and right-hand keypressing reactions. To manipulate the cortical hemisphere responsible for stimulus processing, the words were presented randomly to the left or right ear through earphones. Surprisingly, stimulus location strongly interacted with response location, such that left responses were much faster if the command signal was presented to the left than the right ear, whereas right responses were faster with right-side presentation. Follow-up studies by Simon and colleagues demonstrated that this effect is much more general than one might assume (for an overview, see Lu & Proctor 1995). Similar effects were observed with tone pitch (Simon & Small 1969), visual color (Craft & Simon 1970), or other nonspatial features as relevant stimulus, showing that what matters is the relationship between (irrelevant) stimulus location and (relevant) response location, and not that between (relevant) stimulus meaning and (irrelevant)

stimulus location. Furthermore, hemisphere-specific processing does not substantially contribute to the effect, as it can be obtained even if both stimulus
locations fall into the same visual field (e.g., Craft & Simon 1970) or if
unimanual pointing responses are employed (e.g., Simon 1968).

Over the years, several explanations have been suggested to account for
the "Simon effect", as it is called since Hedge and Marsh (1975), but the
differences between existing models are rather subtle (see Hommel & Prinz
1997, for a recent overview). The very first account proposed by Simon (1968,
1969) attributes the effect to a "natural tendency" to respond toward the
source of stimulation. If, for instance, a signal indicating the left response
appears on the right side, this automatically induces the tendency to respond
"toward the right side". As this tendency is misleading, it needs to be overcome by time-consuming processes, which are not required if the signal had
appeared on the response-corresponding left side. Although this approach
goes not much further than to redescribe the empirical findings, it is interesting to note that it follows the same line of reasoning than that by Ach (1910):
Stimuli might activate overlearned (or even inborn) habits that compete with
intentional translation processes for action control. If such a description really
captures the essence of the Simon effect, the Simon task might be a useful tool
to investigate the relationship and interplay between automatic and intentional
processes of S-R translation.

In fact, the distinction between parallel automatic and intentional routes
from stimuli to responses plays a prominent role in most models on the Simon
effect and similar phenomena, the perhaps most comprehensive approach
being the dimensional-overlap model proposed by Kornblum and colleagues
(Kornblum 1992, 1994; Kornblum et al. 1990). According to the model, the
intentional route works as assumed by most other information processing
models, with stimuli being encoded and translated into the correct response,
followed by retrieval and execution of the corresponding motor program. The
automatic route comes into play if stimulus and response features overlap.
Then the stimulus will automatically prime the feature-overlapping response,
whether this response is correct or not. If it is correct, the same motor program
is activated via two routes, resulting in a speed-up of program retrieval. But if
it is the wrong response, two responses will be active and compete for
execution, which calls for a time-consuming conflict-resolution process that
delays eventual responding.

Although the details of this model are still under debate and in need of clarification, its basic assumption of parallel intentional and automatic routes of S-R translation are shared by many other models in the S-R compatibility domain (e.g., Barber & O'Leary 1997; De Jong et al. 1994; Eimer et al. 1995; Hommel 1993a). This is the more interesting as those dual-route models can be seen as mere translations (though with somewhat more detail) of Ach's theory on the relationship between will and habit from an outdated, phenomenologically inspired language into more fashionable information-processing terms. Of course, the theoretical focus differs slightly between these approaches: Ach was mainly interested in practice-induced automatic translation, whereas compatibility approaches rather focus on automaticity due to feature overlap. However, even though it makes sense to treat practice and feature overlap as distinct factors capable of producing automatic response activation (Hommel 1998; Kornblum et al. 1990), this has no obvious implications for how one conceives of the relationship and interplay between intentional and automatic translation processes as such.

Strong support for the dual-route conception comes from psychophysiological studies. For instance, presenting a lateralized stimulus has been found to prime the corresponding response up to a level that can be observed in lateralized readiness potentials (LRPs; De Jong et al. 1994; Sommer et al. 1993), electromyographical recordings (Zachay 1991), and registrations of subthreshold movements (Zachay 1991) — even when stimulus location is completely irrelevant and even if the correct response is eventually performed. Furthermore, Eimer (1995) showed that merely presenting cues with a spatial meaning (i.e., left- or right-pointing arrow-heads) activates the spatially corresponding response, and this is true even if those cues are not consciously perceived (Eimer & Schlaghecken, 1998; Leuthold & Kopp 1998). So, there is little doubt that stimuli can be translated into response activation even if this runs counter to one's current intention to act, this strongly suggesting parallel intentional and automatic translation.

More evidence on the existence of more than one route from stimulus to response comes from studies on the temporal dynamics of the Simon effect. In several experiments in my lab I consistently observed that the size of the Simon effect decreases with increasing task difficulty. For instance, when I varied the lateral retinal eccentricity of a form stimulus from 0.2° to 6.1°, I found the benefit of S-R correspondence over noncorrespondence to decrease from 23 to -5 ms (Hommel 1993a: Exp. 2) — a rather counterintuitive result. One possible explanation, also suggested by De Jong et al. (1994), assumes a spontaneous decay of automatically induced response activation. Figure 2 shows the logic of this explanation. Assume that presenting a lateralized stimulus automatically activates the corresponding response, but this activation quickly decays over time, just as indicated by the leftmost activation function (see broken lines) in Figure 2. If the relevant stimulus feature is easy to process, it is soon translated into the correct response, as indicated by the activation function in the middle (fast intentional). As the activation of this response temporally overlaps with the automatically activated response, a pronounced Simon effect is obtained: fast responses if both activations refer to the same response, slow responses if they refer to different responses. However, if one makes processing the relevant stimulus feature more difficult (e.g., by presenting it at retinal locations with suboptimal spatial resolution), intentional S-R translation will be delayed, as indicated by the rightmost activation function in Figure 2. With increasing delay the temporal overlap of intentional and automatic activation decreases, so that it becomes more and more likely that the automatically induced response activation has already decayed at the time the response is selected. If so, automatic response activation does no longer affect performance, hence no Simon effect.

According to this temporal-overlap account, intentional and automatic translation processes are independent and can thus be experimentally manipulated separately. This allows for a number of predictions, some of which have already been empirically confirmed. First, one would expect that any manipu-

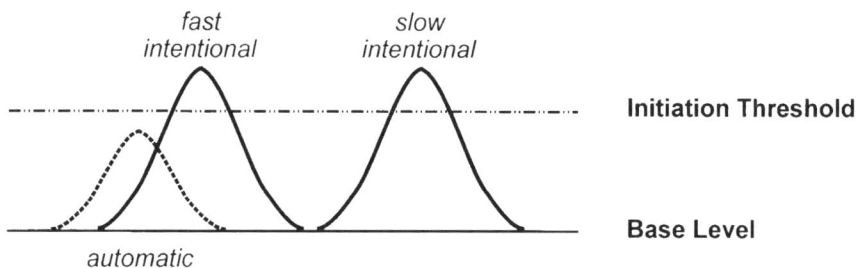

Figure 2. A temporal-overlap model of the Simon effect. Fast automatic translation produces temporary, subthreshold stimulus-induced activation of the corresponding response, followed by quick decay. If intentional translation is fast, there is temporal overlap of automatic and intentional response activation, this yielding facilitation if both converge onto the same response, and conflict if not. If intentional translation is slow, there is no overlap and, hence, no facilitation or conflict.

lation that prolongs the processing of the relevant stimulus feature and/or the activation of the correct response (without affecting location processing) reduces the size of the Simon effect. In fact, marked reductions of effect size (up to the elimination of the effect) have been demonstrated as a consequence of reducing the visual quality of the stimulus through pattern masking (Hommel 1993a), of making the alternative stimuli less discriminable (Hommel 1994; Lu & Proctor 1994), of increasing the size of the memory set the stimuli belong to (Hommel 1995), or of introducing a secondary task (McCann & Johnston 1992).

Second, the Simon effect should not only decrease between conditions of different difficulty, but also within a condition, namely from fast to slow responses of the same subject. That is, if we compute the Simon effect separately for the lower and the upper tails of individual reaction-time distributions, we would expect the Simon effect to be the smaller the longer the reaction times are. In fact, the effect size can be shown to continuously decrease from fast to slow portions of the reaction time distribution (De Jong et al. 1994; Eimer et al. 1995; Hommel 1997; see, however, Zhang & Kornblum 1997, for some caveats as to this kind of analysis).

Third, if the decrease of the Simon effect with increasing task difficulty is really due to the spontaneous decay of automatic response activation, one should be able to work against the effect's decrease by introducing task features that make the location of the stimulus more relevant to the task. Again, the evidence is positive. If one asks the subjects in a Simon task to report the location of the stimulus after each trial, the effect gets even larger than normal (Hommel, submitted a; Simon 1982).

Fourth, the temporal-overlap model suggests that, under certain stimulus conditions, one should be able to completely invert the Simon effect's temporal dynamics. In the standard task, the relevant stimulus feature often takes much longer to process than the irrelevant location information, which is why the "intentional" function in Figure 2 begins to rise only some time after the "automatic" function. However, what if we came up with a relevant stimulus feature that can be processed even faster than stimulus location? Then, the intentional function would start before the automatic one, so that the effect of S-R correspondence should be the more pronounced the longer the relative reaction times are — hence increase from the lower to the upper tail of the reaction time distribution. This prediction is supported by Hommel (1996: Exp. 1), where subjects responded to the mere onset of a lateralized stimulus by performing an already prepared response. Reaction times were not only very quick, they also showed the expected distribution, with longer reaction times being associated with a larger correspondence effect.

Taken in sum, there is ample evidence from Simon tasks that intentional and automatic processes coexist and compete for action control. They are likely to exhibit different time courses — depending on the particular stimulus features and task context — that can be dissociated and selectively manipulated. Although the genesis of automatic translation processes due to S-R feature overlap on the one hand and those due to S-R practice on the other may be different, the implications from compatibility studies and from learning studies nicely converge onto the same theoretical conclusions.

Intentional control of automatic translation processes

The evidence discussed so far clearly rules out the perhaps more intuitive idea that S-R translation is a direct reflection of human will. Rather, it seems that human performance emerges from the interplay of both intentional and automatic translation processes. But does this necessarily imply that intentional and automatic translation processes are of comparable status except that the former are more related to intentions than the latter? Is it really true that automatic processes are autonomous operations that do in no way depend on the intentional states of an acting person, as assumed, among others, by Ach (1910), De Jong et al. (1994), or Kornblum and coworkers (1990)? I will now go on to discuss several empirical reasons — mostly taken from S-R compatibility research (for a broader review, see Hommel, in press) — to doubt the assumption that automatic translation is completely independent from intentions. There is evidence that automatic translation is a more or less direct function of intentional preparation, suggesting that intentional processes do not really compete with, but rather set the stage for automatic processes. Hence, in the words of Bargh (1989), automaticity may (always?) be conditional automaticity, just as suspected by Lewin (1922b).

To begin with, let me use the example sketched in Figure 3 to organize the further discussion. It refers to a typical situation in a Simon task, which in this case requires pressing a left versus right key in response to the green or red color of a visual stimulus, respectively. Let us now assume that a red stimulus appears on the left side, an incompatible situation that induces competition

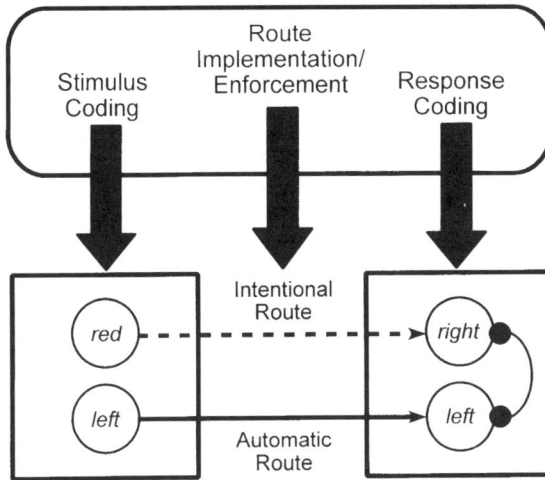

Figure 3. Illustration of possible influences of intentional preparation processes on automatic stimulus-response translation.

between the correct response activated via the intentional route from color to response and the automatically activated, but incorrect stimulus-corresponding response. Logically, there are at least three ways in which translation via the automatic route could be affected by, or depend on, intentional processes. First, intentional processes may be able to influence, or even to determine, whether and how stimuli are cognitively coded (e.g., as LEFT or RIGHT), and thus be able to control the input side of the automatic channel. Second, intentional processes might have an impact on how responses are coded (e.g., as LEFT or RIGHT), and thus be able to control the output side of the automatic channel. Third, intentional processes may even have a direct or indirect influence on the automatic translation process itself, or even have control over its effect on response selection and related processes. In fact, there is evidence for all three kinds of influence.

Stimulus coding and attention

Outside the lab, there are many ways to control even our strongest habits, with one of the best being distraction and ignoring: We avoid getting in touch and view with the stimuli we know to trigger inefficient, unwanted, or unacceptable behavior. But there are more subtle means also, such as ignoring a stimulus we are confronted with, or concentrating on a less critical stimulus attribute. Hence, the way stimuli affect our behavior strongly depends on whether we attend and how we perceive them, which is nicely demonstrated by studies on the impact of perception and attention on the Simon effect.

In the standard Simon task, only one stimulus appears at a time, and it is usually presented to the left or right of a central fixation mark. However, Simon effects can also be obtained with more complex visual displays, displays that require attentional selection of the stimulus. For instance, Grice, Boroughs, and Canham (1984) presented their subjects with two stimuli in each trial, one on either side, one being a to-be-discriminated response-signaling letter and the other a neutral distractor letter. Pronounced Simon effects (i.e., better performance if the target letter corresponded with the response it signaled) were obtained in this study, as well as in studies where target and distractor differed in color (Hommel 1993b; Proctor & Lu 1994) or meaning (O'Leary & Barber 1993). Inasmuch as the Simon effect indicates automatic S-R translation, these findings show that it is not the stimulus information per se that is translated into response activation but the *attended* stimulus information only. Therefore, "automatic" translation processes critically depends on the intention to process a particular stimulus (Stoffer & Umiltà 1997). This is also obvious from a study of Hommel (submitted b), where the stimulus displays looked like the one shown in panel A of Figure 4.

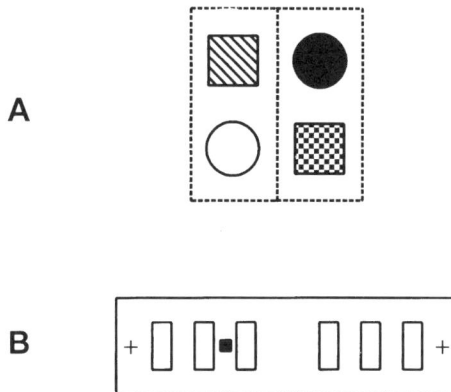

Figure 4. Schematic illustrations of the stimulus displays used in the studies of (A) Hommel (submitted a) and (B) Nicoletti and Umiltà (1989). See text for further explanations.

The display always consisted of four differently colored objects, whose form signaled left and right responses. The actual target was cued by coloring a frame that surrounded the display, hence by presenting the color of the relevant stimulus. Although the stimulus display as such was more or less symmetrical, performance was much better if the cued target was on the same side as the response it required.

Another fine demonstration of the role attentional processes play in controlling automatic S-R translation was provided by Nicoletti and Umiltà (1989), who used a stimulus display as sketched in panel B of Figure 4. Subjects kept their eyes at a fixation mark to the left or right side of a row of six boxes, in which the stimulus appeared. Attention was to be focused on a small solid square located in between two boxes, with the particular location of the square varying randomly from trial to trial. Interestingly, performance did not depend on the side of the fixation mark or the stimulus, but on whether the stimulus appeared to the left or right side of the currently attended location, that is, it was best with correspondence between the location of the stimulus relative to the attended square and the location of the response.

Obviously, the very same stimulus condition can trigger very different responses depending on which part of the stimulus configuration is attended, which stimulus is searched for, and so forth. Given that in the described studies attention was induced and manipulated by means of instruction and, thus, was under voluntary control of the subjects, this means that automatic S-R translation as indicated by the Simon effect cannot be completely automatic and unconditional. Rather, intentional/attentional processes seem to implement a particular state or task set to code, analyze, and perceive the reaction stimuli in a particular way, and it is only this set that allows automatic translation processes to take place.

Response coding and intention

In addition to the input part of overlearned or compatible S-R couplings the output part also provides a means to control S-R translation and its effect on behavior. In fact, there is evidence that S-R compatibility effects strongly depend on the response part, on how a response is coded and interpreted, and on whether it is prepared in advance of the stimulus.

The role of response preparation has been investigated in the study of Hommel (1996). In one experiment, subjects responded during a whole block by pressing the same response key to the onset of a temporally unpredictable green square coming up on the left or right side. On very few occasions, a red square also appeared immediately after a response key was depressed. This signaled a further response with either the same key or, in a separate session, with the opposite key. That is, subjects were required to hold only one response in preparation in one condition, but two responses in the other — although the two responses were no real response alternatives. Interestingly, the two-key condition yielded a much more pronounced effect of (green) S-R correspondence than the one-key condition. This suggests that holding two responses in preparation results in, or even requires, much stronger spatial response coding than preparing only one response. Response coding, in turn, strongly affects automatic translation because, for obvious reasons, translating a left stimulus into a left response, say, only works if one of the responses is actually coded as left.

Further evidence that compatibility phenomena cannot only be affected, but are even determined by response coding, can be taken from the study of Hommel (1993c). In this study, subjects performed left and right keypresses in response to the pitch of a tone. Like in a typical Simon task, the tone was randomly presented through a left or right loudspeaker. In addition, each keypress flashed a light-emitting diode on the opposite side. In one group, the instruction referred to the response keys, hence subjects were asked to "press the left/right key in response to the low/high pitch". A second group performed exactly the same task, but they were instructed to "flash the right/left light in response to the low/high pitch". Given that flashing the right/left light was done by pressing the left/right key, one might not expect any impact of the instruction on a truly automatic translation process. Yet, the typical benefit of stimulus-key correspondence was only obtained under key instruction, whereas the light group showed exactly the opposite result (i.e., better performance with stimulus-light correspondence). Obviously, the light group had coded their responses in terms of light location and as these were always opposite to the keys, the effect was also the opposite.

In sum, processes of response coding and preparation are as effective as stimulus-coding processes in controlling both the degree and direction of "automatic" S-R translation. Given that response coding was a rather direct function of task instructions and the way these instructions were implemented, we see once more that automatic translation strongly depends on intentional processes.

Stimulus-response translation, practice, and task set

Clearly, both stimulus and response coding processes play a decisive role for the occurrence of automatic translation. But there are even more direct influences on the effect of automatic translation processes, as well as on the likelihood and the time of their occurrence, just as indicated by the middle vertical arrow in Figure 3. For example, in the study of Hommel (1994), subjects performed a standard Simon task, except that the frequency of noncorresponding (incompatible) trials was varied from 20% to 80%. As a consequence, the location of the stimulus was no longer as uninformative as with 50% probability. In fact, frequency of noncorrespondence trials had a strong impact on the Simon effect: The effect sharply increased with low frequencies and was eliminated with the highest frequency. Obviously, then, (strategically?) using the information provided by a task-irrelevant stimulus attribute can overrule the effect of automatic S-R translation.

Interestingly, S-R contingencies and the associations and strategies they induce can even transfer to a different task. In the study of Proctor and Lu (1999), subjects performed a Simon task after receiving practice in a standard spatial compatibility task, with either a compatible mapping (left stimulus → left response, right stimulus → right response) or an incompatible mapping (left stimulus → right response, right stimulus → left response). The group practicing with the compatible mapping exhibited a normal Simon effect, with S-R correspondence yielding faster responses than noncorrespondence. However, the group practicing with the incompatible mapping showed the opposite pattern, that is, S-R noncorrespondence was now faster than correspondence. Hence, the association of stimulus and response locations strategically acquired in the practice task must have been involuntarily transferred to the Simon task, where the respective S-R associations counteracted the effect of S-R compatibility.

Strategies and task sets cannot only counteract, but also effectively eliminate automatic translation. An impressive demonstration of that phenomenon comes from Eimer and Schlaghecken (1998). As already mentioned, these authors presented their subjects with subliminal left- and right-pointing arrow-heads before the actual target stimulus, which again signaled a left-vs.-right keypress. If the target was also an arrowhead, the arrow primes produced LRPs indicative of automatic activation of the hand that corresponded to the prime's direction. Of course, this is what one would expect from an automatic-translation approach to S-R compatibility. However, when the arrow targets were replaced by single-letter stimuli, the primes no longer produced an LRP. Therefore, if one attributes the effect of arrowhead primes on lateralized responses to automatic S-R translation, this kind of automaticity must strongly depend on whether and how a person intends to act to a given stimulus. This conclusion is also suggested by a study of Valle-Inclán and Redondo (1998), who measured LRPs in a Simon task with a trial-by-trial variation of the mapping between the relevant stimulus feature (i.e., color) and the response keys. If the mapping appeared before the stimulus, the stimulus elicited the usual LRP related to the spatially corresponding hand, but not if the stimulus preceded the mapping. Inasmuch as LRPs induced by stimulus location can be taken as an indicator of automatic S-R translation, this finding strongly suggests that automatic translation is tightly coupled to, and apparently even depends upon, the subject's intention to act at the time of stimulus presentation. Although this does not always seem to be the case (Eimer 1995), it at least demonstrates that under some circumstances task sets can have full control over automatic translation processes.

Conclusion

To sum up, we have seen that intentions by no means shield our response tendencies from being activated by environmental stimulation. Responses may become automatically activated by a stimulus if they were often paired with that stimulus in the past, and/or if they are compatible (i.e., share features) with it. Automatic S-R translation processes can be experimentally dissociated from intentional processes, they can be independently manipulated, and they can be shown to have different characteristics. Nevertheless, automatic translation processes are not completely independent from intentions. Indeed, intentions can affect automatic processing in many ways, for example by determining whether and how stimuli and responses are cognitively represented, or by defining and preparing intentional translation processes. That is, intentional processes do not so much compete with automatic processes, as assumed by Ach (1910) or later dual-route models, but rather set the stage for automatic processing to take place (Hommel, in press), which is more in line with the position of Lewin (1922b). If this is so, one may doubt whether there is such a thing like a pure intentional or pure automatic process at all. Intentional processes apparently install automatic processes and can therefore never have complete control over their results, whereas automatic processes depend on intentional preparation and are therefore always controlled. Thus, it seems that speaking of intentional and automatic processing is always relative and in a sense even wrong. However, to find out in which sense it is wrong requires a much better understanding of both how intentions are implemented into the human cognitive system, and how this implementation and its consequences are shaped by previous experience.

References

Ach, N. (1910). *Über den Willensakt und das Temperament.* Leipzig: Quelle & Meyer.
Ach, N. (1935). Analyse des Willens. In E. Abderhalden (Ed.), *Handbuch der biologischen Arbeitsmethoden.* Berlin: Urban & Schwarzenberg, Vol. VI.
Allport, A., Styles, E., & Hsieh, S. (1994). Shifting intentional set: Exploring the dynamic control of tasks. In C. Umiltà & M. Moscovitch (Eds.), *Attention and performance XV: Conscious and nonconscious information processing.* Cambridge, MA: MIT Press, 421–452.
Atkinson, R.C., & Shiffrin, R.M. (1968). Human memory: A proposed system and its control processes. *The Psychology of Learning and Motivation, 2,* 89–195.
Baars, B.J. (1987). What is conscious in the control of action? A modern ideomotor theory of voluntary control. In D. S. Gorfein & R.R. Hoffman (Eds.), *Memory and learning: The Ebbinghaus centennial conference.* Hillsdale, NJ: Erlbaum, 253–270.
Barber, P.J., & O'Leary, M.J (1997). The relevance of salience: Towards an activational account of irrelevant stimulus-response compatibility effects. In B. Hommel & W. Prinz (Eds.), *Theoretical issues in stimulus-response compatibility.* Amsterdam: North-Holland, 135–172.
Bargh, J.A. (1989). Conditional automaticity: Varieties of automatic influence in social perception and cognition. In J. S. Uleman, & J.A. Bargh (Eds.), *Unintended thought.* London: Guilford Press, 3–51.
Craft, J.L., & Simon, J.R. (1970). Processing symbolic information from a visual display: Interference from an irrelevant directional cue. *Journal of Experimental Psychology, 83,* 415–420.
De Jong, R., Liang, C.-C., & Lauber, E. (1994). Conditional and unconditional automaticity: A dual-process model of effects of spatial stimulus-response correspondence. *Journal of Experimental Psychology: Human Perception and Performance, 20,* 731–750.
Eimer, M. (1995). Stimulus-response compatibility and automatic response activation: Evidence from psychophysiological studies. *Journal of Experimental Psychology: Human Perception and Performance, 21,* 837–854.
Eimer, M., Hommel, B., & Prinz, W. (1995). S-R compatibility and response selection. *Acta Psychologica, 90,* 301–313.

Eimer, M., & Schlaghecken, F. (1998). Effects of masked stimuli on motor activation: Behavioral and electrophysiological evidence. *Journal of Experimental Psychology: Human Perception and Performance*, 24, 1737–1747.

Gibson, J.J. (1941). A critical review of the concept of set in contemporary experimental psychology. *Psychological Bulletin*, 38, 781–817.

Glässner, G. (1912). *Über Willenshemmung und Willensbahnung*. Leipzig: Quelle & Meyer.

Grice, G.R., Boroughs, J.M., & Canham, L. (1984). Temporal dynamics of associative interference and facilitation produced by visual context. *Perception & Psychophysics*, 36, 499–507.

Heckhausen, H., & Beckmann, J. (1990). Intentional action and action slips. *Psychological Review*, 97, 36–48.

Hedge, A., & Marsh, N.W.A. (1975). The effect of irrelevant spatial correspondences on two-choice response-time. *Acta Psychologica*, 39, 427–439.

Hommel, B. (1993a). The relationship between stimulus processing and response selection in the Simon task: Evidence for a temporal overlap. *Psychological Research*, 55, 280–290.

Hommel, B. (1993b). The role of attention for the Simon effect. *Psychological Research*, 55, 208–222.

Hommel, B. (1993c). Inverting the Simon effect by intention. *Psychological Research*, 55, 270–279.

Hommel, B. (1994). Spontaneous decay of response code activation. *Psychological Research*, 56, 261–268.

Hommel, B. (1995). Conflict versus misguided search as explanation of S-R correspondence effects. *Acta Psychologica*, 89, 37–51.

Hommel, B. (1996). S-R compatibility effects without response uncertainty. *Quarterly Journal of Experimental Psychology*, 49A, 546–571.

Hommel, B. (1997). Interactions between stimulus-stimulus congruence and stimulus-response compatibility. *Psychological Research*, 59, 248–260.

Hommel, B. (1998). Observing one's own action — and what it leads to. In J. S. Jordan (Ed.), *Systems theory and apriori aspects of perception*. Amsterdam: North-Holland, 143–179.

Hommel, B. (in press). The prepared reflex: Automaticity and control in stimulus-response translation. In S. Monsell & J. Driver (Eds.), *Attention and performance*. Cambridge, MA: MIT Press, Vol.XVIII.

Hommel, B. (submitted a). *Decay and maintenance of spatial codes under dual-task conditions*. Manuscript submitted for publication.

Hommel, B. (submitted b). *Automatic spatial coding in perception and memory*. Manuscript under revision.

Hommel, B., & Prinz, W. (Eds.). *Theoretical issues in stimulus-response compatibility*. Amsterdam: North-Holland.

James, W. (1890). *The principles of psychology*. New York: Dover Publications.

Kornblum, S., Hasbroucq, T., & Osman, A. (1990). Dimensional overlap: Cognitive basis for stimulus-response compatibility — a model and taxonomy. *Psychological Review*, 97, 253–270.

Kornblum, S. (1992). Dimensional overlap and dimensional relevance in stimulus-response and stimulus-stimulus compatibility. In G.E. Stelmach & J. Requin (Eds.), *Tutorials in motor behavior*. Amsterdam: North-Holland, Vol.2, 743–777.

Kornblum, S. (1994). The way irrelevant dimensions are processed depends on what they overlap with: The case of Stroop- and Simon-like stimuli. *Psychological Research, 56,* 130–135.

Leuthold, H., & Kopp, B. (1998). Mechanisms of priming by masked stimuli. *Psychological Science, 9,* 263–269.

Lewin, K. (1917). Die psychische Tätigkeit bei der Hemmung von Willensvorgängen und das Grundgesetz der Assoziation. *Zeitschrift für Psychologie, 77,* 212–247.

Lewin, K. (1922a). Das Problem der Willensmessung und das Grundgesetz der Assoziation I. *Psychologische Forschung, 1,* 191–302.

Lewin, K. (1922b). Das Problem der Willensmessung und das Grundgesetz der Assoziation II. *Psychologische Forschung, 2,* 65–140.

Lotze, R.H. (1852). *Medicinische Psychologie oder die Physiologie der Seele*. Leipzig: Weidmann'sche Buchhandlung.

Lu, C.-H., & Proctor, R.W. (1994). Processing of an irrelevant location dimension as a function of the relevant stimulus dimension. *Journal of Experimental Psychology: Human Perception and Performance, 20,* 286–298.

Lu, C.-H., & Proctor, R.W. (1995). The influence of irrelvant location information on performance: A review of the Simon and spatial Stroop effects. *Psychonomic Bulletin & Review, 2,* 174–207.

McCann, R.S., & Johnston, J.C. (1992). Locus of the single-channel bottleneck in dual-task interference. *Journal of Experimental Psychology: Human Perception and Performance, 18,* 471–484.

Monsell, S. (1996). Control of mental processes. In V. Bruce (Ed.), *Unsolved mysteries of the mind*. Hove: Erlbaum, 93–148.

Müller, E. (1932). Beiträge zur Lehre von der Determination. *Archiv für die gesamte Psychologie, 84,* 43–102.

Nicoletti, R., & Umiltà, C. (1989). Splitting visual space with attention. *Journal of Experimental Psychology: Human Perception and Performance, 15,* 164–169.

O'Leary, M.J., & Barber, P.J. (1993). Interference effects in the Stroop and Simon paradigms. *Journal of Experimental Psychology: Human Perception and Performance, 19,* 830–844.

Ouellette, J.A., & Wood, W. (1998). Habit and intention in everyday life: The multiple processes by which past behavior predicts future behavior. *Psychological Bulletin, 124,* 54–74.

Posner, M.I., & Snyder, C.R.R. (1975). Attention and cognitive control. In R. L. Solso (Ed.), *Information processing and cognition*. Hillsdale, NJ: Erlbaum, 55–85.

Proctor, R.W., & Lu, C.-H. (1994). Referential coding and attention shifting accounts of the Simon effect. *Psychological Research, 56,* 185–195.

Proctor, R.W., & Lu, C.-H. (1999). Processing irrelevant location information: Practice and transfer effects in choice-reaction tasks. *Memory & Cognition, 27,* 63–77.

Reason, J.T. (1990). *Human error*. New York: Cambridge University Press.

Shallice, T. (1994). Multiple levels of control processes. In C. Umiltà & M. Moscovitch

(Eds.), *Attention and performance XV: Conscious and nonconscious information processing*. Cambridge, MA: MIT Press, 395–420.

Shiffrin, R.M., & Schneider, W. (1977). Controlled and automatic human information processing: II. Perceptual learning, automatic attending, and a general theory. *Psychological Review*, 84, 127–190.

Simon, J.R. (1968). Effect of ear stimulated on reaction time and movement time. *Journal of Experimental Psychology*, 78, 344–346.

Simon, J.R. (1969). Reactions toward the source of stimulation. *Journal of Experimental Psychology*, 81, 174–176.

Simon, J.R. (1982). Effect of an auditory stimulus on the processing of a visual stimulus under single- and dual-tasks conditions. *Acta Psychologica*, 51, 61–73.

Simon, J.R., & Rudell, A.P. (1967). Auditory S-R compatibility: The effect of an irrelevant cue on information processing. *Journal of Applied Psychology*, 51, 300–304.

Simon, J.R., & Small, A.M. (1969). Processing auditory information: Interference from an irrelevant cue. *Journal of Applied Psychology*, 53, 433–435.

Simoneit, M. (1926). Willenshemmung und Assoziation. *Zeitschrift für Psychologie*, 100, 161–235.

Sommer, W., Leuthold, H., & Hermanutz, M. (1993). Covert effects of alcohol revealed by event-related potentials. *Perception & Psychophysics*, 54, 127–135.

Stoffer, T.H., & Umiltà, C. (1997). Spatial stimulus coding and the focus of attention in S-R compatibility and the Simon effect. In B. Hommel & W. Prinz (Eds.), *Theoretical issues in stimulus-response compatibility*. Amsterdam: North-Holland, 181–208.

Stroop, J.R. (1935). Studies of interference in serial verbal reactions. *Journal of Experimental Psychology*, 28, 643–662.

Valle-Inclán, F., & Redondo, M. (1998). On the automaticity of ipsilateral response activation in the Simon effect. *Psychophysiology*, 35, 366–371.

Zachay, A. (1991). *Diskrete und kontinuierliche Informationsverarbeitungsmodelle zur Erklärung von Reiz-Reaktions-Inkompatibilitäten: Evidenz für einen Antwortkonflikt beim Simon-Effekt*. Unpublished master's thesis, Tübingen, Germany.

Zhang, J., & Kornblum, S. (1997). Distributional analysis and De Jong, Liang, and Lauber's (1994) dual-process model of the Simon effect. *Journal of Experimental Psychology: Human Perception and Performance*, 23, 1543–1551.

Affect Infusion and Affect Control

The Interactive Role of Conscious and Unconscious Processing Strategies in Mood Management

Joseph P. Forgas & Joseph Ciarrochi
University of New South Wales

This chapter argues that unconscious infusion of affect into cognitive processes during constructive, substantive processing, and the conscious cognitive control of affect during motivated processing can be conceptualised as distinct, dissociated mental processes. Nevertheless, these two mental processes interact to produce an automatic, homeostatic mood management system that helps to calibrate and maintain an affective equilibrium in our daily lives. The first part of this chapter reviews the considerable empirical evidence suggesting that even low-key, temporary moods can produce significant mood-congruent cognitive biases . Furthermore, considerable evidence suggests that these affect infusion effects are largely unconscious.

As negative affect produces negative thoughts, and negative thoughts in turn are likely to generate and intensify negative affect, these automatic affect infusion processes clearly must be self-limiting in normal, well-adjusted people. Once a threshold level of negativity is reached, a complementary affect-control strategy is triggered designed to reduce affective extremity to manageable levels. The second part of the chapter reviews extensive complementary evidence indicating that in many circumstances, more conscious and motivated processing strategies may be adopted by people, leading to affect-incongruent cognitive outcomes.

Most of the previous literature looked at affect infusion and affect control as distinct, dissociated cognitive strategies that operate in isolation from each other. In a break with this tradition, the recently proposed Affect Infusion

Model (Forgas 1995) suggests that these processing strategies are selectively recruited in predictable — and testable — situational and psychological circumstances. The mood management model outlined here goes one step further: It suggests that affect infusion and affect control are in fact interactive cognitive processes, representing two aspects of an automatic, homeostatic affect management system.

The notion that affective states such as mood can unconsciously influence our judgments and behaviour has been a source of fascination to artists, philosophers, and lay people since time immemorial, and has been the subject of psychological theorising for nearly a century (Freud 1915). More recently, psychologists have begun to apply systematic experimental methods to investigate this phenomenon (Fiedler 1991; Forgas 1995; Zajonc 1980). An affective state is considered to be unconscious when a person is not aware either of its source, its target, or both (Murphy, Monahan and Zajonc 1995). There is considerable evidence suggesting that unconscious affect is not only very common in everyday life, but also that it has a widespread influence on many cognitive processes (Forgas 1995; Forgas and Moylan 1987; Kunst-Wilson and Zajonc 1980; Murphy and Zajonc 1987; Murphy, Monahan and Zajonc 1995). For example, millions are afflicted with free-floating anxiety, a condition in which the person is unaware of the origin of anxiety (Beck 1976), and everybody may be influenced, at times, with free-floating sadness or joy (Isen 1990). Numerous mundane everyday experiences appear capable of inducing unconscious affect. For example, watching a movie, taking a walk on a sunny day, listening to music, watching a football game, receiving a small gift, drinking a cup of coffee, succeeding or failing at a task, and getting (or not getting) a date on a Friday night can all generate subtle, enduring and frequently unconscious affective states (Forgas 1995).

There is strong evidence that these everyday moods have an automatic, unconscious, mood-congruent influence on many cognitive tasks involving attention, learning, memory, associations and judgments (Bower 1991; Fiedler 1991). There is also strong evidence, however, that once people become aware of their moods, they frequently switch to more targeted, conscious processing strategies designed to limit or eliminate the prevailing affective state (Forgas 1995; Berkowitz 1990; Ciarrochi and Forgas 1997). Such more or less conscious affect control strategies include trying to distract ourselves (Wegner and Petty 1993), focus attention on mood-incongruent information, make affectively rewarding choices (Forgas 1991), or retrieve mood-incongruent information (Forgas & Ciarrochi 1997).

Although there has been growing evidence for the operation of both unconscious, affect-congruent processing strategies, and more conscious, affect-control processes, little attempt has been made previously to link these mechanisms within an integrated affect management model. In other words, affect infusion and affect control have been traditionally understood as independent, dissociated processes. In contrast, this chapter will argue that these mental processes should be considered as interactive, interdependent cognitive mechanisms that jointly constitute a homeostatic mood management system. How do the processes of unconscious affect infusion and conscious affect control interact? Under what conditions will unconscious infusion versus conscious control dominate a processing outcome? This chapter will argue that the mechanisms of unconscious affect infusion and conscious affect control represent two sides of a single, integrated mood management system. Whether a prevailing affective state leads to affect infusion or affect control often depends on subtle contextual differences that may selectively trigger one of two different information processing strategies: elaborate, substantive processing (the major vehicle for affect infusion), or directed, motivated processing (the mechanism for affect control). Extrapolating from the recently proposed Affect Infusion Model (Forgas 1995), the chapter will suggest that affect infusion in the course of substantive processing, and affect control during motivated processing function as two complementary cognitive strategies that together form the dual components of a self-correcting affect management mechanism.

The first part of the chapter presents a detailed interactive model of spontaneous mood management, integrating unconscious and conscious processes within a comprehensive affect management system. It will be argued that this mood management system operates to maintain affective fluctuations within individual limits in the course of normal everyday activities. The model makes specific predictions about when unconscious affect infusion versus conscious control will be likely to dominate a processing outcome. The second part of the chapter will summarise some of the most recent evidence for both the automatic, unconscious and the controlled, conscious aspects of these processes, placing the findings within the context of the mood management model. We will also specifically consider the role of individual difference variables in the operation of such a dual-process mood management system.

The Affect Infusion Model (AIM): When affect is likely to unconsciously colour judgments

Experiences of positive or negative affect accompany us throughout our daily lives. Most of the time these underlying mood states are not intense or salient enough to command conscious attention. Yet there is growing evidence suggesting that transient mood states do have a significant influence both on the content of cognition (what people think), as well as the process of cognition (how people think) (Bower 1981; Forgas 1995a; Schwarz & Clore 1983). For the purposes of this discussion, *affect infusion* may be defined as a process whereby affectively loaded information exerts an influence on, and becomes incorporated into a person's cognitive processes, entering into their constructive deliberations and eventually coloring the outcome in a mood-congruent direction (Forgas 1995a). As we will see shortly, affect infusion in memory, social cognition and judgments is a largely unconscious process.

Affect infusion occurs because processing novel social information usually requires high-level inferential cognitive processes. The classic work of Asch (1946), Heider (1958), and Kelly (1955) established that even the simplest kinds of judgments of brief lists of adjectives are subject to such highly constructive biases. Social information processors can only create a meaningful pattern or Gestalt of the confusing information available to them by the constructive use of their pre-existing thoughts, memories and associations to create a meaningful cognitive representation of the social world. Under certain conditions, the prevailing affective state of a person can become part of the constructive informational base used when interpreting information, producing a judgment or planning a behavior (Fiedler 1991).

There is now clear evidence suggesting that unconscious affect infusion is most likely to occur in the course of such *constructive processing* that involves the substantial transformation rather than mere reproduction of existing cognitive representations. In other words, affect "will influence cognitive processes to the extent that the cognitive task involves the active generation of new information as opposed to the passive conservation of information given" (Fiedler 1990, pp. 2–3). Research has also shown however that affect infusion is not an invariable phenomenon. Frequently, the affective state of a person appears to have no influence on the content of cognition, and may even have an inconsistent, mood-incongruent influence (Erber & Erber 1994; Sedikides 1994). How can we explain these apparently contradictory findings?

The recently proposed *Affect Infusion Model (AIM)* (Forgas 1995a) argues that the nature and extent of unconscious affect infusion into cognition depends fundamentally on what kind of cognitive strategy is adopted by a person in dealing with a particular task. The model identifies four distinct processing strategies, each characterized by different affect infusion potentials. Two of these processing strategies, (1) the *direct access* of pre-existing information, and (2) *motivated processing* in service of a pre-existing goal, represent highly predetermined and directed information search patterns that require little generative, constructive processing, limiting the scope of unconscious affect infusion effects. In contrast, when a cognitive task requires a degree of open, elaborate, constructive processing, people may adopt either (3) a *heuristic*, simplified or a (4) a *substantive*, elaborate processing strategy to compute a new outcome. These are high-infusion strategies, which involve some degree of constructive thinking (Fiedler 1990; 1991; Forgas 1995a) and allow affect to unconsciously infuse outcomes either indirectly (through primed associations; Forgas & Bower 1988) or directly (when people misattribute their affective state to a mistaken source; Schwarz & Clore 1983). A complete description of the AIM and the evidence supporting it is presented by Forgas (1995a), so it will not be reviewed in detail here. The major relevance of the Affect Infusion Model to our discussion is that it seeks to provide a framework within which instances of unconscious affect infusion, as well as instances of more conscious affect control — based on motivated processing — can be characterized within an integrated framework. Together, these two complementary processes may also be considered as part of a single, interactive mood management system.

According to the AIM, most unconscious affect infusion occurs when people employ *substantive processing*. This involves selecting, learning and interpreting novel information, and relating this information to pre-existing knowledge structures. Substantive processing is more likely when the task is complex or atypical, there is adequate cognitive capacity, and there are no specific motivational goals to pre-determine the outcome. Most cognitive theories in psychology implicitly assume that such exhaustive, elaborate and 'dutiful' information processing is the norm. In contrast, the AIM suggests that substantive processing will be adopted only when simpler and less effortful strategies prove unequal to the task. Affect infusion during substantive processing is best understood in terms of memory principles that can account for the role of affect in the selection, learning, interpretation and assimilation of novel information into a pre-existing knowledge base (Bower 1981). The more elaborate and constructive the processing strategy required, the more likely that affectively primed information will become accessible and be incorporated in the cognitive process, eventually infusing its outcome (Fiedler 1991; Forgas 1992b; 1993b).

In contrast, more conscious, targeted and *motivated processing* typically occurs when processing is guided by a specific goal, leading people to employ highly selective, motivated information search and integration strategies designed to produce a preferred outcome. As motivated processing precludes genuinely open, constructive information search and selection strategies, the likelihood of affect infusion is reduced. Motivated processing is the prime technique for achieving mood control, as suggested by several recent studies (Clark & Isen 1982; Erber & Erber 1994; Forgas 1990, 1991; Forgas & Fiedler 1996; Wegner & Erber 1993). Motivated processing as defined here involves more than just a motivation to be accurate (cf. Kunda 1990): It involves a specific goal (such as mood-control) which dominates and guides information search strategies. Motivated processing is particularly likely to occur when people become consciously aware of the causes or consequences of their mood state (Berkowitz & Troccoli 1990; Murphy & Zajonc 1987, 1993; Schwarz & Clore 1983). We shall have more to say about this in the next section.

Distinguishing between the four processing strategies identified by the Affect Infusion Model, and between substantive and motivated processing in particular, has considerable benefits for our understanding of the delicate interplay between affect and cognition, and unconscious affect-infusion and conscious affect-control in particular. Since different processing strategies do imply different affective influences on cognition, and ultimately, behavior, affect control can now be seen as specifically linked to a particular processing strategy — motivated processing — and not to others. Affect infusion in turn is most likely to occur in the course of substantive processing. The AIM predicts that constructive processing (substantive processing in particular) is the prerequisite for unconscious affect infusion to occur, while conscious mood-control should be limited to conditions conducive to motivated processing.

Mechanisms of unconscious affect infusion

Affect infusion occurs because moods can either indirectly (through primed associations) or directly (through the direct use of affect as information) infuse cognitive outcomes. Affect-priming (Bower 1981; Forgas & Bower 1988) is more likely when substantive processing is adopted, while affect-as-information (Schwarz & Clore 1983) should be limited to conditions when heuristic processing is used.

The *affect-as-information* mechanism suggests that "individuals may . . . ask themselves: 'How do I feel about it?' and in doing so, they may mistake feelings due to a preexisting state" as informative about the current situation (Schwarz 1990: 529). Supporting evidence comes from studies reporting mood congruence in certain evaluative judgments (Clore & Parrott 1991). However, many of these results can be equally well explained by alternative, affect-priming models. Further, the affect-as-information model also lacks parsimony, as it deals with mood effects at the retrieval-judgmental stage only. The kind of simple, heuristic processing implied by the affect-as-information approach is most likely when processing resources are limited, prior knowledge and evaluations are not available, and the task is unfamiliar, non-specific, and of little personal relevance. Importantly, affect is only likely to be used as information if people are completely unaware of the source of their mood (Schwarz & Clore 1983; more on this later).

In contrast to the affect-as-information mechanism, the *affect-priming* mechanism suggests that affect can indirectly infuse cognitive processes by facilitating access to related memories and cognitive categories (Bower 1981; Isen 1984). According to this view, affective states have a specific node or unit in memory that is linked with propositions describing events from one's life during which that emotion was aroused. Activation of an emotion node spreads activation throughout the memory structures to which it is connected, increasing the chance that those memories will be retrieved (Bower 1981). The priming model predicts mood congruent biases in attention, encoding, learning (Bower 1981; Forgas & Bower 1987; Forgas 1992b), memory retrieval (Bower 1981; Forgas & Bower 1988), and interpretation (Forgas & Bower 1987).

There is now strong evidence supporting this model. Despite some initial difficulties (Blaney 1986), many studies using rich and elaborate encoding and retrieval cues have reliably demonstrated the predicted mood priming effects (cf. Bower 1981; Forgas 1990, 1992b; Forgas & Bower 1987, 1988; Salovey et al. 1991). The prediction of mood-congruence in conditions that are conducive to substantive processing has also been supported in numerous studies looking at selective attention, learning, retrieval and associative processes (cf. Bower 1981; Forgas 1992b; Forgas & Bower 1987, 1988; Mayer et al. 1992; Salovey et al. 1991). In particular, counter intuitive evidence indicates that the more people engage in substantive processing, the greater the affect infusion and the mood-congruency effects obtained (eg., Forgas 1992b, 1993b, 1995b).

Unlike the affect-as-information mechanism, the affect-priming mechanism may unconsciously influence cognition and judgments even when people can correctly identify the source of their mood (Forgas 1995). Numerous experimental studies demonstrate that mood leads to subtle mood-congruent biases in attention, recall, and judgment even in circumstances when people are certain to be aware of a recent mood induction responsible for their mood states (eg., Forgas 1995). It appears, then, that even people who are likely to be consciously aware of the causes of their moods, may be unaware of the cognitive consequences of their affective states (eg., affect-priming), and do display unconscious affect infusion effects.

Basic predictions of AIM

According to the AIM, choice of processing strategy (and thus, subsequent unconscious affect-infusion or conscious control outcomes) should depend on three sets of factors: features of (1) the *task*, (2) the *person* and (3) the *situation*, respectively (Forgas 1995a). *Task features* include familiarity, typicality, and complexity; *person features* include specific motivation, cognitive capacity, motivation to be accurate, affective state, individual difference variables, and awareness of affective state; *situational factors* include features such as degree of critical scrutiny expected, accuracy expectations, etc. Several testable principles may be derived from this model. For example, cognitive tasks that are highly familiar should be processed using a direct access strategy precluding affect infusion, unless further processing is recruited by other variables (Srull 1983; 1984). A strong prior motivation should also lead to directed and truncated information search strategies, and the absence of affect infusion. Such a pattern was found in several recent experiments looking at mood effects on motivated partner choices (Forgas 1991c) and intergroup decisions (Forgas & Fiedler 1996). Motivated processing however is the primary mechanism that can reverse the usual mood-congruent pattern, as judges selectively process mood-incongruent information, often as a result of growing conscious awareness of the deleterious effects of the prevailing mood state (Erber & Erber 1994; Sedikides 1994).

In the absence of task familiarity or specific motivation, atypical, unusual or complex tasks should recruit more substantive and elaborate processing, and typical or simple targets should recruit more simple, truncated processing. This pattern was supported in several recent studies, showing greater unconscious affect infusion linked to the more substantive processing of complex or atypical targets (Forgas 1992b; 1993b). The model also predicts that all things being equal, personally relevant tasks are more likely to be processed using the motivated strategy (if a prior objective exists), as found in some recent experiments (Forgas 1989, 1991b). Finally, pragmatic situational demands (eg. expected publicity or scrutiny, expectations of accuracy) also impact on processing choices, triggering substantive rather than heuristic or direct access processing (Wegner & Erber 1993).

Within the AIM framework, the ongoing task of mood management can be understood as people routinely and automatically switching between two complementary information processing strategies: substantive processing that results in unconscious affect infusion, and motivated processing that results in conscious affect control outcomes. The mood management model proposed here is thus a refinement and development of the relevant aspects of the earlier and more general Affect Infusion Model (Forgas 1995a). A schematic summary of the mood management hypothesis is presented in Figure 1. As this figure shows, the choice of either a substantive (affect infusion) or motivated (affect control) processing strategy is determined by a combination of input variables, and the extremity of the prevailing affective state of the person. Most of the variables that feed into the mood management system are personal rather than situational. So far, we know that motivated rather than substantive processing is more likely when (a) the task is of direct personal relevance (Forgas 1991c), (b) people are aware of the cause or consequence of their mood (Berkowitz & Troccoli 1990; Schwarz & Clore 1983), (c) they score high on individual differences measures that indicate motivated processing tendencies (Forgas, in press) and (d) they experience extreme or aversive affective state (Weary et al. 1994). Situational variables may also impact on processing choices (Forgas 1995; Wegner & Erber 1993). For example, persons who expect to engage in a demanding interaction with a stranger often prefer to tone down their mood by reading articles that are the opposite in affective tone to their own mood (Wegner & Erber 1993).

A critical feature of this mood management model is that it incorporates a

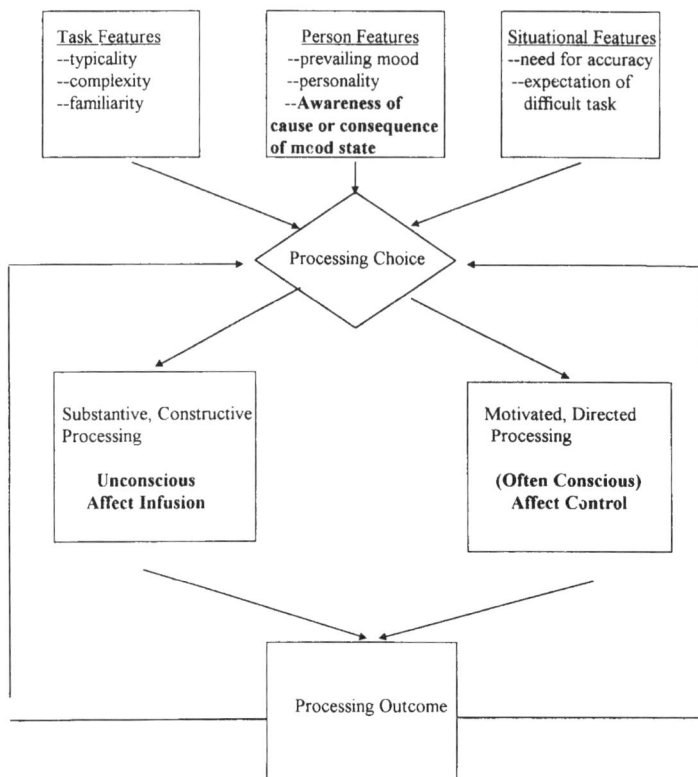

Figure 1. The mood management model, showing the predicted relationship between unconscious affect infusion (during substantive processing) and conscious affect control (during motivated processing), and the variables influencing processing choices.

feedback loop between the valenced outcome of the existing processing strategy and subsequent processing choices. As a consequence, the model provides for the possibility of continuous changes in processing style as a function of the prevailing mood state, a suggestion that is supported by empirical evidence (Clark & Isen 1982; Forgas 1995a; Sedikides 1994). In practical terms, this means that if as a result of an existing substantive processing strategy and ongoing affect infusion processes the level of negativity in a person's thinking — and mood — reaches a threshold level, an automatic correction may take place, that consists of a switch to motivated processing. In the next section we will briefly survey some of the evidence illustrating affect infusion processes in the course of substantive processing. Then, we will discuss the different types of conscious, motivated processes that are often used to counteract unconscious affect infusion.

Evidence for unconscious affect infusion

Numerous studies have found that a person's affective state is likely to infuse cognitive processes in circumstances that, according to the AIM, should trigger constructive, substantive processing strategies. In a particularly challenging early test of the affect infusion hypothesis, even basic interpretations of observed social interactions were significantly distorted in a mood-consistent direction (Forgas et al. 1984). Other researchers used a more realistic personnel selection task and found an almost identical pattern of affect infusion in interviewers' reactions to job applicants (Baron 1987). Affect infusion may also distort highly important personal judgments, such as perceptions of health and illness (Croyle & Uretzky 1987; Salovey & Birnbaum 1989). As implied by the AIM, "negative mood can affect subjective appraisals of health by increasing the accessibility of illness-related memories" (Croyle & Uretzky 1987: 239).

Affect infusion has been demonstrated not only in the laboratory, but also in many real-life situations. In one of the largest unobtrusive field studies on this topic, involving almost a thousand subjects (Forgas & Moylan 1987), we approached people who were just leaving movie theatres having seen happy or sad films and asked them to make a number of judgments about topical issues, political figures, and their life satisfaction in a "street survey". On all questions, happy subjects made significantly more positive and lenient judgments than did sad subjects, without any conscious awareness of the distorting effects of their film-induced moods. Significant affect infusion was also found with stereotype judgments, "consistent with the affect-priming explanation" (Haddock et al. 1994: 203).

Given that affect does indeed colour judgments, what evidence is there that such colouring occurs unconsciously? A number of experiments have now demonstrated that people must be unaware of the consequences of their mood if it is to infuse their judgments (Berkowitz & Troccoli 1990; Murphy & Zajonc 1987, 1993; Schwarz & Clore 1983). For example, Murphy and Zajonc (1990) found that when positive and negative facial expressions were presented subconsciously, neutral Chinese ideographs targets were influenced by the affective prime. If the prime was positive, the otherwise nondescript ideographs were judged more positively; if the prime was negative, the ideographs were judged negatively. However, when the primes were presented consciously, they had no impact on the ideographs. Thus, when people became aware of the source of the affect (the facial expressions), they prevented it from influencing their judgments.

Other studies specifically suggest that if people become consciously aware of their affective states, they will tend to counteract its affects (Berkowitz et al. 1994; Schwarz & Clore 1983). Schwarz and Clore (1983) found, for example, that when survey respondents were asked about their well being, they gave more positive answers on sunny days, presumably because they were in a good mood. However, the effect disappeared when respondents were made to consciously focus on the source of their mood, the weather, by answering a casual question about the weather that day. In another set of studies, Berkowitz et al. (1994) found that negative mood led people to evaluate a target person unfavourably, a typical mood congruence effect. However, when subjects were made to focus on their internal states, and as a result became consciously aware of their negative mood, this eliminated mood congruent responses, and led them to evaluate the target person more *favourably*. Thus, consciously aware subjects not only corrected, but also overcorrected, for potential affective biases in their thinking and judgments.

The examples discussed thus far suggest that when people are unaware of their moods, they are more likely to allow that mood to infuse an unrelated cognitive process and judgments. Thus, moods seem to become easily "detached" from their true source. Schwarz, Servay and Kumpf (1985) provide another striking illustration of this. They had smokers watch a fear-arousing anti-smoking movie and observed the effects of the film on attitudes towards smoking. Before the film, smokers were given a placebo and told that it had either arousing, tranquillizing, or no side effects. Relative to the no side effects group, the subjects who could attribute the fear arousal to the pill reported less intention to quit smoking, and those who expected the pill to be tranquillising reported more intention to quit smoking. In addition, the self reported number of cigarettes smoked during the two-week period that followed the film decreased in both the tranquillizing and no side effects condition, but did not decrease in the arousing side effects condition. These findings suggest that people are often not consciously aware of the true source of their affective states and can be easily misled to misattribute it to an irrelevant source.

Evidence that unconscious affect infusion occurs under substantive processing

Specific evidence for the role of processing strategies in unconscious affect infusion comes from the direct analysis of processing latency and memory data. In one relevant study, happy, control or sad moods were induced by bogus feedback about performance, followed by impression formation judgments and a recall task about persons presented on a computer screen (Forgas & Bower 1987). The experiment found significant mood-congruence. It also found that people took longer to process and encode mood-congruent information into a presumably more extensive, activated associative base, but were faster to produce mood-congruent judgments using a pre-activated mood-congruent associative base, consistent with affect-priming theories and the AIM in particular (Bower 1981; Forgas 1995).

One of the more important and counter-intuitive predictions of the Affect Infusion Model is that the longer and more extensively a person needs to substantively process a task, the more likely that unconscious affect infusion will occur. This prediction was supported in several recent studies. In these experiments, the time required for processing was manipulated and recorded through varying the complexity and typicality of targets to be judged, using people (Forgas 1992b), relationships (Forgas 1995b; Forgas & Moylan 1991; Forgas et al. 1994) and conflict episodes (Forgas 1994) as stimuli. One set of experiments found greater unconscious affect infusion in memory and judgments about atypical rather than typical people (Forgas 1992b), and these greater mood effects were consistently linked to more prolonged processing latencies.

Another series of studies demonstrated greater affect infusion into judgments about unusual, mismatched rather than well-matched couples, due to the more substantive, elaborate processing recruited by such targets (Forgas 1995b; Forgas & Moylan 1991). In one experiment, several features of the target couples were simultaneously manipulated to create various degrees of 'match' between them. Results showed that the size of mood effects on judgments was proportional to the degree of mismatch between the partners, and the length of processing required to produce a reaction (Forgas 1995b; see Figure 2). Thus, more 'mismatched' couple took longer to process, and produced greater affect infusion than did targets that were better matched. Interestingly, these affect infusion effects also occur in highly complex and personally

RELATIONSHIP JUDGMENT   PARTNER JUDGMENT

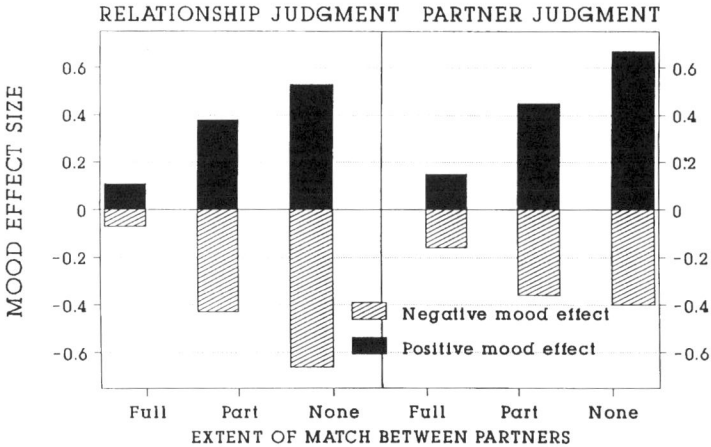

Figure 2. Mood effects on the perception of well-matched, partially matched and badly-matched couples: the size of the mood effect is proportional to the degree of mismatch between the couples (After Forgas, 1995b).

relevant cognitive tasks, such as perceptions of one's real-life intimate relationships (Forgas et al. 1994), and people's explanations for their more or less serious interpersonal conflicts (Forgas 1994). Once again, these mood effects were most extensive for serious, involving conflicts that required longer, more extensive processing, rather than for simple, superficial conflicts, as suggested by the AIM (Forgas 1994; see Figure 3).

To summarize, we have argued that low-level, fluctuating affective states and moods that are typically experienced by all of us in everyday life have a continuous, and often imperceptible cognitive influence on the way we think about, remember and evaluate complex social information. Such unconscious affect infusion processes seem most marked when a person needs to engage in constructive, substantive information processing in response to a problematic task. Several of the experiments described here confirm that the longer and more constructively we need to think about a task, the more likely that affect infusion will have a mood-congruent impact on the outcome. Specifically, mood has been shown to have a significantly greater distorting effect on tasks that are rare, unusual, atypical or complex. Importantly, mood seems to have a distorting affect only when it is unconscious. Unconscious affect infusion is only one side of the mood management equation, however. We now turn to the complementary process of conscious affect control during motivated processing.

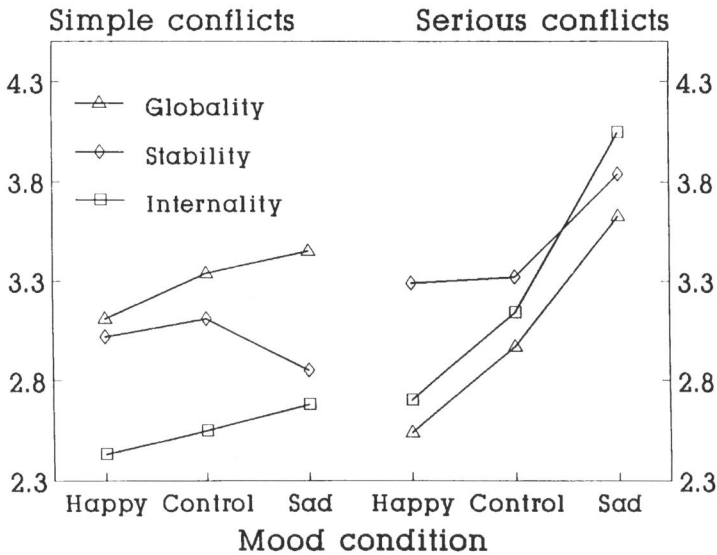

Figure 3. Mood effects on explanations about simple and serious relationship conflicts: mood has greater impact on judgments about serious, complex conflicts requiring longer, more substantive processing (After Forgas, 1994).

Affect control: Motivated processing strategies

Unconscious affect infusion represents one important aspect of the delicate interrelationship between affect and cognition. While affect can and does impact on our cognitive processes, often in ways that we don't realize, the opposite can also occur: targeted, motivated cognitive activity can influence and control our affective states. This reverse process, affect control, occurs in conditions when a motivated processing strategy is adopted in terms of the Affect Infusion Model. *Motivated processing* is most likely to be employed by a person when there are strong and specific motivational pressures for a particular cognitive outcome to be achieved. The defining feature of motivated processing is that people engage in highly selective, guided, and targeted information search and integration strategies designed to achieve a pre-existing motivational objective. Motivated processing is not only a low affect infusion strategy, but is also the major vehicle for balancing affect infusion and achieving mood-incongruent outcomes, often in the service of personal control. Motivated mood control strategies are often, but not always, conscious (Forgas & Ciarrochi 1997). To stay close to the theme of the present paper, we will focus on more conscious mood control strategies and the ways that such strategies are used to counteract and control unconscious affect infusion processes.

There are a number of factors that determine whether or not people will engage in motived mood control. For example, when a task requires high accuracy, people may be motivated to engage in a thorough, unbiased search for information, a motivational drive that may overcome any unconscious affect-infusion processes (Forgas 1995; Janis & Mann 1977). Also, if a person becomes aware of the cause or consequence of a mood, they may become motivated to recall mood-incongruent information in order to counteract mood congruent biases (Berkowitz & Troccoli 1990; Ciarrochi & Forgas 1997). Other factors that predict motivational processing include high personal relevance, strong external pressures or expectations, the likelihood of external scrutiny or evaluation, and an internal need to balance or rectify aversive states (such as aversive mood states). A more detailed discussion of these factors can be found in Forgas (1995), and in Forgas & Ciarrochi (1997).

According to the mood management model proposed here, substantive processing and motivated processing can be regarded as two dissociated, but interactive cognitive strategies that jointly constitute a homeostatic mood management system. Affect-infusion processes lead to increasingly mood congruent biases and increasingly intense mood until a threshold level is reached, at which point more conscious and motivated mood control processes take over. Why might a person spontaneously switch to mood control? One reason is that a negative mood might reach a level of aversiveness that is in excess of what the person can tolerate, thus prompting that person to try to alleviate it. A second reason, more relevant to the present paper, is that a good or bad mood might reach a sufficient level of intensity that a person becomes consciously aware of it, triggering motivated strategies to control and counteract an aversive state (Berkowitz et al. 1994; Schwarz & Clore 1983).

It is important to note that motivated processing, as understood here, does not simply refer to a generic motivation to be careful and accurate (cf. Kunda 1990). Rather, it assumes that information search and processing strategies are directed in the service of a specific, pre-existing goal. Recent studies have demonstrated motivated processing in the service of such goals as mood repair and mood maintenance, self evaluation maintenance, ego enhancement, achievement motivation, and affiliation (Berkowitz 1993; Erber & Erber 1994; Forgas 1991c; Forgas et al. 1990; Tesser 1986). In fact, most of these goals relate to more or less conscious personal control objectives, and affect control in particular.

Despite growing interest in motivated processing (Forgas 1995; Janis & Mann 1977; Kunda 1990; Martin 1986), the precise processing consequences of this strategy have received insufficient attention in the psychological literature, as most studies of social cognition use artificial and relatively uninvolving tasks. Nevertheless, several studies have now shown that affect infusion effects disappear under conditions that are conducive to motivated processing. These conditions include high self-relevance or a high level of awareness about the primed material, when attention is directed to the mood state, in tasks requiring deliberate processing, or when subjects compensate for unbalanced information by "resetting" the input array (Berkowitz et al. 1994; Erber & Erber 1994; Martin 1986). We turn now to a brief discussion of the kind of conscious strategies people use to control their affect. We will then consider the circumstances when, according to the AIM, such conscious control processes are likely to occur and the role of awareness in such processes.

Strategies of conscious affect control

People may use one of a number of motivational strategies to consciously control their affective states. First, they may selectively expose themselves to mood incongruent information, either by putting themselves into mood-incongruent situations (Cialdini & Kenrick 1976; Forgas 1991) or by recalling mood-incongruent memories (Erber & Erber 1994; Parrott & Sabini 1990; Forgas & Ciarrochi 1997). Conscious behavioral strategies can also play a role in affect control, for example when people try to reduce a negative mood by helping others (Baumann et al. 1981; Cialdini & Kenrick 1976; Manucia et al. 1984) or by interacting with rewarding as opposed to competent partners (Forgas 1991). They also may try to reduce bad mood by selectively retrieving positive memories, adjectives, or self-descriptors (Erber & Erber 1994; Parrott & Sabini 1990; Forgas & Ciarrochi 1997).

Another way people may control their moods is by distracting themselves from the source of their mood (Nolen-Hoeksema 1993; Wegner, Erber, & Zanakos 1993). For example, Erber and Erber (1994) put people into a sad or

happy mood and then had them engage in either (1) effortless mood-incongruent recall, (2) effortful (ie., distracting) mood-incongruent recall, (3) or no
recall. The results indicated that high-effort, mood incongruent recall led to
greater reduction of aversive mood than low-effort mood incongruent recall,
which supports the idea that cognitive load itself reduces mood effects,
presumably by disrupting the kind of substantive, constructive processing
strategies affect infusion requires. In another illustration of this effect, Wegner
et al. (1993) had subjects recall a sad life event under high load (ie., 'remember a 9 digit number') or low load instructions. The sad recall instruction
increased negativity of mood in the low load condition, but had no affect on
mood in the high load condition. Again, this study suggests that cognitive load
(distraction) can be used to control mood. In more "real world" settings,
Nolen-Hoeksema (1991) has demonstrated that people who ruminate or focus
on their depression tend to show longer depression than people who take
action to distract themselves from their symptoms. These results suggest that
open, constructive processing and the availability of cognitive resources
enhances affect infusion, while a reduction of processing resources has the
opposite effect.

Yet another way people may control affect is through cognitive distortion
(Janis & Mann 1977; Mann et al. 1969; Pervin & Yatko 1965) or cognitive "reappraisal" (Nolen-Hoeksema 1992). For example, Pervin and Yatko (1965)
demonstrated that smokers try to reduce negative affect by cognitively minimising the validity of smoking-related findings or by minimising the personal
danger of smoking. In related study, Mann, et al. (1969) demonstrated that
people will try to reduce the anxiety related to a difficult decision by exaggerating the value of one choice alternative and minimizing the value of the other
alternatives. In their study, subjects were forced to choose between two similar,
unpleasant physiological stimulants and were told that they either would or
would not be given additional information about the side effects of the
stimulants. Physiological measures indicated that the choice was stressful to
subjects. The main results indicated that subjects in the no-information-
expected condition showed significant spreading of alternatives, which indicated that they engaged in biased, motivated processing aimed at increasing the
"attractiveness" of one alternative and decreasing the attractiveness of the
other. Subjects in the information expected condition showed no such biases.
The findings are consistent with the idea that if individuals feel aversive affect,
but do not believe that they can do anything 'rational" about it, then they will

attempt to reduce their aversive affect by engaging in motivated thinking to bolster one alternative over another. It is important to note that the cognitive reappraisal strategy may have both conscious and unconscious elements. People may be aware of their aversive mood and may consciously try to re-appraise the information at hand (eg., information about the hazards of smoking), but may be unaware that they are actually distorting that information in mood-incongruent directions.

The evidence for conscious affect control and motivated processing

Having considered the kinds of conscious strategies people may use to control their affect, we turn now to the evidence concerning when they use such strategies. The mood management model (Figure 1) predicts that negative mood leads initially to unconscious affect-infusion and mood congruent recall until a threshold level of negativity is reached, at which point people are likely to become aware of their mood. This awareness is expected to prompt them to switch to conscious mood control and mood-incongruent, positive recall. In an initial test of this hypothesis, Sedikides (1994) gave sad subjects a guided imagery mood induction; subsequently, they were asked to generate open-ended self-descriptions. Initial responses showed a clear mood congruent pattern, consistent with the operation of unconscious affect infusion mechanisms. With the passage of time self-descriptions in the negative mood group changed, becoming more positive and less negative. This result suggests that subjects came to adopt a motivated affect control strategy to "repair" their sad mood, but only after the initial negative mood effects due to affect infusion generated a sufficiently aversive state. One potential limitation of this study, however, was that it does not allow us to determine conclusively whether the effects were due to the motivated recall of incongruent materials (as hypoth-esized in our mood repair model), or simply to sad mood wearing off over time.

To remedy this limitation, Forgas and Ciarrochi (1997) conducted 3 additional studies, which attempted to test the hypothesis that mood leads first to unconscious affect infusion, and that once mood reaches a threshold level of intensity, a more conscious, mood-incongruent affect control strategy will be adopted. In study 1, subjects were put into a good or bad mood by having them recall a sad or happy event from their past. Then, they were asked to generate, as quickly as possible, trait adjectives (eg., "gloomy," "intelligent"). We found that people in a negative mood tended to initially generate mood congruent adjectives, but that over time, they switched to generating mood incongruent (positive) adjectives in a pattern that is consistent with a conscious affect control strategy. People in a positive mood, in contrast, generated first congruent adjectives, and gradually reverted to more neutral adjectives. These findings are consistent with the idea that negative, but not positive, mood prompts people to overcome unconscious affect infusion by intentionally recalling mood incongruent information (Figure 4).

In study 2, we attempted to replicate study 1 using the same mood induction but a different and more time sensitive dependent measure. Happy and sad subjects were asked to complete words given a starting letter (eg., "t" might lead to "terrible" or ''terrific''). A time-series regression analysis was used to assess subtle changes in the valence of generated words (as rated by two independent raters) over time. The analyses revealed that sad subjects rapidly changed from affect-congruent to affect-incongruent recall. Happy subjects, in contrast, more gradually changed from affect-congruent to neutral recall. Thus as in study 1, after affect infusion was the dominant pattern in the

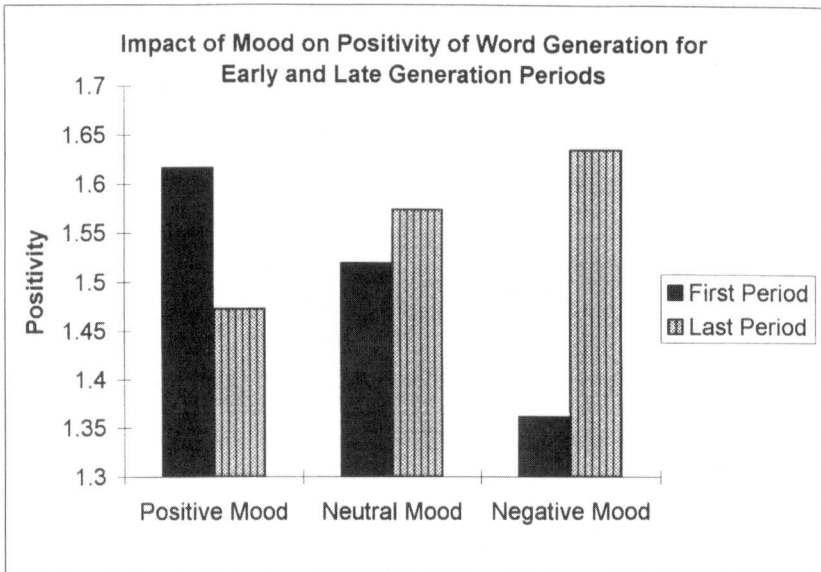

Figure 4. Evidence for motivated mood management over time: initially mood-congruent associations (indicating affect infusion) spontaneously become incongruent over time, as participants seek to control their affective states.

early stages of this generative cognitive task. It appears that once a threshold level of negativity was reached due to affect infusion processes, sad subjects switched to motivated, incongruent recall as if seeking to control and eliminate their aversive mood.

Study 3 attempted to extend the previous findings by using different mood induction procedures and different dependent measures. This study also explored the role of individual difference variables such as self-esteem in these affect management strategies. Previous work suggests that people low in self-esteem are less likely than others to engage in conscious affect control (Smith & Petty 1995). Thus, we expected that such people would be less likely and slower to switch from congruent to incongruent recall. That is, we expected their thoughts to be dominated by unconscious affect infusion and not by conscious affect control. To induce mood, participants performed a false feedback task, in which they were led to believe they did very well (good mood) or very poorly (bad mood) on a spatial abilities task. Next, they were asked to complete as fast as possible a long series of sentences beginning with "I am_." Results again indicated a clear 'first congruent, then incongruent pattern', and this result was particularly marked for high SE people. Those scoring high on self esteem were able to rapidly eliminate a mood-congruent bias in their associations by producing mood-incongruent, positive words after initially negative responses. Low SE people showed mood congruent recall across the entire time period. This finding suggests that, at least when the cognitions are self-referencing (eg., 'I am a loser'), low SE people are unable or unwilling to effectively adopt conscious and motivated affect control strategies to stop affect from infusing their cognitions.

In summary, the pattern or results found by both Sedikides (1994) and Forgas and Ciarrochi (1997) are consistent with the kind of homeostatic feedback-loop model of affect control proposed here as part of an integrated mood management system (Figure 1). Initially, unconscious affect-infusion dominates processing. Over time, people overcome such processes by engaging in more conscious, mood incongruent recall (Figure 4).

One of the important assumptions of the mood management model is that becoming aware of a mood can prompt a person to switch from unconscious affect infusion to conscious affect control. What evidence is there for this? Numerous studies (Clore & Parrott 1991; Schwarz 1990; Schwarz & Clore 1983) suggest that simply making people aware of the source of their mood will lead them to counteract its effects. For example, Schwarz and Clore put people into a good or bad mood by having them write about a happy or sad event in their recent past. Later, participants answered questions about how satisfied they were with their life. In addition to mood, the salience of a possible external cause for their feelings was varied. The experiment was conducted in a small and unusual soundproof room with its own ventilation and lighting system. Before beginning, half the subjects were led to believe that the sound proof room might make them tense. Thus, they had something salient on which to blame their mood. The results indicated that making people aware of a plausible external cause of the their feelings eliminated the normal mood congruency effect. Aware people stopped mood from influencing their judgments.

The most dramatic evidence that conscious awareness leads to affect control is provided by studies that show people over-controlling for the mood once they become aware of it (Berkowitz 1993; Berkowitz et al. 1994; Martin et al. 1990). Berkowitz et al. (1994), for example, had subjects listen to a job applicant talk about herself while they were either relatively comfortable (their extended arm rested on a table) or much more uncomfortable (because their arm was unsupported for several minutes). Half the subjects rated their feelings so that they were made highly aware of their discomfort, whereas the remaining subjects were given an equally long extraneous task and presumably were less conscious of their unpleasant feelings. Immediately afterward, when all of the subjects indicated their impressions of the job applicant's personal qualities, only those who were not consciously aware of their feelings allowed their negative mood to infuse the judgments: the more negative they felt, the more negative were their judgments. The relationship was actually reversed for subjects who were made consciously aware of their feelings. The worse they felt, the more *positive* became their judgments. As Berkowitz et al. (1994) put it, it was as if aware subjects "leaned over backwards" to avoid letting their bad feelings affect their judgments.

Being aware of one's mood is not always sufficient to prompt a person to engage in conscious mood control. Martin, Seta, and Crelia's (1990) research suggests that people must also have sufficient cognitive resources. These authors asked subjects to read and then write about statements that were either positive or negative. Immediately afterwards, they gave subjects a written description of a target person and required them to form an impression of the person. Importantly, the researchers distracted half the subjects as they read the description by also having them listen to a voice read a random string of numbers or letters. The distracted subjects displayed the usual affect-priming result: they assessed the target more positively after the positive as compared to the negative priming experience. In contrast, the non-distracted subjects showed an affect-incongruent effect, making more positive judgments following the negative priming experience. These results are consistent with the idea that all subjects were aware of the potential biasing influence of the affective prime but only subjects that were undistracted had the cognitive resources to actually correct for them

Most research so far considered shows that conscious processing can be triggered to control negative, aversive affective states. There are also situations, however, in which excessively positive mood states may have equally deleterious effects, calling for motivated thinking to tone down euphoria (Parrott 1993). For example, when people expect to undertake a complex, demanding task (such as meeting a stranger for the first time), they may prefer to enter this situation in a calm, low-key affective state. The role of the surrounding social situation in the regulation of both good and bad moods was first emphasized by Goffman (1974), and this point was recently reiterated by Wegner and Erber (1993). In an interesting study illustrating the engagement of motivated processing to control positive mood, these authors used music to induce good or bad mood in subjects, who expected to either interact with a stranger or spend some time alone. They then had an opportunity to chose to read either depressing, neutral or cheerful newspaper articles. Results showed that people who expected to be alone preferred mood-consistent articles. However, subjects who expected a demanding interaction with a stranger preferred to read articles that were the opposite in affective tone to their own mood, as if trying to tone down their prevailing affective state. These results nicely illustrate that when people are aware of their mood and believe the mood will interfere with a future social interaction, they will engage in conscious, motivated affect control (eg., selective reading of negative articles) in order to eliminate the mood.

Individual differences, awareness, and mood control

Individual differences may play an important role in determining the extent to which people who are aware of their moods have sufficient resources to engage in conscious mood control. Steele, Spencer, and Lynch (1993) have argued that low self-esteem (SE) people have fewer "affirmational resources" on which to draw when their self-concepts are threatened. This hypothesis suggests that low SE people may be less able to repair a negative mood, especially when that mood is related to their self-esteem (eg., a bad mood due to a failure experience). Consistent with this hypothesis, Smith and Petty (1995) found that sad mood prompted high SE subjects to generate more positive than negative stories in response to TAT items and recall more positive memories from their school days, consistent with the idea that they were engaging in mood repair. However, low SE people showed the opposite pattern of responding, generating more negative information when in a negative mood. Thus, low SE people seemed more susceptible to unconscious affect infusion. In a related study, Forgas and Ciarrochi (1997) found that sad mood led high SE subjects to initially generate mood congruent associations (consistent with unconscious affect-infusion mechanisms), but as time passed to generate increasingly mood-incongruent associations (consistent with conscious affect-control mechanisms). Low SE people, in contrast, never overcame their mood biases, generating mood-congruent associations throughout the entire time period. These results are consistent with the idea that low SE people may be less able to switch to conscious mood control strategies, and are thus more susceptible to unconscious affect-infusion.

Trait Anxiety is another important individual difference variable that may influence whether or not people overcome unconscious affect infusion with conscious affect control. High trait anxious people experience aversive moods more often than low trait anxious people do (Spielberger 1983) and as a consequence, may become more skilled at recognizing their own aversive moods. If they do become more aware, then they should be more likely to engage in conscious affect-control (Berkowitz 1993). In a study relevant to this hypothesis, Ciarrochi and Forgas (1997) placed high and low trait anxious subjects into an aversive or neutral mood and then asked them to make judgments related to a racial out-group (eg., "How dangerous is this group"). The findings indicated that aversive mood led to unconscious affect-infusion among low trait anxious people but affect-control (consistent with mood awareness) among high trait anxious subjects. That is, bad mood led low trait anxious people to evaluate the racial out-group as more dangerous, untrustworthy, and racist, but led high trait anxious people to evaluate the out-group as relatively less dangerous, untrustworthy, and racist. High trait anxious people appeared to be more aware of their aversive moods and "bent over backwards" in an attempt to prevent it from infusing their judgments.

Conclusions

This chapter proposed that two processes that were previously considered dissociated, affect infusion and affect control, may in fact be best conceptualised as complementary parts of an interactive, homeostatic affect management system. The evidence reviewed here lends considerable support to this hypothesis, even though specific research on this topic is relatively recent. Affect management and the role of consciousness in this domain remains one of the more intriguing areas of contemporary psychological theorising. It is hoped that the ideas outlined here will stimulate further interest in this important and promising domain.

Acknowledgments

Work on this chapter was supported by the Research Prize by the Alexander von Humboldt Foundation, Germany, and by a Special Investigator Award from the Australian research Council to the first author. Please address all enquires in connection with this chapter to Joseph P. Forgas, School of Psychology, University of new South Wales, Sydney 2052; e-mail: JP.Forgas@unsw.EDU.AU;internet: http://www.psy.unsw.edu.au/~joef/jforgas.htm.

References

Asch, S.E. (1946). Forming impressions of personality. *Journal of Abnormal and Social Psychology*, 41, 258–290.

Baron, R. (1987). Interviewers' moods and reactions to job applicants: The influence of affective states on applied social judgments. *Journal of Applied Social Psychology*, 16, 911–926.

Baumann, Cialdini, & Kendrick (1981). Altruism as hedonism. Helping and self-gratification as equivalent responses. *Journal of Personality and Social Psychology*, 40,(6), 1039–104.

Beck, A.T. (1976). *Cognitive Theory and the Emotional Disorders*. New York: International University Press.

Berkowitz, L. & Troccoli, B. (1990). Feelings, direction of attention, and expressed evaluations of others. *Cognition and Emotion*, 4, 305–325.

Berkowitz, L. (1993). Towards a general theory of anger and emotional aggression. In T. K. Srull & R. S. Wyer (Eds.), *Advances in social cognition*. Hillsdale, New Jersey: Lawrence Erlbaum, Vol.6, 1–46.

Berkowitz, L., Jo, E., Troccoli, B.T. & Monteith, M. (1994). *Attention-activated regulation of feeling effects*. Unpublished manuscript, University of Wisconsin, Madison.

Blaney, P.H. (1986). Affect and memory: A review. *Psychological Bulletin, 99,* 229–246.

Bower, G.H. (1981). Mood and memory. *American Psychologist, 36,* 129–148.

Cialdini, R.B. & Kenrick, D.T. (1976). Altruism as hedonism: A social development perspective on the relationship of negative mood state and helping. *Journal of Personality and Social Psychology,* 34, 907–914.

Ciarrochi, J. and Forgas, J.P. (1997). On being tense yet tolerant: the paradoxical effects of aversive mood and trait anxiety on intergroup judgments. Manuscript submitted for publication.

Clark M.S. & Isen, A.M. (1982). Towards understanding the relationship between feeling states and social behavior. In A.H. Hastorf & A. M. Isen (Eds), *Cognitive social psychology.* Amsterdam: Elsevier/North-Holland, 73–108.

Clore, G.L. & Parrott, G. (1991). Moods and their vicissitudes: Thoughts and feelings as information. In J.P. Forgas (Ed.), *Emotion and social judgments.* Elmsford, NY: Pergamon Press, 109–123.

Croyle, R.T. & Uretsky, M.B. (1987). Effects of mood on self-appraisal of health status *Health Psychology,* 6, 239–253.

Erber, R. & Erber, M.W. (1994). Beyond mood and social judgment: Mood incongruent recall and mood regulation. *European Journal of Social Psychology,* 24,79–88.

Fiedler, K. (1990). Mood-dependent selectivity in social cognition. In W. Stroebe & M. Hewstone (Eds.), *European review of social psychology.* New York: Wiley, Vol.1, 1–32.

Fiedler, K. (1991). On the task the measures and the mood in research on affect and social cognition. In J.P. Forgas (Ed.), *Emotion and social judgments.* Elmsford, NY: Pergamon Press, 83–104.

Forgas, J.P., Bower, G.H. & Krantz, S. (1984). The influence of mood on perceptions of social interactions. *Journal of Experimental Social Psychology,* 20, 497–513.

Forgas, J.P. & Bower, G.H. (1987). Mood efforts on person perception judgments. *Journal of Personality and Social Psychology,* 53, 53–60.

Forgas, J.P. & Moylan, S.J. (1987). After the movies: The effects of transient mood states on social judgments. *Personality and Social Psychology Bulletin,* 13, 478–489.

Forgas, J.P. & Bower, G.H. (1988). Affect in social judgments. *Australian Journal of Psychology,* 40, 125–145.

Forgas, J.P. (1989). Mood effects on decision-making strategies. *Australian Journal of Psychology,* 41, 192–214.

Forgas J.P. (1990). Affective influences on individual and group judgments. *European Journal of Social Psychology,* 20, 441–453.

Forgas, J.P. Bower, G.H. & Moylan, S.J. (1990). Praise or blame? Affective influences on attributions for achievement. *Journal of Personality and Social Psychology,* 59, 809–818.

Forgas, J.P. (Ed). (1991b). *Emotion and social judgments.* Elmsford, NY: Pergamon Press.

Forgas, J.P. (199lc). Mood effects on partner choice: Role of affect in social decisions. *Journal of Personality and Social Psychology,* 61, 708–720.

Forgas, J.P. (1992b). On bad mood and peculiar people: Affect and person typicality in impression formation. *Journal of Personality and Social Psychology,* 62, 863–875.

Forgas, J.P. (1993b). On making sense of odd couples: Mood efforts on the part of mismatched relationships. *Personality and Social PsychologyBulletin,* 19, 59–71.

Forgas, J.P. (1994). Sad and guilty? Affective influences on the explanation of conflict episodes. *Journal of Personality and Social Psychology*, 66, 56–68.

Forgas, J.P., Levinger, G. & Moylan, S.J. (1994). Feeling good and feeling close: Affective influences on the perception of intimate relationships. *Personal Relationships*, 1, 165–184.

Forgas, J.P. (1995a). Mood and judgment: The affect infusion model (AIM). *Psychological Bulletin*, 117, 39–66.

Forgas, J.P. (1995b). Strange couples: Mood effects on judgments and memory about prototypical and atypical targets. *Personality and Social Psychology Bulletin*, 21, 747–765.

Forgas, J.P. & Fiedler, K. (1996). Us and Them: Mood effects on intergroup discrimination. *Journal of Personality and Social Psychology*, 70, 39–70.

Forgas, J.P. & Ciarrochi, J. (1997). Evidence for automatic mood management: Mood congruent and incongruent thoughts over time. Paper presented at Midwestern Psychological Association, (May).

Forgas, J.P. (in press). On feeling good and getting your way: Mood effects on negotiating strategies and outcomes. *Journal of Personality and Social Psychology*.

Freud, S. (1915). *The unconscious*. London: Hogarth Press, Vol. XIV.

Goffman, E. (1974). *Frame analysis*. Harmondsworth: Penguin.

Haddock, G., Zanna. M.P. & Esses, V.M. (1994). Mood and the expression of intergroup attitudes: The moderating role of affect inten*sity*. *European Journal of Social Psychology*, 24, 189–206.

Heider, F. (1958). *The psychology of interpersonal relations*. New York: John Wiley.

Isen, A. (1984). Towards understanding the role of affect in cognition. In R.S. Wyer & T.K Srull (Eds.), *Handbook of social cognition*. Hillsdale, New Jersey: Lawrence Erlbaum, Vol.3, 179–236.

Isen, A. (1990). *Affect and Social behavior*. In B.S. Moore & A.M. Isen (Eds.), New York: Cambridge Press.

Janis, I.L. & Mann, L. (1977). *Decision making: A psychological analysis of conflict, choice and commitment*. New York: Free Press.

Kelly, G.A. (1955). *The psychology of personal constructs*. New York: Norton.

Kunda, Z. (1990). The case for motivated reasoning. *Psychological Bulletin*, 108, 331–350.

Kunst-Wilson, W.R. & Zajonc, R.B. (1980). Affective discrimination of stimuli that cannot be recognized. *Science*, 207, 557–558.

Mann, L., Janis, I.L. & Chaplin, R. (1969). Effects of anticipation of forthcoming information on predecisional processes. *Journal of Personality and Social Psychology*, 11(1), 10–16.

Manucia, G.K., Baumann, D.J. & Cialdini, R.B. (1984). Mood influences on helping: Direct effects or side effects? *Journal of Personality and Social Psychology*, 46, 357–364.

Martin, L., Seta, J. & Crelia, R. (1990). Assimilation and contrast as a function of people's willingness and ability to expend effort in forming an impression. *Journal of Personality and Social Psychology*, 59, 27–37.

Murphy, S. & Zajonc, R.B. (1987). *Affect and awareness: Comparisons of subliminal and supraliminal affective priming*. Paper presented at the 95th Annual Convention of the American Psychological Association. New York, NY.

Murphy, S. & Zajonc, R.B (1993). Affect, cognition, and awareness: Affective priming with suboptimal and optimal stimulus. *Journal of Personality and Social Psychology,* 64, 723–739.

Murphy, S., Monahan, J. & Zajonc, R. (1995). Additivity of nonconscious affect: Combined effects of priming and exposure. *Journal of Personality and Social Psychology,* 69, 589–602.

Nolen-Hoeksema, S. (1991) Responses to depression and their effects on the duration of depressive episodes. *Journal of Abnormal Psychology,* 100, 569–582.

Nolen-Hoeksema, S. (1992). Children coping with uncontrollable stressors. *Applied and Preventive Psychology,* 1, 183–189.

Nolen-Hoeksema, S. (1993). Sex differences in control of depression. In D. M. Wegner & J.W. Pennebaker (Eds.), *Handbook of Mental Control.* Englewood Cliffs, NJ: Prentice Hall, 306–324.

Parrott, W.G. & Sabini, J. (1990). Mood and memory under natural conditions: Evidence for mood incongruent recall. *Journal of Personality and Social Psychology,* 59, 321–336.

Parrott, W.G. (1993). Beyond Hedonism: Motives for inhibiting good moods and for maintaining bad moods. In D.M. Wegner & J. W. Pennebaker (Eds.), *Handbook of mental control.* Englewood Cliffs, NJ: Prentice Hall, 278–305.

Pervin, L.A. & Yatko, R.J. (1965). Cigarette smoking and alternative methods of reducing dissonance. *Journal of Personality and Social Psychology,* 30–36.

Salovey, P. & Birnbaum, D. (1989). Influence of mood on health-related cognitions. *Journal of Personality and Social Psychology,* 57, 539–551.

Salovey, P., O'Leary, A., Stretton, M., Fishkin, S. & Drake, C.A. (1991). Influence of mood on judgments about health and illness. In J. P. Forgas (Ed.), *Emotion and social judgments.* Elmsford, NY: Pergamon Press, 241–262.

Schwarz, N. & Clore, G.L. (1983). Mood, misattribution and judgments of well-being: Informative and directive functions of affective states. *Journal of Personality and Social Psychology,* 45, 513–523.

Schwarz, N., Servay, W. & Kumpf, M. (1985). Attribution of arousal as a mediator of the effectiveness of fear-arousing communication. *Journal of Applied Social Psychology,* 15(2), 178–188.

Schwarz, N. (1990). Feelings as information: Informational and motivational functions of affective states. In E.T. Higgins & R. Sorrentino (Eds), *Handbook of motivation and cognition: Foundations of social behavior.* New York: Guilford Press, Vol.2, 527–561.

Sedikides, C. (1994). Incongruent effects of sad mood on self-conception valence: It's a matter of time. *European Journal of Social Psychology,* 4, 161–172.

Smith, S. & Petty, R. (1995). Personality moderators of mood congruency on cognition: The role of self-esteem and negative mood regulation. *Journal of Personality and Social Psychology,* 68, 1092–1107.

Spielberger, C.D. (1983). *State-Trait Anxiety Inventory for Adults.* Palo Alto, CA: Mind Garden.

Srull, T.K (1983). Affect and memory: The impact of affective reactions in advertising on the representation of product information in memory. In R. Bagozzi & A. Tybout (Eds.), *Advances in consumer research.* Ann Arbor, MI: Association for Consumer Research, Vol.10, 244–263.

Srull, T.K. (1984). The effects of subjective affective states on memory and judgment. In T. Kinnear (Ed.), *Advances in consumer research*. Provo, UT: Association for Consumer Research, Vol.11, 530–533.

Steele, C.M., Spencer, S.J. & Lynch, M. (1993). Self-image and dissonance: The role of affirmational resources. *Journal of Personality and Social Psychology,* 64, 885–896.

Tesser, A. (1986). Some effects of self-evaluation maintenance on cognition and action. In R. M. Sorrentino & E. T. Higgins (Eds.), *The handbook of motivation and cognition: Foundations of social behavior*. New York: Guilford Press, 435–464.

Weary, G., Marsh, K.L. & McCormick, L. (1994). Depression and social comparison motives. *European Journal of Social Psychology*, 24, 117–130.

Wegner, D.M. & Erber, R. (1993). Social foundations of mental control. In D.M. Wegner & J.W. Pennebaker (Eds.), *Handbook of mental control*. Englewood Cliffs, NJ: Prentice Hall, 36–56.

Wegner, D.M., Erber, R. & Zanakos, S. (1993). Ironic processes in the mental control of mood and mood-related thought. *Journal of Personality and Social Psychology*, 65, 1093–1104.

Wegner, D.M. & Pennebaker, J.W. (1993). Changing our minds: An introduction to mental control. In D.M. Wegner & J.W. Pennebaker (Eds.), *Handbook of mental control*. Englewood Cliffs, NJ: Prentice Hall, 1–12.

Zajonc, R.B. (1980). Feeling and thinking: Preferences need no inferences. *American Psychologist*, 35, 151–175.

From an Implicit to an Explicit "Theory of Mind"

Josef Perner
University of Salzburg

Wendy A. Clements
University of Sussex

Introduction

"Theory of mind" means the field that investigates the nature, evolution and development of the conceptual system underlying our mental state attributions like knowing, thinking (believing), wanting, feeling, etc. It is named after a paper by Premack and Woodruff (1978) who asked whether chimpanzees have a theory of mind. Whether our (or the chimpanzee's) body of knowledge about the mind (i.e., our naive folk psychology) deserves to be called *a theory* is controversial. We use "theory" here only as the usual descriptor of the field of investigation.

Our theory of mind is often referred to by its two core concepts as "belief-desire psychology". Belief and desire are core concepts because — as reflected in Aristotle's Practical Syllogism — information of a person's desire and belief about how to reach the desired state allows one to predict how that person is likely to act. Children's acquisition of these two concepts, in particular, that of belief has been extensively investigated (for reviews: Astington 1993; Mitchell 1996; Perner 1991, 1995; Wellman 1990). Most investigations of children's grasp of belief employ variations of the false belief task (Wimmer & Perner 1983) in which children typically are told a story about a protagonist who does not witness an unexpected transfer of an object from one location to another. Children's understanding that the world looks different in the protagonist's mind from how it really is as a result of the unseen and unexpected transfer, is tested by asking them directly, "where does the protagonist *think* the object is", or by asking them to predict where the protagonist will *look* for the object. The typical finding is that very few children at the age of 3 years (3;0) give correct answers. Almost all answer incorrectly that the protagonist will look for the object where it really is, i.e., in the object's current location. By about 4 or 4½ years most children answer correctly that he will look in the now empty, original location of the object.

Although the knowledge the child has to acquire to be able to give correct answers may not be a theory in the sense of scientific theories, it certainly is abstract knowledge. It is abstract because it is not simply knowledge about the physical world but knowledge — once removed — about how the physical world is seen by other people. It is, therefore, interesting that Clements and Perner (1994) reported a dissociation between the younger children's visual orienting responses to the correct location (suggestively an expression of precocious implicit knowledge) and their wrong answers to the explicit question.

The dissociation between an earlier and later understanding of false belief

In the study by Clements & Perner (1994) children were told a false belief story and a true belief (control) story. In the false belief story Sam the Mouse put some cheese into the box in front of the left entrance to his dwellings (location A). While Sam is asleep inside, his friend discovers the cheese and carries it over to the box in front of the right entrance (location B). Then Sam wakes up hungry and declares a wish to retrieve the cheese. At this point children's eye gaze was monitored within a 2 second time window on video in order to record whether they looked at location A or B in expectation of Sam's reappearance. In order to be able to interpret children's looking at A (where Sam erroneously thinks his cheese is) as a sign of understanding Sam's mistaken belief a control condition is required, in which everything is the same except that Sam witnesses the transfer of his cheese to B before going to sleep. Thus, he knows that his cheese is in B (true belief control). Only to the degree that children do not look at location A in this control condition can their looking to A in the false belief condition be interpreted as indicative of understanding false belief. In fact, only children in the youngest group, who were younger than 3 years ever looked to A in the control condition.

The upper line in Figure 1 shows the number of children who looked to A in the false belief condition but not in the true belief condition. As one can see, although there was no sign of such 'implicit' understanding of belief in the under 3s, after a sharp developmental onset almost 80% of children at the age of 3 years (2;11–3;2) did show implicit knowledge. And there was a large gap at this age between visually orienting to A and answering the question where Sam will go to look for his cheese with A, as the lower line in Figure 1 shows. In fact it takes practically a full year (at 4 years) before the level of 80% correct responses is reached in their responses to the direct question.

In further studies Clements and Perner (1997) found similar levels of precociously correct responses in children's spontaneous action. This was possible in a new action condition in which Sam made his way to each box by a slide. To soften his arrival the child had to move a mat to the slide which the

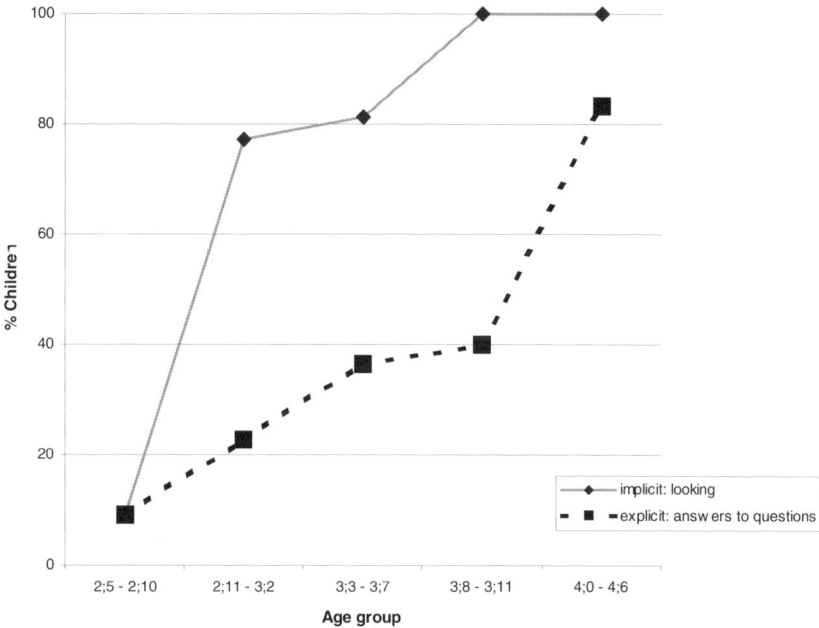

Figure 1. Percentage of children responding with location A in false belief story and with location B in true belief control story (from: Clements & Perner 1994)

child thought Sam might come down on. In the analysis of results it became apparent that one had to distinguish between responses that were given spontaneously and quickly, and those where children hesitated and needed some prompting before responding.

Figure 2 shows that in the verbal condition (where children had to answer the question "Which slide will Sam come down on?") the original result of more children looking to the correct location A than children answering with A was replicated. And it made little difference whether their answers were given quickly or after some prompting. In contrast, as many — if not more — children spontaneously moved the mat to location A as looked at A. For this response mode it mattered a great deal whether responses were given quickly or after prompting.[1] This pattern of results can be summarised as follows:

1. The precociously correct A response occurs more often in action (visual orienting responses and manual manipulations) than in answers to questions.

2. Action responses are only precociously correct when they are given quickly.

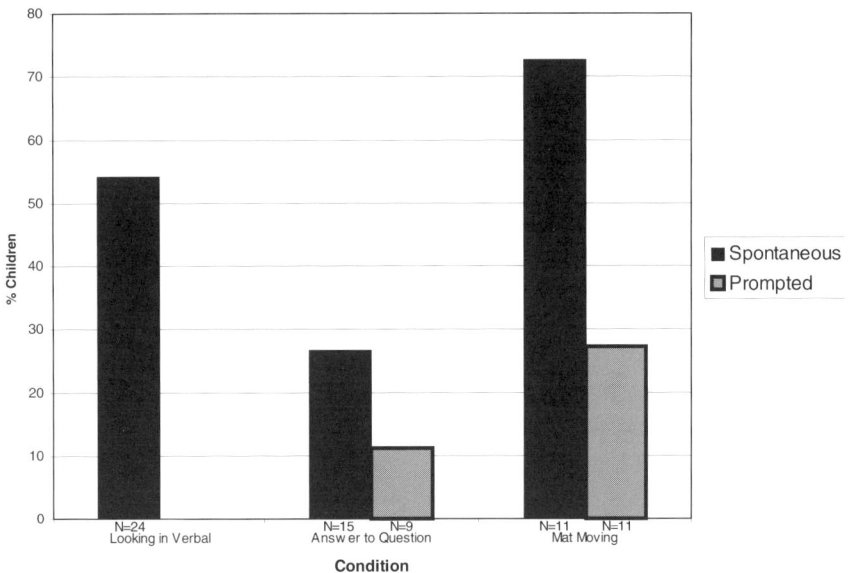

Figure 2. Percentage of children responding with location A in false belief story and with location B in true belief control story (from: Clements & Perner 1997 Exp. 2)

This summary brings out an interesting parallel between the two knowledge bases underlying precociously and later developing correct responses and the two streams of visual information processing posited by, e.g., Milner and Goodale (1995). The one feature is that the implicit knowledge is not accessible to declarative expressions (saying or pointing) of where something is, yet is used for moving something to a location. The other feature is that time delays reduce the successful use of the implicit knowledge.

Wong and Mack (1981) report that despite the phenomenal appearance of a dot's movement in one direction and participants' indication that the dot moved in that direction, saccades remain fixed at the dot's actual location or followed the actual movement in the opposite direction.. However, when instructed to look to the original, remembered location participants had to rely on the conscious illusory location of the dot. Bridgeman (Bridgeman 1991; Bridgeman et al. 1981; this volume) reported for a similar visual illusion (the induced Roelofs effect) that all participants are subject to the illusion in their verbal report of where the dot has moved but that only half the participants show it in their pointing and that none show it in their hand movement to the dot's location (Bridgeman, personal communication). Again, after a delay of some seconds even the hand movement to the dot becomes subject to the illusion.

Blindsight patients (Weiskrantz 1988) who have no phenomenal awareness of most events in their blind field are able to move their finger to a visual event quite accurately. Their accuracy in detecting the presence of an event is higher for an action response like an eye blink than a verbal yes-no response and the accuracy of quick blinking responses is higher than for delayed blinking responses (Marcel 1993). Blindsight patients can also bring their hand into the right orientation in order to insert it into a slot within their blind field but fail to indicate verbally or with their hand what the direction of the slot is (Perenin & Rossetti 1993, 1995, Rossetti 1998; Pisella & Rossetti, this volume). Similarly a numb-sense patient (Paillard et al. 1983) who has no phenomenal awareness of being touched on her right hand can fairly accurately move her left finger to the point of touch. However, if the pointing is not a movement to the actual point of touch but an indicative action of showing on a drawing of her hand where the touch occurs, this ability is lost (Rossetti, 1998). Further evidence that implicit knowledge is only available for immediate action but not for delayed action or symbolic acts is reviewed in Rossetti (1998; Pisella & Rossetti, this volume).

The dominant explanation of these dissociations is physiological, namely that these characteristics are due to the information being processed by different, to a large degree independent processing strands. For visual information the dorsal path (visual cortex to dorsal parietal areas) processes information for *how* to act and this information remains unconscious, while the ventral path (from the visual cortex to the inferior temporal lobe) represents *what* there is in the perceived environment (Milner & Goodale 1995). The fact that the observed dissociation of knowledge about understanding false belief shows such a parallel to these perceptual dissociations is then particularly interesting, because it suggests that the characteristics of the different information processing strands are not due to the physiology of perceptual information processing. It makes it more likely that it is due to functional differences that become relevant for quite distinct information processed in quite different parts of the brain, e.g., for perceptual information about one's immediate surroundings and for knowledge about what goes on in someone else's mind.

This parallel between our developmental findings and these findings from adult psychology provide important support for the intuition that the knowledge base for the earlier understanding of false belief is 'implicit'. For, to establish that it is 'implicit' it would be critical to ascertain whether children lack awareness of their thought of Sam going to location A which governs their visual orienting responses and spontaneous mat movings. We know for the implicit knowledge phenomena gained from adults that they are based on implicit knowledge because of the phenomenal experience of not being aware of this correct information. If we were dealing with adults, who like three year olds predicted that Sam would go to location B, we could validate that their looking and mat movings to location A are based on implicit knowledge by probing their phenomenal experience. If they deny altogether having looked at A and wonder themselves why they moved the mat to A (e.g.: "Oops, I made a mistake — no idea why I moved it to A when Sam is coming down the B slide") then we could conclude that the knowledge that made them look to A and move the mat to A is 'implicit' and unconscious. Unfortunately, this direct validation of probing phenomenal experiences is not possible with 3 year old children. Validation can, if at all, only be gained indirectly. One way of indirectly assessing that knowledge is 'implicit' is to show that it behaves like knowledge in adults that is in their phenomenal experience unconscious. And what we have shown is that the precocious understanding of false belief behaves like implicit knowledge of perceptual information: it is not available for answers to questions, only for spontaneous, quick actions.

There is one aspect in our findings that appears to differ from the dissociation between two knowledge bases in visual information processing. In one experiment (Clements & Perner 1997; Exp. 2) we also checked where children looked AFTER their answers to the question. Of particular interest are those children who in the false belief condition looked to A but then answered wrongly that Sam would appear at B. Of the 8 children who showed this pattern of behaviour 7 looked back to location A right after their B answer to the question. In contrast, of those 11 children who had not looked to A initially and answered with B only one looked subsequently to A. This strong tendency to look back to A after a verbal or gestural (pointing) response to B could mark a difference to the dissociation found in psychophysical studies. In particular, as described above, Wong and Mack (1981) found that eye movements to remembered locations were based on the explicit (conscious) representation and not, like the spontaneous saccades, on the implicit (unconscious) representation. In analogy one might expect that eye movements after the explicit B response should also be to B.

However, that our children move their eyes to A instead need not be a violation of the parallel to Wong and Mack's results because there is an important difference in instructions. Eye movements to remembered locations are voluntary eye movements in response to an instruction: "Look to where the dot was before it moved!" The strictly corresponding case in our study would be eye movements in response to instructions: "look to where Sam is coming down!" There is then no reason to suspect that in response to this instruction children would look anywhere but to B, where they said he'd come down. So, the fact that children's spontaneous (and presumably unconscious, unreflected) eye movements go back to A does not constitute a difference from how eye movements behave in Mack and Wong's psychophysical study.

We have now described our findings that indicate an earlier implicit understanding of false belief. We now turn to speculation of how this earlier, implicit understanding might relate and integrate with the later, explicit understanding. This speculation is based on the theoretical analysis by Dienes and Perner (1996, 1999) of the different ways in which knowledge can be 'implicit' and finds some support in our pilot data. We first try to lay out the basic intuition behind Dienes and Perner's analysis.

A theory: Implicit and explicit predication

A central distinction in Dienes and Perner's analysis hinges on the notion of 'predication', as familiar from predicate logic where the logical form of sentences is given as a Predicate (P, Q,...) being predicated to an individual or particular (a, b, x, y, ...), i.e., Pa. The most common examples are quantified sentences like "All humans are mortal," which are formalised as "$\forall$x (Hx $\supset$ Mx)." In this formula H stands for being human, M for being mortal and $\supset$ for material implication and it means something like, for every individual x it holds that if x is human then x is also mortal. Elaborating Strawson's (1959) word playing game, imagine a situation where one is presented with an individual and one has to identify it, e.g., when presented with a cat, one has to say "cat". What the utterance "cat" represents is the fact that the presented individual is a cat, but only the property of being a cat is made explicit (is reflected in the linguistic expression of "cat" as opposed to "dog", etc.). The fact that it is the presented individual that is a cat is left 'implicit'. In contrast, a sentence like "This is a cat", would also make the predication of cat-ness to the presented individual explicit.

Similarly, if by looking at a cat one forms the mental representation "cat" then this mental representation represents that the individual which gave rise to this representation is a cat, but only its cat-ness is represented (known) explicitly. The fact that it is a particular individual that is a cat remains implicit. Dienes and Perner (1996, 1998; Perner 1993, 1996) speak of 'predication implicit'. For our purposes this basic idea needs to be extended from individual objects and their predicates to event sequences (which is not common in standard predicate logic but corresponds to the distinction between situations and situation types in situation semantics, Barwise & Perry 1983). For instance, I can observe a particular happening which is of the type of a dog chasing a cat. If I represent this event by "dog chasing cat" then I make the event type explicit but leave implicit that this type of event applies (is predicated) to the particular event I am observing. As in the case of objects the predication does exist in the causal link of the particular event causing the representation. One could, therefore, say that it represents the particular event in a 'causally indexical way' (Campbell 1993, 1994).

The claim we want to make is that the dissociations between im- and explicit knowledge that we have discussed can be mapped onto the distinction whether predication is left implicit or made explicit. An important question, then, is when it is important to make predication explicit and when we can get away with leaving it implicit. This should enable us to explain why answers to questions draw on explicit representation and why spontaneous action draws on implicit representations.

Predication needs to be explicit when information about the same individual in different mental spaces (Fauconnier 1983/ 1985; mental models, Johnson-Laird 1983) needs to be co-ordinated. Different mental spaces are needed to enable representation of contradictory basic propositions. This is best explained by one of the prime examples: change with time. If the lovely big balloon pops then it is not big anymore. So we have two contradictory propositions: The balloon is big. The balloon is not big. To avoid confusion these propositions must be put into different spaces or contexts. Since they represent the size of the balloon at different times, the needed contexts are temporal. At t1: the balloon is big. At t2: the balloon is tiny. Now the problem is that this representation loses the distinction between one balloon being big at t1 and another being tiny at t2, versus the same balloon being once big then tiny. For this reason it is essential to represent that balloon-ness and different sizes are predicated to the same individual over time. The for us important implication is that memory of past states needs explicit predication.

Another relevant case where different mental spaces become necessary is the co-ordination of what we perceive to be the case and what we are told about it. Verbal information can easily be wrong and therefore needs to be separated from perceived information in a different mental space. Hence, the second important implication for us is that verbal communication needs explicit predication.

A third, particularly relevant case that requires different mental spaces are representations of what people think, want, believe as distinct from what is the case. This provides a link to consciousness if one accepts at least a weak version of the Higher-Order-Thought theory of consciousness (e.g., Carruthers 1996; Rosenthal 1986), at least for 'access consciousness' (if not for phenomenal consciousness, Block 1995). The basic insight behind different variants of this theory is that to be conscious of some state of affairs (e.g., that the animal in front of me is a cat) then I am also aware of the mental state by which I behold this state of affairs (i.e., that I *see* that the animal is a cat). There is something intuitively correct about this claim, because it is inconceivable that I could sincerely claim, "I am conscious of this being a cat" and at the same time deny to have any knowledge about whether I see the cat, or hear about it, or just know of it, or whether it is me who sees it, etc. That is, it is a necessary condition for consciousness of a fact X that I entertain (or at least: to be able to entertain) a higher mental state (second order thought) that represents the first order mental state with the content X. Now, to represent my mental state about X requires a separate mental space, which in turn requires explicit predication. Hence a third important implication for our purposes is that conscious awareness requires explicit predication.

Explaining the dissociations in visual information processing

We can now see how the distinction between representations that make predication explicit and those that leave it implicit can be related to the different paths of visual information processing. Much of visual information is about the current state of the immediate environment within which we move and act. The dorsal path(Milner & Goodale 1995) processes information for action. Since action takes place within the current state of the world a single mental space (model of the world) is required. According to our argument, it does not need explicit predication of properties to individuals.[2] Assuming that it does not have explicit predication we can explain why one cannot use it for communicative purposes, verbal or gestural answers to questions, why it remains inaccessible to consciousness, and why it does not support memory of previous locations (Wong & Mack 1981). One can also understand why the information fades with time (Bridgeman 1991; this volume; Rossetti, 1998; Pisella & Rossetti, this volume; Rossetti et al. 2000), since it is useless, or even dangerous, to represent in one's state of the world model the last location of a potentially moving object that has become invisible.

In contrast, the ventral stream (Milner & Goodale 1995) processes the incoming information by making predication explicit. This allows representation of the state of the world at different times, makes this information accessible to communicative exchanges and to conscious awareness. Now it is clear why neurological patients whose ventral stream is severely impaired, as in blindsight patients, can show correct action above guessing when their action is not delayed for too long, and why they have no awareness of the stimulus and cannot indicate its location or shape in communication (see Rossetti, 1998, for condensed review).

In the case of observed dissociations under perceptual conditions that create illusions, an interesting question is why only the information along the ventral path is subject to the illusion but not the information along the dorsal path. In the case of the movement induced illusions used by Wong and Mack and by Bridgeman our analysis provides a straight forward reason. Since the dorsal path only processes information about the current state of the world and does not attempt to relate it to previous states it is not subject to the illusion which critically depends on the perceived changes over time. To explain the dissociation for static illusions like the Titchener circles used by Agliotti et al (1995) is less straight forward and much more speculative. Perhaps the illusion occurs when the stimulus is analysed beyond a three dimensional layout into objects that have individual identity and can be moved independently. We do not know any evidence for this possibility for the Titchener illusion but one of the explanations of the Müller-Lyer illusion, for which the dissociation between action and conscious experience has also been reported (Gentilluci et al. 1995), might fit that explanation. One suggested reason (Gregory 1966) why the line with arrows is seen as shorter than the line with inverted arrows is that the visual system tries to interpret the lines as part of a three dimensional object of which the line connecting the arrows is the nearest part with the arrow lines receding into depth. Since retinal images of objects judged near are interpreted as larger than same size retinal images of objects judged distant, the two lines (interpreted as parts of objects) appear to be of different length. The depth cue leading to the illusion only affects the ventral system that tries to "interpret" the scene as objects. The dorsal path might only use depth cues that are not dependent on identifying objects in the scene.

Explaining the developmental gap in understanding belief

It is clear that explicit predication is required to understand a story that unfolds over time. So the implicit understanding of belief identified in our experiments cannot be without some explicit predication. However, one can apply this analysis at a higher level. The complicated temporal sequence of events itself can be a higher order predicate (event type) that can be predicated to a particular event. To use our earlier example, I can predicate cat-ness to an individual, and I can turn the event involving a particular dog and cat into a higher order predicate, 'Fido chasing our cat', and predicate it to an individual event. To individuate the event allows us to identify the event in different ways, i.e., 'Fido chasing the cat', or 'What I just saw'. And we can use one description to identify the individual event and then add new information about that event: 'Looking out the window I saw *something* '. '*What* I saw was Fido chasing the cat.'

We need to individuate events in order to re-identify them across different spaces. Unlike objects, re-identification across time is less important, though not negligible, e.g., "the party was rather dull to begin with but in the end it was very lively". At time 1 the party was dull, at time 2 it was lively, and it was the same party. And as for objects we need individuated events in order to co-ordinate what we experience with what is being talked about (communication) and in order to represent mental states about it (a prerequisite for conscious awareness according to the higher-order thought theory).

An important question is how one can learn that certain events tend to go together and form a typical sequence. Such filtering of statistical patterns of possible combinations does not need representation of individual events and inferences from individual events to all possible events. Rather it is a process of pattern formation and recognition for which connectionist systems are good (e.g., to classify different feature patterns into letters, e.g., Bechtel & Abrahamsen 1991). The encountered combinations of letters in artificial grammar tasks have a similar effect and can be particularly well modelled by connectionist networks (Dienes 1992). Although individual instances shape the connections between units and, hence, the association between the properties that these units represent, there is no representation of the individual instances.[3] Connectionist work also shows that such pattern generalisation also leads to pattern completion. If many elements of a typical pattern are present then the network tends to generate representations of the missing bits. This is important, because such pattern completion processes can produce expectations of what is to come on the basis of what has so far happened. And the, for us, important implication is that such associative expectation is possible without explicit predication.

This makes it possible to anticipate correctly where Sam will go to get his cheese in our false belief stories without explicit predication to a particular occasion, i.e., without representing *that* he will go there. So, according to our above discussion, such a representation of the mere event form 'Sam going to location A' and hence, 'Sam at location A' as part of a pattern completion process, can guide visual orienting responses and spontaneous actions because such a representation can trigger an existing action schema waiting to be executed. It cannot be used for communication because it lacks predication to an individual event which can be re-identified across mental spaces, i.e., between the space of anticipation and the space of verbal description. It cannot sustain uncertainty, since it does not support a self-reassuring check about where Sam *will* come down since without explicit predication there is no representation stating *that* he will go anywhere. And that is the pattern of results we observed in the precociously correct responses: they were high only in spontaneous action and visual orienting responses.

The basis for this prediction was that the anticipation be based on ob-served behavioural regularities. For instance, by observing persons putting things into boxes then returning to that location even when the object has been moved may lead to abstraction of such a behaviour pattern: "Puts object into location A, looks for object, returns to where he had put object." Another observed regularity may be: "Tells another person to put object into a location, then looks for object in that location." By way of pattern completion, observ-ing the first part of these patterns may associatively evoke the typical ending. If we now construct a story where typically observed patterns are mixed so that each initial pattern would predict a different ending, then no clear — or at least much weaker — anticipation should result. This is what Clements (1995, Chapter 5) undertook.

A pilot test of our explanation

Clements (1995) used variations of the false belief story employed by Perner, et al. (1987) to test the generality of explicit understanding of belief. One story is the traditional (Unexpected Transfer) story in which the desired object is put by the protagonist in location A and is then unexpectedly moved without the protagonist witnessing the move to location B. This is contrasted with a new (Forget Transfer) story in which the protagonist puts the object in location B and later tells a friend to move the object to location A but the friend forgets without informing the protagonist. Now notice, in the traditional story ob-served regularities like "looks where last put" or "looks where last seen" all support the correct anticipatory response of looking to location A. Whereas, in the new Forget Transfer story these regularities support a wrong response of looking to B. Only the regularity "looks where he told other to put object" supports the correct anticipatory looking. Figure 3 shows that of 38 children between the ages of 2 years 5 months and 4 years 6 months, as predicted, about 20% more children looked at location A in the traditional Unexpected Transfer story than in the new Forget Transfer story.

Figure 3 also shows that the difference between stories is fairly minimal for answers to questions — replicating the original finding by Perner et al. (1987, a difference of 63% vs.50%) and also Doherty & Perner (1998, 50% vs. 48%). This provides some support for the claim that explicit responding is less dependent on observed regularities than implicit responses. Rather, explicit responses reflect children's understanding of the causal information processing mechanism underlying belief (Leslie 1988; Perner 1991; Wimmer et al. 1988). The child's theory might consist of pieces like the following: "If a person sees an object put into a box, the person believes the object is in that box and remains there until one has information about a transfer. If a person instructs another to transfer an object and the person does not receive information to the contrary, the person believes the object to be in the new location. People look for objects where they believe them to be." This theory reflects a deeper understanding of belief than the mere generalisations of observed regularities and yields the correct answer in both stories.

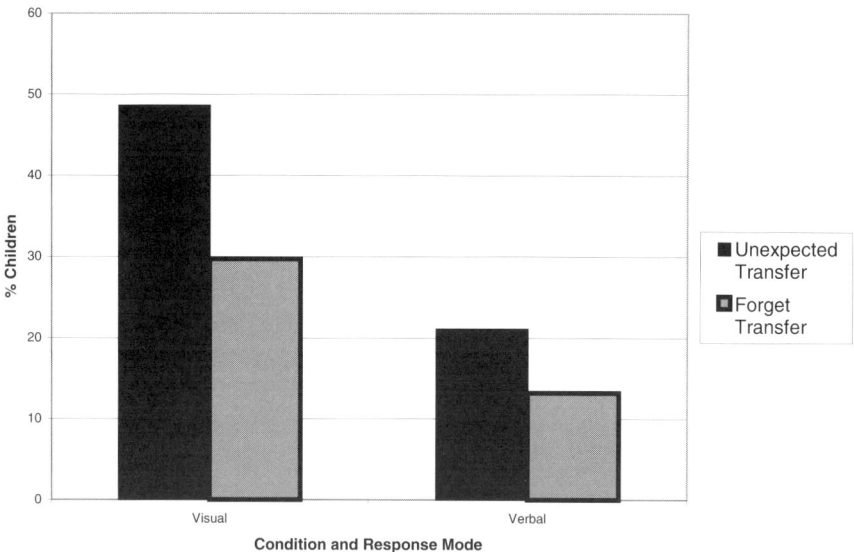

Figure 3. Percentage of children responding with location A in false belief story and with location B in true belief control story (Clements 1995, Chap. 5)

We do not know how such a theory is acquired, but it seems that such a theory goes beyond mere generalisations of observed regularities and constitutes genuine causal understanding of the underlying processes (see Gopnik, 1993; Perner, 1991, for indications of theory use). Causal understanding cannot be achieved by mere pattern matching and pattern completion but must employ explicit predication since causal reasoning is counterfactual supporting (Lewis 1986; Salmon 1984). Counterfactual support means that one understands that if the conditions were different then the result would be different, and such reasoning requires different mental spaces for contrasting the actual facts with their counterfactual oppositions. For these reasons, responses that are based on a causal theory of belief should also be accessible to communication (answers to questions) and be robust against doubt (hesitating action). The available findings for answers to questions support this connection. Correct answers to questions (requiring explicit predication) tend not to differ much between the Unexpected Transfer and the Forget Transfer conditions which indicates that children go beyond mere pattern generalization and use a proper causal understanding of belief (requiring explicit predication).

But interaction?

We have not said much about 'interaction' between the earlier implicit and the later explicit understanding of belief. Correct responding of one kind simply precedes the other. There may, however, be a more intimate connection, namely that implicit understanding is a precondition for training explicit understanding. This claim has been made and tested in a somewhat different domain of knowledge where a dissociation between gesture and speech has been reported.

For instance, the gesture-speech mismatch literature (e.g., Church & Goldin-Meadow 1986; Goldin-Meadow et al. 1992; Goldin-Meadow et al. 1993b) reports precocious expression of Piagetian conservation concepts and arithmetical notions in gesture over verbal answers. On the surface this seems different from our findings since we did not report a gesture vs. speech mismatch but rather a gesture/speech vs. looking/action mismatch. However, if one considers that the gestures that mismatch with speech are spontaneous concomitants of the thinking process and not a means of declarative communication, then the same difference in knowledge could underlie the observed dissociation in these and in our studies.

The interesting claim about interaction is that the onset of implicit understanding marks the Vygotskian (1978) 'Zone of Proximal Development' where explicit mastery of a concept can be profitably trained. For instance, Church and Goldin-Meadow (1986) found that children who show in their gestures implicit understanding of the to be acquired concept could be successfully trained to acquire this concept also for their explicit verbal interactions whereas children who did not show any implicit gestural understanding could not be thus trained.

Clements, Rustin and McCallum (2000) tested this claim with reference to false belief understanding. Children were given a pre-test which consisted of one false belief story as used in Clements and Perner (1994). Eye gaze was monitored as well as verbal responses. In the training phase, children were allocated to one of three groups: In the *Explanation* group, two false belief stories were administered and feedback together with explanations was given about why the correct answer was correct and why the incorrect answer was incorrect. In the *Practice* group, two false belief stories were administered but no explanations were given. Children simply received feedback in form of seeing the outcome of the story (i.e. the protagonist re-appearing at location A). In the Control group, children listened to two stories which were completely unrelated to false belief. At post-test, seven to ten days later, children were administered one false belief story.

Table 1 shows for each training condition how many children gave the same response in pre- and post test, how many improved from answering with B on the pretest to answering A on the post test, and how many deteriorated from A to B. In the Control group there was no systematic improvement. About as many children deteriorated (4) from pre- to post test as improved (3). In the Practice group only one child improved. The only training that had a reliable and sizeable effect was the Explanation condition. Here 11 children improved and only one child deteriorated: McNemar's $\chi^2(1, N=29) = 8.33$, p < .01.

Table 1. Number of children classified according to their improvement from Pre- to Posttest (from Clements, Rusttin & McCallum, 2000)

Condition	Change from pre- to posttest		
	No change	B → A	A → B
Control	25	3	4
Practice	29	1	0
Explanation	17	11	1

The fact that only children in the Explanation condition but not in the Practice condition improved on the post test underlines our earlier discussion about explicit answers depending on a causal understanding of belief. Observing the behavioural regularities in the Practice condition does not influence answers to questions on the post test. Only when an explanation is given of why the protagonist goes to the wrong place does the training have an effect on answers to questions. Unfortunately, children's looking responses on the post test were not recorded. The prediction would be that in the Practice group children should show more looking to A on the post test than on the pretest since they experience behavioural regularities during Practice training.

Table 2 shows the importance of initial implicit understanding for the effectiveness of explanation training. The first column shows children's explicit understanding on the pretest, i.e., whether they answered the question with A or B. If we concentrate on those children who gave wrong B answers (last two rows), we see that 13 of them did not show any implicit understanding in their looking. For these children training had a minimal effect. Only 3 of the 13 improved their answer from pre- to post test (23%). In contrast, of the 8 children who gave a wrong B answer but did show implicit understanding (looking to A), all 8 of them improved on the post test (answering with A). A reliable difference to those who did not show any implicit understanding: $\chi^2(1, N=21) = 11.75$, $p < .001$.

Table 2. Children in the explanation group classified by their implicit and explicit understanding in the pre- and posttest performance (from Clements, Rusttin & McCallum, 2000)

Pretest explicit answer	Looking	n	Posttest answer	
			A	B
A	A	8	7	1
	B	0	0	0
B	A	8	8	0
	B	13	3	10

Conclusion

We have found a dissociation between an earlier, precocious understanding of the behavioural consequences of a false belief (where someone will go on the basis of such a belief) expressed in visual orienting responses and spontaneous action, and a later understanding expressed in answers to questions and deliberate action. Since the earlier knowledge does not influence deliberate action and declarative communication it is reminiscent of implicit knowledge in perceptual information processing.

We speculated that implicit knowledge of this kind consists of knowledge that does not make predication to particular instances explicit. With this assumption we tried to account for the fact that implicit knowledge cannot be used for symbolic expression (communication), cannot represent changes over time, cannot be used for deliberation (indicated by hesitant action), and escapes access to consciousness. Another consequence is that such knowledge is limited to being acquired through abstraction of observed regularities. In line with this speculation, pilot data indicated that implicit knowledge expressed in visual orienting responses is more likely when the mistaken person's future action can be anticipated on the basis of observed regularities (traditional Unexpected Transfer condition) than when such regularities provide contradictory anticipations (Forget Transfer condition). We also found that experience of behavioural regularities (Practice group) had no effect on explicit answers in a post test but explanations of the deeper (causal) reasons did have a clear effect. Since understanding of causal reasons requires explicit predication it is to be expected that knowledge thus gained is expressible in answers to questions.

The training study also showed that the earlier, implicit knowledge is not unrelated to the later emerging explicit understanding. Rather it constitutes a necessary prerequisite for achieving explicit understanding. Only children who had prior implicit understanding profited from explanation training in their explicit answers.

Notes

1.   Figure 2 suggests that the difference between spontaneous and prompted responses influences the number of A responses more strongly in the action than in the verbal condition. However the data were not strong enough to show a statistically significant

interaction term. Both main effects of verbal versus action condition ($\chi^2(1, N=71) = 7.87$, p=.02) and spontaneous versus prompted responses ($\chi^2(1, N=71) = 8.19$, p=.004) were significant after potentially confounding age differences had been partialled out.

2.   This holds only for action for which a response schema is set up (Perner, 1998). If the action has to be computed on the basis of fresh verbal instructions of what to grasp or move one's finger to then explicit predication is required for co-ordinating the verbal description (one mental space) with the perceived world (second mental space). Accordingly, one claim inherent in this analysis is that the psychophysical type experiments show a dissociation between action information and declarative responses (e.g., Bridgeman, 1991; Aglioti, et al., 1995) because they are based on a large number of repetitions of the same response, so that the response does not have to be computed on each single trial on the basis of a verbal goal description but can be executed on the basis of an existing response schema that is triggered by the presented stimulus.

3.   For this reason one can speak of association but not of inference. For, inferences go from state of affairs to state of affairs, i.e., reasoning of the form 'whenever X is the case then Y must be the case.' But that means X and Y are predicated to particular occasions. That associative processes are possible implicitly and without consciousness but not inferences is reminiscent of Sloman's (1996) suggestion that implicit knowledge is tied to associative processes and explicit knowledge to rule governed inference processes.

References.

Aglioti, S., DeSouza, J.F.X. & Goodale, M.A. (1995). Size-contrast illusions deceive the eye but not the hand. *Current Biology, 5*(6), 679–685.

Astington, J.W. (1993). *The child's discovery of the mind.* Cambridge, MA: Harvard University Press.

Barwise, J. & Perry, J (1983). *Simulations and attitudes.* Cambridge, MA: MIT Press. A Bradford Book.

Bechtel, W. & Abrahamsen, A. (1991). *Connectionism and the mind.* Oxford: Blackwell.

Block, N. (1995). On a confusion about a function of consciousness. *Behavioral and Brain Sciences, 18,* 227–287.

Bridgeman, B., Kirch, M. & Sperling, A. (1981). Segregation of cognitive and motor aspects of visual function using induced motion. *Perception and Psychophysics, 29,* 336–342.

Bridgeman, B. (1991). Complementary cognitive and motor image processing. In G. Obrecht & L.W.Stark (Eds.), *Presbyopia research: From molecular biology to visualadaption.* New York: Plenum Press, 189–198.

Campbell, J. (1993). The role of physical objects in spatial thinking. In N. Eilan, R. McCarthy & B. Brewer (Eds.), *Spatial representation.* Oxford: Blackwell, 65–96.

Campbell, J. (1994). *Past, space and self.* Cambridge: MIT Press.

Carruthers, P. (1996). *Language, thought and consciousness. An essay in philosophical psychology.* Cambridge: Cambrige University Press.

Church, R.B. & Goldin-Meadow, S. (1986). The mismatch between gesture and speech as an index of transitional knowledge. *Cognition, 23,*43–71.

Clements, W.A. (1995). Implicit theories of mind. Unpublished doctoral dissertation, University of Sussex.

Clements, W.A., Rustin, C. & McCallum, S. (2000). Promoting the transition from implicit to explicit understanding: A training study of false belief. *Developmental Science, 3,* 81–92.

Clements, W.A. & Perner, J. (1997). When Actions Really Do Speak Louder Than Words but only implicitly: Young Children's Understanding of False Belief in Action. Unpublished Manuscript, University of Sussex.

Dienes, Z. (1992). Connectionist and memory-array models of artificial grammar learning. *Cognitive Science*, 16, 41–79.

Dienes, Z. & Perner, J. (1996). Implicit knowledge in people and connectionist networks. In G.Underwood (Ed.), *Implicit cognition*. Oxford: Oxford University Press, 227–255.

Dienes, Z. & Perner, J. (1998). A theory of implicit and explicit knowledge. *Behavioral and Brain Sciences, 22,* 735–755.

Doherty, M. & Perner, J. (1998). Metalinguistic awareness and theory of mind: Just two words for the same thing? *Cognitive Development, 13,* 279–305.

Fauconnier, G. (1985). *Mental spaces: Aspects of meaning construction in natural language.* Cambridge, MA: MIT Press.

Gentilucci, M., Chieffi, S. & Daprati, E. (1995). Visual illusion and action. *Neuropsychologia, 34,* 369–376.

Goldin-Meadow, S., Nusbaum, H., Garber, P. & Church, R.B. (1993). Transitions in learning: Evidence for simultaneously activated strategies. *Journal of Experimental Psychology: Human Perception and Performance*, 19 (1), 92–107.

Goldin-Meadow, S., Alibali, M.W. & Church, R.B. (1993). Transitions in concept acquisition: Using the hand to read the mind. *Psychological Review*, 100, 279–297.

Johnson-Laird, P.N. (1983). *Mental models.* Cambridge: Cambridge University Press.

Leslie, A.M. (1988). Some implications of pretense for mechanisms underlying the child's theory of mind. In J.W. Astington, P.L. Harris & D.R. Olson (Eds.), *Developing theories of mind*. New York: Cambridge University Press, 19–46.

Lewis, D. (1986). Causal Explanation. In D. Lewis (Ed.), *Philosophical Papers*. Oxford: Oxford University Press.

Marcel, A.J. (1993). Slippage in the unity of consciousness. In *Experimental and theoretical studies of consciousness*. Chichester: Wiley, 168–186.

Milner, D.A. & Goodale, M.A. (1995). *The visual brain in action*. Oxford: Oxford University Press.

Mitchell, P. (1996). *Acquiring a conception of mind*. Hove, East Sussex: Psychological Press.

Paillard, J., Michel, F. & Stelmach, G. (1983). Localization without content. A tactile analogue of 'Blindsight'. *Archives of Neurology*, 40, 548–551.

Perenin, M.T. & Rossetti, Y. (1993). Residual grasping in a hemianoptic field. *European Brain and Behaviour Society (EBBS)*.

Perenin, M.T. & Rossetti, Y. (1995). Saisir sans voir dans un champs hémianopsique: un autre exemple de dissociation entre perception et action. *Annual meeting of the French Neuroscience Society*.

Perner, J. (1993). Implicit, explicit, … and even consciousness. Paper presented at the

Biennial Meeting of the Society for Research in Child Development, New Orleans.
Perner, J., Leekam, S.R. & Wimmer, H. (1987). Three-year olds' difficulty with false belief: The case for a conceptual deficit. *British Journal of Developmental Psychology*, 5, 125–137.
Perner, J. (1991). *Understanding the representational mind.* Cambridge, MA: MIT Press.
Perner, J. (1995). The many faces of belief: Reflections on Fodor's and the child's theory of mind. *Cognition*, 57, 241–269.
Perner, J. (1996). Simulation as explicitation of predication-implicit knowlegde about the mind: Arguments for a simulation-theory mix. In P.Carruthers & P.K.Smith (Eds.), *Theories of theories of mind.* Cambridge: Cambridge University Press, 90–104.
Perner, J. (1998). The meta-intentional nature of executive functions and theory of mind. In P. Carruthers & J. Boucher (Eds.), *Language and Thought: Interdisciplinary themes* (270–283). Cambridge: Cambridge University Press.
Premack, D. & Woodruff, G. (1978). Does the chimpanzee have a theory of mind? *The Behavioral and Brain Sciences*, 1, 516–526.
Rosenthal, D.M. (1986). Two concepts of consciousness. *Philosophical Studies*, 49, 329–359.
Rossetti, Y. (1998). Implicit short-lived motor representation of space in brain-damaged and healthy subjects. *Consciousness and Cognition*, 7, 520–558.
Rossetti, Y. (2000). Implicit perception in action: short lived motor representations of space. In P. Grossenbacher (Ed.), *Finding consciousness in the brain.* (pp. 131–178). Amsterdam: Benjamins.
Rossetti, Y., Pisella, L., Pélisoon, D. (2000). Eye blindness and hand sight: temporal aspects of visuo-motor processing. *Visual Cognition*, in press.
Salmon, W.C. (1984). *Scientific explanation and the causal structure of the world.* Princeton, NJ: Princton University Press.
Sloman, S.A. (1996). The empirical case for two systems of reasoning. *Psychological Bulletin*, 119 (1), 3–22.
Strawson, P.F. (1959). *Individuals.* London: Methuen.
Vygotsky, L.S. (1978). *Mind in society.* Cambridge, MA: Harvard University Press.
Weiskrantz, L. (1988). Some contributions of neuropsychology of vision and memory to the problem of consciousness. In A.J. Marcel & E. Bisiach (Eds.), *Consciousness in contemporary science.* Oxford: Clarendon Press, 183–199.
Wellman, H.M. (1990). *The child's theory of mind.* Cambridge, MA: MIT Press. A Bradford Book.
Wimmer, H. & Perner, J. (1983). Beliefs about beliefs: Representation and constraining function of wrong beliefs in young children's understanding of deception. *Cognition*, 13, 103–128.
Wimmer, H., Hogrefe, G.J. & Sodian, B. (1988). A second stage in children's conception of mental life: Understanding sources of information. In J.W.Astington, P.L Harris & D.R.Olson (Eds.), *Developing theories of mind.* New York: Cambridge University Press, 173–192.
Wong, E. & Mack, A. (1981). Saccadic programming and perceived location. *Acta Psychologica*, 48, 123–131.

Consciousness and the Zombie Within

A Functional Analysis of the Blindsight Evidence

Ullin T. Place

University of Leeds and University of Wales Bangor

The evolution of a theory

In this chapter I develop a theory of consciousness and its unconscious counterpart which I call the "zombie-within". It has its source in two lines of research both of which originated in the 1950s, now more than forty years, ago. One of these was an attempt made by the present author in two papers published in the *British Journal of Psychology*, 'The concept of heed' (Place 1954) and 'Is consciousness a brain process?' (Place 1956), to examine the implications for the science of psychology of the work of Wittgenstein (1958; 1953) and Ryle (1949) on the linguistic analysis of what Ryle calls "the logical geography of our ordinary mental concepts". The other was the late Donald Broadbent's (1958) experimental and theoretical analysis of the phenomenon of selective attention in his book *Perception and Communication*.

Place 'The Concept of Heed' (1954) and 'Is Consciousness A Brain Process? (1956)

In *The Concept of Mind* Ryle (*op.cit.*) shows that many of our most common psychological verbs, verbs such as 'know', 'believe', 'understand', 'remember', 'expect', 'want' and 'intend', do *not*, as had been traditionally supposed, refer to processes within the individual of whom they are predicated to which he or she has "privileged access" through the process known as "introspection". These verbs refer to *dispositions* or *performance characteristics* of the individual which are manifested as much in what he or she publicly says and does as in his or her private mental processes. However, the application of these same techniques of linguistic analysis also shows

> "an intractable residue of concepts clustering around the notions of consciousness, experience, sensation and mental imagery, where some sort of inner process story is unavoidable." (Place 1956: 44)

It was this "intractable residue" to which I was referring when I argued in the same paper that

> "the thesis that consciousness is a process in the brain is a reasonable scientific hypothesis, not to be dismissed on logical grounds alone" (Place 1956: 44)

Central to this concept of consciousness was the idea that the verb phrase 'paying attention to _____' refers to an *internal non-muscular activity* whereby the individual

> "exercises a measure of control over the vividness or acuteness of his consciousness of (a) the sensations to which he is susceptible at that moment, or (b) such features of the environment as are impinging on his receptors, without necessarily adjusting his receptor organs or their position in any way." (Place, 1954: 244)

In contrast to Ryle who had argued that to pay attention was to perform whatever task one was engaged in at the time with a disposition to succeed in it, I pointed out that

> "close attention to his own activity will be of no avail to the unskilled person because he has not learnt to discriminate between the relevant and irrelevant features. On the other hand an acute consciousness of the details of his own activity in relation to the environment may actually detract from the efficiency of performance in the case of an individual who has learnt to make many of the adjustments involved automatically." (Place 1954: 247)

Here we have the germ of two ideas which are fundamental to the theory expounded below, (a) the idea that conscious experience is *not*, as it has been too often portrayed by philosophers, a mere passive spectator of what is going on inside and outside the organism, but, when properly focussed, is an integral part of the process whereby the behaviour of the organism is brought into an adaptive relation to the environmental contingencies, and (b) the idea that in order to perform that function successfully, the implementation of the *tactical details* of a skilled performance must be handed over, as it were, to what I am

here calling the "automatic pilot" or "zombie-within" in order to free consciousness to concentrate on those features of the task where important
strategic decisions are called for.

Although I did not emphasise this point at the time, it will be apparent that
the role assigned in this account to consciousness in general and conscious
experience in particular is one which has as much application to the control of
animal behaviour as it has to that of human beings. What I did not then
appreciate is that the other function of consciousness which I emphasised both
in 'The concept of heed' and in 'Is consciousness a brain process?', that of
enabling the individual to give a verbal description of those aspects of the
current situation on which attention is focussed, also has its roots in a mechanism which plays a key role in animal problem-solving. For, as is shown by
research on the effects of lesions of the striate cortex in man and monkey
("blindsight"), without conscious experience of the stimuli involved a monkey
is unable to categorize and thus recognise either individuals or things of a kind
(Humphrey 1974). What I *did* emphasise, particularly in 'Is consciousness a
brain process?', was the idea that the remarkable ability of human subjects to
give a running commentary on their private experiences, either at the time or
shortly thereafter, is a *by-product* of the ability to give a description of and
running commentary on that individual's current stimulus environment *in so
far as* attention and consciousness are focussed upon it.

*Broadbent's 'Perception and Communication' (1958) and 'Decision and
Stress' (1971)*

This theory of the functions of attention and consciousness, as I was later to
discover (Place 1969), bears a remarkable resemblance to the theory of
selective attention expounded by the late Donald Broadbent (1958) in his
book *Perception and Communication*. Basing his conclusions on results obtained from the *dichotic listening experiment* in which conflicting auditory
messages are fed by earphones into the two ears, Broadbent introduced the
idea that there is a central information processing unit in the brain that is a
"limited capacity channel" in the sense that it can only process a limited
amount of information coming in from the sense organs at any one time. Such
a limited capacity channel or LCC requires a *selective attention mechanism*
which protects it from overload, partly by excluding aspects of the current
total input which are unproblematic and thus do not need to be processed, and

partly by holding other inputs that need to be processed in a short term memory store or *"buffer"* until the LCC-entry bottleneck clears.

In *Decision and Stress* Broadbent (1971) introduced a number of modifications to the model he had outlined in the 1958 book. Three are particularly important for our present purpose:

(1) He introduced the term *"state of evidence"* (i.e. "evidence" about the current state of the environment) to refer to the output of the selective attention mechanism and the input into the limited capacity channel, a notion which corresponds to that of "raw" or uninterpreted experience in traditional psychology.

(2) He proposed that the function of the limited capacity channel is to "pigeon-hole" and "categorize" the "evidence" passed through from the selective attention mechanism, where 'to pigeon-hole' is to routinely assign an unproblematic input to its classification and 'to categorize' is either to create a new classification or to extend or otherwise modify an existing classification so as to accommodate an otherwise unclassifiable input. However, as is shown by the "blindsight" evidence described below, the kind of routine automatic behaviour which on the present hypothesis is assigned to the zombie-within requires no conscious experience to supply the "evidence" and no categorization of objects in the affected part of the visual field. Nevertheless, the individual is able to perform routine visually guided tasks, such as reaching for objects and, in the case of the monkey at least, avoiding obstacles. I infer from this that no classification of the input is necessary for the automatic routine control of behaviour by visual stimuli or those in the other sensory modalities which, on this hypothesis, is mediated by the automatic pilot or zombie-within, and that, therefore, Broadbent's routine "pigeon-holing" of non-problematic inputs does not exist. The only classification of sensory inputs that occurs is the categorization in consciousness of problematic inputs.

(3) He proposed that the parts of the input that are not in the current focus of attention are not filtered out completely, as proposed in 1958, but rather contribute, to a lesser extent than the part that is in the focus, to what Broadbent calls *"the category state"*, the final outcome of the categorization process. Although Broadbent himself does not use that terminology, another way of putting the point would be to say that the input in the focus of attention stands as *figure* to the inputs outside the focus as *ground*.

Humphrey's 'Vision in a Monkey without Striate Cortex' (1974)

In his 1974 paper Nicholas Humphrey writes:

> "In 1965 Weiskrantz removed the visual striate cortex from an adolescent rhesus monkey, Helen. In the 8 years between the operation and her death in 1973 this monkey slowly recovered the use of her eyes, emerging from virtual sightlessness to a state of visual competence where she was able to move deftly through a room full of obstacles and could reach out and catch a passing fly." (Humphrey 1974: 241)

Nevertheless,

> "After years of experience she never showed any signs of recognizing even those objects most familiar to her, whether the object was a carrot, another monkey or myself". (Humphrey 1974: 252).

The full significance of this observation for the theory of consciousness has only become apparent in the light of two subsequent discoveries. The first of these was Weiskrantz's (1986) demonstration that in addition to retaining the same visual abilities (apart possibly from the ability to avoid obstacles which is not demonstrable in a subject with only a partial lesion of the striate cortex) lesions of the striate cortex in man have the effect of completely abolishing visual conscious experience in the affected part of the visual field. The second discovery was Cowey and Stoerig's (1995; 1997; Stoerig & Cowey 1997) demonstration that lesions of the striate cortex in the monkey have the same effect in abolishing visual conscious experience of stimuli in the "blind" field as they do in human subjects, despite the fact that the animal can reach for objects in that part of the visual field with almost the same accuracy as for objects in the intact field.

When combined with these subsequent discoveries and interpreted in the light of Broadbent's model, Humphrey's observations show (a) that the function of conscious experience is to provide the "evidence" on which categorization of current inputs is based and without which no categorization of those inputs is possible, (b) that relying only on the sub-cortical visual inputs available to it, the unconscious "automatic pilot" or "zombie-within" can learn by the process of trial-and-error to make many very accurate visual discriminations including the ability to reach for objects and avoid obstacles by sight, and (c) that the behaviour controlled by the unconscious "automatic pilot" or "zombie-within" (e.g., reaching for "unseen" objects and avoiding "unseen" obstacles in the visual field) does *not* require any categorization of the inputs to which system is responding (human subjects describe such responses as "pure guesswork").

Weiskrantz's Blindsight *(1986)*

As already mentioned, Weiskrantz has shown that the effect of lesions of the striate cortex in man is to abolish conscious experience in the affected part of the visual field. It does so, presumably, by depriving the cortex of the "raw material" from which the "evidence" on which categorization of inputs is based. Nevertheless, as we have also seen, patients such as Weiskrantz's subject D.B., show some remarkable visual discrimination abilities, such as the ability to reach for objects in the blind field with considerable accuracy, the phenomenon to which Weiskrantz has given the name "blindsight". For our present purposes, the two most important additional points to emerge from Weiskrantz's study are (a) that the visual discrimination abilities displayed by the blindsight patient always fall short of the ability to judge spontaneously *what kind of a stimulus* has been presented to the "blind" field (thereby confirming Humphrey's observation that without striate cortex categorization of a visual input is impossible), and (b) that human subjects with striate cortical lesions can only be induced to display the considerable discrimination abilities they retain in the "blind" part of the visual field, by persuading them to *guess* the location of something or which of two specified alternatives was present in a case where they insist that they *"saw nothing"*, showing thereby that *without conscious experience of the input* the subject has no way of checking his judgment against "evidence" on which such judgments are normally based.

Cowey and Stoerig's 'Blindsight in Monkeys' (1995)

In addition to showing that we can use Humphrey's (1974) study as evidence of the effect of completely depriving an organism of its visual conscious experience, Cowey and Stoerig's (1995) paper also provides us with the first conclusive evidence that Descartes was mistaken in thinking that, because only humans have language, because only *they* can describe what their conscious experiences *are like,* conscious experience is an exclusively human phenomenon. It also provides us with a methodology which, when suitably adapted to the species in question, should allow us to demonstrate the "blindsight" phenomenon in other species of mammal, in birds, in other vertebrates, and perhaps even in some invertebrates. If this latter prediction is fulfilled, it will show beyond serious doubt that conscious experience has been present in the brains of free-moving living organisms for a very long time indeed. Even with only the monkey evidence available, the idea, supported by many contemporary philosophers, that conscious experience is a functionless epiphenomenon which appears only with the emergence of *homo sapiens* can no longer be sustained.

The ventral and dorsal visual pathways

Recent neuropsychological research on visual agnosias (Farah 1990; Milner & Goodale 1995) has drawn attention to the functional significance of an anatomically identified bifurcation within the visual areas of the brain between two "streams" or "pathways", the *ventral stream* and the *dorsal stream*. As originally defined by Ungerleider and Mishkin (1982), these two pathways bifurcate downstream of the striate or primary visual cortex (V1). The ventral stream travels *via* the extra-striate visual areas (V2-V5) to the *infero-temporal cortex*. The dorsal stream travels upwards to "terminate" in the *posterior parietal cortex*. In other words, the bifurcation between the two pathways lies entirely within the cerebral cortex.

Studies of the behaviour of patients with lesions restricted to one or other of these two pathways show that lesions of the ventral stream result, depending on the site and extent of the lesion, in a variety of functional disorders involving the loss or disturbance of visual conscious experience associated with a loss or disturbance of the ability to recognise objects and the situations in which they occur, conditions such as *prosopagnosia* (loss of the ability to recognise faces) and *simultanagnosia* (loss of the ability to recognise the relations between multiple objects in a visually presented scene). Lesions of the dorsal stream, on the other hand, result in disturbances of the visual control of voluntary movement.

Since the two pathways bifurcate downstream of the striate cortex (V1), they cannot be invoked to explain the phenomena of "blindsight", i.e., the visual functions that survive lesions of V1. However, as is shown on Figure 1 which is reproduced with the permission of the authors and publisher from Milner and Goodale (*op.cit.*, p. 68), there is *another* pathway converging on the posterior parietal cortex most of which consists of structures lying outside

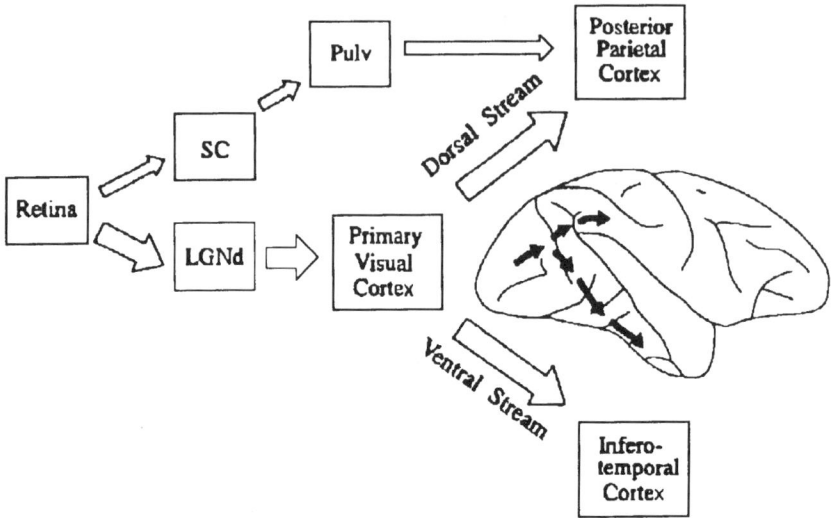

Figure 1. The ventral and the dorsal streams (After Milner & Goodale, 1995, Figure 3.1, p.68)

the cortex in the midbrain (*superior colliculus* and *pulvinar*). I call this the "*sub-cortical (S-C) to dorsal[1] pathway*". For although it is shown for conve-nience on Figure 1 above both the dorsal *and* ventral streams properly so-called, in fact, until it reaches its "destination" in the posterior parietal cortex, it is composed of structures (the *superior colliculus* and *pulvinar*) which lie *below* the cortex in the midbrain and thus below both dorsal *and* ventral streams.

As is apparent from Figure 1, identifying the S-C to dorsal pathway gives us a second pair of visual pathways with the same "destinations" as the dorsal and ventral streams (the posterior parietal and infero-temporal cortices respec-tively), but bifurcating *at the retina* rather than downstream of the primary visual cortex (V1). Balancing the S-C to dorsal pathway is what we may call the "*ventral pathway*" (to distinguish it from the ventral stream which forms part of it) consisting of the *lateral geniculate nucleus*, the *primary visual cortex* (V1), the *ventral stream* (V2-V5) and the *infero-temporal cortex*. The two pathways so-defined differ in two respects:

(1) Apart from the lateral geniculate nucleus, all the structures composing the ventral pathway are in the cortex, whereas all the structures composing the S-

C to dorsal pathway, apart from its final "destination", the posterior parietal cortex, are sub-cortical.

(2) Unlike the ventral pathway all of whose component structures apart from its "destination", the infero-temporal cortex, are concerned only with the processing of *visual* information, all the structures composing the S-C to dorsal pathway without exception process information from all sensory modalities.

Recent work on attention

Recent work on the phenomenon of selective attention within conceptual analytic philosophy, experimental cognitive psychology and neuroscience has shown that Broadbent's conclusions are in need of considerable modification and elaboration. A recent development which supports the notion that one of the functions of selective attention is to protect consciousness, considered as a limited capacity channel, from overload by alerting it only to those inputs that are problematic for one reason or another comes from conceptual analysis as practised by philosophers in the ordinary language tradition. At a one day conference on 'Attention and Consciousness' held in the Department of Philosophy, University College, London, on 26th May 1995 the Oxford philosopher Paul Snowdon presented an analysis of the concept of attention in ordinary language in which he drew a distinction between what he calls "Attention-N" ("N" for 'noticing') represented by passive voice expressions such as *Her attention was caught by an unusual* ____ and what he calls "Attention-A" ("A" for 'active') represented by active voice expressions such as *She paid close attention to the colour and shape of the object* or *to what she was doing*. It looks as though Attention-N is an unconscious involuntary mechanism for ensuring that problematic inputs and only such inputs are processed by consciousness, while attention-A is mechanism for ensuring that the focus of consciousness is maintained on a problematic input until it has been adequately categorized. There is evidence to suggest that the involuntary catching of attention by problematic inputs is a midbrain function mediated primarily by the superior colliculus and pulvinar;[2] while the conscious voluntary active holding of the focus onto an input until adequate categorization is achieved is mediated by the posterior parietal cortex.[3]

From a neuroscientific perspective, Michael Posner (Posner & Petersen 1990; Posner & Dehaene 1994) has adduced evidence that in addition to the function which it shares with the intra-cortical dorsal pathway of mediating the visual control of voluntary movement, the S-C to dorsal pathway "(posterior parietal cortex, pulvinar and superior colliculus)" also has an important role in the control of selective attention, constituting, as it does, what he calls (Posner & Dehaene, *op.cit.*: 76) "the posterior attention system".

The posterior system would seem to have two functions, (a) that of bringing problematic inputs into the focus of attention in the first place (Snowdon's "Attention-N"), and (b) that of maintaining such inputs in the focus attention until an adequate categorization is achieved (Snowdon's "Attention-A"). Of these two functions the first involves a mechanism which is necessarily *unconscious* and *involuntary* in the sense that the individual cannot decide or, in the true sense of that word, be instructed to notice things. We often say *Notice this* or *Notice that*; but such instructions only work if they are accompanied either by pointing at or otherwise highlighting the feature in question or by a verbal description of what is to be noticed, thereby creating an expectation of what is to be noticed. In either case the effect of the instruction is to *facilitate* rather than directly *induce* the noticing which remains essentially involuntary. By contrast the function of maintaining the focus of attention on a problematic input, once it has been noticed, until an adequate categorization has been achieved is an activity which is subject to conscious and voluntary control. If, as the evidence seems to suggest, tasks involving conscious and voluntary control are mediated by the cerebral cortex, while those that are unconscious and involuntary are mediated by the mid- and hindbrains, it looks as though Snowdon's Attention-A is mediated by the posterior parietal cortex and his Attention-N by the superior colliculus and pulvinar, with superior colliculus controlling the peripheral aspects (the orientation of the receptor organs) and the pulvinar the ingate into consciousness.

The other attentional system which Posner distinguishes, "the anterior attention system (anterior cingulate and basal ganglia)" would seem, in light of the evidence adduced by Pashler discussed below, to have the function of initiating and maintaining concentration on the processes of response-selection and response-execution. This type of selective attention, like that which maintains focus of attention on a problematic input until adequate categorization of it is achieved, is under conscious and voluntary control and is to that extent also part of Snowdon's Attention-A.

Finally there is the recognition for which I am personally indebted to Harold Pashler (1991; 1997) that Broadbent's threefold system of *limited capacity channel* with a *"bottleneck"* or *"filter"* which protects the LCC from overloading by restricting input access to it, and a *buffer* which holds prospective inputs until the bottleneck clears has more than one embodiment in the brain. Pashler has shown in his experimental studies of dual-task that the response-selection system is also a limited capacity channel protected by a filter or bottleneck restricting access into it from what Broadbent calls the "category states" generated by *his* limited capacity channel, the input categorization system. A similar bottleneck is to be expected restricting access into the response-execution system. Similar bottlenecks may also exist in the human cerebral cortex to control access to the name-concept selection system (Wernicke's area) and the sentence articulation system (Broca's area). As we have seen, controlling access into the response-selection and response-execution systems and maintaining the focus of attention on these tasks until an appropriate response has been selected and its execution is complete would seem to be functions performed by Posner's anterior attentional system.

The complementary functions of consciousness and the unconscious zombie-within

The picture that emerges from the various strands of evidence described above is of two parallel, but complementary and continuously interacting input-to-output transformation systems in the brain which I shall refer to respectively as "consciousness" and the unconscious "automatic pilot" or "zombie-within".

Consciousness as an input-output transformation system

On this hypothesis, *consciousness* is a *"limited capacity channel"* (LCC) or rather a sequence of three such channels which, together with what I call "the *emotion-servo*", have four sequentially ordered functions, (a) the function of *categorizing* on the basis of what Broadbent (1971) calls the "evidence" and which I equate with conscious experience any input that is identified by the zombie-within as *problematic*, in that it is either *unexpected* or *motivationally significant*, i.e., significant relative to the individual's current or perennial motivational concerns (LCC 1), (b) the function of *reacting emotionally* to inputs which have been identified as problematic, both before ("physical" pleasure/pain) and after they have been categorized ("mental" pleasure/pain), thereby ensuring that the subsequent processes of response-selection and response-execution are brought into an adaptive relation to the individual's current and perennial motivational concerns (the Emotion-Servo), (c) the function of *selecting a response* appropriate both to the presence of a thing of that kind and to the individual's motivational concerns with respect to it (LCC 2), and (d) the function of initiating and monitoring the *execution* of the response selected (LCC 3).[4]

The evidence suggests that although much of what goes on is unconscious (in the sense that the details are not available to be described or reported by the human subject), the whole of the cerebral cortex in mammals is devoted to the implementation of consciousness *in this functional sense*. In general it would seem that what the human subject reports are the *outcomes* of the processes of selective attention, categorization, emotional reaction, response-selection and response-execution, rather than the processes themselves. The exceptions to this rule are the process of *sensory conscious experience* which can, to some extent, be described independently of the way it is finally (as opposed to tentatively) categorized, and the thoughts (images and sub-vocal speech) which contribute to, but do not exhaust, the process of response-selection, just as conscious experience of the feedback from the output as it develops contributes to, but does not exhaust, the process of response-execution.

The unconscious "automatic pilot" or "zombie-within"

The functions of the *unconscious automatic pilot* or *zombie-within* are (a) that of continuously *scanning* the total current input so as to alert consciousness to any input it identifies as *problematic*, (b) that of *protecting consciousness from overload* either by ignoring those non-problematic inputs which require no response or by responding appropriately, but automatically and *without categorization*, to those for which there already exists a well practised skill or other "instinctive" response pattern.

Like its namesake in popular mythology, the zombie-within is a creature of habit, routine and unquestioning conformity to the instructions it receives from consciousness. Anything out of the ordinary is immediately passed on for processing by consciousness. The one respect in which it differs from the traditional picture of its mythical namesake is in its capacity to learn from experience, limited though that is to the progressive shaping of minor variations in behaviour by their immediate consequences.

The evidence suggests that, with one possible exception, all the functions of the zombie-within are mediated by structures in the midbrain and brainstem. The one possible exception is in the case of the visual functions of reaching for objects and avoiding obstacles which are retained when visual conscious experience is abolished by lesions of the striate cortex (V1), thus occluding the ventral visual pathway and yielding the phenomenon of "blindsight". The dorsal visual pathway which is known to mediate these functions, though composed in the main of midbrain structures such as the superior colliculus and pulvinar, also includes the posterior parietal cortex. It may be, however, that although the functions of reaching for objects and avoiding obstacles do not require *visual* conscious experience and are, to that extent, to be regarded on the present hypothesis as functions of the zombie-within, they *do* require the integration of visual information supplied by the zombie along the S-C to dorsal pathway with conscious experience of the *somaesthetic feedback* from the movements involved as they develop, and that this integration is the contribution to these functions made by the posterior parietal cortex.

Interactions between the two systems

Although, as the blindsight phenomenon shows, there are other forms of interaction between the two systems, the three most important interactions between consciousness and the zombie-within are (a) the action of the zombie in alerting consciousness in general and conscious experience in particular to problematic inputs, (b) the gradual transfer to the zombie-within of stimulus-stimulus expectations and stimulus-response connections formed within consciousness as they become habitual (for PET scan evidence of this process, see Raichle et al. 1994), and (c) the integration of the two systems in a well-developed motor skill where, as the syntactic organization of movement becomes increasingly automatised, i.e., gets taken over by the zombie, the easier it becomes for the mechanisms of selective attention to ensure that consciousness is focussed on those aspects of the task that are crucial from the point of view of effective strategic decision-making and the timely initiation of the selected response.

Modules within consciousness and the zombie-within

The multiple functions identified within both consciousness and the zombie-within imply a multiplicity of modules within both systems. Figure 2 shows

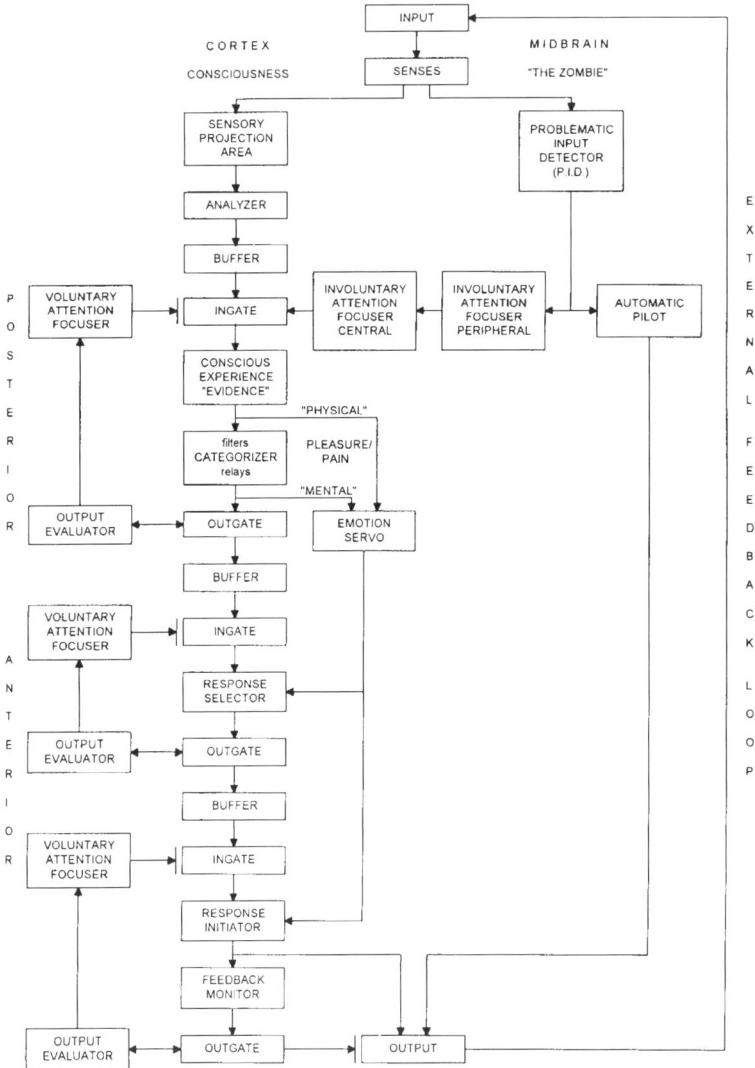

Figure 2. Consciousness and the zombie-within- Suggested layout of modules

the arrangement of these modules as I currently construe it. As you will see, the diagram shows the output from the sense organs splitting into two streams, *consciousness* on the left, the *zombie* on the right.

Modules within the zombie

The zombie is shown as consisting of four functionally defined modules, (a) the *problematic input detector (PID)* which separates inputs into problematic and non-problematic on the basis of relatively coarse criteria of unexpected/ expected and motivationally significant/insignificant, and transmits the former *via* (b) the *involuntary attention-focuser (peripheral)* which mobilises and directs movements of the head eyes and body so as to bring the *source* of the problematic input within the range of all relevant sense organs, (c) the *involuntary attention-focuser (central)* which attracts the focus of *conscious experience* to that part of the sensorium where the problematic input is located, while either ignoring or routing non-problematic inputs to output *via* (d) the *automatic pilot.*

Modules within consciousness

Consciousness, as shown here, consists of three sequentially ordered limited capacity channels (LCCs), concerned respectively with *input-categorization (perception)*, *response-selection* and *response-execution*. The concept of the *limited capacity channel* comes from Broadbent (1958) whose 1971 book *Decision and Stress* restricts its application to the process of input categorization. The evidence that there is more than one such channel in the brain comes from Pashler (1991; 1997). In order to protect it from overloading, Broadbent's model requires that each LCC be provided with a system of subordinate modules, including (a) an "ingate" which *controls access* to the LCC, (b) a *buffer* or short term memory store in which inputs waiting to obtain access to the LCC are held until the ingate clears, (c) an *attention-focuser* which maintains the focus of attention on the task in hand until it is satisfactorily completed, and (d) an *output evaluator* which checks the candidate outputs of the LCC and allows the attention-focuser to open the ingate to a new input once the previous information processing task has been satisfactorily completed, while at the same time opening (e) an *outgate* which allows the approved output schema to proceed either directly to the initiation of a response or into the buffer of the next LCC in line.

In the case of the input-categorizing LCC the limited capacity channel is shown as divided into two separate modules, *conscious experience* which, to use Broadbent's (1971) term, provides the "evidence" on which categorization is based and without which the blindsighted subject's judgments become "pure guesswork" and the *categorization* response itself. A similar division is shown within the response-executor LCC between *response initiation* and *feedback control*.

Lying outside this system of three limited capacity channels are two modules, the ANALYZER and the *emotion servo*. The existence of the ANALYZER is suggested by the known functions of the visual cortical areas V1-V5. Recordings from individual cells in these areas have revealed what are known as "feature detectors", cells which fire in response to the presence within the current retinal input of various features and patterns which are relevant for the identification of objects and situations in the organism's visual environment. The features which are detected in this way become more and more abstract and involve responding to activity spread over a wider and wider area of the visual field the further they are from V1. Recent research by Steve Luck and Nancy Beach (1996) confirming the Feature Integration Theory (FIT) of Ann Treisman and her colleagues (Treisman 1988; Treisman & Gelade 1980; Treisman & Gormican 1988) suggests that the effect of the module here identified as *conscious experience* is to "bind" the "information" provided by these individual feature detectors into a single *Gestalt*, thereby generating the "evidence" on which categorization or interpretation of the input is subsequently based.

Whereas the ANALYZER is construed as a module which precedes and prepares the ground for the process of input-categorization, the *emotion servo* is brought into play by the action of the input-categorization LCC. This activation occurs both before categorization in response to "raw" uninterpreted conscious experience, as in the case of "physical" pleasure and pain, and after categorization, as in the case of "mental" pleasure and pain. Its function is to provide motivation both for response-selection and for response-execution.

The problematic input detector (PID)

Fundamental to the system whereby behaviour is controlled by the brain as set out on Figure 2 is the *problematic input detector* (PID). The PID is that part of the zombie-within which determines whether a current input is or is not problematic, alerting consciousness to it if it is, either ignoring it or allowing it to proceed automatically to the selection and execution of a response if it is not.

In order to understand how the PID works two questions need to be answered:

(1) What sorts of input qualify as *problematic*?

(2) How, given that input-categorization does not occur before consciousness has been brought into play, are such inputs *detected* by the zombie?

Varieties of problematic input. An input is problematic if (a) it is *unexpected*, or, (b) if expected, it is *motivationally significant*, i.e., significant relative to the individual's current or perennial motivational concerns. An input is *motivationally significant* if it is (c) something the individual is *searching* or *on the look out* for, (d) a stimulus which is *intrinsically pleasant* or *unpleasant* (i.e., one whose pleasantness or unpleasantness does not depend on how it is categorized or interpreted) e.g., the pleasantness of the sensation of being stroked or the unpleasantness of the sensations of pain and nausea, and (e) a stimulus which has been associated with a motivationally significant past event, such as Plato's lyre that reminds the lover of his beloved.

How different varieties of problematic input are detected

The unexpected. Given the principle of association by contiguity, it can be predicted that an organism will build up a vast number of *stimulus-stimulus expectations* based on observed regularities in the way an input of one type is invariably succeeded by an input of another type. Given a background of such expectations, a second input which differs from that expected on the basis of past experience, given the first input, is going to stand out like a sore thumb.

Objects of search. We may suppose that the PID is sensitized to respond to the objects of search by the *active disposition which initiates the search* and guides it until either the object is found or the search is abandoned.

Intrinsically pleasant and unpleasant stimuli. Although any such effect, if it exists, is concealed by the fact that intrinsically pleasant and unpleasant stimuli immediately attract conscious attention, there is some evidence to suggest that emotional reactions elicited by conscious experience of the stimuli before categorization may also be elicited by the alternative input system which serves the zombie-within. A study by Zihl, Tretter & Singer (1980) cited by Weiskrantz (1986: 125–6) reports "an autonomic electroder-mal response . . . to [moving] visual stimuli in the absence of 'seeing'" in a case of blindsight; while Tranel & Damasio (1985), also cited by Weiskrantz (1986: 137–8), "showed that two prosopagnosic patients who failed to recog-nize familiar faces verbally nevertheless displayed a clear and strong skin conductance response to photographs of familiar faces relative to control faces." This evidence raises the possibility that emotional reactions to intrinsi-cally pleasant and unpleasant stimuli may not be, as it subjectively appears, a response to conscious experience of the stimuli in question. It may rather be *a response to a preconscious input reaching the zombie-within* which, in turn, attracts the focus of conscious attention to the stimulus and emotional reaction as a unitary *Gestalt*. It suggests that these emotional reactions are triggered by a direct connection between the problematic input detector (PID) and the emotion servo. But since its only function would appear to be to ensure a more rapid mobilisation of motivational resources than if it were routed through consciousness, this connection has been omitted from Figure 2 in favour of the phenomenologically more significant contrast between emotional reactions which do and do not depend on the way the experience is conceptualised.

Associations with motivationally significant past events. It is suggested that the function of the *dream imagery* characteristic of REM sleep is to "stamp in" associations between events that have occurred during previous waking peri-ods and motivationally significant past events at the expense of motivationally neutral associations formed during the same period. In REM sleep conscious experience is, as it were, being allowed to "freewheel" when decoupled from sensory input, thus leaving it free to generate images, particularly visual ones, whose form is determined only by the new *associative links* formed as a result of the attention-focusing and categorizing of problematic inputs which has taken place during the preceding period of waking, and by the individual's current *emotional preoccupations*.

Conscious/Phenomenal Experience

Conscious/phenomenal experience, on this view, is the first stage in the process whereby problematic inputs are processed by consciousness. Its func-tion is to provide the "evidence" on which the categorization of problematic inputs is based, by modifying the *figure-ground relations* (Figure 3) within the central representation of the input until an adequate categorization is selected.

Figure 3. Figure-ground reversal *(After Rubin 1915)*

Intrinsic figure-ground differentiation versus *imposed figure-ground organization.* Two kinds of figure-ground relation need to be distinguished. On the one hand there is the *intrinsic figure-ground differentiation* whereby one part of the current input (the figure) stands out from, is more salient and thus catches the attention more readily than, the rest (the ground), simply by virtue of the sharpness and magnitude of the contrast between the two. The other is the *figure-ground organization* properly so-called which is *imposed* on the input from the sensory projection areas of the cortex by the process whereby conscious/phenomenal experience is generated.

The two forms of figure-ground differentiation are connected in that the sharper the intrinsic figure-ground contrast the more *strongly structured* and, therefore, less malleable is the input which is available for moulding by conscious experience. In other words, the larger and simpler the intrinsic contrast between figure and ground (salience) the less room there is for conscious experience to impose a different pattern of figure-ground organization.

Conscious/phenomenal experience as imposed figure-ground organization. We have seen that on the present hypothesis it is the output or *"evidence,"* as Broadbent (1971) calls it, which is generated by the process of *selective attention* which constitutes the *conscious/phenomenal experience* to which the introspecting subject is responding when she describes what it is like either to receive sensory input from a particular input source in the environment or to imagine being exposed to it. The "luminosity" or "phosphorescence" which is the most striking feature of conscious/phenomenal experience from the standpoint of the introspective observer enables a linguistically competent human to give a running commentary both on the sequence of events in her stimulus environment and her conscious/phenomenal experience of those events at the time and to provide a first hand report on some of them subsequently. It also enables the organism to check its categorization of a problematic input against the "evidence" on which the categorization is based. Without this check the blindsighted subject loses all confidence in the sometimes remarkably accurate discriminations he is able to make relying solely on the sub-conscious system. Such discriminations, he insists, are "pure guesswork." This lack of confidence may also explain the inability of blindsighted patients to initiate voluntary action based upon their blind field discriminations to which Marcel (1988) has drawn attention.

Mental imagery. Mental imagery is a form of conscious experience which occurs in a variety of different contexts, in dreams, in daydreaming, in the recollection of past events and in planning the future. Phenomenologically it resembles and can sometimes be confused with the kind of sensory conscious experience which provides the "evidence" for the categorization of an input. Moreover, there is evidence from a study (Kosslyn et al. 1995) using positron emission tomography (PET) that when a subject forms a visual image of a picture he or she has just been shown, the same pattern of activity develops in all the principal visual areas of the cortex, including V1, as occurs when the subject is looking at the actual picture. This re-instatement of the cortical activity involved in sense perception in the absence of the input otherwise required for its occurrence is undoubtedly the substance behind Hume's much criticised claim

> "That all our simple ideas in their first appearance are deriv'd from simple impressions, which are correspondent to them, and which they exactly represent" (Hume 1740/1978: 4).

Aside from the fact that its form is not determined by *current* sensory input, the principal difference between a mental image and a perceptual experience is its relation to the process of categorization. We have seen that in sense perception conscious experience precedes and provides the "evidence" on which categorization is subsequently based. In the case of a mental image, as Kant (1781/1787/1929, pp. 182–183) demonstrates in developing his concept of the "schema", the construction of a mental image presupposes a prior categorization or conceptualization of what the image is to be an image of.

In order to account for this kind of control over the process of conscious experience on the present model as laid out on Figure 2, we would have to include a number of "re-entrant" (Edelman 1987) or "recurrent" (Jordan 1986) circuits feeding back from the CATEGORIZATION and RESPONSE-SELECTION modules.[5] Not only are such circuits well-attested anatomically, Jordan (*op.cit.*) has shown that, along with the reverberatory circuits (Hebb 1949) required to bridge the gap between the offset of the first stimulus and the onset of the second, such circuits are an essential feature of any neural network that can learn to "expect" or "anticipate" the *second* of two sequentially ordered stimuli on presentation of the *first*. As we have already seen, an extensive repertoire of such expectations is required as a background against which an unexpected input will stand out as the figure and thus be referred to consciousness by the zombie-within.

It seems that the recurrent circuits required to account for the generation of mental imagery would need to feedback from the CATEGORIZATION and RESPONSE SELECTION modules to the SENSORY PROJECTION AREAS (such as V1 in the case of a visual image) to ensure that conscious experience is supplied with the necessary "raw material", to the ANALYZER to ensure that it is given the necessary structure, to the relevant INGATE to ensure access into CONSCIOUS EXPERIENCE, and to the VOLUNTARY ATTENTION FOCUSER to ensure the maintenance of the image until it has served whatever purpose it was intended to fulfil. However, in order to avoid too much complication these circuits are not shown on Figure 2. The only recurrent circuits shown are those connecting the OUTGATE of each of the three LCCs to its respective INGATE and the EXTERNAL FEEDBACK LOOP connecting the motor output to sensory input.

It is suggested that in the case of a *mental image* these recurrent circuits impose a pattern of figure-ground organization on a field that is *intrinsically weakly structured* (Figure 4) and does not, therefore, restrict the pattern of organization that can be imposed on it in the way a more salient and strongly structured input would do. This results in a pattern of figure-ground organization which in the extreme case bears no relation to any objective structure in the input source. In the case of vision, the Rorschach (1932/1942) ink blots provide a classic example of a series of such weakly-structured fields which permit and thus promote the formation of a wide variety of such images.[6]

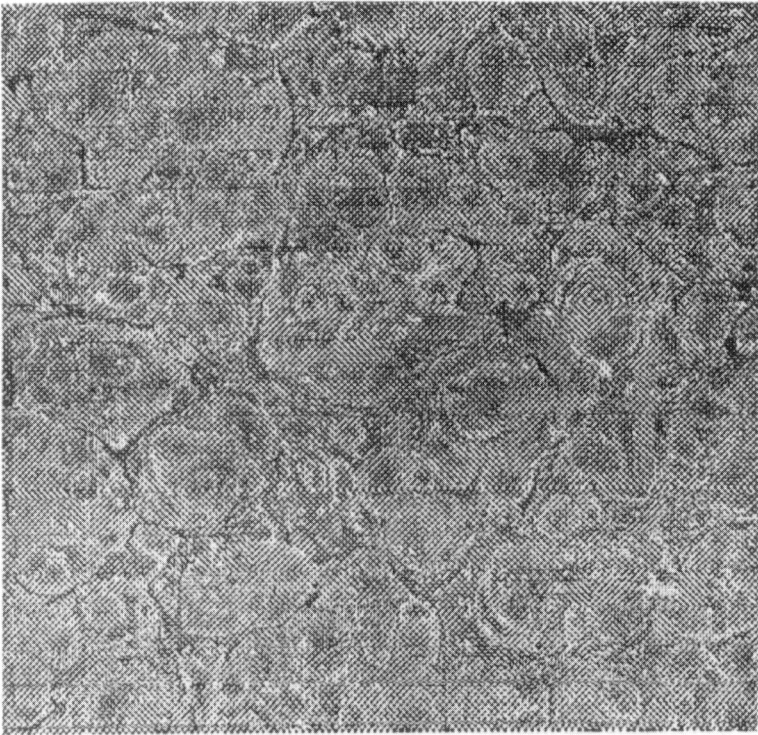

Figure 4. A weakly-structured field

We know from the introspective reports of human subjects that such images occur both in waking consciousness as part of the thought process whereby solutions to problems are generated and as the predominant feature of the dreams that occur during the rapid-eye-movement (REM) phase of sleep. In the latter case there is strong circumstantial evidence for the occurrence of such imagery in the sleep of those mammals in which it occurs.[7] Although there is at present no corresponding evidence for the occurrence of mental imagery as an aid to animal problem-solving, it would be surprising if an ability which is almost certainly present during sleep were not exploited for more obviously practical purposes during waking.[8]

Categorization

Categorization is the process whereby problematic inputs are classified according to the kind of object or situation of whose presence in the organism's stimulus environment the input is a reliable indicator. It is the function of categorization to ensure that the universal, kind or category under which an input is subsumed lines up with what Skinner (1969) calls the "contingencies" operating in the organism's environment. A *contingency* for Skinner is a sequence of events whereby under certain *antecedent* conditions *behaving* in a certain way will have certain predictable *consequences*. By classifying its problematic inputs in a way that enables it to anticipate the consequences of selecting one form of behaviour rather than another, the organism puts itself in a state of readiness to select a successful behavioural strategy appropriate both to the presence of an object or situation of that kind and to whatever may be the organism's current behavioural objectives as and when the occasion for action arises.

Two components of categorization: the input filter and the output relay. We have seen that Broadbent (1971) distinguishes two processes within what we are here calling "categorization", namely, "pigeon-holing" and "categorization" proper. On his view, "pigeon-holing" is simply a matter of slotting an input into a pre-existing category, whereas "categorization" in his sense involves either creating a new category altogether or modifying the boundaries of an existing category so as to fit a new instance. This way of construing the matter is mistaken in so far as it assumes that the organism cannot respond adaptively to an input without specifically classifying it as an encounter with an object or situation of a particular kind. On the present hypothesis, it is only problematic inputs that require classification in this way. Once a behaviour pattern has become habitual, direct input-to-output transformations replace responses mediated by categorization and motivational choice. Evidence for just such replacement of one pattern of brain activity by another as behaviour becomes habitual comes from the recent study by Raichle et al. (1994) mentioned above.

The categories which make up an individual's conceptual scheme to one of which every problematic input must be assigned in order for the process of categorization to succeed have two components. One component is the *filter* which selects those inputs which satisfy the entry criteria for the concept in question and rejects those otherwise similar inputs which do not satisfy them. The other component is what we may think of as a *relay* which pre-selects all those behavioural strategies which can be relied on to yield a predictable consequence, when emitted in the presence of an object or situation of that kind. Once this set of behavioural strategies has been pre-selected, a choice is made between them in the light of subsequent environmental conditions and the organism's motivational attitude to the expected consequences of adopting one course of action rather than another. In the case of a linguistically competent human being, an important group of behavioural strategies which are pre-selected in this way are strategies for selecting appropriate words and sentence frames for describing objects and situations of the kind in question.

The emotion servo

Skinner's concept of the "three-term contingency" (*antecedent* conditions, *behaviour* called for under those conditions and the *consequences* of so behaving) not only provides a clue to the nature of the concepts or categories the organism uses in classifying its problematic inputs, it is also the key to understanding the operation of what we are calling the "emotion servo." As we have seen, the function of this module is to modulate behaviour in such a way as to bring it into conformity with the organism's motivational objectives. As the contingency unfolds and as its conformity or lack of conformity to those objectives becomes apparent, so the organism's emotional reaction changes. The same sequence of events will evoke a different sequence of emotional reactions depending on the organism's motivational attitude to the anticipated or actual consequences of its behaviour. If the consequence is attractive, anticipating its appearance produces excitement, its actual occurrence, pleasure, its failure to appear when expected, first anger then misery or depression. If the consequence is repulsive or, as Skinner would say, "aversive", anticipating its appearance produces fear or anxiety, its actual occurrence, first anger then misery or depression, its failure to appear when expected, relief.

Each different variety of emotional response is characterized (a) by the type of situation that evokes it, i.e., whether it is *prospective* as in excitement and fear, *retrospective* as in anger, relief and depression, or *focussed on the moment* as in pleasure and disgust, (b) by its position on the *pleasant-unpleasant* dimension, pleasant in the case of excitement, pleasure and relief, unpleasant in fear, disgust and depression, mixed in the case of anger and apathy, (c) by its position on the *arousal* dimension, high in the case of excitement, anger and fear, moderate in pleasure and disgust, low in relief, apathy and depression, and (d) by a characteristic *impulse*, the impulse to sigh in relief, to smile in pleasure, to jump for joy in excitement, to attack in anger, to freeze or run away in fear, to vomit in disgust, to do nothing or punish oneself in depression.

Locating these modules within the brain

Evidence from a variety of sources, neurology, electrophysiology, and, most recently, the newly discovered brain-imaging techniques, makes it possible to propose a tentative identification of the modules shown on Figure 2 with specific anatomically defined structures within the brain.

The ventral and S-C to dorsal pathways

For the most part, I shall confine my remarks on this score to the "upstream" portion of Figure 2, that which precedes the transition within consciousness from CONSCIOUS EXPERIENCE to CATEGORIZATION. For this is the area to which the neurological evidence described in Section 1.6 above relates. That evidence shows that in order to account for the visual functions which survive lesions of primary visual cortex (V1) and the consequent loss of visual conscious experience, the phenomenon known as "blindsight", we must suppose that the residual visual functions are mediated by what we are calling the "sub-cortical (S-C) to dorsal pathway" which proceeds by way of the *superior colliculus* and *pulvinar* to the *posterior parietal cortex*. This S-C to dorsal pathway bifurcates at the retina from the *ventral pathway* consisting of the *lateral geniculate nucleus*, the *primary visual* or *striate cortex (V1)*, and the *extra-striate visual areas (V2-V5)* to the *infero-temporal cortex*. These two pathways, together with the intra-cortical dorsal and ventral streams distinguished by Ungerleider & Mishkin (1982) which bifurcate "downstream" of V1, are shown on Figure 1 (taken from Milner & Goodale 1995: 68).

Whereas all the structures composing the ventral pathway, with the doubtful exception of the infero-temporal cortex,[9] are exclusively visual in function. Those composing the S-C to dorsal pathway (superior colliculus, pulvinar and posterior parietal cortex) subserve all sensory modalities. This is consistent with Posner's (Posner & Petersen 1990; Posner & Dehaene 1994) hypothesis that the function of these structures, in their capacity as the "posterior attention system", is to control the focus of sensory attention as it switches from one modality to another or concentrates different modalities on the same area of environmental space. This concatenation of evidence allows us, in the case of the visual modality, to identify the bifurcation between consciousness and the zombie-within as shown on Figure 2 with the bifurcation at the retina between a *ventral* pathway consisting of the *lateral geniculate nucleus*, the *primary visual* or *striate cortex* (V1), the *extra-striate visual areas* (V2-V5) and the *infero-temporal cortex* corresponding to the upstream portion of what I am calling "consciousness", and the *S-C to dorsal pathway* consisting of the *superior colliculus* and *pulvinar*, but almost certainly excluding its "destination", the *posterior parietal cortex*, corresponding to the zombie. These relationships are shown on Figure 5. It is a re-drawing of Milner & Goodale's diagram (Figure 1 above) which, for the sake of clarity, omits the dorsal stream properly so-called (connecting V1 to the posterior parietal cortex) and is arranged in the same format as the upper part of Figure 2 with the ventral pathway on the left and the S-C to dorsal pathway on the right.

Given the identification of the ventral pathway as the route whereby information is passed from the retina into consciousness and the S-C to dorsal pathway as the route into and through the zombie-within, what are we to say about the one exception, the posterior parietal cortex, which is the terminus of both the S-C to dorsal pathway and the intra-cortical dorsal stream? There would seem to be a connection here between the posterior parietal and the visual functions of reaching for objects (Weiskrantz 1986; Cowey & Stoerig 1995) and avoiding obstacles (Humphrey 1974)[10] which are retained when visual conscious experience is abolished by lesions of the striate cortex (V1),

```
                                    INPUT  ◄─────────────────────┐
        C O R T E X                                              │
     VENTRAL PATHWAY                  │           M I D B R A I N │
      CONSCIOUSNESS                   ▼        S-C -> DORSAL PATHWAY
                                   RETINA          "THE ZOMBIE"      E
                                                                    X
                                                                    T
                                 LATERAL                            E
                                GENICULATE        SUPERIOR          R
                                 NUCLEUS         COLLICULUS         N
                                                                    A
                                                                    L

      STRIATE                                                       F
      CORTEX                                     PULVINAR           E
       (V1)                                                         E
                                                                    D
                                                                    B
     VENTRAL          POSTERIOR                                     A
     STREAM           PARIETAL  ◄────────────────────────          C
     (V2-V5)           CORTEX                                       K

      INFERO-                                                       L
     TEMPORAL                                                       O
      CORTEX                                                        O
                                                                    P
```

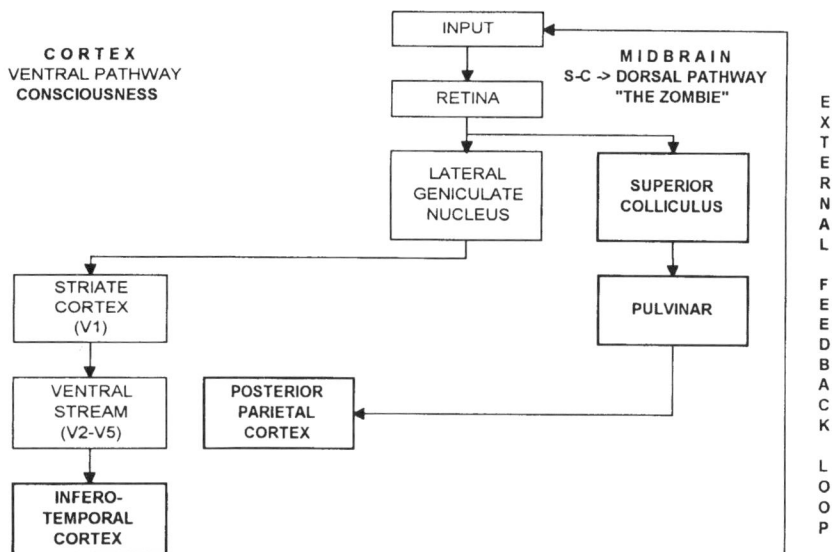

Figure 5. The dorsal and the ventral pathways — multimodal modules in bold

thus occluding the ventral visual pathway and yielding the phenomenon of 'blindsight.' Although it is clear from the performance of human subjects with lesions of the striate cortex ("blindsight") that the functions of reaching for objects and avoiding obstacles do not require *visual* conscious experience of the relevant stimuli and are, to that extent, to be regarded on the present hypothesis as functions mediated by the zombie-within, the fact that the subject in such cases is induced to reach for an object he does not "see" by an appropriate instruction to *guess* where it was shows that conscious experience of *some* kind is involved in the production of such behaviour. A plausible hypothesis would be that reaching and obstacle-avoiding behaviour, though it does not require *visual* conscious experience, *does* require the integration of visual information supplied by the zombie along the S-C to dorsal pathway with conscious experience of the *somaesthetic feedback* from the movements involved as they develop, and that this integration is the contribution to these functions made by the posterior parietal cortex. However, some recent evidence (Rossetti, Rode and Boisson 1995; Rossetti 1997) on the somaesthetic counterpart of blindsight which the authors refer to as "numb-sense" shows that a patient (J.A.) with this condition can use his "normal" left hand to point accurately at the location of stimuli applied to the "numb" right hand which he cannot consciously feel. This shows that, provided the blindsight or numb-sense subject can be induced to guess at the location of the target object by pointing at it, successful voluntary movement does not require conscious experience, whether visual or somaesthetic, of the target towards which the movement is directed. What the evidence does not show is that such voluntary movement is possible without conscious experience of the feedback from the movement itself, whether visual, somaesthetic or both.

Although, as this evidence clearly demonstrates, the S-C to dorsal pathway has a *secondary* function in the visual control of voluntary movement, the fact that all its structures process information from *all* sensory modalities, when combined with the brain-imaging and neurophysiological data reviewed by Posner and Dehaene (1994) and the evidence of disorders of attention, such as unilateral neglect, resulting from lesions of these structures, suggest that its *primary* function is to integrate the *involuntary* alerting of conscious attention to problematic inputs from all sensory modalities mediated by the two mid-brain structures, the superior colliculus and pulvinar, with the *voluntary* maintenance of the focus of attention on such inputs until an adequate categorization of them is achieved mediated by the posterior parietal cortex. On this hypothesis the posterior parietal is construed as having two functions, (a) a *general* function which is to *maintain* the focus of conscious attention within and between the different sensory modalities (acting on structures such as those in the ventral stream in the case of vision) on inputs to which the focus has been initially attracted by the "zombie" (in the shape of the superior colliculus and pulvinar) until such time as an adequate categorization of those inputs has been achieved,[11] and (b) a *specific* function which is to control voluntary movement by integrating, through the same mechanism of conscious attention focusing, the visual and somaesthetic feedback from such movements as they develop.

Provisional anatomical conclusions

Assuming that this analysis is approximately correct, we are in a position to make some tentative identifications of the modules shown on Figure 2 with some of the actual structures that have been identified anatomically within the brain as laid out on Figures 1 and 5. These tentative identifications are set out on Figure 6 which is a re-working of Figure 2 with the names of the neural structures substituted for the functional descriptions of the modules with which they have been provisionally identified in the preceding discussion in the special case of vision.

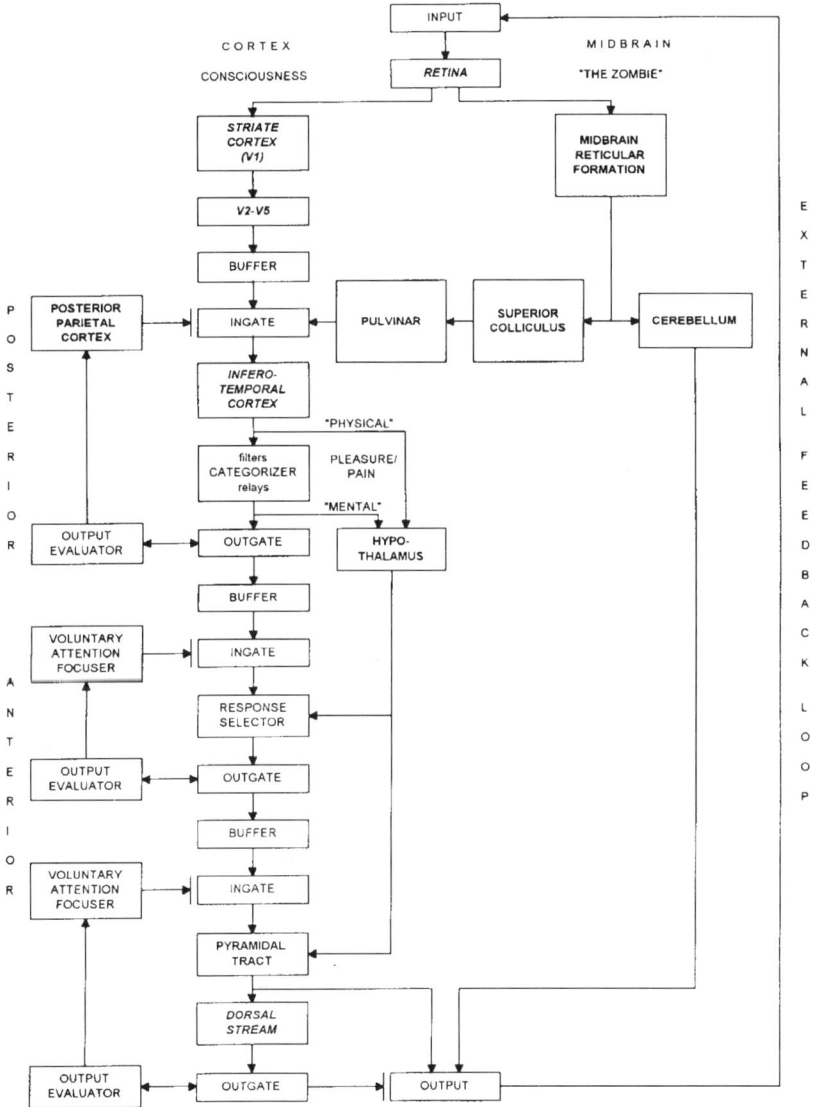

Figure 6. Consciousness and the zombie-within — Tentative identifications in bold — visual structures in italics

Thus, in place of the SENSES we have, in the case of the visual modality, the RETINA. In place of the SENSORY PROJECTION AREA we have, in the case of the visual modality, the STRIATE CORTEX. In place of the ANALYZER we have, in the case of the visual modality, V2-V5. In place of the PROBLEMATIC INPUT DETECTOR (P.I.D.) we have, for all modalities, the MIDBRAIN RETICULAR FORMATION.[12] In place of the AUTOMATIC PILOT we have the CEREBELLUM. In place of the INVOLUNTARY ATTENTION FOCUSER — PERIPHERAL we have the SUPERIOR COLLICULUS.[13] In place of the INVOLUNTARY ATTENTION FOCUSER — CENTRAL we have the PULVINAR.[14] In place of the VOLUNTARY ATTENTION FOCUSER we have the POSTERIOR PARIETAL CORTEX. Finally, in place of CONSCIOUS EXPERIENCE "EVIDENCE" we have, at least in the case of vision, the INFERO-TEMPORAL CORTEX.[15] You will notice that Figure 6 omits the connection between the PULVINAR and the POSTERIOR PARIETAL CORTEX shown on Figures 1 and 5 and which is needed to explain the visual control of reaching for objects and obstacle avoidance when the relevant parts of V1 have been destroyed ("blindsight"). This has been done in order not to obscure the functionally much more important connection between the PULVINAR and the INGATE controlling access to the INFERO-TEMPORAL CORTEX *alias* CONSCIOUS EXPERIENCE. Further "downstream" the only identification to have emerged at all clearly from the preceding discussion is that between the FEEDBACK MONITOR and the DORSAL STREAM.[16] However, two other identifications have been included on the basis of what has been known for a long time, that between RESPONSE INITIATION and the PYRAMIDAL TRACT and between the EMOTION-SERVO and the HYPOTHALAMUS. Likewise the recent work on "numb-sense" mentioned above will doubtless soon make possible the identification of the somaesthetic counterparts of the purely visual structures shown on Figure 6. It may be that similar identifications can already be suggested for other sensory modalities. If not, future research will doubtless allow us to fill these gaps too.

But there, for the present, I shall let the matter rest. I hope I have said enough to persuade you that we are now in a position to answer the question which has remained unanswered since my (Place 1956) paper 'Is consciousness a brain process?', namely, 'If consciousness *is* a brain process, which of the various processes in the brain that we now identify neuroanatomically is it?' It turns out in the light of what has been said above that that question is too simplistic. But complicated though it is, I hope I have persuaded you that the rudiments of an answer are within our grasp.

Acknowledgments

For the courage to embark on this attempt to explore the neuropsychological implications of my 1956 paper 'Is consciousness a brain process?' and for their individual contributions to giving it such merits as it has I am indebted above all to the late Donald Broadbent and in the temporal order of their contribution to Larry Weiskrantz, Rodolfo Llinás, Gerald Edelman and members of the staff of the Neurosciences Institute, then in New York, while I was a Visiting Fellow at the Institute in 1991; Kathleen Taylor, Alan Cowey, Colin Blakemore, and the editors of this volume, Yves Rossetti and Antti Revonsuo.

Notes

1. "Dorsal" here only in the sense that, like the dorsal stream properly so-called, it "terminates" in the posterior parietal cortex.

2. The evidence described in footnotes 9 and 10 (Section 4.2 below) suggests that the function of the superior colliculus is to control the orientation of the relevant sense organs towards the location of a problematic input in environmental space, and that the function of the pulvinar is to control the access of such inputs into consciousness.

3. See footnote 8 (Section 4.1 below).

4. There is reason to think that in human brain there are two more limited capacity channels, one which selects the name assigned to the concept or category in question by the natural language spoken by the individual concerned and another which constructs a syntactically articulated sentence appropriate to the "thought" which emerges from a further stage in the categorization process.

5. I am indebted to Pim Haselager of the University of Nijmegen for drawing my attention to the need to emphasize this point.

6. The "non-objects" used by Vanni, Revonsuo and Hari (1997) in their experiments are another example.

7. The inhibition of the skeletal musculature during this phase of sleep makes sense only as a device whose function is to prevent the massive and obviously maladaptive somnambulism which would otherwise occur in response to such imagery.

8. Tim Shallice (1988; Burgess & Shallice1996) has drawn my attention to a hypothesis proposed by Schank (1982) which suggests that the original function of mental imagery was to allow the organism to remind itself of the past consequences of the various courses of action suggested by the current stimulus situation as possible solutions to the problem that situation presents.

9. There is evidence (Gibson and Maunsell 1997) of cells in IT which respond to cross-modal associations between visual and auditory stimuli in a delayed match-to-sample memory task.

10. There is at present no evidence that human blindsighted subjects can learn to negotiate

obstacles in the absence of visual stimulation routed via V1, as Humphrey's monkey subject Helen learned to do. But all the human blindsighted subjects studied thus far have been able to rely on the unaffected portion of the visual field to do this. If, like Helen, they had been compelled to rely on visual information arriving from the retina via the sub-cortical route, my guess is that they too would have learned to avoid obstacles in the absence of V1.

11. Evidence confirming the suggestion that the posterior parietal cortex performs this function is provided by a recent study by Vanni, Revonsuo and Hari (1997) which shows that the magnetic alpha rhythm generated in the parieto-occipital sulcus (POS) is sup-pressed by object targets to a much greater degree than non-objects, a finding which is readily interpreted as showing the persistence of activity in this area when a stimulus is not readily categorized, as compared with the rapid shut down when it is.

12. As shown by Moruzzi and Magoun (1949).

13. For the role of the superior colliculus in coordinating, at a pre-conscious level, the position and sensitivity of the different sense organs in relation to particular locations in environmental space see Stein and Meredith (1995). For the role of the superior colliculus in controlling the reflexive orienting response whose absence on the affected side of the body is characteristic of the phenomenon of unilateral neglect see Rafal and Robertson (1995).

14. A study by Vanni, Revonsuo and Hari (1997) provides evidence suggesting that the pulvinar is involved in modulating activity in the ventral stream (V2-V5), where object recognition or, as I would think, the preparation of the "evidence" for it occurs and that the effect of such modulation is to "select the next target for ventral processing". If this may be interpreted to mean that the pulvinar controls which parts of the total visual input are currently subject to "ventral processing" and hence in the focus of conscious atten-tion, it supports the suggestion that the function of this structure is to regulate the involuntary attraction of the focus of conscious attention to problematic inputs by processes which are themselves necessarily pre-conscious, i.e., part of what I am calling the "zombie-within".

15. Evidence confirming this identification is provided by Sheinberg and Logothetis (1997). They showed that in a binocular rivalry experiment 90% of the cells in a monkey's IT respond to whichever of the two rival stimuli is currently in the focus of attention; whereas in V1, V4 and V5 only 20–25% of cells do so. But, apart from that cited in footnote 9 above, there is no evidence of the involvement of other sensory modalities beside the visual in IT. It is, therefore, unlikely that the "unity of consciousness" across sensory modalities which is demanded, as much by functional considerations as by phenomenology, is secured by concentration in a single anatomical location. For this a better candidate is the synchronous firing of cells in different parts of the cortex.

16. Needless to say, this identification rides roughshod over a number of complexities. The dorsal stream is a body of linked cortical modules connecting the [VISUAL] PROJECTION AREA (V1) with the POSTERIOR PARIETAL CORTEX. It is of similar complexity to that of the ventral stream which appears on Figures 2 and 6 as the [VISUAL] ANALYZER (V2-V5) connecting V1 to the INFERO-TEMPORAL CORTEX. The posterior parietal cortex appears to have two functions (a) the function emphasised on Figures 2 and 6 where it is identified as the VOLUNTARY ATTENTION FOCUSER and the function which it presumably shares with the

dorsal stream as a whole and which is the basis for this identification of providing the integration of visual and somaesthetic information required for the FEEDBACK MONITORING of voluntary movement. A further complexity is added by recent evidence (Gallese 1998; Rizzolatti & Arbib 1998) demonstrating the role of the pre-motor cortex (the counterpart of the posterior parietal on the anterior side of the fissure of Rolando), not only in the visual feedback control of voluntary movement, but in the visual interpretation of the movement of others. As in the case of the role of mental imagery in response selection, to do justice to these complexities on a diagram such as that on Figures 2 and 6 would seriously detract from the sense of a flow of information within consciousness from input to output.

References

Broadbent, D.E. (1958). *Perception and communication*. Oxford: Pergamon.

Broadbent, D.E. (1971). *Decision and stress*. London: Academic Press.

Burgess, P.W. & Shallice, T. (1996). Confabulation and the control of recollection. *Memory*, 4, 359–411.

Cowey, A. & Stoerig, P. (1995). Blindsight in monkeys. *Nature,* 373, 6511, 247–9.

Cowey, A. & Stoerig, P. (1997). Visual detection in monkeys with blindsight. *Neuropsychologia*, 35, 929–939.

Edelman, G.M. (1987). *Neural darwinism: The theory of neuronal group selection*. New York: Basic Books.

Farah, M.J. (1990). *Visual agnosia: Disorders of object recognition and what they tell us about normal vision*. Cambridge, MA: MIT Press.

Gallese, V. (1998). From neurons to meaning: Mirror neurons and social understanding. Paper presented to the Second Annual Conference of the Association for the Scientific Study of Consciousness, Bremen, Germany, June 21st 1998

Gibson, J.R. & Maunsell, H.R. (1997). Sensory modality specificity of neural activity related to memory in visual cortex. *Journal of Neurophysiology*, 78 (3), 1263–1275.

Hebb, D.O. *The organization of behavior*. New York: John Wiley.

Hume, D. (1740/1978). *A treatise on human nature*. L.A. Selby-Bigge (Ed.), 2nd Edition, P.H. Nidditch (Ed.), Oxford: Clarendon Press.

Humphrey, N.K. (1974). Vision in a monkey without striate cortex: a case study. *Perception*, 3, 241–255.

Jordan, M.I. (1986). Attractor dynamics and parallelism in a connectionist sequential machine. *Proceedings of the Eighth Annual Conference of the Cognitive Science Society*. Hillsdale, NJ: Erlbaum.

Kant, I. (1781/1787/1929). *Kritik der reinen Vernunft*. First and Second Editions, Riga: Hartknoch. English translation by N. Kemp Smith as *Immanuel Kant's critique of pure reason*, London: Macmillan.

Kosslyn, S.M., Thompson, W.L., Kim, I.J. & Alpert, N.M. (1995). Topographical representations of mental images in primary visual cortex. *Nature*, 378, 496–498.

Luck, S.J. & Beach, N.J. (1996). Visual attention and the binding problem: a neurophysiological perspective. In R. Wright (Ed.) *Visual attention*. Oxford: Oxford University Press.

Marcel, A.J. (1988). Phenomenal experience and functionalism. In A.J. Marcel & E. Bisiach (Eds.) *Consciousness in contemporary science,* Oxford: Clarendon Press.

Milner, A.D. & Goodale, M.A. (1995). *The visual brain in action.* Oxford: Oxford University Press.

Moruzzi, G. & Magoun, H.W. (1949). Brain stem reticular formation and activation of the EEG. *Electroencephalography and Clinical Neurophysiology,* 1: 455–473.

Pashler, H.E. (1991). Shifting visual attention and selecting motor responses: distinct attentional mechanisms. *Journal of Experimental Psychology: Human Perception and Performance,* 17, 1023–1040.

Pashler, H.E. (1997). *The psychology of attention.* Cambridge, MA: MIT Press.

Place, U.T. (1954). The concept of heed. *British Journal of Psychology,* 45, 243–255.

Place, U.T. (1956). Is consciousness a brain process? *British Journal of Psychology,* 47, 44–50.

Place, U.T. (1969). Burt on brain and consciousness. *Bulletin of the British Psychological Society,* 22, 285–292.

Posner, M.I. & Petersen, S.E. (1990). The attention system of the human brain. *Annual Review of Neuroscience,* 13, 25–42.

Posner, M.I. & Dehaene, S. (1994). Attentional networks. *Trends in Neuroscience,* 17, 75–79.

Rafal, R. & Robertson, L. (1995). The neurology of visual attention. In M.S. Gazzaniga (Ed.) *The cognitive neurosciences.* Cambridge, MA: MIT Press, ch.40, 625–648.

Raichle, M.E., Fiez, J.A., Videen, T.O., MacLeod, A.-M.K., Pardo, J.V., Fox, P.T. & Petersen, S.E. (1994). Practice-related changes in human functional anatomy during non-motor learning. *Cerebral Cortex,* 4, 8–26.

Rizzolatti, G. & Arbib, M.A. (1998). Language within our grasp. *Trends in Neuroscience,* 21, 188–194.

Rorschach, H. (1932/1942). *Psychodiagnostik.* Berne: Hans Huber. English translation as *Psychodiagnostics* by P. Lemkau & B. Kronenberg, W. Morganthaler (Ed.). New York: Grune & Stratton.

Rossetti, Y., Rode, G. & Boisson, D. (1995). Implicit processing of somesthetic information: a dissociation between Where and How? *Neuroreport,* 6 (3), 506–510.

Rossetti, Y. (1997). Implicit perception in action: short-lived motor representations in space. P.G. Grossenbacher (Ed.) *Advances in consciousness research.* Amsterdam: John Benjamins.

Rubin, E. (1915). *Synsoplevede Figurer.* København: Gyldendalska.

Ryle, G. (1949). *The concept of mind.* London: Hutchinson.

Schank, R.C. (1982). *Dynamic memory: A theory of reminding and learning in computers and people.* New York: Cambridge University Press.

Shallice, T. (1988). *From neuropsychology to mental structure.* New York: Cambridge University Press.

Sheinberg, D.L. & Logothetis, N.K. (1997). The role of temporal cortical areas in perceptual organization. *Proceedings of the National Academy of Sciences, USA,* 94, 3408–3413.

Skinner, B.F. (1969). *Contingencies of reinforcement: A theoretical analysis.* New York: Appleton-Century-Crofts.

Snowdon, P. (1995). Perception and attention. Paper presented to a one-day conference on 'Attention and Consciousness: Psychological and Philosophical Issues', Department of Philosophy, University College London, 26th May 1995.

Stein, B.E. & Meredith, M.A. (1993). *The merging of the senses*. Cambridge, MA: MIT Press.

Stoerig, P. & Cowey, A. (1997). Blindsight in man and monkey. *Brain*, 120, 535–559.

Tranel, D. & Damasio, A.R. (1985). Knowledge without awareness: an autonomic index of facial recognition by prosopagnosics. *Science*, 228, 1453–1455.

Treisman, A. & Gelade, G. (1980). A feature integration theory of attention. *Cognitive Psychology*, 12, 97–136.

Treisman, A. (1988). Features and objects: The Fourteenth Bartlett Memorial Lecture. *Quarterly Journal of Experimental Psychology*, 40, 201–237.

Treisman, A. & Gormican, S. (1988). Feature analysis in early vision: Evidence from search asymmetries. *Psychological Review*, 95, 15–48.

Ungerleider, L.G. & Mishkin, M. (1982). Two cortical visual systems. In D.J. Ingle, M.A. Goodale, & R.J.W. Mansfield (Eds.) *Analysis of visual behavior*. Cambridge, MA: MIT Press.

Vanni, S., Revonsuo, A. & Hari, R. (1997). Modulation of the parieto-occipital alpha-rhythm during object-detection. *Journal of Neuroscience*, 17 (18), 7141–7147.

Weiskrantz, L. (1986). *Blindsight*. Oxford: Clarendon Press.

Wittgenstein, L. (1953). *Philosophical investigations*. English Translation by G.E.M. Anscombe. Oxford: Blackwell.

Wittgenstein, L. (1958). *The blue and brown books*. Oxford: Blackwell.

Zihl, J., Tretter, F., & Singer, W. (1980). Phasic electrodermal responses after visual stimulation in the cortically blind hemifield. *Behavior and Brain Research*, 1, 197–203.

The Zombies Among Us

Consciousness and Automatic Behaviour

Antti Revonsuo
Center for Cognitive Neuroscience, University of Turku

Mirja Johanson, Jan-Eric Wedlund & John Chaplin
Stora Sköndal Hospital, Sweden

Introduction

The concept of "zombie" has been used in a variety of ways in philosophy and consciousness studies, but the common underlying theme in all these usages appears to be the idea that there is a living creature (or at least some sort of a behaving system) that manifests relatively complex behaviour, but is, in one sense or another, devoid of consciousness or subjective experience. While philosophers have engaged themselves in debates about the metaphysical possibilities of behavioural zombies (creatures that behave just like a normal human being but are nonconscious) and neurophysiological zombies (creatures that are physically and biologically identical with a normal human being but nonconscious), empirical scientists have recently applied the concept of "zombie" to such neurocognitive mechanisms that perform complex transformations of sensory input to motor output nonconsciously or implicitly. For example, U.T Place (this volume) proposes that there is a non-conscious automatic pilot system, "the Zombie within", that can respond automatically and appropriately to many stimuli for which there exists a pre-programmed response pattern. In September 1998, *New Scientist* featured research on implicit perception and action with a cover story entitled "Zombies: They are inside you". In that article, the implicit processing systems revealed in e.g.

Milner and Goodale's well-known research were called "The (visuo-motor) Zombie".

Why should consciousness researchers be interested in these empirically actual zombies? Obviously because they reveal that the control of many aspects of our behaviour is handled by neurocognitive mechanisms devoid of consciousness. Thus, these dissociations between consciousness and behaviour are bound to raise questions about the causal powers of conscious perception and about the interaction between conscious and nonconscious processes. If so many complex input-output functions can be handled perfectly well in the absence of phenomenal experience, does our brain need consciousness at all when it guides the complex motor actions of our body? How do conscious states interact with the nonconscious ones in the control of behaviour? What is the special contribution, if any, that conscious phenomenal states bring along?

Lahav (1993) provides an illuminating analysis of implicit (i.e. nonconscious) and explicit (i.e. consciously experienced) information, arguing that their effects on behaviour are profoundly different. Implicit information can only affect "narrow and isolated islands of fixed behavioural responses" (p. 76). Nonconscious information is not integrated with other information in the system, and is limited to exerting specific, isolated or rigid effects on behaviour. Lahav characterizes "automatic behaviour" as behaviour that is governed by relatively simple input-output relationships; nonconscious information can only give rise to automatic behaviour. By contrast, explicit knowledge, or information represented in conscious experience, has the causal power to evoke a wide range of behaviours; different sources of explicit information are integrated with each other; and the response to explicit information is not obligatory but can be selected from a huge repertoire of behavioural responses. Lahav (1993) concludes that conscious experience expresses information that is available for an entire spectrum of global, integrated and flexible, non-automatic behaviours. Thus, consciousness certainly seems to have causal powers in the control of behaviour radically different from nonconscious information.

In order that our behaviour would express this special contribution of conscious states, conscious information needs to modulate the functioning of several behavioural mechanisms which themselves may be nonconscious, but can be informed by both nonconscious and conscious information. At some stage a transformation from a conscious mode of representation to a nonconscious one must happen. What happens if no such transformation occurs, or if, for some reason, there is no conscious information available? Do we end up with a zombie, or does all behaviour simply stop? Dissociations between consciousness and automatic behaviour provide us with interesting clues to these questions.

In the clinical literature several phenomena can be found that involve curious dissociations between consciousness and the control of behaviour. For example, sleepwalking (somnambulism), nocturnal wandering, and automatic behaviours during epileptic seizures are, *prima facie*, cases where a totally nonconscious person engages in incredibly complex behaviours. These cases often seem even more puzzling than implicit information in neuropsychological patients, for here we do (at least apparently) have global and goal-directed behaviours going on in the absence of consciousness. However, these dissociations between consciousness and behaviour and their theoretical implications for consciousness research have not been treated with any detail in the current discussions on consciousness. Churchland (1988) mentions sleepwalking as problematic for the view that we consciously control our behaviour, and Searle (1992) discusses epileptic automatisms, based on the anecdotes reported by Penfield (1975), and concludes that such behaviours are not as flexible as those guided by consciousness.

Our aim in the present paper is to review and analyse the dissociations between consciousness and automatic behaviours from the viewpoint of consciousness research. We will present detailed descriptions from the clinical literature of the behaviour of such patients as well as descriptions on epileptic automatisms collected by one of the present authors (MJ) in her clinical practice. Based on these data we will evaluate the following questions:

(1) Are the individuals truly nonconscious when they manifest complex behaviours, or only non-reflective or in a confused state of consciousness during the experience, and / or totally amnesic about the experience afterwards? The assumption in the medical and forensic science literature appears to be that if a person is asleep, he is not conscious, and if there is no consciousness, then acts done by the person cannot be criminal, for he does not know what he is doing (Beran 1992; Mahowald et al. 1990). However, it seems the term "conscious" here refers to something like "aware of one's surroundings and of what one is doing" which implies a degree of reflective consciousness. This leaves open the question whether the person nevertheless had phenomenal experience of some kind, if only vague, partial or distorted.

(2) How complex are the actual behaviours of the patients in the allegedly nonconscious state? Are there any well-documented cases of truly elaborate, non-routine automatic behaviours that ordinarily are accompanied by conscious experience and cannot be realized without it?

(3) Does the data cast doubt on the hypothesis that consciousness possesses causal powers unlike those of nonconscious processing systems? Is automatic behaviour quite as adaptive and reasonable as the voluntary behaviour we execute consciously? What is the contribution of consciousness to behaviour normally, and how is it integrated with nonconscious forms of the control of behaviour?

There are difficult methodological problems involved in this exploration.

First, we have no independent means of checking whether or not the person truly was nonconscious during the automatic behaviour. The only criterion we can use is the person's subjective retrospective report as to his experiences during the episode. If the person is completely amnesic about the episode, and/or reports losing consciousness before it and regaining consciousness after it, and describes the episode as a complete blackout, then we assume that she was to all intents and purposes nonconscious. But of course there still is no absolute guarantee that this was truly the case.

Second, how should we rate the behaviours manifested during these episodes? What is the criterion of behaviour that normally requires consciousness? After all, we can carry out many highly complicated tasks, say driving to work or walking home or eating sweets, without paying any attention to the task and being only very dimly aware of our surroundings as our attention is turned elsewhere, to inner thoughts or future plans, for example. Therefore, an apparently nonconscious person carrying out a routine task that can be normally done with minimal consciousness is no evidence of true zombiehood, but only evidence of the activation of highly overlearned action schemata. Still, it is a remarkable achievement if a nonconscious person can successfully move from one location to another or can accurately pick up objects from the surroundings because such actions require relatively complex interactions with the environment. Furthermore, this is more than what e.g. blindsight patients can typically do, for they cannot avoid obstacles or pick up objects they cannot see (Weiskrantz 1992). We shall regard automatic behaviours that are routine and could be normally carried out without focal awareness as evidence of Weak Zombiehood.

What, then, would be evidence of Strong Zombiehood? It would be: to successfully carry out tasks that are non-routine or otherwise require high awareness of surroundings or objects one is in interaction with. Examples of such tasks would be finding one's way in unfamiliar surroundings; looking up an unfamiliar phone number and making a phone call; writing a letter; drawing a picture. These tasks are open-ended, require decisions and choices, and the content of the task and the meaningfulness of the surrounding objects need to be appreciated. If such tasks can be carried out by persons who otherwise, to all intents and purposes, appear nonconscious, then we have evidence of Strong Zombiehood.

Consequently, we will evaluate the automatic behaviour as providing evidence of (1) No Zombiehood if the person is at least dimly conscious during the behaviour, or if the behaviour is completely reflexlike during nonconsciousness; (2) Weak Zombiehood if the person is nonconscious but can only carry out routine action programs; (3) Strong Zombiehood if the person can carry out non-routine tasks involving new decisions and the processing of the meaning of the task and the surrounding objects. Strong Zombiehood, if it exists, means that there are (temporary) zombies around us, who can perform almost any task even in the absence of consciousness.

Sleep-related dissociations of consciousness and behaviour

There are several diagnostic categories referring to complex motor attacks occuring during sleep: night terrors, sleepwalking (somnambulism), nocturnal paroxysmal dystonia, nocturnal wandering, nocturnal seizures, and REM sleep behaviour disorder (RBD). All of them, apart from RBD, tend to arise during NREM sleep and it is unclear whether they are manifestations of basically similar or qualitatively different types of phenomena occurring in the sleeping brain. Descriptions of these automatisms are given below.

NREM-related nocturnal wandering: Case descriptions

Schenck & Mahowald (1995)
Subject: A 43-year old man who showed frequent and violent nocturnal behaviours 1–3 hours after sleep onset.
Documented complex behaviours: He often engaged in strenuous activity that he could not duplicate in the daytime (e.g. lifting a large mattress over his head

or pushing a heavy dresser across the room) and running out of the house. Once he left the house in pajamas by running through a screen door, entered his automobile and drove eight kilometers to his parents' home where he awakened them by pounding on their door. He frequently injured himself while colliding with doorways and furniture, and from falling down the staircase.

Contents of consciousness during automatic behaviour: The subject was often but not always amnesic about the attacks afterwards. During the attack it was impossible to communicate with the patient or break the spell. His eyes were wide open, but he did not actually see the environment as it was, but e.g. instead of seeing his wife, he often perceived a dreamed object or person with extremely threatening content. For example, the episode of somnambulistic automobile driving was initiated by the belief, formed during dreaming, that someone was in the house and about to attack him. While driving he was only aware that he was driving to his parents' home to escape an intruder at his own home.

Zombie rating: No Zombiehood. This person is not completely nonconscious during the behavioural attacks; instead, he is in an altered state of consciousness, involving distorted perceptions of the surroundings and delusions of threats.

Kushida et al. (1995)
Subject: A 51-year-old man who would abruptly arise in the night and have violent outbursts for 3–4 hours.
Documented complex behaviours: He smashed dishes, threw anything within reach, crawled on his hands and knees throughout the house, chased the cats, removed his clothes, walked out of the house partially clothed and attempted to drive the automobile.
Contents of consciousness during automatic behaviour: The subject's eyes were open, but he had a "glazed" appearance and seemed to be completely removed from the environment. Although he often injured himself during these episodes, he could not recall the cause of his injuries upon awakening in the morning. Immediately after an episode of nocturnal wandering, the patient was confused and disoriented, not able to state his name, not oriented to time or place, and unable to repeat phrases or follow simple commands.
Zombie rating: Weak Zombiehood. There is no evidence of consciousness during the behaviours, although an altered state of consciousness cannot be ruled out. The behaviours are complex, involving interactions with the envi-

ronment and its objects. However, the behaviours are manifestly bizarre and indicate that the meaningfulness of the surroundings or its objects cannot be appreciated. Instead, primitive aggressive and defensive behavioural programs are activated.

Maselli et al. (1995)
Subjects: 12 patients with nocturnal wandering.
Documented complex behaviours: Attacks that were stereotyped for a given patient and consisted of complex automatisms ranging from crawling movements to running through hallways. One patient would drag his wife around the bedroom by her hair, another would kneel at her bed and appear to be praying.
Contents of consciousness during automatic behaviour: Four patients reported stereotyped frightening images that consisted of moving objects, animals or persons but no dream-like plot or narrative. Patients were only dimly aware of their behaviour, and seemed surprised when the attacks were described by outside observers.
Zombie rating: Weak or No Zombiehood. Some patients were in an altered state of consciousness, some may have been completely nonconscious, but the behaviours were routine and/or bizarre.

Guilleminault et al. (1995)
Subjects: 41 patients with nocturnal wandering.
Documented complex behaviours: Subjects could make series of gestures that were very decisive or threatening (e.g. fist movements, leg kicks, assumption of a defensive posture). One subject threw his wife on the floor, ran to his two children, took them into his arms and ran out of the house.
Contents of consciousness during automatic behaviour: Subjects were unresponsive, appeared distant and unaware of their surroundings. They sometimes ran into furniture and objects, due to what witnesses felt was a lack of awareness of objects that were in their way. The subjects had incomplete memory of the episodes, but often had vague recollections of nightmarish imagery that was always terrifying and always involved some type of perceived threat to the subject or a loved one. Subjects appeared to attempt an escape from a danger that they alone perceived, but their movements were not appropriate for the real situation and surroundings. Onlookers were often ignored or pushed aside. The subject who ran out of the house with his children said afterwards that he had believed the house was on fire.

Zombie rating: Weak or No Zombiehood. As in the previous report, some patients probably were in an altered state of consciousness and perceived a distorted environment, some may have been completely nonconscious, but their behaviours were routine and/or bizarre.

Plazzi et al. (1995)
Subjects: Four patients with epileptic nocturnal wanderings.
Documented complex behaviours: Patient 1 gets up, walks around, opens the door, steps into the garden and then goes back to bed. In the sleep laboratory, he jumped out of bed, tried to open the door and started to jump on and around the bed. When questioned immediately after the episode, he could not report any dream. Patient 2 sat on the bed, got up and left the bed, moving around the room with a motionless facial expression and speaking unintelligibly. Afterwards he was aware that something had happened during the night. Patient 3 would suddenly sit up in bed, scream and jump out of bed, walk around the bedroom, unresponsive to calls and with an expressionless face. Afterwards, he could not remember what happened. Patient 4 also gets out of bed, then puts his clothes on, screams, and goes back to sleep. He cannot remember the episodes the morning after. In the sleep lab, he pulled the electrodes out of his head and tried to get off the bed. Although alert immediately after the episode, he could remember nothing.
Contents of consciousness during automatic behaviour: Nonexistent or non-reportable due to amnesia.
Zombie rating: Weak Zombiehood. All of the patients seem to be quite nonconscious during the episodes, but the behaviours they manifest are not particularly demanding.

NREM-sleep automatisms: conclusion

These cases described above represent a mixture of sleepwalking, sleep terrors, nocturnal seizures etc. Remarkably complex behaviours are realized by these patients during sleep, but as far as it is possible to tell, some of the patients do not appear to be entirely nonconscious during the behaviour. In many cases some sort of frightening imagery or perceived threat is experienced and sometimes its content is later recalled. This mental content obviously motivates and causes the observed, often violent behaviours. The behaviours are frequently quite rational and adequate in the light of the perceived threat: the patients attempt to save themselves and their loved ones from e.g. threatening intruders or a fire. For example, when aged ten, one patient had risen from sleep, rushed into the sitting room where his parents were still sitting, and thrown the butter dish out of the window, believing it to be a bomb (Oswald & Evans 1985).

The patients have their eyes open and there is at least some registration of the environment, since in many cases (if not always) objects of furniture are bypassed or stairs negotiated safely. However, even if there is a degree of conscious experience involved in this registration, they do not perceive the environment properly nor can proper judgment be exercised (Mahowald 1993). There is little evidence that the patients manifesting extremely complex automatic behaviours should be invariably regarded as completely nonconscious zombies. Rather the contrary: the patients seem to be in an altered and confused state of consciousness, a mixture of wakefulness and NREM sleep (Mahowald & Schenck 1992, 1998). In this state, one's subjective consciousness is focused on one internally generated, usually terrifying image or belief. Appropriate threat avoidance behaviour is often realized automatically, violently and effeciently, in the absence of reflective thought, without an awareness of one's altered state, one's actions, or their actual consequences. We should take into consideration that such a state of consciousness coupled with the kinds of behaviour described above might well be entirely appropriate in a corresponding real situation.

Some cases with moderately complex behaviour coupled with dense amnesia for the events may, however, indicate nearly complete absence of subjective experience during the episode. Even if in those cases the patients can be regarded as totally nonconscious zombies, their behaviour is far from the flexible and integrated types of behaviour guided by a consciously apprehended model of the world. Sleep-related automatisms without any remembered mental content tend to consist of routine actions or stereotyped violent behaviours that are not particularly adaptive for the individual. The patients may even be seriously injured by their own actions when bumping into obstacles they are not aware of. This kind of behaviour may well be the best that can be managed without the contribution of a consciously experienced model of the world. There is no evidence of rational, adaptive and flexible behaviour taking place in the complete absence of consciousness, i.e., no evidence of Strong Zombiehood. But in our rating scale, these cases do fulfill the criterion of Weak Zombiehood.

REM sleep behaviour disorder (RBD)

REM sleep is normally a state of essential paralysis. Thus, for complex behaviour to be manifested during REM sleep, the neural mechanisms responsible for maintaining muscular atonia have to be defective. RBD refers to a condition in which muscular atonia is removed during REM sleep and complex, often violent behaviours are manifested. Some illustrative cases are described below.

Dyken et al. (1995) describe the case of a 73-year old man. On occasion, he unintentionally struck his wife. Once he jumped off the end of the bed and awoke on the floor with a bloody lip, head, and knee. During another episode, the patient leaped from his bed, fell, and struck the right side of his face on a corner of a chest, causing him to wake up immediately. This accident resulted in subdural hemorrhage. In the sleep laboratory during REM sleep, the patient suddenly exhibited explosive running movements, followed by an arousal. The patient's actions clearly corresponded to what he was dreaming about at the time of the observed behaviours. He got the subdural hemorrhage when he dreamed of working on a loading dock and saw a man running. Someone yelled "Stop him!", and the patient had tried to do just that when he jumped out of his bed with the unfortunate consequences.

Boeve et al. (1998, p. 363–370) describe a patient who, on one occasion, "held his wife's head in a headlock and, while moving his legs as if running, shouted: 'I'm gonna make that touchdown!' He then attempted to throw her head down toward the foot of the bed. When woken up, he recalled a dream in which he was running for a touchdown, and he spiked the football in the end zone".

Comella et al. (1998) describe a group of patients with RBD. If these patients were woken up during an episode of abnormal sleep behaviour, none of them recalled that they had executed violent movements, although all recalled violent dreams at the time of wakening: being pursued by an enemy; trying to protect family members from unknown intruders; or fighting off unidentified assaillants.

Schenck (1993) describes a patient whose EEG, EMG and EKG were polysomnographically recorded during an attack of violent behaviour. The muscle tone was increased and the arms and legs showed bursts of intense twitching, accompanied by observable behaviour. After a spontaneous awakening, the man reported a dream in which he was running and trying to escape skeletons that were awaiting him.

One of the present authors (A.R.) has, during several years, recorded three dreams in which a violent dreamed action has led to a corresponding movement of a limb. On one occasion, he dreamed that he was lying on the ground and somebody was coming towards him riding a bicycle. He saw the bicycle wheel rapidly approaching his face, at which point he made a rapid defensive motion, straightening his arm in front of him in order to stop the bikewheel and protect his face. He woke up when his hand hit the bedroom wall. On another occasion he dreamed that he was in a corridor in a big unfamiliar building. From behind one corner, a gorilla suddenly appeared and started attacking him. He tried to lift one knee in order to strike the gorilla on the chest and to protect his own body. He woke up when his knee hit the bedroom wall. On the third occasion he dreamed that he was trying to defend his house against a violent intruder. He saw the intruder in the staircase going down in front of him. He jumped and attempted to kick the intruder in the head. He did hit the intruder's head (with the dreamed leg), but at the same time his real leg kicked the bedroom furniture, resulting in his waking up (with a couple of aching toes).

In conclusion, in RBD there is typically a very close correspondence between the virtual action within the dream and the observed real action, which thus is simply the acting out of the dreamed behaviours. During dream enactment the dreamer is far from a nonconscious zombie. Quite on the contrary, he is right in the center of a vivid subjective dream world, perfectly unaware of the real surroundings. The complex behaviours observed in RBD are guided by the contents of consciousness, but the subject's consciousness is totally immersed to the dream world. His actions consequently reflect his attempts to interact with and adapt to the phenomenal world immediately present in consciousness. As there is a radical mismatch between the real physical environment and the model of the world in consciousness, the physical actions of the subject are highly maladaptive in the real world, often resulting in injuries to the patients and their bedfellows. As Schenck (1993) notes, in RBD an ironical situation commonly occurs that in his dreamworld a husband is desperately fighting to defend his wife from some impending threat while in the real world he is actually beating her up in bed.

It is clear that RBD provides no evidence of zombiehood. However, it shows that consciousness of a dream world can lead to behaviour that would be adaptive and reasonable in that world, although it is not so in relation to the real world. RBD thus shows the power of phenomenal consciousness in determining the framework of our voluntary actions.

Automatic behaviour during epileptic seizures

Dissociations between consciousness and behaviour during epileptic seizures have been described in the literature, although it is by no means quite clear what exactly the patients can do and whether they actually are completely nonconscious during the episode. A well-known formulation of this dissociation is by Penfield (1975). He notes that when epileptic discharge confines itself to one functional mechanism, it will selectively paralyze that mechanism. Consequently, if the mechanisms indispensable for consciousness are involved, then they can be selectively put out of action, which, according to Penfield, converts the individual into a "mindless automaton". Penfield locates these areas critical for consciousness in the subcortical grey matter in higher brain stem (thalamus and basal ganglia); inactivation of these areas produces unconsciousness. Epileptic discharges initiated locally in the temporal or prefrontal cortex may spread to this subcortical network and produce an attack of automatism:

> In an attack of automatism the patient becomes suddenly unconscious, but, since other mechanisms in the brain continue to function, he changes into an automaton. He may wander about, confused and aimless. Or he may continue to carry out whatever purpose his mind was in the act of handing on to his automatic sensory-motor mechanism when the highest brain mechanism went out of action. Or he follows a stereotyped, habitual pattern of behavior. In every case, however, the automaton can make few, if any, decisions for which there has been no precedent. He makes no record of a stream of consciousness. Thus, he will have complete amnesia for the period of epileptic discharge. (Penfield 1975, p. 39).

Penfield mentions a patient who could automatically continue playing the piano during a seizure, another one who walked home from work, and yet another who drove the car home, although occasionally through red traffic lights. Automatisms are realized by a sensory-motor mechanism which is normally in interaction with but can become disconnected from consciousness. The behaviour of the automaton reveals, as Penfield observes, what the brain without consciousness can still do:

> The human automaton, which replaces the man when the highest brain mechanism is inactivated, is a thing without the capacity to make completely new decisions. ... The automaton is incapable of thrilling to the beauty of a sunset or of experiencing contentment, happiness, love, compassion. These, like all awarenesses, are functions of the mind. The automaton is a thing that makes use of the reflexes and the skills, inborn and acquired, that are housed in the computer. ... This automatic coordinator that is ever active within each of us, seems to be the most amazing of all biological computers. (Penfield 1975, p. 47).

Thus, Penfield's automaton surely deserves to be described as some sort of zombie, evidently the kind we would classify as Weak Zombiehood.

Since little attention has been paid theoretically to the dissociations between consciousness and behaviour in epilepsy, we collected reports of behaviour during seizures from epileptic patients and their family members. The patients were furthermore interviewed about their memories of experiences during seizures, in order to find out whether there was any evidence of subjective experiences during the state commonly believed to involve a loss of consciousness. The detailed case reports will be published elsewhere, but some of the most interesting ones are briefly described below.

Before we can assess whether the patients had some sort of consciousness during the seizures, we need to define the concept of consciousness more clearly. By *reflective consciousness* we mean such states in which the subject not only experiences something but, in addition, can take this experience as an object of further thought. Thus, the ability to somehow evaluate, compare, classify, internally comment or verbally report one's experience indicates reflective consciousness. Self-awareness, voluntary control and planning require reflective consciousness. *Primary consciousness* refers to all varieties of subjective experience, be it sensory, perceptual, emotional, or thought-like. *Peripheral consciousness* refers to subjective experience on the borderline between conscious and nonconscious: it is something we only vaguely or dimly experience, although by focusing our attention on some content in peripheral consciousness we can usually bring it to primary consciousness and be fully aware of it. All the rest is *nonconscious* (Farthing 1992).

Case reports

M.C. is a 35-year-old female diagnosed one year ago with complex partial epilepsy. Prior to a major seizure she experiences a gradual decrease of consciousness. Perception can become distorted, but emotions, sensations and thoughts may remain normal. For example, during a recent seizure she was sitting at the lunch table with some other people when she noticed that she did not understand any more what the others were saying. She also was no longer aware of the visual surroundings in the same way as before the seizure. However, she thought that she should try to remember her experiences in order to report them to the neuropsychologist. Thus, M.C.'s seizure is associated with a restricted primary consciousness and an indication of preserved reflective awareness. No automatic behaviours were reported.

W.W. is a 55-year-old female suffering from complex partial epilepsy with secondary generalisation, diagnosed in 1994. She experiences a seizure as a strange feeling in the head and as distance or derealization, although she can continue to see and hear what is going on around her. She does not bump into things around her. She is usually not capable of formulating sentences, but she might answer with a single word. She does not do what she is asked to do. During one seizure that she reported afterwards, she felt as if she was wandering around in a fog and was unable to think clearly. She was unable to lock the door with a key, although she usually manages such things during a seizure. She kept repeating the question: "Where are the children?", although they were right beside her. She did not remember that part of the seizure. The utterances may be considered as an unconscious automatism, akin to repetitive sleeptalking.

She also has attacks during sleep: she may stand up, mumble incomprehensibly, or walk into the wall. She might go to the kitchen, eat something, and leave the refrigerator door open. She has no recall of such events in the morning. Such attacks closely resemble sleepwalking and another sleep pathology named "nocturnal sleep-related eating disorder" (Schenck & Mahowald 1994). There seems to be no reflective consciousness present during such actions, and even the presence of primary consciousness may be questioned. Automatic behaviour such as sleepwalking and sleep-eating can probably be supported by mechanisms subserving peripheral consciousness or unconscious sensorimotor functions. This patient's behaviour is a manifestation of Weak Zombiehood.

E.M. is a 37-year-old female who has complex partial epilepsy with secondary generalization and epileptiform activity in the right temporal lobe. Her seizures start with a nasty feeling in the stomach, followed by a blurred consciousness, distorted images and voices, and progressively decreasing awareness. During one seizure she was aware of her state and she realized that she was only able to say "yes" to whatever she was asked. Thus also M.E. can retain even reflective consciousness during a seizure, but full voluntary control and ability to communicate are lost. No automatisms were reported.

D.D. is a 38-year-old female also suffering from complex partial epilepsy for over 10 years, an epileptic focus in the left temporal lobe. Once she had a seizure while on her way to lunch with her colleagues. She recalls nothing of what happened during the seizure. When she regained consciousness she found herself back in the office with a portion of chicken salad (which she does not like) for lunch. Her colleagues told that she had got out of the car and walked into a nearby restaurant where she never goes. The restaurant personnel told that she had not said anything, but had just pointed to the salad, bought it, smiled, but avoided eye contact. Thus, here we have an example of complex behaviour certainly without reflective consciousness, and possibly guided only by nonconscious or peripherally conscious information. The goal chosen prior to the seizure (to buy lunch) had been preprogrammed and was therefore carried out automatically though erroneously — the patient bought something she would not have liked to eat and would not have bought in her normal state of mind. This is one of the most complex automatisms so far, involving object recognition (restaurant, food), choice (chicken salad), gestural communication, and complex interaction with objects and persons when paying for the salad. However, the whole behavioural episode constitutes a fairly well overlearned script of "buying lunch", so that it can still be regarded only as evidence, even if quite remarkable, of Weak Zombiehood. The error in choosing something one doesn't like reveals that the meaning of the surrounding objects was not fully available during the episode.

J.T. is a 48-year-old female with complex partial epilepsy and a left temporal focus. She reported a seizure that began with the feeling that she was on the point of vanishing into thin air. She did not remember anything of what happened during the next hour. She fell sideways on the sofa, her body first tensed and then relaxed. After about ten minutes she got up. She turned some lights off. Then she took some children's toys and placed them next to the kitchen sink. Now and then she mumbled incomprehensibly. She was able to walk without bumping into objects. She finally undressed and put her nightgown on, although with some difficulties. The whole time her mouth was distorted and she had a blank stare in her eyes. She went to bed and regained consciousness after some time, but a strong sense of unreality remained long afterwards.

In this case we have genuine automatisms (turning off lights, picking up things, undressing and dressing), some of which at least were unreasonable, in the complete or near-complete absence of conscious experience. The automatisms are again quite closely reminiscent of the behaviours manifested by ordinary sleepwalkers. Placing toys next to the kitchen sink reveals that the toys were not recognized but handled as if they were dishes. Therefore, this is another case of Weak Zombiehood: complex interaction with the environment, nonconscious registration of the surroundings, but no evidence of having access to the full meaning of the objects and one's interactions with them.

L.C. is a 26-year-old female with complex partial epilepsy. During a recent seizure she was cooking. She wanted to buy red onion, went to the shop, but came back with yellow onion. She placed it on the floor. She hallucinated hearing the neighbors speaking, and then she realized that she was having a seizure. She called a friend and then lost consciousness. She woke up in bed, and was delighted to see her friend at the bedside. Then she looked at her own hands and saw that they were badly burnt; she was shocked and started to feel the pain. She thought that she must have put her hands on the hot stove while she was nonconscious during the seizure, but she has no recollection of this.

This seizure is very interesting, for it strongly suggests that even an intensive painful stimulus was not consciously registered during the seizure; the patient most likely had been deeply nonconscious — but also behaving in a most unreasonable manner — to have burnt her hands that badly. Again, Weak Zombiehood.

Automatic behaviours from a neuropsychological perspective

There are some neuropsychological findings which may illuminate the mechanisms behind automatic behaviours. Lhermitte et al. (1986) describe two types of behaviours that arise in connection of frontal lobe damage. Utilization behaviour refers to the tendency of perceived objects to trigger corresponding motor programs in which the objects are involved, although no request to use the objects is made. Thus, a comb placed on a table induces combing of one's hair; a glass of water, drinking; a newspaper, reading, and so on. Imitation behaviour refers to the repetition of whatever behaviours are observed to be done by the examiner (or other people). Such patients seem to be very much dependent on environmental cues, but in the absence of external cues they often showed apathy. Lhermitte (1986) calls this the environmental dependency syndrome, in which the autonomy of the patient seems to be compromised.

The explanation for such bizarre behaviour is that frontal lobe mechanisms normally excerting control over action schemata have become defective, which leads to the automatic activation of action programs, executed without any reflection. This account is consistent with the theory by Stuss et al. (1995) according to which frontal attentional mechanisms control the monitoring, energizing, inhibiting, and competition between rival schemata. Schemata or routine input-output transformations can become automatically activated by sensory input or other schemata, but frontally based attentional mechanisms can modulate this activation and thereby implement a degree of choice.

In the absence of consciousness action schemata could still be activated by the same triggers as normally, but since there is no inhibition or monitoring of the activity, the action programs would be released without reflection and perhaps in a state of a very low level of awareness of surroundings. Therefore epileptic patients may carry out complex tasks which nevertheless are somehow inappropriate; they do things they would not do if they were able to control their actions and monitor their behaviour. Sleepwalkers often do the same sort of things: the mechanisms for releasing the behaviours are basically the same in both cases, although the reason why consciousness is suppressed may be different in these two groups.

Weak Zombiehood is probably based on the automatic activation of action programs that can be guided by nonconscious registration of the overall spatial layout of the surroundings, leading to the observed interactions with the environment.

Conclusions

Our purpose in this paper was to examine the possibility of Real Zombies or Strong Zombiehood existing among us: pathological disorders of consciousness that would abolish subjective experience but preserve complex and entirely normal-looking behaviour. We examined various sleep-related behaviours and epileptic automatisms. We found that only in a few cases do we have reason to believe subjective consciousness to have been completely lost. However, as far as we can tell, this may sometimes happen during sleepwalking or epileptic seizures; at least the patient reports experiencing loss and regaining of consciousness and all memory for the events in between are completely lost, even when the patient is interviewed only a few minutes after the episode. Behaviour during such episodes is often surprisingly complex, but at the same time clearly abnormal. The nonconscious registration of the environment seems to be restricted in the way that the meaning of the surrounding objects is not available for guiding behaviour. A motor program or even an event script can be carried out, but in a mechanical way that reveals only superficial classification of objects. The meaningfulness of objects, surroundings and one's own actions seems to be lost with the loss of conscious perception. There is little reason to believe that such a zombie could manage any genuinely novel situation requiring adaptive responses.

In many cases, especially sleepwalking and nocturnal wandering, we found that the patients are not entirely nonconscious, but simply in a confused state of consciousness. They may have one strong image or belief or emotion in mind, and a somewhat distorted awareness of the surroundings. Nevertheless, when the patients perform complex adaptive feats, such as escaping from their houses and driving a car, they are usually in the grips of a horrible delusion, e.g. that somebody is after them or that their house is on fire. In some restricted ways they are orientated to the surroundings, but their focus is extremely narrow and they are unable to monitor or reflect on their own behaviour or thinking. Therefore, it is fair to say that such patients do not know or realize what they are doing: they lack reflective consciousness. They should not be blamed or put into legal responsibility for the things they do during such episodes. However, they are not completely nonconscious zombies either; they experience emotions, perceptions, hallucinations, delusions, and so forth. The same is true of patients with REM sleep behaviour disorder; the difference is that the subjective world of these patients does not have any ingredients of the real surroundings incorporated. The patients' brains hallucinate a complete dream world, and the patients then try to interact with that world, but collide with the real one. This is a powerful demonstration of how the contents of consciousness can guide behaviour even when they do not in any way reflect the real physical surroundings of the subject.

In conclusion, we did not find convincing evidence of any pathological dissociation where consciousness would be completely absent but complex adaptive non-routine behaviour would be possible in the same way as it is during normal waking consciousness. Thus, as Lahav (1993) argued, it appears that consciousness possesses causal powers in the initiation or guidance of behaviour unlike those of any purely nonconscious processing systems in the brain. Consciousness forms a *meaningful* model of the world in the brain, and the brain attempts to interact with and adapt to this semantically transparent world as represented in the content of consciousness. Even though the brain can be said to somehow *register* the environment nonconsciously, this registration is a far cry from the meaningful consciously apprehended model of the world. Consciousness is needed to program, initiate, guide and evaluate meaningful, integrated, adaptive, and flexible behavioural sequences, although many components of these sequences are actually nonconscious.

Nonconscious registration of surroundings can initiate and guide behavioural sequences whose overall goal has been preprogrammed consciously before the loss of consciousness occurred. Nonconsciously guided behaviour is often inflexible or unreasonable, showing a lack of insight into what the overall meaning of the action is supposed to be. This pattern suggests that goals, once consciously activated, can modulate behaviour through nonconscious behaviour, as if the goals had been translated into a sequence of action representations that are coded and released at a nonconscious level. Goal descriptions may thus be an important form of high-level outputs normally fed from consciousness to nonconscious systems. A significant part of the normal interaction between conscious and nonconscious processing might be realized by using such representations.

If the conscious model of the world is missing or only extremely weakly activated, all the brain can do is to let sensory stimulation guide behavioural schemata in automatic ways that rarely lead to flexible and adaptive responses. If the model in consciousness reveals that monsters are attacking us or that our house is on fire, the brain initiates complex patterns of defensive behaviours, even if the world-model is based on radically incorrect or distorted information. People with REM sleep behaviour disorder or nocturnal wandering clearly demonstrate this. But for better or worse, there appear to be no Real Zombies. Nevertheless, all the dissociations actually occurring between behaviour and consciousness that we have reviewed are remarkable in themselves and may teach us important lessons about the role of consciousness in the guidance of human behaviour.

Acknowledgements

A.R. was supported by The Academy of Finland (project 36106).

References

Beran, R.G. (1992). Automatisms — the current legal position related to clinical practice and medicolegal interpretation. *Clinical and Experimental Neurology,* 29, 81–91.

Boeve, B.F., Silber, M.H., Ferman, T.J., Kokmen, E., Smith, G.E., Ivnik, R.J., Parisi, J.E., Olson, E.J. & Petersen, R.C. (1998). REM sleep behavior disorder and degenerative dementia: an association likely reflecting Lewy body disease. *Neurology,* 51, 363–70.

Churchland, P.S. (1988). Reduction and the Neurobiological Basis of Consciousness in: A.J. Marcel & E. Bisiach (Eds.), *Consciousness in Contemporary Science.* Oxford, Oxford University Press, 273–304.

Comella, C.L., Nardine, T.M., Diederich, N.J. & Stebbins, G.T. (1998). Sleep-related violence, injury, and REM sleep behavior disorder in Parkinson's disease. *Neurology,* 51, 526–9.

Dyken, M.E., Lin-Dyken, D.C., Seaba, P. & Yamada, T. (1995). Violent sleep-related behavior leading to subdural hemorrhage. *Archives of Neurology,* 52, 318–321.

Farthing, W.G. (1992). *The Psychology of Consciousness.* Englewood Cliffs, NJ: Prentice Hall.

Guilleminault, C., Moscovitch, A. & Leger, D. (1995). Forensic sleep medicine: Nocturnal wandering and violence. *Sleep,* 18, 740–748.

Kushida, C.A., Clerk, A.A., Kirsch, C.M., Hotson, J.R. & Guilleminault, C. (1995). Prolonged confusion with nocturnal wandering arising from NREM and REM sleep: A case report. *Sleep,* 18, 757–764.

Lahav, R. (1993). What neuropsychology tells us about consciousness. *Philosophy of Science,* 60, 67–85.

Lhermitte, F., Pillon, B. & Serdaru, M. (1986). Human autonomy and the frontal lobes. Part I: Imitation and utilization behavior: A neuropsychological study of 75 patients. *Annals of Neurology,* 19, 326–334.

Lhermitte, F. (1986). Human autonomy and the frontal lobes. Part II: Patient behavior in complex and social situations: The "Environmental Dependency Syndrome". *Annals of Neurology,* 19, 335–343.

Mahowald, M.W., Bundlie, S.R., Hurwitz, T.D. & Schenck, C.H. (1990). Sleep Violence — Forensic science implications: Polygraphic and video documentation. *Journal of Forensic Sciences,* 35, 413–432.

Mahowald, M.W. & Schenck, C.H. (1992). Dissociated states of wakefulness and sleep. *Neurology,* 42(suppl 6), 44–52.

Mahowald, M.W. (1993). Sleepwalking. In M. Carskadon (Ed.) *Encyclopedia of Sleep and Dreaming.* New York: Macmillan, 579–9.

Mahowald, M.W., Woods, S.R. & Schenck, C.H. (1998). Sleeping dreams, waking hallucinations, and the central nervous system. *Dreaming,* 8, 89–102.

Maselli, R.A., Rosenberg, R.S. & Spire, J.P. (1988). Episodic nocturnal wanderings in non-epileptic young patients. *Sleep,* 11, 156–161.

Oswald, I. & Evans, J. (1985). On serious violence during sleep-walking. *British Journal of Psychiatry,* 147, 688–691.

Penfield, W. (1975) *The Mystery of the Mind.* Princeton, NJ: Princeton University Press

Place, U.T. (this volume) Consciousness and the zombie within: A Functional analysis of the blindsight evidence. In: Y. Rossetti & A. Revonsuo, *Beyond Dissociation.* (Advances in Consciousness Studies). Amsterdam: John Benjamins, Vol. 22.

Plazzi, G., Tinuper, P., Montagna, P., Provini, F. & Lugaresi, E. (1995). Epileptic nocturnal wanderings. *Sleep,* 18, 749–756.

Schenck, C.H. (1993). REM sleep behavior disorder. In M. Carskadon (Ed.), *Encyclopedia of Sleep and Dreaming.* New York: MacMillan, 499–505.

Schenck, C.H. & Mahowald, M.W. (1995). Review of nocturnal sleep-related eating disorders. *International Journal of Eating Disorders,* 15, 343–356.

Schenck, C.H. & Mahowald, M.W. (1995). A polysomnographically documented case of adult somnambulism with long-distance automobile driving and frequent nocturnal violence: Parasomnia with continuing danger as a noninsane automatism? *Sleep,* 18, 765–772.

Searle, J.R. (1992). *The Rediscovery of the Mind.* Cambridge, MA: The MIT Press.

Stuss, D.T., Shallice, T., Alexander, M.P. & Picton, T.W. (1995). A multidisciplinary approach to anterior attentional functions. *Annals of the New York Academy of Sciences,* 769, 191–211.

The Zombie Within (1998, September 5) *New Scientist* 159: 31.

Weiskrantz, L. (1992). Introduction: Dissociated Issues. In A.D. Milner & M.D. Rugg (Eds.), *The Neuropsychology of Consciousness.* New York: Academic Press, 1–10.

Dissociation and Interaction

Windows to the Hidden Mechanisms
of Consciousness

Antti Revonsuo and Yves Rossetti

1. Introduction

The dissociation between conscious and nonconscious information is one of the main sources of empirical evidence in contemporary consciousness research. Blindsight, numb-sense (or blindtouch), implicit memory, implicit control of goal-directed actions, implicit processing of unseen objects in unilateral neglect and implicit knowledge of the familiarity of faces in prosopagnosia: without the recent discoveries of such robust but surprising phenomena, it is doubtful whether empirical consciousness research would ever have got off the ground (Rossetti and Revonsuo, introduction chapter).

In this concluding chapter we will try to clarify why exactly these phenomena are so valuable for progress in the scientific understanding of consciousness. We will argue that the study of dissociations and interactions between conscious and nonconscious phenomena in the brain is a prime example of a certain research strategy widely used in the biological sciences: mechanistic explanation. It has proved to be highly successful elsewhere in the life sciences. Therefore, if we accept the view that consciousness ultimately is a biological phenomenon in the brain, we have every reason to believe that the hidden mechanisms of consciousness can be uncovered by using such an approach, if at all.

Although the merits of this research strategy may seem quite obvious to the empirical cognitive neuroscientist, the same is not necessarily true across the multidisciplinary field of consciousness studies. There are several theoretical approaches in that field that accept neither the view that consciousness is a real biological phenomenon in the brain nor the methodology of mechanistic explanation in the study of conscious phenomena. To mention just a few well-known views that do not accept the mechanistic research strategy and the biological view of consciousness: Dennett (1991) claims that subjective phenomenology does not really exist at all, and that it is impossible to draw a clear line between conscious and nonconscious processes in the brain. Chalmers (1996) argues that in order to explain consciousness it is not enough for us to understand the brain as a biological organ. McGinn (1991) readily accepts the view that consciousness has a hidden structure that should be uncovered before genuine explanation of how consciousness is linked with the brain is possible. However, he believes that the hidden structure of consciousness is radically unknowable to us. We can at best have good reasons to believe that a hidden level must exist, but we are doomed to remain completely ignorant as to its nature.

The above views deny either the basic assumptions or the explanatory value of empirical research on the dissociations between conscious and non-conscious phenomena in the brain. The naturalistic biological explanation of consciousness is, therefore, far from generally accepted in the field of consciousness studies. The best way to defend the naturalistic approach against all the philosophical naysaying is simply to show that it works. Our empirically-based understanding of the neural correlates of consciousness and of the borderline between the conscious and the nonconscious in the brain is increasing all the time, no matter what the philosophical resistance to this empirical progress may be. Since the naturalistic approach will anyway be advocated by an army of cognitive neuroscientists, it would be useful for philosophers to try to figure out what exactly is going on within empirical research, instead of comfortably retreating back to the proverbial armchair after having philosophically defeated the pitiful attempts of the empirical scientist to search for a naturalistic explanation of consciousness.

In the present paper we will try to understand the ongoing empirical research on the dissociation and interaction between the conscious and the nonconscious from a metatheoretical viewpoint. In Section 2 we will describe the research strategy of mechanistic explanation and show that studies on the dissociation between conscious and nonconscious processes conforms to this strategy. In Section 3 we will give an overview of what the current empirical findings (largely covered in the other chapters of the present volume) tell us about consciousness, and in what theoretical direction the results are leading us. In Section 4, we will connect the dissociation / interaction -issue with another prominent theme in consciousness research: the binding problem. Both of these empirical approaches to consciousness are at bottom attempts to understand what the components of a complex biological system — the conscious brain — are, how those components bring about their causal effects, and how the components interact in order to generate coherent phenomenal experience and integrated adaptive behaviour.

2. Mechanistic explanation and the study of consciousness

In the biological sciences, mechanistic explanation is coupled with the standard hierarchical view of the natural world: natural phenomena are realized at several different levels of organization and, in order to understand a given phenomenon, we need to describe the level of organization at which the phenomenon is realized, and subsequently figure out how that level is realized by the underlying lower levels of organization. To explain a complex system mechanistically is, first, to describe the system accurately at its own level of description and, second, to reveal the causally relevant parts that the system is composed of, and how those parts are interactively organized to bring about the structure and behaviour of the complex system in question.

It is not too difficult to grasp how this sort of mechanistic explanations are constructed in, say, molecular biology and cytology. But how are we to use a similar strategy in the study of consciousness and the brain? One of the most crucial stages in developing a mechanistic explanation of a system is to determine what the components of the system are and what they do (Bechtel & Richardson 1993). However, an intact, smoothly operating system rarely reveals its components and their organization directly. But when the system breaks down in one way or another, and the system is only partially functional, the underlying mechanisms may become exposed. Neuropsychological patients who have suffered brain injury provide us with examples of permanent lesions to the system we are interested in. And, as the vast literature on blindsight and related implicit phenomena shows, sometimes this kind of breakdown of the brain-mind system reveals the hidden mechanisms that would otherwise have gone unnoticed (see Rossetti and Revonsuo (introduction chapter)). As stated in a provocative way in our introduction breaking down one system (i.e. the human body) into dissociable pieces should not prevent us from keeping in mind that the only entity we are facing in this analysis is the whole human being. Identifying components of this entity is nevertheless a productive approach to the relationship between implicit and explicit processing.

One of the most significant contributions of dissociation research to consciousness studies is the undeniable fact that consciousness (or "explicit" information) constitutes a separable functional "component" of the human information processing system that must be distinguished from all the nonconscious components of the system (Schacter et al. 1988). This component of the system has features and causal powers that it shares with none of the nonconscious components of the system; it seems that in consciousness information from several sources is brought together into one coherent representation which is involved in the initiation of global, flexible and integrated behaviour (Lahav 1993).

Thus, the theoretical implication derived from dissociation research is that the human cognitive system is decomposable into component functions, and that one of the most important divisions between them is the conscious-nonconscious dichotomy. Most components of the human cognitive system are completely nonconscious whereas at least one of them realizes phenomena that are subjectively experienced. Several theoretical models have been put forward that attempt to specify the relations between the conscious and the nonconscious components in the human cognitive system. In a recent review Köhler and Moscovitch (1997) divide these models into three categories: Disconnection models, Distinct Knowledge models and Degraded Representation or threshold models.

In Disconnection models (e.g. Schacter et al. 1988), nonconscious domain-specific modules normally produce output that feeds into one common Conscious Awareness System (CAS). If the nonconscious modules become disconnected from the CAS but remain otherwise intact, they cannot feed information to consciousness any more. However, they have other output connections through which the same information may be implicitly processed. Thus, disconnection models see implicit information as information that is supposed to be fed into the conscious component of the system but, due to the disruption of the connections, it never reaches its proper destination. In this model, implicit information is produced by modules that are "earlier" than consciousness in a linear, serial processing chain, but normally in tight interaction with it. Implicit information is nonconscious because it resides at an earlier stage in the processing chain; it is supposed to be transformed into conscious information once it enters (or modulates the states of) the one and only unified Conscious Awareness System.

In Distinct Knowledge models the idea is that implicit information resides in processing systems that never were supposed to feed their information into consciousness in the first place: they are thoroughly nonconscious by their very nature. Such processing systems operate in parallel with the one(s) subserving explicit knowledge or consciousness, but are usually hidden from view, only exposed in exceptional cases where the conscious processing system is malfunctioning. In such situations, the nonconscious parallel systems go on as ever, transforming specific forms of input into specific forms of output, thus modulating observable behavior nonconsciously.

Degraded Representation models assume that the very same system that generates conscious states also produces nonconscious states, if the system is inadequately activated or partially damaged. Nonconscious states result if the representations that the system produces are degraded or if the activation that the system receives is insufficient. In any case, conscious and nonconscious information (of the same stimulus) does not reside in two different systems, but manifests two different states of the very same system.

Köhler and Moscovitch (1997) conclude that the Distinct Knowledge model can explain most of the available data on implicit visual processing, whereas the two other models seem more restricted. The most convincing evidence for the Distinct Knowledge model comes from implicit processing in blindsight and visual object agnosia, and has been argued for especially by Milner and Goodale (1995). Several papers in the present volume also advocate this kind of an interpretation of implicit processing. Bridgeman says that there is overwhelming evidence for the existence of two branches of visual processing, one cognitive branch supporting conscious perception, the other a sensorimotor branch supporting visually guided behavior. Pisella and Rossetti show that there are two distinct ways of encoding spatial information for action: one system using perceptual or semantic representations at the explicit or conscious level, one sensory-motor system using short-lived motor representations at the implicit or nonconscious level (see also Bhalla and Proffitt; Jackson). Hommel argues that the Simon effect provides evidence for the coexistence of independent but parallel automatic (nonconscious) and intentional (conscious) routes for stimulus-response transformations. In addition he shows that altering the focus of attention can modify implicit visual process-ing so as to become explicit, and then produce a different effect on behaviour. Interestingly the implicit to explicit translation of proprioceptive information produces a similar modification of the way the same piece of information is used to control action (Imanaka and Abernethy). Place presents a model of visual information processing with two parallel input-output transformation systems: consciousness and the nonconsious zombie-within. According to this model, the nonconscious route is mostly subcortical, while the conscious route is mostly cortical, corresponding to the ventral visual stream. Revonsuo et al. suggest that in some forms of automatic behaviour, complex behaviour is guided by nonconscious representations, some of which may have their origin in information represented earlier at the conscious level.

Thus, it is nowadays generally accepted that there are completely non-conscious systems that take in sensory input, process and transform it in complex ways, and deliver representations that modulate external reactions or behaviour in various ways. These nonconscious systems bypass conscious-ness entirely, although they may be in interaction with or influenced by it to some extent. For example, Pisella and Rossetti (this volume) present an initial analysis of the nature of the interaction between implicit and explicit spatial representations: it seems that time — the speed and latency of an action — is a very important factor in determining which representations primarily guide the action and what the degree and direction of interaction between the explicit and implicit representations will be.

It is important to uncover the nonconscious zombie systems and their contribution to the modulation of behavior, for those systems tell us what consciousness definitely is *not*, and the anatomical basis of those systems reveals to us which kinds of neural systems can guide behavior in the total absence of consciousness. An understanding of the biology and the behaviour of the nonconscious information processing systems in the brain can then be contrasted with a positive view of consciousness: if consciousness is *not* realized in *these* neural systems and *not* carrying out *these sorts* of input-output transformations, then it is probably realized elsewhere and its tasks are likely to be complementary to the ones that can be carried out nonconsciously.

However, there is no compelling reason to believe that all instances of implicit information should be explained by referring to two entirely separate systems. Covert recognition of faces in prosopagnosia is a case in point. Young (this volume) argues that, although the implicit effects related to autonomic activation (e.g. those affecting skin conductance responses) are probably realized by neural systems different from the ones supporting overt recognition of faces, the behavioural implicit effects, such as associative priming, can be best explained by a Degraded Representation model. The basic idea of such a model is that, due to dysfunctional connections, the component modules containing the representations of face and person identity do not receive sufficient excitation from earlier stages of processing. Thus the activation received is not enough to reach above the critical threshold for producing overt recognition, but it is enough to support the implicit behavioral effects. A first argument for this model comes from the developmental studies presented by Perner and Clements (this volume), showing that the same information appears to be gradually transformed from implicit to explicit representations. Also Bar (this volume) puts forward a threshold explanation, but his paper is concerned with the effects of subliminal visual priming. He argues that subliminal presentation of a visual image is not sufficient to induce conscious recognition, probably because the areas subserving conscious identification in the inferotemporal cortex receive insufficient activation. However, even subliminal presentations of stimuli leave their mark at some earlier, nonconscious stage in the processing system (possibly in V4). When the same stimulus is presented again, this nonconscious representation facilitates the further processing of the stimulus, leading to threshold-crossing activation in the inferotemporal cortex.

These interpretations of implicit, nonconscious information suggest that such information exists in several different forms in the brain. With all likelihood no single model can account for all of them. In some cases it seems clear that nonconscious information is routed along completely different neural pathways from those of conscious information in the brain. The two serve entirely different functions and the one is neither a preliminary nor a degraded form of the other. However, in other cases it seems more reasonable to think that the implicit information resides within the very same processing route as conscious information does. Along this route there are stages of completely nonconscious processing which in the normal case modulate the conscious stage, but in a disrupted system all the effects remain nonconscious, either because of disconnection between processing modules or degradation of certain processing stages (or some combination of these malfunctions).

So far all this seems to tell us quite a lot about the nature of *nonconscious* information in the brain, and the *separation* of the nonconscious effects from the conscious ones in the brain. Perhaps the more intriguing question, however, is what we can learn about consciousness itself, and of the *interaction* between the nonconscious and the conscious; defining the possible interaction between the components of a system is a crucial step in the development of mechanistic explanations.

3.   Interactions between the conscious and the nonconscious

How far apart from each other are the conscious and the nonconscious in the light of the data reviewed in the present volume? We must remember that the answer to this question is dependent on the specific type of nonconscious information we are considering. If the nonconscious information resides in a processing system that is separate from conscious forms of information, we are looking for interactions between two separate processing systems. But if nonconscious information is simply a preliminary stage or weakly activated form of conscious information inside the same processing system where conscious information itself resides (e.g. Perner and Clements, this volume), then we are not looking at two independent neural systems interacting with each other, but two different stages of information processing within the same neural system influencing each other.

Prime examples of systems transforming input into output, independent of but in interaction with consciousness, are Hommel's automatic processing route and Bridgeman's sensorimotor branch of vision that uses short-lived motor representations (see also Bhalla and Proffitt; Pisella & Rossetti, this volume). How do these nonconscious systems cooperate with consciousness? First, we should note that these systems do indeed most of the time cooperate with consciousness instead of competing with it. These systems do not have goals of their own that are fully independent of those determined at the level of conscious intention (It should be noticed however that because of different time constraints applied to automatic and voluntary processes, these two systems may be in conflict over a very short range of time, as demonstrated by Pisella and Rossetti). In fact, these systems appear to be more like slave systems which ensure that whatever the goals determined at the level of consciousness are, these fast zombies go for them without asking any questions. Thus, as Hommel agrees, intentional processes (i.e. the consciously represented and attended goals of the person) set the stage for the automatic processes to carry out their job fast and efficiently, blindly serving the purposes of consciousness. Without the conscious selection of goals, the automatic system would not be able to take any behavioral initiative of its own. And vice versa, without the automatic systems, consciousness would not be able to guide all the details required in programming goal-directed behavior successfully and carrying it out rapidly. For other, more complex systems, such as mood management, the conscious and the unconscious processing remain even more difficult to disentangle.

Second, as Bridgeman argues, information processed during a given action can flow from the conscious system to the nonconscious one, but not the other way round (see also Bhalla and Proffitt; Pisella and Rossetti). In some cases, e.g. when a delayed response to the stimulus is required, the nonconscious system cannot store the relevant representations, but must rely on those delivered by the conscious system. This also shows clearly that the nonconscious system is a servant of the consciously selected goals. Interestingly, the information delivered by the conscious system is not as accurate for the purposes of motor programming as the normal direct on-line input of this system is, for the representations filtered through the conscious system include distortions and illusions that the nonconscious system is not otherwise inclined to generate. Unfortunately we do not know as yet what the anatomical connections are that allow such interaction to take place. Knowing the anatomy of the connections might give us a clue to the location of the systems supporting consciousness, for the information influencing the nonconscious system is likely to have its origins in the neural systems that realize consciousness (e.g. the ventral stream?). In addition, the fact that the opposite interaction may be observed when a longer time-scale is being considered (e.g. Bhalla and Proffitt; Pisella and Rossetti), strongly supports the idea that reciprocal interactions and thus interconnections can be observed between the two systems.

The above mentioned interactions between the conscious and the nonconscious systems are relatively straightforward. In cases where the conscious and nonconscious information are parts of the same processing system, the interaction is also relatively easy to model. Repeated activation of similar nonconscious processing stages or representations may accumulate and result in the information subsequently crossing a critical threshold and entering consciousness. This is how Bar (this volume) suggests that subliminal priming works. Young (this volume) cites an interesting study in which the presentation of multiple instances of faces from the same semantic category sometimes led to overt recognition of a face in a prosopagnosic patient, suggesting that the increased activation within a narrow semantic field in memory led to a crossing of a critical threshold that could not otherwise be crossed anymore. Converging evidence from studies on binocular rivalry suggest that activity in areas along the ventral visual stream increase when the stimulus represented in those areas becomes the dominant one and enters awareness (without any changes in the retinal stimulation taking place). Sheinberg and Logothetis (1997) showed that single cells increase their firing rate in the inferotemporal cortex when their preferred stimulus enters awareness. Tong et al. (1998) discovered by using fMRI that in humans during binocular rivalry between stimuli depicting faces and places, the fusiform face area activates when the face stimulus enters awareness, and the parahippocampal place area activates when the place stimulus dominates in visual consciousness. Furthermore ffytche et al. (1998) showed that areas in the ventral stream are activated during hallucinations of e.g. faces and objects.

Taken together, the message from these findings is that for conscious perception to occur, one needs, first, the involvement of the kind of processing system that is specialised in generating consciousness, not the automatic slave systems and, second, within this processing system, one needs sufficient activation of specific processing modules or specific types of representations; otherwise the information will not cross the critical threshold and enter consciousness. But we are still entirely ignorant about the *kind* of neural activation that is required for consciousness. We have little idea how the electrophysiological activity is organized at the higher levels when millions of neurons and billions of synapses are involved in creating complex electrophysiological patterns and states. Single cell studies tell about what a few neurons out of millions are doing, and fMRI reveals that a greater proportion of oxygenated blood is flowing to some brain areas in the conscious than in the unconscious condition. Neither of these methods can really capture those levels of organization that directly realize consciousness. Therefore, at present we have no idea what an area is doing when the stimulus it represents is transformed from a nonconscious representation into a consciously experienced representation. Just saying that the area is "active" amounts to no more than saying that the area is doing *something*, but we don't have the slightest idea what that might be. The twilight zone where the nonconscious crosses the threshold of consciousness remains mysterious.

We have no reason to believe that the uncharted area between the nonconscious and the conscious will be easily explicable. On the contrary, it will probably prove to be at least as complicated and multilayered as the path from nonliving simple parts such as organic molecules to living entities such as cells. We may come to realize this by exploring the borderline between conscious and nonconscious in specific cases. Things do get a bit complicated when we consider the evidence presented by Jackson (this volume) on blindsight and pathological visual completion. It shows that the so-called "blind" visual field (scotoma) in a cortically blind patient may not be absolutely blind after all. Specific types of visual stimulation may create visual experience that reaches into the blind field. The stimuli that can do this involve a holistic gestalt that at least partially extends to the intact parts of the visual field. However, nothing that depends entirely on the damaged field can be visually experienced. How should we interpret these findings? It appears that spatial grouping and gestalt perception are realized at a processing stage that is not entirely dependent on input from V1, as long as the stimulus falls at least partly on intact parts of V1. The highly interesting questions that, unfortunately, cannot be answered at this point are: What are the neural mechanisms that provide information about those parts of the stimuli that fall into the blind field? And what are the neural systems where the consciously perceived gestalt is represented? Obviously, V1 is not among those systems; somehow the gestalt information must originate and be realized in systems outside the damaged primary visual cortex. Furthermore, the generation of the perceived gestalt must be the result of complex interactions taking place within multiple different visual maps, some of which, it would seem, must be activated by the information in the blind field, but in a way that necessarily bypasses V1.

Even more curious are the findings cited by Ladavas et al. (this volume) on unilateral neglect. They suggest that visual awareness requires the combination of two independent and intact representations: space representation coding the "where" aspects of the stimuli, and object representation coding the "what" aspects. In unilateral neglect the representation of space is compromised, whereas object representations are relatively intact. This is sometimes dramatically revealed when objects or parts of objects actually residing in neglected space are in fact perceived within the intact space. This happens presumably because the objects can be recognised and represented, but there is no phenomenal space in the "correct" location where the object should appear; consequently the object representation, if it is to enter consciousness at all, must be bound to an incorrect location in the available perceptual space. Ladavas et al.

go on to argue that space representation depends on the integration of the activity in multiple different spatial maps. The balance between these maps is lost in neglect, which results in a limited and sometimes changeable conscious representation of perceptual space. Interestingly, Pisella & Rossetti (this volume) discuss striking evidence on the effects of prism adaptation to neglect: it seems that if the damaged spatial representations can be influenced or activated by exposure to an optical alteration of the visual field, dramatic improvement of neglect symptoms may follow.

These findings and theories of neglect bring the issue of conscious — nonconscious interaction very close to the binding problem. Ladavas et al. (this volume) argue that certain in-themselves-nonconscious representations must be bound together in order that a conscious representation of space — the phenomenal space around us — can be constructed in the brain. And the phenomenal representation of space is also necessary for the conscious perception of objects, for otherwise there would be no perceived space in which the perceived objects could be located. The situation may be something like that in dorsal simultanagnosia or Balint's syndrome, where only one object at a time can be recognized, but even that object cannot be located in space — space representation is severely disrupted.

4. The conscious, the nonconscious, and the levels of organisation in the brain

The dissociation and interaction between conscious and nonconscious processes ultimately bring us close to the deep unsolved questions in contemporary consciousness studies: the neural correlates of consciousness and the binding problem. In fact it seems that these questions cannot be completely separated from each other.

At the beginning of this chapter we argued that the empirical study of dissociations and interactions is an application of mechanistic explanatory strategies in consciousness research, and that such research strategies have proved to be quite fruitful in other branches of biological science. The strategy aims at finding out the component parts (or functions) of a system and their interactions and localizing such parts within the system, and finally explaining the contribution of each part by shifting into a lower level of description and trying to figure out how the component functions themselves are put together.

It seems that this sort of mechanistic explanatory strategy is helping to get a grip on consciousness as well. The studies in the present volume reveal that the brain has several different processing systems. Some of them are intrinsically nonconscious input-output transformers: no states or representations or stages of processing are ever conscious in those systems. There is no phenomenal level of organization in such systems. Then there is at least one system that realizes a higher level of organization we call consciousness or the phenomenal level. Even in this system (or at least in close interaction with this system) there are several processing stages or below-threshold representations that are intrinsically nonconscious, only preparing information for inclusion into consciousness at later stages (cf. the unconscious brain inferences postulated by von Helmholtz). However, once the information does enter the level of consciousness, it seems to acquire qualitatively distinct properties (Lahav 1993): it can be widely integrated with other conscious information from any sense modality or explicit memory system, it can be used to control global behavior very flexibly; no fixed input-output transformations determine the ways in which conscious information is used.

We do not really know what the levels of organization immediately below and necessary for the conscious level are. Is the binding of multiple nonconscious spatial maps absolutely necessary for any kind of conscious visual perception to take place at all? This reminds us of the Kantian view that the category of space is a necessary prerequisite for human perception. Then how can patients with Balint's syndrome lose the awareness of visual space but retain awareness of single objects? Does consciousness require widespread neural synchronization to create visual awareness (Engel et al., 1999) or are conscious experiences realized as a multitude of "micro-consciousnesses" (Zeki & Bartels, 1999) that need not be bound together before they can enter awareness? By asking these questions we can begin to realize that there are several levels of description between the conscious and the nonconscious that we are unaware of at the moment. Somehow the level of consciousness is based on those levels.

Once we can close in on the level of consciousness itself we must face the question: how is it possible to explain phenomenal consciousness by referring to the lower levels of organization? As long as we just chart the *relations* between conscious and nonconscious processing systems, we can avoid facing the *internals* of consciousness itself, but at some point we will need to start explaining that too. The levels of description and explanation needed in that task will probably be quite different from the ones we are currently familiar with in cognitive neuroscience.

In conclusion, if we strive for a mechanistic explanation of the mind-brain, the task before us is clear enough: to describe the relatively independent components of the system and the interaction of those components with each other in the production of coherent behavior. Dissociations between functions reveal, at least sometimes, what the independent components of the system may be. Interactions reveal how the components are causally related with each other in order to generate the causal effects that the system as a whole has. We should expect to end up with lots of nonconscious systems and lots of nonconscious stages of processing, and few conscious systems or stages or only one. The nonconscious systems we might be able to describe exhaustively by referring to standard cognitive and neural levels of explanation, but in order to explain consciousness, we first need to construct a phenomenal level of description to systematically capture the phenomenon we are trying to explain (Revonsuo 1997). We have only faint ideas at this point how we should go about doing that. But we should not even expect more than that: scientific discoveries are not something that can be imagined before they have actually been made. If they were, we could all just retreat to our armchairs and start imagining, like some philosophers are still inclined to do, with the result that they cannot imagine how consciousness could ever be explained. Too bad for them that the discoveries that may explain consciousness have to be actually *made*, not imagined. The empirical study of the dissociation and interaction of conscious and unconscious phenomena in the brain is a good way to launch into that quest.

Acknowledgements

A.R. is supported by the Academy of Finland (projects 36106 and 45704) and Y.R. by the Center for Consciousness Studies (Tucson, Arizona) and by Région Rhône-Alpes (France).

References

Bar, M. (2000). Conscious and Nonconscious Processing of Visual Identity. This volume, 153–175.
Bechtel, W. & Richardson, R.C. (1993). *Discovering Complexity. Decomposition and Localization as Strategies in Scientific Research*. Princeton, NJ: Princeton University Press.

Bhalla, M. & Proffitt, D.R. (2000). Geographical slant perception: dissociation and coordination between explicit awareness and visually guided actions. This volume, 99–128.

Chalmers, D.J. (1996). *The Conscious Mind*. Oxford: Oxford University Press.

Dennett, D.C. (1991). Consciousness Explained. Boston: Little, Brown.

Engel, A.K., Fries, P., König, P., Brecht, M. & Singer, W. (1999). Temporal Binding, Binocular Rivalry, and Consciousness. *Consciousness and Cognition* 8(2): 128–151.

Ffytche, D.H., Howard, R.J., Brammer, M.J., David, A., Woodruff, P. & Williams, S. (1998). The anatomy of conscious vision: an fMRI study of visual hallucinations. *Nature Neuroscience* 1: 738–742.

Imanaka, K. & Abernethy, B. (2000). Distance-Location Interference in Movement Reproduction: An Interaction between Conscious and Unconscious Processing? This volume, 41–73.

Jackson, Stephen R. (2000). Perception, Awareness and Action: Insights from Blindsight. This volume, 73–99.

Köhler, S. & Moscovitch, M. (1997). Unconscious visual processing in neuropsychological syndromes: a survey of the literature and evaluation of models of consciousness. In: MD Rugg (Ed.) *Cognitive Neuroscience*, 305–373. Cambridge, MA: MIT Press.

Lahav, R. (1993). What neuropsychology tells us about consciousness. Philosophy of Science 60, 67–85.

McGinn, C. (1991). The Problem of Consciousness. Oxford: Basil Blackwell.

Milner, A.D. & Goodale, M.A. (1995). *The Visual Brain in Action*. Oxford: Oxford University Press.

Perner, J. & Clements, W.A. (2000). From an Implicit to an Explicit "Theory of Mind". This volume, 273–295.

Pisella, L. & Rossetti, Y. (2000). Interaction between Conscious Identification and Non-Conscious Sensory-Motor Processing: Temporal Constraints. This volume, 129–153.

Revonsuo, A. (1997). How to take consciousness seriously in cognitive neuroscience. *Communication & Cognition* 30: 185–206.

Revonsuo, A., Johanson, M., Wedlund, J.-E. & Chaplin, J. (2000). The Zombies Among Us: Consciousness and Automatic Behaviour. This volume, 331–353.

Rossetti, Y. & Revonsuo, A. (2000). Introduction. Beyond Dissociations: Reassembling the Mind-Brain After All? This volume, 1–16.

Schacter, D.L., McAndrews, M.P. & Moscovitch, M. (1988). Access to consciousness: Dissociations between implicit and explicit knowledge in neuropsycho-logical syndromes. In: L. Weiskrantz (Ed.): Thought without Language, 242–278. Oxford: Oxford University Press.

Sheinberg, D.L. and Logothetis, N.K. (1997). The role of temporal cortical areas in perceptual organization. *Proceedings of the National Academy of the Sciences*, USA 94: 3408–3413.

Tong, F., Nakayama, K., Vaughan, J.T. & Kanwisher, N. (1998). Binocular rivalry and visual awareness in human extrastriate cortex. *Neuron* 21: 753–759.

Young, A.W. & Ellis, H.D. (2000). Overt and Covert Face Recognition. This volume, 195–220

Zeki, S. & Bartels, A. (1999). Towards a theory of visual consciousness. *Consciousness and Cognition* 8(2): 225–259.

Index

27. McMILLAN, John and Grant R. GILLETT: *Consciousness and Intentionality.* n.y.p.
28. ZACHAR, Peter: *Psychological Concepts and Biological Psychiatry. A philosophical analysis.* n.y.p.
29. VAN LOOCKE, Philip (ed.): *The Physical Nature of Consciousness.* n.y.p.